Lecture Notes in Economics and Mathematical Systems

Managing Editors: M. Beckmann and W. Krelle

Economic Theory

205

Ramu Ramanathan

Introduction to the Theory of Economic Growth

Springer-Verlag
Berlin Heidelberg New York 1982

Managing Editors
Prof. Dr. M. Beckmann
Brown University
Providence, RI 02912, USA

Prof. Dr. W. Krelle
Institut für Gesellschafts- und Wirtschaftswissenschaften
der Universität Bonn
Adenauerallee 24–42, D-5300 Bonn, FRG

Author
Prof. Ramu Ramanathan
Department of Economics
University of California, San Diego, D-008
La Jolla, CA. 92093, USA

ISBN 3-540-11943-4 Springer-Verlag Berlin Heidelberg New York
ISBN 0-387-11943-4 Springer-Verlag New York Heidelberg Berlin

Library of Congress Cataloging in Publication Data:
Ramanathan, Ramu, 1936- Introduction to the theory of economic growth.
(Lecture notes in economics and mathematical systems; v. 205) Bibliography: p. Includes index.
1. Economic development. I. Title. II. Series.
HD82.R28 1982 338.9'001 82-16973
ISBN 0-387-11943-4 (U.S.)

Printing and binding: Beltz Offsetdruck, Hemsbach/Bergstr.
2142/3140-543210

The standard Heckscher-Oklin static open economy model is presented first. This is then extended to the dynamic case analyzed by Uzawa and Oniki. Finally, a dynamic open economy model with a monetary sector is explored in detail.

Many of my own contributions in journals have been integrated with the rest of the literature, especially in Chapters 5,6,7,8 and 11. Each chapter has a set of exercises for the students to practice on and a set of review questions are at the end of the book. Many of these questions are significant extensions to the models presented in the book and have been asked in Ph.D. qualifying examinations at UCSD. In the interest of keeping the book as structured as possible, I have been forced to eliminate a vast amount of important contributions. I can only offer my apologies to the authors of those contributions.

In writing this book I have accumulated a hugh intellectual debt. Again, I can mention only a few names. My first interest in growth theory was stimulated by Murray Kemp when he was a Visiting Professor at the University of Minnesota in Fall 1965. My colleagues John Conlisk and Robert Russell have read earlier drafts of the book and have made substantial comments. I have benefited greatly from Conlisk's lecture notes on growth theory when he was on the faculty of the University of Wisconsin. Christopher Bliss, Ronald Britto and Michael Intriligator also made penetrating criticisms. Class handouts which formed the basis of the book were tried on several batches of UCSD graduate students and I am grateful for their suggestions for improvements, especially those made by Emmanuel Garon and Arthur Abraham. Needless to say, none of these persons is responsible for any omissions and defects that are present. I also extend my thanks to my secretaries, Jane Nizyborski, Judy Lyman and Dorothea Smits, who prepared innumerable handouts and typed several draft versions of this manuscript. Finally, the book could not have been completed without the understanding and cooperation of my family, my wife Vimala, and my children, Sridhar, Pradeep and Sadhana, to whom this book is dedicated.

La Jolla, September 1982 Ramu Ramanathan

PREFACE

This book is an outgrowth of years of teaching and doing research at the University of California, San Diego (UCSD), in the area of economic growth. Although there have been several books on this topic published in the last eight years, I have been dissatisfied with them for several reasons. First, books such as those by Wan, Burmeister and Dobell are uneven in their technical difficulty and, while they are excellent, are apparently difficult for first year graduate students and advanced undergraduates. Solow's expository book, on the other hand, is at the other extreme. Furthermore, many of the books seem to be aimed at the authors' peers rather than the students. My primary objective in writing this book is to bridge this gap and to pitch, very appropriately I hope, at the level of a typical student enrolled in a beginning course in growth theory. Secondly, almost all the growth models in the literature can be recast in a single analytical framework. Although the various authors have not written so as to conform to any particular pattern, it is the function of a textbook writer to identify such a pattern, if it exists, and present the theory in that framework. Many authors make implicit assumptions about their models which are either never specified or sometimes specified in footnotes. Here, the assumptions of a particular model are clearly stated in a formal algebraic form, the analysis is then carried out in a standard way and the implications examined. It is perhaps already evident that there is a great deal of emphasis in this book on the analytical framework. Some readers may be impatient with this approach but from my experience at UCSD I am convinced that the emphasis is quite appropriate. Once the reader has mastered this standard framework, he/she can confidently go on to build his/her own models. The specifics of the framework are spelled out in the introductory chapter and again in Chapter 3.

The coverage in this introductory book excludes multisector growth models, but includes a chapter on international trade and economic growth and another on the speed of adjustment. The book starts with the simple Harrod-Domar, Solow-Swan models and gradually takes the reader to more complicated models involving technical progress, money and growth, optimum growth, two-sector models, etc. The prerequisites needed here are no more than intermediate level micro and macro economics and a working knowledge of calculus. Rudiments of differential equations are covered in the book itself.

The layout of the book is as follows. After an introductory chapter, production functions and their properties are reviewed in detail in Chapter 2. The basic Harrod-Domar and Solow-Swan models are presented in Chapter 3. The appendix to this chapter has a discussion of differential equations, phase diagrams etc., with several illustrative examples. Technical progress is discussed in Chapter 4. Here again my approach is different from that in many books. All the various forms of technical progress (including endogenous change, induced bias, vintage models etc.) are systematically examined in one chapter rather than scattered in various chapters. Measurement of technical progress is also briefly discussed here. Chapter 5 explores monetary growth models. Besides Tobin's simple neo-classical model, the Levhari-Patinkin approach of treating money alternatively as a consumer and producer good is examined as is the more recent Keynes-Wicksell approach of Stein and others. A synthesis of both approaches is also presented here. The Kaldor-Pasinetti saving behavior with two separate income classes is explored in Chapter 6 under the neo-classical framework. A monetary version of this model is also discussed there. Chapter 7 alludes, but only briefly, to the Cambridge school's criticisms of the neo-classical approach. The speed of convergence to the long run equilibrium, a topic usually neglected entirely, is discussed in Chapter 8.

Chapters 9 and 10 provide introductions to optimal growth and two-sector growth models respectively. International Trade and Economic Growth is discussed in Chapter 11 at some length. That topic is not covered in any of the leading books on growth theory.

CONTENTS

CHAPTER 1

INTRODUCTION

An examination of the experience of advanced countries over long periods of time brings out certain empirical facts. Real wages and real per capita output have increased, but by rates which cannot be accounted for by capital accumulation alone. The relative shares of wages and profits and the real rate of interest have been constant in the long run, even though they have fluctuated during business cycles. The overall capital-output ratio and the saving-income ratio have also been nearly constant. Samuelson called these results the _stylized facts of capitalism_.[1]

For several decades, economists have constructed theoretical frameworks which attempted to explain these stylized facts, and the last twenty years have seen a phenomenal rise in the literature on growth theory. Dynamic models of economic systems have been formulated and their implications for long period growth examined. There has also been an increasing interest in the roles of technical progress and money supply in generating growth with full employment.

The purpose of this book is to introduce the modern theories of economic growth to students majoring in economics by bringing together a large collection of papers on aggregate growth theory, and casting them into a single framework of analysis. In the following paragraphs we discuss the general framework of analysis and systematic steps used in this text to analyze growth models and their implications.

Structural equations: Every theoretical framework of analysis is based on a set of assumptions or conditions. These may take the form of behavioral assumptions, technological requirements, equilibrium conditions or simple definitions. The _structural equations_ of an economic system are a set of simultaneous

---

[1]Paul A. Samuelson, "Rejoinder: Agreements, Disagreements, Doubts and the Case of Induced Harrod-Neutral Technical Change," _Review of Economics and Statistics_, November 1966.

equations specifying the relationships between a number of endogenous variables and other endogenous variables, exogenous variables and parameters. A variable is said to be exogenous if its value is determined not from within the economic system the model represents but from outside considerations. It may be a non-economic variable or an economic variable whose behavior is not under study. If the value of a variable is obtained from within the system, the variable is said to be endogenous. A system also depends on a number of different constants which are called parameters. The best way to illustrate these concepts is with the help of a simple model. The following model of income determination will be familiar to every reader:

(1.1) $$C = a + bY$$

(1.2) $$Y = C + I$$

C is the aggregate consumption expenditure of an economy, Y is its aggregate income and I is aggregate investment. Suppose firms decide on a given level of investment I regardless of income or other considerations. Then I is an exogenous variable. Equation (1.1) describes consumption behavior. Equation (1.2) states that income is the sum of consumption and investment. a and b are assumed to be known constants and are thus parameters. With regard to the above model, we can ask the question: "what are the values of consumption and income consistent with a given level of investment and the set of known parameters a and b?" The endogenous variables are therefore consumption and income. The above system thus consists of two equations in the endogenous variables C and Y. Substituting for consumption from (1.1) into (1.2) and solving for Y, we obtain.

(1.3) $$Y = \frac{a + I}{1 - b}$$

Similarly,

(1.4) $$C = \frac{a + bI}{1 - b}$$

The question raised above can now be answered by simply substituting the values for a, b and I. We thus have the solution to the structure specified in (1.1) and (1.2). Equations (1.3) and (1.4) are called the reduced form which, by definition, relates each endogenous variable to the exogenous variables and the parameters.

The first step in analyzing any economic system is then to represent it by a set of structural equations. This will clearly bring into focus the foundations on which the entire model rests. An additional advantage of proceeding this way is that contrasts between the assumptions and conclusions of different models can be clearly distinguished.

Basic differential equations: In the simple static model presented above, we could readily derive the reduced form from the structure. Such a simple reduction is generally not possible in a dynamic model, that is, a model describing the behavior of an economy over time. In dynamic models we must first reduce the system to one or more basic equations of motion specifying the behavior over time of a subset of the endogenous variables. In growth theory, all variables are assumed to be continuous functions of "time" which also changes continuously.

The second step in the analysis of a growth model is then to reduce the system to a set of equations of motion called the basic differential equations. A differential equation is simply a relationship between one or more variables and their derivatives. The appendix to Chapter 3 discusses them in more detail. Although the above step might seem formidable, it is indeed one of the easiest steps to carry out. In most cases, the system can be reduced to a differential equation in a single endogenous variable or utmost to two differential equations in a pair of endogenous variables.

The steady state: Although the system is reduced to one or two differential equations, explicit solutions are generally not obtained. Instead, the long run implications of the model are derived by focusing on the steady state. A steady state, as defined in growth theory, is a situation in which all the endogenous variables in the system grow exponentially at constant rates. More specifically, the time path of a variable X(t) will have the form $X(t) = X_o e^{gt}$ where g is the constant growth rate. For some of the variables g may be zero implying that they are constant along the steady state path. In most models, we will assume that only a few endogenous variables grow exponentially at constant rates and then deduce that the others also grow exponentially or remain constant. Along a steady state path, the relative shares of factors in total output is generally constant. For this reason a steady state is also referred to as a balanced growth path. Several questions arise in connection with a steady state: "Does a steady state exist? Is it unique or are several steady state paths possible? Is it stable, that is, if there is a disturbance to the system throwing it off the steady state path, will the system return to the path?" These questions thus relate to the existence, uniqueness and stability of a steady state.

Comparative dynamics: In static models we often ask a question such as: "what happens to income and employment if there is a change in the tax rate or money supply?" The technique used in static models to analyze the effects of changes in the exogenous variables or parameters on the endogenous variables is called comparative statics. In growth theory, we would like to know how monetary and fiscal policies would affect the time paths of aggregate output, real wage rate, real rents, etc. For example, we might be interested in knowing whether an increase in the saving rate or the rate of monetary expansion might increase the rate of growth of output and per capita income. These issues are discussed under the heading of comparative dynamics.

In the presentation of the models that follow, we essentially follow the above outline. After the first few models, the reader will find the technical analysis routine and can concentrate on the assumptions and implications.

CHAPTER 2

REVIEW OF PRODUCTION FUNCTIONS AND THEIR PROPERTIES

The basic results of the theory of the firm under perfect competition are summarized in this chapter. The analysis will be confined to the situation in which there are two variable _factors_ of production or _inputs_ and a single commodity produced or _output_. Output is determined by the aggregate production function represented by the relation $Y = F(K,L)$ where Y is aggregate output, K is a variable factor of production labeled _Capital_ and L is _Labor_, the other variable factor of production.[1] The form of the production function is determined by the nature of the technology which combines labor and capital to produce the commodity. It may be possible to combine given levels of capital and labor in several ways to generate different levels of output. The production function defined above presupposes technical efficiency and stands for the maximum possible output for specified levels of the two inputs. Thus the function $F(K,L)$ is single-valued, i.e. for given levels of labor and capital there is a unique level of output.

2.1 Production with Fixed Coefficients

If capital and labor have to be combined in a fixed proportion to produce the output, then we have a technology with _fixed coefficients_. In this case the inputs are complimentary and there is no possibility of substituting capital for labor and vice versa. Suppose that to produce each unit of output we need α units of capital and β units of labor. These constants are called capital and labor coefficients respectively. This production technique can be represented by an _isoquant_, which is the locus of all combinations of the inputs yielding a specified level of output. Figure 2.1 shows the isoquants corresponding to output levels 1 and 2. The point A represents β units of labor and α units of capital, which input combination will yield one unit of output.

---

[1] This assumes that such an aggregate production function can be defined. For an excellent summary of the problems of aggregation see Fisher [5] and Green [6].

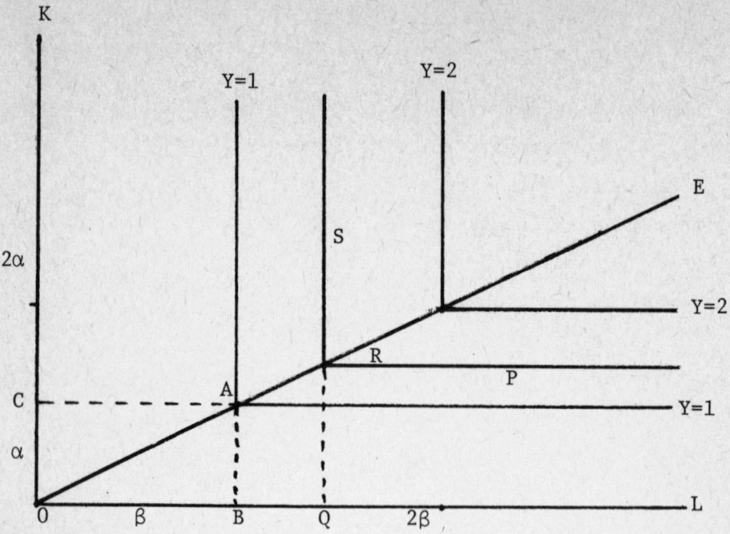

Figure 2.1

Because capital and labor have to be used in a fixed proportion, additional amounts of one input with the other input held at a constant level will not result in an increased output. Therefore the isoquant corresponding to an output of one unit is the right angle marked Y = 1. Similarly, all the isoquants are right angles with their corners lying along the line OAE which has the slope α/β.

Let the point P represent (L,K) the total quantities of labor and capital available. Then the maximum possible output is given by the isoquant which passes through P. The same output might have been obtained by combining OQ units of labor (call it $\bar{L}$) with QR units of capital (K). This would have resulted in a lower cost of production. Output is given by K/α which is the same as $\bar{L}/\beta$ and $K/\alpha < L/\beta$. Therefore, assuming cost minimization, the amount of labor actually employed ($\bar{L}$) is smaller than the amount of labor available (L) and hence there is surplus labor. If the factor endowment, i.e. the levels of capital and labor available, was a point like S then $L/\beta < K/\alpha$ and the actual output would have been

L/β with surplus capital, again assuming cost minimization. Thus the output Y is the smaller of K/α and L/β and the production function for the fixed coefficients case is given by

$$Y = F(K,L) = \min\,(K/\alpha,\ L/\beta) \tag{2.1}$$

It is clear that full employment of both types of resources is possible if and only if $K/\alpha = L/\beta$.

The production function (2.1) exhibits constant returns to scale, i.e. if the levels of both inputs are multiplied by a positive factor λ then output is also multiplied by the factor λ.

2.2 Substitution Between Capital and Labor

In the fixed coefficients case there was only one technique available, that of combining capital and labor in a fixed proportion. There was thus no possibility of substituting one factor for another. At the other extreme, we assume that an infinite number of techniques are available and that capital and labor can be continuously substituted for each other.[1] More specifically, we will assume that the production function F(K,L) is continuous with continuous first and second order partial derivatives. The first partials F_K and F_L are the marginal products of capital and labor respectively. The ratio of F_L/F_K is the rate of technical substitution (RTS) between capital and labor, and the ratio $k = K/L$ is the capital-labor ratio, also known as the capital intensity. If the production function F(K,L) is strictly quasi-concave then the isoquants will have the conventional shape shown in Figure 2.2.[2] Strict quasi-concavity of F is assured if the Hessian matrix of F, viz.

$$\begin{bmatrix} F_{KK} & F_{KL} \\ F_{LK} & F_{LL} \end{bmatrix}$$

---

[1] For a detailed analysis of this case see Henderson and Quandt [7], or Intriligator [11].

[2] The bordered Hessian condition implies strict quasi-concavity of F. For a definition and discussion of concave and quasi-concave functions see Lancaster [8].

is <u>negative definite</u>, that is the <u>quadratic form</u> $Q = K^2 F_{KK} + 2KL F_{KL} + L^2 F_{LL} < 0$ for all K and L both $\neq 0$ (see Intriligator [9]). This implies that the second partials are both negative; $F_{KK} < 0$ and $F_{LL} < 0$.

Let w be the real wages and r be the real rate of return to capital. The total cost of production is then given by wL + Kr. The loci of input combinations for which the total costs are constant are called <u>isocost lines</u> and are downward sloping parallel straight lines (for given w and r) of slope w/r (see Figure 2.2). The loci of tangency points of isocost lines with the isoquants are known as <u>expansion paths</u>.

2.2.1 Homogeneity and Euler's Theorem

Y = F(K,L) is said to be <u>homogeneous of degree μ</u> if

$$F(\lambda K, \lambda L) = \lambda^{\mu} F(K,L) \tag{2.2}$$

for all positive λ, K and L. <u>Euler's Theorem</u> states that if F(K,L) is homogeneous of degree μ and its first partials exist

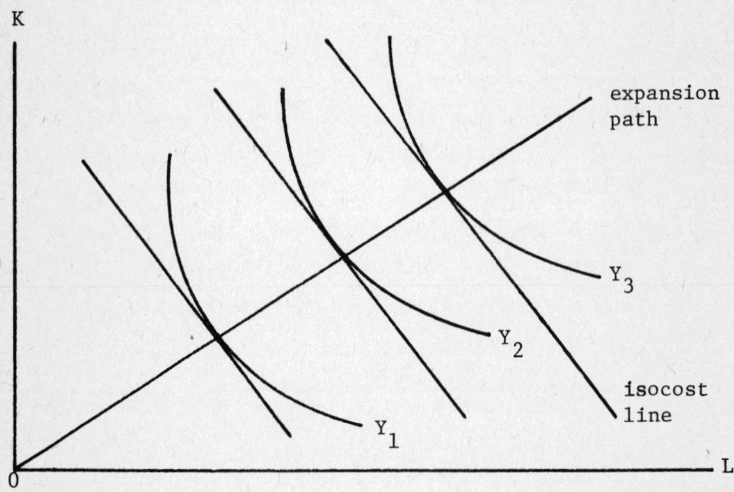

Figure 2.2

everywhere, then for any K and L

$$(2.3) \qquad KF_K + LF_L = \mu F(K,L)$$

This theorem is easily proved by partially differentiating (2.2) with respect to λ and then setting $\lambda = 1$.[1] For homogeneous production functions the expansion paths are straight lines through the origin as in Figure 2.2 (Exercise 2.6).

2.2.2 Share of Capital and the Elasticity of Substitution

Aggregate profits, that is real output less total cost, are given by $Y - wL - Kr$ (since there is only one commodity, it can be treated as *numeraire* and its price assumed to be one). Under perfect competition (i.e. when all the economic units treat the commodity and factor prices as given) and profit maximization we get the following results which are obtained by partially differentiating the expression for profits with respect to K and L and equating to zero:

$$w = F_L \quad \text{and} \quad r = F_K$$

Thus for profit maximization under competition the marginal products must equal the real factor prices. This condition holds whether or not the production function is homogeneous. Under this marginal productivity theory, LF_L is the wage bill and KF_K is the rental bill. If $F(K,L)$ is such that $\mu = 1$, then the sum of wage and rental bills is Y by Euler's theorem. The total product is thus exactly distributed between the two factors. If $F(K,L)$ is homogeneous of degree μ, wage and rental bills add up to μY which is not equal to Y.[2] The total factor payments will therefore more or less than exhaust the total output depending on whether $\mu > 1$

---

[1] Partial differentiation with respect to λ gives $K\partial F/\partial(\lambda K) + L\partial F/\partial(\lambda L) = \mu\lambda^{\mu-1}F(K,L)$. Setting $\lambda = 1$ in this, we obtain (2.3).

[2] But this would violate the profit maximizing conditions. To avoid this difficulty it is generally assumed that $\mu = 1$. Factors can then be paid their marginal products and the total product is exhausted with zero aggregate profits.

or < 1. In this case the factors may be paid proportionately to their marginal products in such a way as to exactly distribute the total product. If this is done, the wage rental ratio will be equal to the marginal rate of substitution which is a necessary condition for cost minimization (or output maximization). The wage and rental bills would then be LF_L/μ and KF_K/μ respectively. The ratio, $\pi = KF_K/\mu Y$ is the relative Share of Capital in the income distribution and lies between 0 and 1. The extreme case when π is either 0 or 1 is uninteresting and is ruled out by assumption.

The Elasticity of Substitution (σ) between capital and labor is defined as

$$\sigma = \left(\frac{dk}{k}\right)\Big/\left(\frac{dR}{R}\right) = \frac{d(\log k)}{d(\log R)} = \frac{(F_L/F_K)}{(K/L)} \cdot \frac{d(K/L)}{d(F_L/F_K)}$$

where $R = F_L/F_K$ is the rate of technical substitution and $k = K/L$ is the capital-labor ratio. When factors are paid their marginal products, R is the same as the ratio of wages to rent, i.e. the relative wages. Loosely speaking, the elasticity of substitution between capital and labor is a numerical measure of the percentage change in the capital-labor ratio (dk/k) per one percent increase in the relative wages (dR/R). As relative wages increase, firms would substitute capital for labor and capital intensity would rise. The elasticity of substitution would therefore have a positive value. The actual value of σ depends on the extent to which diminishing marginal products operate for each factor. In a subsequent section we illustrate different elasticities of substitution and discuss their properties.

Theorem 2.1: Let F(K,L) be homogeneous of degree μ with continuous first and second partials F_K, F_L, F_{KK}, F_{LL} and F_{KL}. Then the rate of technical substitution, the share of capital and the elasticity of substitution are all functions of k alone.

To prove this first define a new function f(k) which is given by the relation $f(k) \equiv F(k,1) = F(K/L,1)$. Since F(K,L) is homogeneous of degree μ, setting $\lambda = 1/L$ in (2.2) we get $F(K,L) = L^{\mu}f(k)$. Differentiating this partially with respect to K and using the chain rule of differentiation we obtain $F_K = L^{\mu}f'(k) \cdot 1/L = L^{\mu-1}f'(k)$. Similarly, $F_L = L^{\mu-1}[\mu f(k) - kf'(k)]$. It is easily verified that the above marginal products are homogeneous of degree $\mu-1$ (See exercise 2.1). From these, the rate of technical substitution is given by $R(k) = F_L/F_K = [\mu f(k) - kf'(k)]/f'(k)$ which is a function of k alone. The share of capital is given by $\pi(k) = KF_K/\mu F = kf'(k)/\mu f(k)$ which also depends on k only. Differentiation of R(k) with respect to k gives $R'(k) = [(\mu-1)f'^2 - \mu ff'']/f'^2$. Therefore, the elasticity of substitution is given by

$$\sigma(k) = \frac{R(k)}{kR'(k)} = \frac{f'(k)[\mu f(k) - kf'(k)]}{k[(\mu-1)f'^2 - \mu f(k)f''(k)]}$$

This again depends only on k.

2.2.3 Linearly Homogeneous Production Functions

A major portion of the discussion in later chapters will be based on production functions that are linearly homogeneous, i.e. homogeneous of degree one.[1] Some of the results obtained above take simpler forms in this case. Setting $\mu = 1$ we obtain the following results:

(2.2a) $\quad Y = F(K,L) = Lf(k)$

(2.4) $\quad F_K = f'(k)$

(2.5) $\quad F_L = f(k) - kf'(k)$

(2.6) $\quad \pi(k) = kf'(k)/f(k)$

(2.7) $\quad \sigma(k) = \dfrac{-f'(k)[f(k) - kf'(k)]}{kf(k)f''(k)}$

Differentiating $\pi(k)$ with respect to k and using (2.7) it can be shown that

(2.8) $\quad \pi'(k) = \dfrac{kf''(k)}{f(k)} [1-\sigma(k)]$

Since $F_{KK} < 0$, it follows by differentiating (2.4) partially with

---

[1] If $\mu = 1$, the function F(K,L) is not strictly concave but strict quasi-concavity might be preserved.

respect to K that $f''(k) < 0$. From (2.8) we then see that

(2.9) $\quad \pi'(k) \lesseqgtr 0$ according as $\sigma \lesseqgtr 1$

We have therefore established the following result:

Theorem 2.2: If the elasticity of substitution of a linearly homogeneous production function with continuous first and second partials is less than one, then an increase in the capital intensity lowers the relative share of capital in total output. If $\sigma > 1$, the relative share of capital is raised and if $\sigma = 1$, changes in the capital intensity do not affect the income distribution.

The conclusion of Theorem 2.2 can also be reached by arguing intuitively. Suppose σ is less than one, say equal to one-half. This means that if relative wages go up by 10 percent then firms will substitute capital for labor and capital intensity will go up. But since $\sigma = \frac{1}{2}$, k will go up by only 5 percent (approximately). Since the rate of return to capital went down relatively (when relative wages went up) and capital intensity has not gone up as much, we can expect the share of capital to go down. If $\sigma > 1$ say equal to 2, then a 10 percent increase in real wages would raise capital intensity by about 20 percent and thus capital's share would increase.

It will be useful to depict some of the results obtained above in a diagrammatic form. It is seen from equations (2.2a) and (2.4) that $f(k)$ is the average product of labor and $f'(k)$ is the marginal product of capital. A typical form of $f(k)$ is shown in Figure 2.3. The diagram makes the following assumptions, $f(0) \geq 0$, $f'(k) > 0$ and $f''(k) < 0$ for all k. In other words, output is always nonnegative, the marginal product of capital is positive for all capital intensities and this marginal product diminishes with increases in k. OA is the capital intensity and AB is the corresponding average product of labor. The slope of the tangent at B is $f'(k)$ the marginal product of capital. In other words, $f'(k) = AB/AC$. The slope of the line OB is $f(k)/k$ (=AB/OA), the average product of capital. It is evident from the figure that the average product of capital is always higher than the mar-

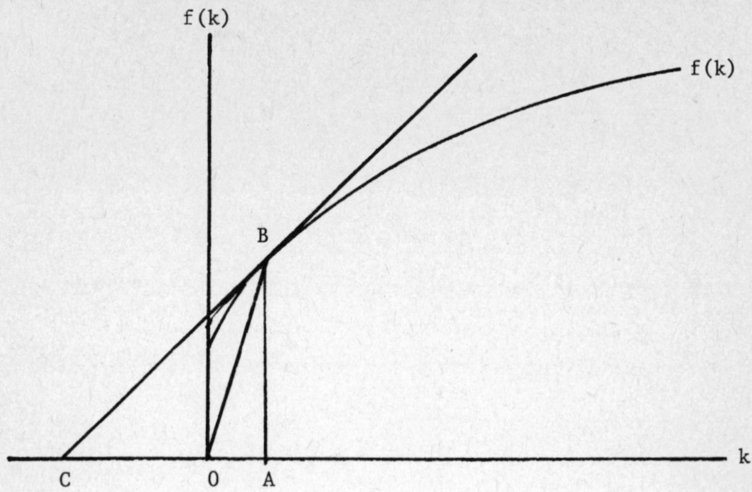

Figure 2.3

ginal product of capital which implies that the marginal product of labor $f(k) - kf'(k) > 0$. This result can be obtained mathematically by using the mean value theorem together with the three conditions on f(k) stated above.

We just showed that $f'(k) = AB/AC$. Since $AC = k + OC$ and $AB = f(k)$, the relation for f'(k) can be rewritten as $f'(k) = f(k)/(k+OC)$. Solving for OC we obtain

$$OC = \frac{f(k) - kf'(k)}{f'(k)} = \frac{F_L}{F_K} = R(k) \tag{2.10}$$

Thus OC is the marginal rate of substitution. Under perfect competition and profit maximization it is also the wage-rental ratio. If capital intensity is increased, the point B moves to the right. Because of diminishing marginal product, the slopes of both OB and CB decrease. This means that both the average and marginal product curves for capital are downward sloping with the average product curve lying everywhere above the marginal product curve. Similarly, an increase in k increases OC and therefore the wage-rental ratio (relative wages) is an increasing function of k and vice versa. This last result can also be derived by arguing that when the wage-rental ratio goes up, firms will substitute capital for labor and therefore the capital intensity would go up thereby raising F_L and lowering F_K. This implies that relative wages and capital intensity move in the same direction.

2.2.4 The Cobb-Douglas Production Function

A special kind of production function is of the Cobb-Douglas type [4]. It is defined as

$$(2.11) \qquad Y = aK^{\alpha}L^{\beta}$$

where a, α and β are all positive parameters. The Cobb-Douglas production function is homogeneous of degree $\alpha + \beta$. Since output is zero when K or L is zero, both inputs are needed to produce a positive output. The following results are readily obtained:

$$\pi(k) = \alpha/(\alpha+\beta)$$
$$R(k) = \beta k/\alpha$$
$$\sigma(k) = 1$$

It can be shown that a linearly homogeneous production function will be of the Cobb-Douglas type if and only if the elasticity of substitution is one (Exercise 2.3).

2.2.5 The CES Production Function

A generalization of the Cobb-Douglas production function, proposed by Arrow, Chenery, Minhas and Solow, is the Constant Elasticity of Substitution (CES) production function which has the property that the elasticity of substitution is a constant for all capital intensities [3]. Thus $\sigma(k)$ is independent of k. The explicit form is given in (2.12).

$$(2.12) \qquad Y = \begin{cases} a[\alpha K^{\rho} + (1-\alpha)L^{\rho}]^{\frac{\mu}{\rho}} & \text{for } \rho \neq 0 \\ a(K^{\alpha}L^{1-\alpha})^{\mu} & \text{for } \rho = 0 \end{cases}$$

$$a > 0, \quad \mu > 0, \quad 0 < \alpha < 1, \quad \rho \leq 1.$$

The CES production is homogeneous of degree μ. When $\rho = 0$ it reduces to the Cobb-Douglas form. This can be shown by first taking logarithm of Y and then applying L'Hospital's Rule. Thus the Cobb-Douglas production function is a limiting case of the constant elasticity of substitution production function.

Differentiation of (2.12) partially with respect to K and L gives

$$F_L = a[\alpha K^\rho + (1-\alpha)L^\rho]^{\frac{\mu}{\rho}-1} \cdot \mu(1-\alpha)L^{\rho-1}$$

$$F_K = a[\alpha K^\rho + (1-\alpha)L^\rho]^{\frac{\mu}{\rho}-1} \cdot \mu\alpha K^{\rho-1}$$

Hence $R(k) = F_L/F_K = (1-\alpha)/\alpha \cdot k^{1-\rho}$ and $R'(k) = (1-\alpha)(1-\rho)k^{-\rho}/\alpha$. Therefore the elasticity of substitution is $\sigma(k) = R(k)/[kR'(k)] = 1/(1-\rho)$, a constant. The share of capital is given by $\pi(k) = \alpha/[\alpha + (1-\alpha)k^{-\rho}]$.

The following statements regarding the CES production function can easily be verified (Exercise 2.5):

1. When $\sigma = \infty$ ($\rho = 1$), the two factors are perfect substitutes and the isoquants are straight lines of slope $(1-\alpha)/\alpha$ in absolute value.

2. When $1 < \sigma < \infty$ ($0 < \rho < 1$), it is possible to obtain a positive output when one of the factors is zero. Thus the isoquants will intersect the axes in this case.

3. When $\sigma = 1$ ($\rho = 0$), the isoquants are tangent to the axes.

4. When $0 < \sigma < 1$ ($-\infty < \rho < 0$), the isoquants are asymptotic to the straight lines $K = Y_o^{1/\mu}/(a\,\alpha^{1/\rho})$ and $L = Y_o^{1/\mu}[a(1-\alpha)^{1/\rho}]$.

5. When $\sigma = 0$ ($\rho = -\infty$), there is no possibility of substitution between capital and labor. This is the fixed coefficients case.

REFERENCES

[1] Allen, R. G. D.: Mathematical Analysis for Economists, St. Martin's Press, 1967.

[2] Allen, R. G. D.: Macro-Economic Theory, St. Martin's Press, 1967.

[3] Arrow, K. J., H. B. Chenery, B. S. Minhas, R. M. Solow: "Capital-labor Substitution and Economic Efficiency," Review of Economics and Statistics, Aug. 1961.

[4] Bronfenbrenner, M., and P. H. Douglas: "Cross Section Studies in the Cobb-Douglas Function," Journal of Political Economy, Dec. 1939.

[5] Fisher, Franklin M.: "The Existence of Aggregate Production Functions," Econometrica, Oct. 1969.

[6] Green, H. A. J.: Aggregation in Economic Analysis: An Introductory Survey, Princeton University Press, 1964.

[7] Henderson, J., and R. Quandt: Microeconomic Theory, McGraw-Hill, 1971, 2nd Edition.

[8] Lancaster, K.: Mathematical Economics, Macmillan, 1968.

[9] Leontief, W. W.: "Introduction to a Theory of the Internal Structure of Functional Relationships," Econometrica, 1947.

[10] Solow, R. M.: "The Production Function and the Theory of Capital," Review of Economic Studies, 1955-56.

[11] Intriligator, Michael D., Mathematical Optimization and Economic Theory, Prentice-Hall , 1971.

EXERCISES

2.1 Verify that if F(K,L) is homogeneous of degree μ then F_K and F_L are homogeneous of degree μ-1.

2.2 Show that for a Cobb-Douglas production function, $\pi(k) = \alpha/(\alpha+\beta)$, $R(k) = \beta k/\alpha$ and $\sigma = 1$.

2.3 Prove that a linearly homogeneous production function is of the Cobb-Douglas type if and only if $\sigma = 1$.

2.4 By taking the logarithm of (2.12) and using L'Hospital's rule show that for $\rho = 0$, $Y = a(K^{\alpha}L^{1-\alpha})^{\mu}$.

2.5 Graph a typical isoquant and the function f(k) = F(K/L,1) for the CES production function in the following cases: $\sigma = 0$, $0 < \sigma < 1$, $\sigma = 1$, $1 < \sigma < \infty$ and $\sigma = \infty$.

2.6 Show that for homogeneous production functions the expansion paths are straight lines through the origin (Hint: Use Theorem 2.1).

CHAPTER 3

BASIC NEO-CLASSICAL GROWTH MODELS

The models of aggregate economic behavior that represent short-period analysis demonstrate that the necessary condition for full employment is that the level of investment generated in an economy be offset by the volume of saving made at the full employment income. This conclusion is based on the assumption that the labor force and the productive capacity of a given economy are fixed. In the short run these assumptions are realistic but labor force as well as productive capacity change over time. Population may be increasing and therefore what is full employment today may not be full employment tomorrow. Secondly, investment in a given year adds to the productive capacity of the economy thereby increasing its potential output. It is this dual aspect of investment (i.e. investment on the one hand offsetting saving and on the other increasing productive capacity) that is central in theories of economic growth. A second reason why productive capacity might increase is technical progress. Improvements in technology bring about increases in the efficiency of the factors of production thereby raising potential output.

In this and succeeding chapters we will examine the conditions under which a given economy can achieve and maintain full employment with the level of real income increasing over time. The simplest framework of analysis and the starting point of all modern theories of economic growth is the Harrod-Domar model. The models originally proposed by Roy F. Harrod and Evsey D. Domar [2,5,6] differ in a number of respects but since the basic structure is similar, the initial presentation will be in terms of a single model. Later on, however, we do discuss Harrod's arguments regarding the instability of the growth path.

3.1 The Harrod-Domar Model

The model makes the following assumptions.

(i) Production function: It is assumed that there is a single commodity which can be consumed or saved and used as an input in the production of more of the same commodity. The output of this commodity at time t is denoted by Y(t). There are two factors of production, capital denoted by K(t) and labor denoted by L(t). It takes α units of capital and β units of labor to produce each unit of output. Production techniques are thus given by fixed coefficients with no possibility of substitution between labor and capital.

It was seen in the last chapter that the above assumptions imply the following (aggregate) production function.

$$Y(t) = F(K,L) = \min[K(t)/\alpha,\ L(t)/\beta] \tag{3.1.1}$$

When capital and labor are fully employed (3.1.1) is simply the aggregate supply of the commodity in question at full employment. The assumption of fixed coefficients with no substitution possibilities may be realistic in the short run but in the long run, labor can certainly be replaced by capital and vice versa. This production function is therefore hard to justify in the context of a growth model. It should also be pointed out that Harrod himself did not assume fixed coefficients. He assumed rigidities in the economy so that the interest rate was fixed. Given this fixed interest rate firms would choose a capital intensity which will remain constant over time. There is thus an ex post fixity of coefficients implicit in Harrod's theory (see Exercise 3.8). In spite of this distinction, let us stick to the above production function and examine the long run properties of the model. The assumption will be relaxed in Section 3.2.

(ii) Saving behavior: The second assumption is behavioral and relates to saving (consumption) behavior. Aggregate saving S(t) is assumed to be a constant fraction s of aggregate output. Equivalently,

(3.1.2) $S(t) = sY(t)$

The overall saving-income ratio is therefore a fixed parameter. It is not implied that every individual consumes the same fraction of income. Individuals may differ in their consumption patterns but the overall fraction of income saved is a constant for all time periods. It may be possible to change this constant by fiscal policy. In the case of the United States there is some empirical justification for this assumption. Simon Kuznets, for example, found that the overall percentage of real income saved in the U.S., by decades, has been remarkably steady for a very long period [7]. Goldsmith's study of savings in the United States has also supported this result [3].

In order to have equilibrium in the economy, aggregate supply of the commodity, $Y(t)$ should equal aggregate demand $C(t) + I(t)$ where $C(t)$ is consumption ($C \equiv Y - S$) and $I(t)$ is investment. From this we have the following well-known condition for equilibrium

(3.1.3) $S(t) \equiv Y(t) - C(t) = I(t)$

So far we are in the realm of short run economics. Additional conditions which will make the model dynamic are now added.

(iii) Labor supply: The third assumption of the Harrod-Domar model is that the labor force grows at the constant rate n which is a parameter determined exogenously, i.e. by considerations outside the model. It will be assumed that n is not negative, that is that the labor force does not decline. The change in the labor force at any instant is given by $dL(t)/dt$, the time derivative of the function $L(t)$. To simplify the notation this will be denoted by $\dot{L}(t)$ where a dot above a variable stands for the time derivative. The rate of growth of labor force at the time t is given by $\dot{L}(t)/L(t)$.[1] The assumption made above implies the following relation:

---

[1]The term rate of growth of a variable $X(t)$ is used to denote the proportionate rate of growth $\dot{X}(t)/X(t)$ which is the derivative with respect to t of the logarithm of $X(t)$.

(3.1.4) $\dot{L}(t)/L(t) = n$

This relation can also be represented in another form. Integration of both sides of the above relation with respect to t yields log L(t) on the left hand side and nt plus an arbitrary constant of integration on the right hand side, i.e. $\log L(t) = nt + A$. Taking the exponential of both sides results in $L(t) = e^A \cdot e^{nt}$. Setting $t = 0$ we get $L(0) = e^A$ and therefore

(3.1.5) $L(t) = L(0)e^{nt}$

Thus a constant rate of growth of labor force is equivalent to an exponentially increasing time path for L(t).

Capital formation: The level of investment is I(t). To simplify the analysis assume that capital does not depreciate. Then all of I(t) will go into the formation of new capital thus adding to the existing stock of capital. Therefore, if K(t) denotes the level of capital at time t, $\dot{K}(t)$ which is the change in capital, is the same as current investment. This leads to the following equation:

(3.1.6) $\dot{K}(t) = I(t)$

The five equations (3.1.1), (3.1.2), (3.1.3), (3.1.5), and (3.1.6) completely specify the economic system. There are five endogenous variables, i.e. variables the time paths of which are to be determined within the system. They are Y(t), K(t), L(t), S(t) and I(t). The saving rate s and the rate of growth of labor force n are known parameters which may be changed by appropriate policies.

3.1.1 The Warranted and Natural Rates

Let us now examine how an economy characterized by the Harrod-Domar model will behave over time. Assume that initially the economy is at full employment with the level of capital given by K_o and an initial labor force of L_o. These two inputs can be combined to yield the output level specified by the production function (3.1.1). Of this, the proportion (1-s) is consumed and the rest saved. In order to maintain full employment equilibrium, this level of saving must be offset by an equivalent amount of investment. It is well-known from standard macro-economic theory that if adequate investment is not forthcoming, real income will drop below the full employment level. If savings equal investment, the capital stock at the next instant will be higher by the amount of current saving (less depreciation if there is any). Labor force also grows according to (3.1.5). The aggregate output at the next instant will therefore be higher. The process will repeat itself resulting in higher and higher levels of aggregate output. We can thus generate the time path of aggregate output from which the time paths of the other endogenous variables may be derived by using the appropriate equations.

While the above line of argument is generally valid, the assumption of a fixed coefficient production function places certain constraints on the long-run behavior of the economy. To explore this further, assume that aggregate output is always given by $Y(t) = K(t)/\alpha$ which means capital is never redundant.[1] Taking logarithms of both sides of the equation we get $\log Y(t) = \log K(t) - \log \alpha$. Differentiation with respect to t gives[2] $\dot{Y}(t)/Y(t) = \dot{K}(t)/K(t)$. The left hand side represents the rate of growth of aggregate output while the right hand side stands for the rate of growth of the capital stock. Thus a necessary condition for capital to be always fully utilized with no excess capacity is that capital and output must grow at the same rate. From (3.1.1), (3.1.2), (3.1.3) and (3.1.6), $\dot{K}(t) = I(t) = S(t) = sY(t) = sK(t)/\alpha$. From this it follows that $\dot{K}(t)/K(t) = s/\alpha$. Therefore in order for investment to equal saving with full utilization of capital, aggregate output and capital must grow at the <u>warranted rate</u> (s/α) which is the ratio of the saving coefficient to the capital-output ratio.

---

[1] Such a situation is typical of less developed countries where capital is the bottleneck and limits total output.

[2] This procedure of first taking logarithms of a variable and then differentiating with respect to t is called <u>logarithmic differentiation</u> and will be used often.

In Harrod's analysis since the interest rate is constant, firms choice of techniques (i.e. the capital intensity or the capital-output ratio) will also remain constant. In order for firms to be continuously satisfied with this choice of technique, growth must be at the warranted rate.

A similar condition may be derived for the full employment of labor. Assuming that $Y(t) = L(t)/\beta$, which holds if labor is not redundant and is more likely in advanced economies, a similar derivation gives $\dot{Y}(t)/Y(t) = \dot{L}(t)/L(t) = n$. This means that if full employment of the labor force is to be maintained, a necessary condition is that output must grow at the <u>natural rate</u> n which is the rate at which labor grows. If both factors are to be fully employed, then the following condition must be satisfied.

(3.1.7) $\quad s/\alpha = n$

Thus the powerful conclusion of the Harrod-Domar model is that for equilibrium growth with full employment of both factors, it is necessary that the warranted rate of growth (s/α) which depends on the saving habits of people and the production technique, should equal the natural rate (n) which depends on the growth of labor force. Since the saving rate, capital coefficient and the rate of growth of labor force are determined independently, equation (3.1.7) will not be satisfied except in special cases. If equality between the warranted and natural rates is not maintained, there will be ever increasing unemployment or excess capacity. Suppose, for example, s/α is larger than n which means capital stock accumulates faster than labor grows. Since capital and labor have to be used in a fixed proportion, labor will be a bottle-neck. So the capital which is <u>in use</u> will be smaller than capital <u>in existence</u>. The result will be excess capacity. If s/α is smaller than n, the argument is simply reversed. Not enough capital is accumulated resulting in unemployment of labor.

If the natural rate (n) exceeds the warranted rate (s/α), then in the long run aggregate output will grow at the rate s/α, per capita output will steadily decline and there will be ever increasing unemployment. When labor grows slower than capital, aggregate output will ultimately grow at the rate n, per capita output will be constant and there will be ever rising excess capacity. The above conclusions are formally shown in the next section.

3.1.2 Analysis of Long-run Behavior[1]

The formal analysis of the model will be simplified if the system is expressed in terms of the capital-labor ratio $k = K/L$. Omitting all time subscripts, the production function is rewritten as $Y = \min[K/\alpha, L/\beta]$. Since this function is linearly homogeneous in K and L, the left hand side and each of the arguments on the right hand side may be multiplied by $1/L$ without changing the equality. We therefore get

$$Y/L = \min[k/\alpha, 1/\beta] \tag{3.1.8}$$

Taking logarithms of both sides of the relation $k = K/L$ we get $\log K = \log K - \log L$. Differentiation of this with respect to t results in

$$\dot{k}/k = \dot{K}/K - \dot{L}/L \tag{3.1.9}$$

But $\dot{K} = I = S = sY$ and $\dot{L}/L = n$. Substituting these in (3.1.9) we obtain $\dot{k}/k = sY/K - n$, or by multiplying both sides by k and using (3.1.8), $\dot{k} = sY/L - nk = s \min[k/\alpha, 1/\beta] - nk$. Define the function $\psi(k)$ to be $\psi(k) = s \min[k/\alpha, 1/\beta]$. Then

$$\dot{k} = \psi(k) - nk \tag{3.1.10}$$

Since s, α, β and n are all given parameters, it is seen from (3.1.10) that $\dot{k}(t)$ is a function of $k(t)$ alone, that is, the time rate of change of the capital-labor ratio at each instant depends on the level of the capital-labor ratio at that time. Thus (3.1.10) is a first-order ordinary differential equation in k and $\dot{k}$.[2] Some of the qualitative characteristics of its solution can

---

[1] The analysis here follows that of Robert Solow [9]. This section may be skipped by any reader not interested in the details of the analysis.

[2] See the appendix to this chapter for a discussion of ordinary differential equations. Explicit solutions to this differential equation are obtainable (see Solow [9, pp. 73-76]).

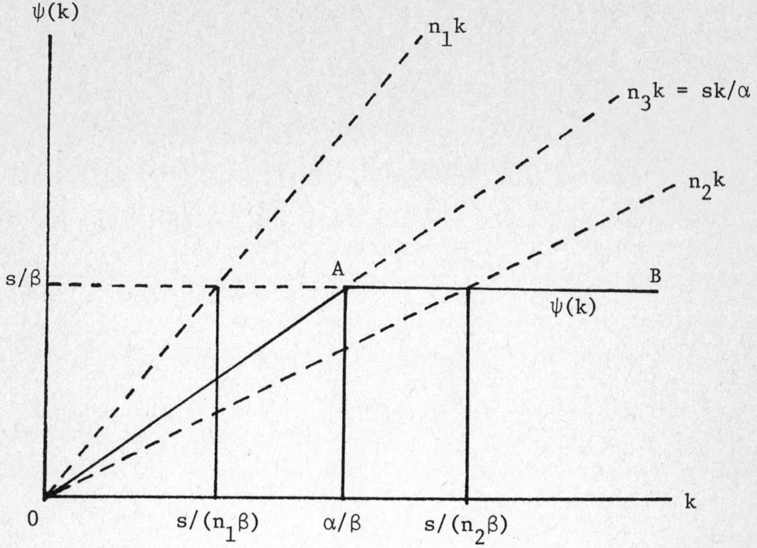

Figure 3.1

be obtained from Figure 3.1.

For $0 < k < \alpha/\beta$, $k/\alpha < 1/\beta$ and $\psi(k) = s \min[k/\alpha, 1/\beta] = sk/\alpha$. In this range $\psi(k)$ is represented by the line segment OA. When $k > \alpha/\beta$, $1/\beta < k/\alpha$ and therefore $\psi(k)$ is a constant equal to s/β and is represented by AB. Thus the entire representation of $\psi(k)$ is the line OAB. The line nk is a straight line through the origin with slope n.

Case 1: $n_1 > s/\alpha$: Suppose the natural growth rate (n_1) exceeds the warranted growth rate which means labor force grows faster than capital. Then in the long run, there will be ever increasing unemployment, aggregate output will grow at the rate s/α and per capita output would steadily decline.

The above conclusions may be reached by arguing as follows: If $n_1 > s/\alpha$, then the line n_1k is always above OAB which stands for $\psi(k)$. If follows from (3.1.10) that since $\psi(k) < n_1k$, $\dot{k}$ is always negative which implies that k is forever declining and will ultimately tend to zero. Thus, whatever the initial position of the economy, given enough time the capital intensity will drop below α/β. When this happens, K/α is less than L/β and therefore output will be K/α. Since capital and labor must be used in a fixed proportion, output will also be $\bar{L}/\beta$ where $\bar{L}$ is the employed labor force. Therefore, $\bar{L} = \beta K/\alpha$ and $\bar{L}/L = \beta k/\alpha$ giving us the employment rate. We just saw that k will steadily decline which means the proportion of the labor force actually employed will steadily decline while the labor force grows resulting in ever rising unemployment.

"Will the aggregate output also decline?" The answer is no. Aggregate output will ultimately grow at the rate s/α. This is so because in the very long run (i.e. for large t) $Y = K/\alpha$. Therefore, $\dot{Y}/Y = \dot{K}/K = sY/K = s/\alpha$. Thus output and the stock of capital will grow at the rate s/α. Let y be the per capita output Y/L. Since Y grows at the rate s/α and L grows at the rate n_1, y will grow at the rate $s/\alpha - n_1$ which is negative. Thus in the long run, per capita output would decline even though actual output is growing.

<u>Case 2: $n_2 < s/\alpha$:</u> If the warranted rate exceeds the natural rate (n_2) then the line n_2k will be as drawn in Figure 3.1. In this case, there will be ever rising excess capacity, aggregate output will grow at the rate n, in the long run, and per capita output will be constant. This is seen as follows.

For all capital intensities below $s/n_2\beta$, $\psi(k) > n_2k$ which means $\dot{k}$ is positive and capital intensity will increase until it reaches $s/n_2\beta$. When k is higher than $s/n_2\beta$, $\psi(k) < n_2k$ and therefore $\dot{k} < 0$ which means k will decline to $s/n_2\beta$. It is thus evident that no matter where the economy starts, the capital intensity will ultimately reach the level $s/n_2\beta$. But at this point $K/\alpha > L/\beta$ (because $k = s/n_2\beta > \alpha/\beta$) and output is given by L/β. Output is also equal to $\bar{K}/\alpha$, where $\bar{K}$ is the actually utilized capital. Hence $\bar{K} = \alpha L/\beta$ and $K - \bar{K} = K - \alpha L/\beta = (k - \alpha/\beta)L = (k - \alpha/\beta)L_o e^{nt}$. But $k > \alpha/\beta$ which means $K - \bar{K}$ is positive implying that there will be excess capacity which according to the above equation will steadily increase. Since aggregate output is L/β or $L_o e^{nt}/\beta$, it will grow at the same rate as the labor force.

Per capita output will be constant at $1/\beta$.

Case 3: $n_3 = s/\alpha$: If the initial capital intensity were to the right of α/β, $\psi(k) = s/\beta = n_3\alpha/\beta < n_3k$ and therefore $\dot{k} < 0$ which means k will decline. This will continue until k reaches α/β, which corresponds to the full employment of both inputs. To the left of α/β, $\psi(k) = n_3k$ and $\dot{k} = 0$ implying that the capital-labor ratio will be unchanged from its initial value. If the initial capital intensity $k_o \leq \alpha/\beta$ then $K/\alpha \leq L/\beta$ and hence capital will be fully employed. But labor will be fully employed if and only if it was initially fully employed. Otherwise whatever percentage of unemployment there was initially, will be preserved.

3.1.3 Instability of the Warranted Rate and the Knife-edge

Harrod was concerned not just with the inequality of the warranted and natural rates as an obstacle to steady growth with full employment of resources. He argued that the warranted rate itself may be unstable irrespective of whether the two rates are equal or not. For instance, suppose investment rises above the level required for the economy to grow along the warranted path. Harrod argued that income would then rise faster than the capital stock through the multiplier effect. This implies a fall in the capital-output ratio and a consequent rise in the real return to capital. This will induce higher levels of investment moving the acutal growth rate away from the warranted growth rate. The economy is thus at best balanced on a knife-edge. Even a slight deviation from equality of the warranted and actual rates would trigger increasing deviations between them.

Harrod made no attempt to formalize his arguments for the instability of the warranted growth path. Several studies have since been written which attempted to study the disequilibrium dynamics of Harrod's model. In the following pages we present two alternative formulations, one demonstrating the instability of the warranted rate and the other reaching the opposite conclusion. Our presentation is a synthesis of the papers by Phillips [12,13], Rose [14], Hahn and Mathews [4], and Jorgenson [15].

Model 1: Let K be the actual stock of capital, X the desired capital stock, Y the actual output, z* the desired rate of capital accumulation (i.e. $\dot{X}/X$) and z the actual rate of accumulation of capital (i.e. $\dot{K}/K$). Given Y, the desired capital stock is assumed to be given by the relation $X/Y = \alpha$. The next assumption of the model is that the desired rate of accumulation of capital is determined by the following partial adjustment mechanism:

$$z^* = s/\alpha + \lambda(X - K)/K \qquad \lambda > 0 \tag{3.1.11}$$

The actual rate of accumulation changes according to the following adaptive rule:

$$\dot{z} = \mu(z^* - z) \qquad \mu > 0 \tag{3.1.12}$$

Thus if the desired capital stock exceeds the actual capital stock (i.e. $X > K$), then the desired rate of accumulation increases. If this desired rate exceeds the actual rate, then there is an increase in the actual rate of accumulation of capital. λ and μ are adjustment coefficients. We also have the result that $z = \dot{K}/K = sY/K$. Given the above four relations, it is easy to derive the following differential equation in z(t):

$$\dot{z} - \mu(\lambda\alpha/s - 1)z = \mu(s/\alpha - \lambda) \tag{3.1.13}$$

It will be seen from the Appendix to this chapter that the above differential equation is of the form (A.10). By proceeding as described in the Appendix, we can solve for z(t) as follows:

$$z(t) = s/\alpha + (z_o - s/\alpha)e^{\mu(\lambda\alpha/s - 1)t} \tag{3.1.14}$$

where z_o is the actual rate of accumulation of capital at time zero.

For the system to be stable the actual rate z(t) must converge to the warranted rate s/α. In other words,

$$\lim_{t\to\infty} z(t) = s/\alpha$$

This is possible if and only if $\lambda < s/\alpha$. Thus a necessary and sufficient condition for the stability of the warranted rate of growth is that the speed of adjustment λ must be less than the warranted rate. Will this condition be satisfied in practice? Reasonable intervals for s and α will be $.05 \le s \le .15$ and

$1.5 \leq \alpha \leq 3$. This implies that $.017 \leq s/\alpha \leq .1$. Thus for stability, λ must be less than .1 or equivalently firms must take a minimum of approximately 10 years ($1/\lambda$) to bridge the gap between desired capital stock and actual capital stock. Since this seems an excessively long period, the stability condition is not likely to be satisfied in practice. Thus the actual rate is likely to diverge from the warranted rate giving rise to the knife-edge.

Model 2: An alternative specification of the disequilibrium dynamics leads to a stable warranted growth rate at least for small discrepancies. Let x be the incremental capital-output ratio and z be the capital-output ratio. Thus $x(t) = \dot{K}/\dot{Y}$ and $z(t) = K/Y$. As before, capital accumulation ($\dot{K}$) is equal to saving (sY). However, firms change their production technique, as represented by changes in the incremental capital-output ratio, if the actual capital-output ratio $z(t)$ differs from the desired ratio α. More specifically,

$$\dot{x}(t) = P(x,z) = b[\alpha - z(t)] \qquad b > 0 \tag{3.1.15}$$

How will this system behave in the long run? It is not possible to characterize the above system in a single differential equation of the form in (3.1.13). However, the system can be reduced to two differential equations in x and z which can be used to analyze long run behavior. Logarithmically differentiating $z = K/Y$ with respect to t we get,

$$\frac{\dot{z}}{z} = \frac{\dot{K}}{K} - \frac{\dot{Y}}{Y} = \frac{sY}{K} - \frac{\dot{K}}{xY} = \frac{s}{z} - \frac{s}{x}$$

We thus have,

$$\dot{z} = Q(x,z) = s(1 - z/x) \tag{3.1.16}$$

The equations of motions of the system have therefore been reduced to the two first order differential equations (3.1.15) and (3.1.16). Note that neither of the equations explicitly involves time. The stability of the system can be analyzed by referring to the techniques discussed in the Appendix [See equation (A.15)].

First note from (3.1.15) that when the capital output ratio

(z) is α then $\dot{x} = 0$, that is, x has no tendency to change. But this situation will not prevail forever because z will change by equation (3.1.16). If, however, $z = x$, then $\dot{z} = 0$ which means z will tend to be unchanged. At the point $x = \alpha = z$ we have $\dot{x} = 0 = \dot{z}$ which implies that once an economy reaches this point, the capital-output ratio remains at the desired level α for all time periods. Such a position is therefore called a steady state or long run equilibrium. It is clear that a steady state exists, but the important question is whether the system will eventually reach the steady state point (α,α) if initially x had some value x_o and z had a value z_o. To examine this we resort to Theorems (A.3) and (A.4) of the Appendix. Define $a_{11} = \partial\dot{x}/\partial x$, $a_{12} = \partial\dot{x}/\partial z$, $a_{21} = \partial\dot{z}/\partial x$ and $a_{22} = \partial\dot{z}/\partial z$ all of which are evaluated at the equilibrium point (α,α). We then have $a_{11} = 0$, $a_{12} = -b$, $a_{21} = s/\alpha$ and $a_{22} = -s/\alpha$. The necessary and sufficient conditions for local stability (i.e. small deviations from equilibrium) are given by $a_{11} + a_{22} < 0$ and $a_{11}a_{22} - a_{12}a_{21} > 0$. It is easy to verify that both these conditions are satisfied. Thus for small deviations from the steady state, the system will return to it. It is left as an exercise to the reader (Exercise 3.9) that if the deviations are large, stability is not assured. Cyclical behavior is possible. Thus global stability (i.e. stability from any initial position) is not assured but local stability is.

It is evident from these two models that different conclusions are possible regarding the instability of the warranted path depending on how the disequilibrium mechanism is specified. The question then is: which is a good theory of investment behavior? Neither of the two mechanisms discussed above can claim approximations to reality. The adjustment behavior is specified a priori rather than derived from some kind of optimization process. As will be seen in future chapters, this weakness is common to a majority of growth models.

3.1.4 Modifications of the Model

Whether we assume fixity of production coefficients a priori or ex post because of a fixed interest rate, it is clear from the above analysis that for capital and labor to be fully utilized with steady growth, it is necessary that $s/\alpha = n$. Since s, α, and n are independently determined, the above equation is not likely to be satisfied except by coincidence. To have a model in which the two rates can become equal, it is necessary to modify one or the other of the assumptions of the Harrod-Domar model.

One of the assumptions made above was that production coefficients are fixed. This can be relaxed by assuming substitutability between the factors. A class of growth models which assume that capital and labor are smoothly substitutable has come to be known as <u>Neo-Classical</u> growth models. A simple version of it, originally presented by Robert Solow and T. W. Swan, is discussed in section 3.2. It will be seen that the inequality of the warranted and natural rates will disappear in the long run if the production possibilities can be varied continuously. Moreover, stability can also be achieved.

<u>Neo-Keynesian</u> variations (often known as Cambridge growth models) of the Harrod-Domar model place the burden of adjustment on the saving rate. For example, wage-earners and profit-receivers could be saving at different rates. The overall saving rate will then vary with the distribution of income between the two classes. The equality of warranted and natural rates can be brought about by suitably varying the distribution of income. Models of this type have been analyzed by Kaldor, Pasinetti, Robinson and others and will be discussed in Chapter 7. Neo-classical models with varying saving rates are discussed in Chapter 6.

Another modification is to assume that the rate of growth of population (n) is not fixed but is endogenously determined. For example, n might depend on per capita income or on the gap between current real wages and subsistence wages. Models of this type are considered in the exercises at the end of the chapter with hints as to their long run behavior.

3.2 The Solow-Swan Model

It was found in the last section that when capital and labor have to be used in a fixed proportion in the production of a commodity, steady growth with full utilization of both factors cannot be achieved unless the rate of growth of labor force was equal to the ratio of the saving rate to the capital-output ratio. One of the ways in which this phenomenon can be avoided is to assume that production possibilities can be varied continuously. A growth model with this modification was originally proposed independently by Robert Solow and Trevor Swan [9,10]. The contributions of these two economists has sparked substantial interest in a class of growth models in which capital and labor can be continuously substituted for each other. Models of this type are known as Neo-Classical growth models. In this section, the long-run properties of the Solow-Swan model, which is the simplest of all neo-classical growth models, are discussed in full detail. The analysis also brings out the basic techniques used in analyzing models of economic growth.

The basic assumptions of the model are the following:

(i) Production function: The earlier assumption of fixed coefficients in production is now dropped. The production possibilities are represented by the production function $Y = F(K,L)$ which is single-valued with continuous first and second order partial derivatives.[1] Capital and labor are therefore continuously substitutable. It is also assumed that production exhibits constant returns to scale implying that the function $F(K,L)$ is linearly homogeneous. It was seen in Chapter 2 (equation 2.2a) that a linearly homogeneous production function $F(K,L)$ can be written as follows.

$$Y = F(K,L) = Lf(k) \tag{3.2.1}$$

where $f(k) = F(k,1)$ and

$$k \equiv K/L \tag{3.2.2}$$

---

[1]The t arguments in the variables are omitted from now on in order to simplify the notation.

$f(k)$ is Y/L the average product of labor. Recall from equations (2.4) and (2.5) that the marginal product of capital is given by $f'(k)$ and that of labor is $f(k) - kf'(k)$. The average product of capital is $f(k)/k$.

(ii) Saving behavior: The assumption regarding the saving behavior is the same as before. The overall saving-income ratio $(s > 0)$ is a fixed parameter.[1] Thus aggregate saving is

(3.2.3) $$S = sY$$

As before, equilibrium in the commodity market implies that aggregate saving should be equal to gross investment. The term gross is used here because we will presently introduce depreciation of capital.

(3.2.4) $$S = I$$

(iii) Labor force: As in the Harrod-Domar model, the labor force, L, is assumed to grow at the exogenous rate $n(n > 0)$. This gives

(3.2.5) $$\dot{L}/L = n \quad \text{or} \quad L = L_o e^{nt}$$

(iv) Depreciation: In our analysis of the Harrod-Domar model depreciation of capital was ignored. Zero depreciation is equivalent to assuming that capital stock is infinitely durable. This is obviously not realistic. A straightforward way of introducing depreciation in the analysis is to assume that capital depreciates at the constant proportional rate $\delta(\delta > 0)$. That is, a proportion δ of the existing capital "disappears" from the production scene.[2] If depreciation is denoted by D, then

(3.2.6) $$D = \delta K$$

---

[1] This assumption is relaxed in Chapter 6. Neo-classical growth models in which workers and firms have different saving rates are discussed in that chapter.

[2] Other types of assumptions are possible. For a summary of these assumptions and their implications to growth models see Hahn and Mathews [4].

Capital formation: Since capital stock is depreciating, not all of saving or gross investment will go into the formation of new capital. Part of gross investment will be used to replace the depreciated capital. Thus the change in capital stock is given by net investment which is gross investment less depreciation. In other words,

$$\dot{K} = I - D \tag{3.2.7}$$

(v) Factor prices: In analyzing the long-run behavior of an economic system we are not just interested in the movement of aggregate output or capital over time. It is of considerable interest to examine how the prices of factors -- real wage rate (w) and real rate of return to capital (r) -- behave over time. We would also like to learn how the factor shares (e.g. the share of capital π encountered in Chapter 2) would be altered.

In order to describe the movement of factor prices, we need a mechanism to first determine these entities. Neo-classical growth models make the following crucial assumptions which enable the determination of the factor prices. The assumptions are: (a) there is perfect competition and (b) aggregate profits are maximized. Aggregate profits are given by $F(K,L) - wL - rK$. The necessary conditions for maximizing aggregate profits are those given by the marginal productivity theory. These are $w = \partial F/\partial L$ and $r = \partial F/\partial K$. These equations are obtained by partially differentiating the expression for profit with respect to K and L and setting the results to zero. If the bordered Hessian conditions stated in Chapter 2 (section 2.2) hold, then the isoquants will have the shape indicated in Figure 2.2. Profits will then be maximum at the points at which the above equations are satisfied. The equations state that the real returns to the factors are given by their respective marginal products.[1] Since the marginal products

[1] A number of economists (in particular Hahn, Kaldor, Pasinetti, Robinson, and Stein) have questioned the validity of these assumptions. They argue that there are imperfections in the market which cast some doubts on the marginal productivity conditions. Neo-Keynesian variations in these assumptions proposed by these economists are discussed in Chapter 7.

of capital and labor are respectively f'(k) and f(k) - kf'(k), the following relationships hold.

(3.2.8) $$w = f(k) - kf'(k)$$

(3.2.9) $$r = f'(k)$$

Structural equations: Equations (3.2.1) through (3.2.9) completely describe the behavior of the economy and are called the Structural equations. It would be useful to reproduce them all in one place, and rearrange them in terms of markets.

(3.2.1)	Production function	$Y = Lf(k)$
(3.2.2)	Definition	$k \equiv K/L$
(3.2.3)	Commodity market	$S = sY$
(3.2.4)		$S = I$
(3.2.7)	Capital market	$\dot{K} = I - D$
(3.2.6)		$D = \delta K$
(3.2.9)		$r = f'(k)$
(3.2.5)	Labor market	$L = L_o e^{nt}$
(3.2.8)		$w = f(k) - kf'(k)$

The above structural equations represent basically three markets. In the commodity market the level of consumption (and hence saving) depends on the aggregate supply of goods. The supply of goods is determined by a production function relating output to two factors of production -- capital and labor (represented by firms and workers for convenience). It is assumed that at each instant there is full employment equilibrium represented by the equality of saving and investment. This is achieved through perfectly flexible wages and rents. The second market is the capital market. The supply of existing capital is increased by the amount of net investment at any instant. Since there is only one commodity which can be consumed or invested, the distinction between the commodity and capital markets is only for descriptive purposes. By perfect competition and profit maximization, firms will choose that capital intensity which equates marginal products to the respective factor prices. The marginal product of capital is thus equal to the real rent on capital. At each instant, the depreciation of capital is a fixed fraction of the existing stock. Finally we have the labor market. The supply of labor grows at an exogenously given rate. The demand for labor is determined by setting the marginal product of labor equal to the real wage. Since wages are also flexible, full employment of labor is assured.

The structure consists of nine simultaneous equations in the nine jointly determined (endogenous) variables Y,K,L,S,I,D,k,w and r. The known parameters of the system are s,n and δ. The exogenous variable is "time" denoted by t.

Basic differential equation: The analysis of the system will be substantially simplified if some of the variables are eliminated by substitutions. For example, in equation (3.2.7) substituting for I and D from the relationships (3.2.3), (3.2.4) and (3.2.6) and then using (3.2.1) we obtain the following: $\dot{K} = sY - \delta K = sLf(k) - \delta K$. Dividing through by K and using the relation $k = K/L$ we obtain

(3.2.10) $$\dot{K}/K = sf(k)/k - \delta \equiv \phi(k)$$

It will be noted that $\phi(k)$ is nothing but the warranted rate of growth, i.e. the rate at which capital stock will grow if it is fully employed. If $\delta = 0$ and the aggregate output is given by $Y = K/\alpha$, as in the Harrod-Domar model, then $f(k)/k$ which is the average product of capital is $1/\alpha$. Thus the warranted rate of growth reduces to s/α which is what we had before.

First taking logarithms of both sides of (3.2.2) and then differentiating with respect to t we get

(3.2.11) $$\dot{k}/k = \dot{K}/K - \dot{L}/L = \phi(k) - n$$

or

(3.2.12) $$\dot{k}/k = sf(k)/k - (n + \delta)$$

Equation (3.2.12) is the basic differential equation of the Solow-Swan model. As before, the time rate of change ($\dot{k}$) of the capital intensity at time t depends only on the capital intensity

(k) at that time. Explicit solution to the above first-order differential equation is obtainable only if the exact form of the function f(k) is known. Assume that (3.2.12) can be solved explicitly to give the time path of the capital-labor ratio k(t). The time path of labor L(t) is known from (3.2.5). From these, the time path of aggregate output is obtained from the relation (3.2.1) and that for capital by multiplying k(t) by L(t). Once k(t) is known, the time paths for w and r are given by (3.2.8) and (3.2.9) respectively. We thus have the time paths for output, capital, capital intensity, real wages and real rents. Since we are assuming that wages and rents are flexible, they will adjust suitably in order to maintain full employment of both capital and labor at each point of time.

3.2.1 Steady-state Properties

In growth theory, the focus of the analysis is on steady-state which is the analogue of the equilibrium in static theory. A steady-state path is defined as that path along which capital and output grow at the same constant rate. In other words,

$$\dot{Y}/Y = \dot{K}/K \equiv g \tag{3.2.13}$$

By integrating each of the two equations and then taking exponentials (similar to the derivation of equation 3.1.5) we obtain $Y = Y_o e^{gt}$ and $K = K_o e^{gt}$. Thus a steady-state path is an exponential time path. Along this path the capital-output ratio is a constant because $K/Y = K_o/Y_o$ for all t.

"Can capital and output grow at constant but different rates?" The answer is no, not if the aggregate saving ratio is constant. Suppose that capital stock grows at the constant rate g. Then from (3.2.10), $\dot{K}/K = sY/K - \delta = g$ for all t. Since s, δ and g are constant, this implies that Y/K must be constant in the steady state. This is possible only if output is growing at the same rate as capital. Thus constancy of the overall saving ratio implies that when capital grows at a constant rate then output must grow at the same rate. If the saving rate changes appropriately, then capital and labor can grow at different rates.

The assumption of constant returns to scale implies that in steady state the capital-labor ratio k is also a constant. This can be seen as follows. By linear homogeneity, $Y = F(K,L) = KF(1,1/k)$. Therefore the capital-output ratio is a constant if and only if $F(1,1/k)$ is a constant for all t, which is possible only if k is a constant at all time periods, i.e. $\dot{k} = 0$. Thus, in the steady state, capital, labor and aggregate output will all grow exponentially at the same rate. It is easy to see that consumption and investment will also grow exponentially and the consumption-investment ratio will be a constant. Since k is a constant, w and r will also remain constant which means the factor shares will be constant. Because the relative factor shares are constant on the steady state path, it is commonly referred to as the balanced growth path. Once an economy follows the balanced growth path, thereafter income distribution and commodity distribution remain constant with no factor receiving an increasing or decreasing share of income. In advanced countries, the capital-output ratio and relative factor shares have both been nearly constant in the long run. This constancy is the reason why in the literature on economic growth so much emphasis is placed on the steady-state path. Henceforth, we will use the terms steady-state, balanced growth and long run equilibrium to stand for equivalent states. Three basic questions arise in connection with the steady state, viz, existence, stability and comparative dynamics. Each of these is now discussed in turn.

Existence: The first is the existence of the steady state. Given the structure of the system, does a balanced growth path exist? It was seen in the Harrod-Domar model that full employment steady growth was not possible unless $s/\alpha = n$ where α is the fixed capital-output ratio. We are also interested in knowing whether the balanced growth path is unique or whether several steady states exist. More specifically, we would like to know the conditions under which a unique steady state exists.

It was just seen that steady state is achieved when capital intensity is constant. Setting $\dot{k} = 0$ in (3.2.11) we obtain the relation

$$(3.2.14) \qquad \phi(k) = sf(k)/k - \delta = n$$

As was noted earlier, $\phi(k)$ is the warranted rate of growth. The above condition therefore implies the equality of the warranted and natural growth rates. In the Harrod-Domar model the capital-output ratio was fixed and therefore equality between the warranted and natural rates was improbable since these rates were obtained independently. But in the Solow-Swan model the capital-output ratio is flexible. Under certain conditions it is possible to find a capital intensity k* satisfying (3.2.14).

By assumption the function f(k) is continuous and hence $\phi(k)$ is also continuous. If there exists a capital intensity k_1 at which the warranted rate exceeds the natural rate and another capital intensity k_2 at which the natural rate exceeds the warranted rate, then it is clear by the continuity of $\phi(k)$ that a capital intensity k* will exist such that these rates are equal. Thus a sufficient condition for the existence of at least one solution to (3.2.14) is the following:

There exist k_1 and k_2 such that

$$(3.2.15) \qquad \phi(k_1) > n \quad \text{and} \quad \phi(k_2) < n$$

A second set of sufficient conditions, stronger than the above but more interesting, are the following:

$$(3.2.16) \qquad \text{(a)} \lim_{K \to 0} F_K = \infty \quad \text{(b)} \lim_{K \to \infty} F_K = 0 \quad \text{(c)}\ f(0) \geq 0$$

These conditions are called <u>boundary conditions</u>. The first condition says that when capital is used in small quantities (near zero) the extra output obtained when capital is increased slightly will be infinitely large. Condition (b) implies that when a very large amount of capital is used the marginal product of capital is almost zero. The third condition says that when capital intensity is zero the average product of labor is zero or positive. If $f(0) = 0$, this means that some capital is necessary in order to produce a positive output. For example, the Cobb-Douglas production function $Y = K^{\alpha}L^{1-\alpha}$ for which $f(k) = k^{\alpha}$ satisfies this property. $f(0) > 0$ implies that even if capital is zero, a positive output can be obtained by labor alone. An example of this kind is the CES production function with elasticity of substitution greater than 1. Both of these production functions satisfy the conditions (a) and (b).

Let us now examine how (3.2.16) implies the existence of at least one steady state solution. Since $F_K = f'(k)$, conditions (a) and (b) imply that $f'(0) = \infty$ and $f'(\infty) = 0$. Next consider the average product of capital $f(k)/k$. By L'Hospital's rule, $\underset{k\to\infty}{\text{lt}}\, f(k)/k = \underset{k\to\infty}{\text{lt}}\, f'(k) = 0$. If $f(0) > 0$, then $\underset{k\to o}{\text{lt}}\, f(k)/k = \infty$. If $f(0) = 0$, then by L'Hospital's rule $\underset{k\to o}{\text{lt}}\, f(k)/k = f'(0) = \infty$. Therefore, both the average and marginal products of capital are infinite at the origin and zero when capital-labor ratio is infinite. Since $\phi(k)$ depends on $f(k)/k$, it follows that $\phi(0) = \infty$ and $\phi(\infty) = -\delta$.

These conditions imply that $\phi(k)$ starts at infinity and ultimately goes below zero. Since $\phi(k)$ is continuous, it is evident that $\phi(k)$ must equal n for some k*. Thus there exists at least one solution to (3.2.14). Multiple solutions are possible as shown in Figure 3.2. The reasons for the arrows in the diagram will be presented later.

<u>Uniqueness</u>: Multiple equilibria can be ruled out by requiring, in addition, that $\phi(k)$ be monotonic. If at least one solution exists and $\phi(k)$ is monotonic, clearly there will be only one k* such that $\phi(k^*) = n$, as shown in Figure 3.3. Since $\phi(0) = \infty$ and $\underset{k\to\infty}{\text{lt}}\, \phi(k) = -\delta$, $\phi(k)$ must be monotonically decreasing, that is $\phi'(k) < 0$ is a sufficient condition for uniqueness of the steady state. But $\phi'(k) = s(kf' - f)/k^2$ and therefore $\phi'(k) < 0$ if and only if $f(k)/k > f'(k)$ or the marginal product of capital must be smaller than the average product of capital, for all capital-labor ratios. We saw in Chapter 2 (Figure 2.3) that the conditions

(3.2.17) $\quad$ (a) $f'(k) > 0$ $\quad$ and $\quad$ (b) $f''(k) < 0$

together with the condition $f(0) \geq 0$ imply that the marginal product of capital is smaller than its average product with average

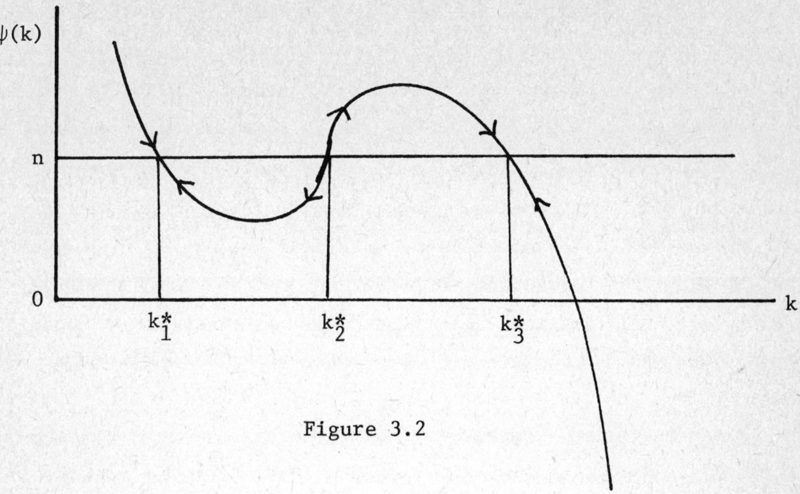

Figure 3.2

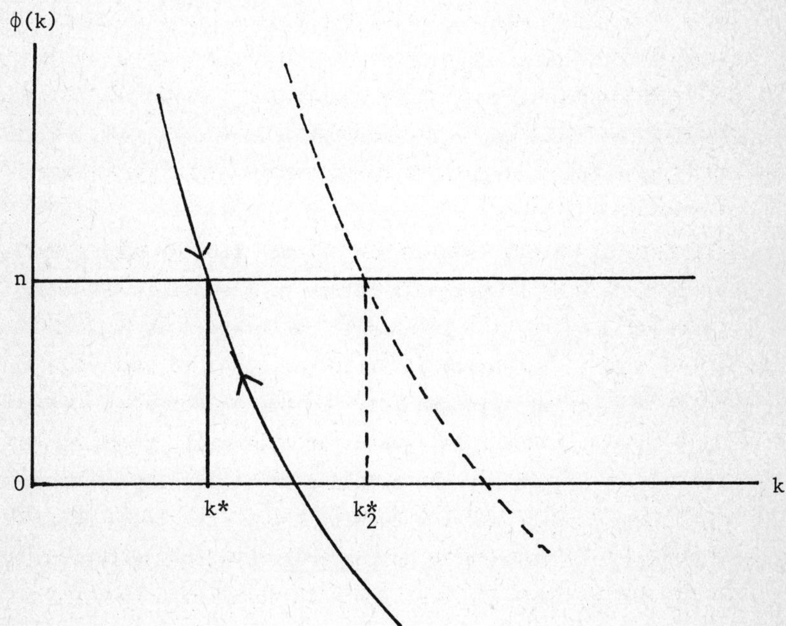

Figure 3.3

product naturally declining. Thus a set of sufficient conditions for the uniqueness of the steady state (assuming the conditions for existence) are given by (3.2.17). These are called the interior slope conditions. The first condition states that capital's marginal product is always positive and the second that there is diminishing marginal product. The condition $f - kf' > 0$ implies that the marginal product of labor is always positive. The conditions specified by equations (3.2.16) and (3.2.17) are commonly known as the neo-classical conditions, also known as Inada conditions [16]. These conditions imply that a unique steady state exists.

Stability. If a steady state solution exists, will the economic system spontaneously move towards it if it were not initially on the steady state path? In other words, is the system stable? Recall that the basic equation of motion of the system is expressed in terms of the capital-labor ratio. In equilibrium (which is the same as steady state), $\dot{k} = 0$ at the capital intensity k^*. The system is said to be stable if $\underset{t\to\infty}{\text{lt}}\, k(t) = k^*$, i.e. given enough time, the capital-labor ratio converges to the constant k^*. We must distinguish between two kinds of stability, local stability and global stability. A solution k^* is said to be locally stable if when a "small" disturbance from the equilibrium position is made, the system will return to the original steady state corresponding to k^*. If a small disturbance is made from k^* and the new capital intensity is $k(t)$ (not equal to k^*), then the further behavior of $k(t)$ is specified by the equation of motion (3.2.12). If the movement is towards k^* ultimately reaching it, (i.e. $\underset{t\to\infty}{\text{lt}}\, k(t) = k^*$) we say the solution k^* is locally stable. If $k(t)$ moves away from k^* never returning to it the steady state corresponding to k^* is said to be unstable. Supposing for any arbitrary initial position (except unstable equilibrium positions), the system will ultimately reach some locally stable position. If this happens, we say there is global stability.

To answer the question of stability of the Solow-Swan world, first assume that there is a unique steady state as in Figure 3.3.

For all capital intensities to the left of k^*, $\phi(k) > n$. From (3.2.12) we see that this implies that $\dot{k}$ is positive which means k will increase. This will continue as long as $k < k^*$ and in the end k^* will be reached. Similarly when $k > k^*$, $\phi(k) < n$ and $\dot{k}$ is negative which means k will decline to k^*. Thus, for any arbitrary initial position, the capital intensity will ultimately reach k^*. This situation is therefore globally stable (which implies local stability). The arrows drawn in Figure 3.3 indicate this.

We can give a straightforward economic explanation for the stability of this case. If initially $\phi(k) > n$, the warranted rate of growth exceeds the natural rate. This implies that capital is accumulating faster than labor and is relatively more plentiful. Rents would therefore decline. Firms would substitute capital for labor and therefore capital intensity would rise. Since the average product curve is downward sloping, an increase in k will lower the average product of capital, thus reducing the warranted rate. If the new warranted rate is still larger than n, the process will continue until the two rates are equal. The mechanism is similar when labor grows faster than capital. Thus, unlike the Harrod-Domar model, there is a mechanism which brings about the equality of natural and warranted rates of growth. This automatic adjustment is possible because of the flexibility of the capital-output ratio.

Suppose there are several possible steady states as in Figure 3.2. When $k < k_1^*$, $\phi(k) > n$ and therefore $\dot{k}$ is positive and k will increase. When $k_1 < k < k_2$, $\phi(k) < n$ and k will decrease. By a similar argument, as long as $k_2 < k < k_3$, k will increase. To the right of k_3, $\phi(k) < n$ and hence k will decline. Thus the directional arrows describing the movement of $\phi(k)$ are as drawn in Figure 3.2. It is evident that k_1^* and k_3^* are locally stable because if we are in their neighborhood, we will move towards them. But if there is a slight disturbance from k_2^*, the system will move away from it to k_1^* or k_3^*. Therefore k_2^* is an unstable equilibrium. From Theorem A.2 of the appendix to this chapter, any equilibrium position at which $\phi(k)$ crosses the straight line n from above (i.e. has a negative slope) will be locally stable and if the crossing is from below, the position is one of instability. The system as a whole is globally stable because from any initial position (except k_2^*) the system will reach either k_1^* or k_3^* both of which are stable. Even if there are more solutions the system will be globally stable provided the solutions are all distinct.[1]

Comparative Dynamics: In static macro models we often ask the question: "what would happen if one of the parameters of the system were changed?" For example, we might be interested in finding out the effect on the equilibrium gross national product, of an increase in the tax rate or money supply. This is Comparative Statics, where we investigate the changes in a system from one position of equilibrium to another without regard to the transitional process. Similar questions also arise in dynamic models. We would, for example, be interested in knowing the effect of an increase in the saving rate on the steady state growth rate of aggregate output or real wages. These come under the subject of Comparative Dynamics. It should be emphasized that the analysis is concerned with comparing two steady states. We do not ask what happens in the transitional period from one steady state to another.

To begin with, assume that there exists a unique solution to (3.2.14). Otherwise the results may be ambiguous. Uniqueness is ensured by presupposing the neo-classical conditions (3.2.16) and (3.2.17). The first entity we would be interested in is the long run (i.e. steady state) growth rate (g) of aggregate output. Logarithmic differentiation of the production function, $Y = Lf(k)$ with respect to t yields $\dot{Y}/Y = \dot{L}/L + \dot{k}f'(k)/f(k)$. In steady state $\dot{k} = 0$. Therefore $g = (\dot{Y}/Y)^* = \dot{L}/L = n$. The star (*) indicates that the steady state value is obtained. Also, by definition,

---

[1]Since $\phi(0) = \infty$, $\phi(k)$ will first cross n from above and therefore that solution will be stable. Similarly, since $\lim_{k\to\infty} \phi(k) < 0$, at the largest solution also $\phi(k)$ will cross from above. So the two extreme positions are stable.

capital and output grow at the same rate in the steady state. Therefore

$$g = (\dot{Y}/Y)^* = (\dot{K}/K)^* = \dot{L}/L = n \tag{3.2.19}$$

Thus capital and output grow at the same constant rate n as the labor force. The long run growth rate is therefore independent of the saving rate, the rate of depreciation and the form of the production function. Thus $\partial g/\partial s = \partial g/\partial \delta = 0$ and $\partial g/\partial n = 1$. The only way to raise the steady state rate of growth of output is to raise the growth rate of the labor force.

This is a somewhat unhappy result because intuitively we would expect that if the saving rate is higher, more investment will take place and capital as well as aggregate output would grow faster. This is indeed true in the short run (as seen from Exercise 3.1) but in the limit, the growth rate will converge back to n. In Figure 3.3 the dotted curve is $\phi(k)$ corresponding to a higher saving rate. Suppose the economy were initially on the steady state at k*. If suddenly the saving rate increases to s_2, $\phi(k)$ goes up. The new warranted rate of growth is higher than the natural rate, i.e. capital stock will start to grow faster than labor. But this cannot go on indefinitely because rents will fall and firms will substitute capital for labor and capital intensity would rise. The average and marginal products of capital would then decline slowing down the rate of growth of capital stock, and the warranted rate, which went up in the short run, will ultimately go back to n. The capital intensity, however, will not remain at k* but will move to a higher value k_2^*.[1] An increase in n with no change in the other parameters, will move the straight line n higher which corresponds to a lower capital intensity. Similarly, an increase in δ would lower k*. We thus have $\partial k^*/\partial s > 0$, $\partial k^*/\partial n < 0$ and $\partial k^*/\partial \delta < 0$.

---

[1]This can also be derived mathematically by differentiating (3.2.14) partially with respect to s and then solving for $\partial k/\partial s$. This gives $\partial k/\partial s = kf(k)/[s(f-kf')]$. Since $f - kf' > 0$, $\partial k/\partial s > 0$. A similar procedure may be adopted for changes in the other parameters.

The equilibrium capital intensity would go up when the saving rate goes up and go down when capital depreciates faster or labor grows faster. Once the nature of the changes in k* are known, the changes in other variables of interest are obtained in a straightforward manner. It was seen in Chapter 2 that the wage rate and capital intensity move in the same direction. If wages go up, firms would substitute capital for labor and k will go up. Analogously, rents (r) will move in the opposite direction. We thus have

$$\frac{\partial w^*}{\partial s} > 0, \quad \frac{\partial r^*}{\partial s} < 0, \quad \frac{\partial w^*}{\partial n} < 0, \quad \frac{\partial r^*}{\partial n} > 0, \quad \frac{\partial w^*}{\partial \delta} < 0, \quad \frac{\partial r^*}{\partial \delta} > 0$$

"What will be the effect on the share of capital $\pi(k^*)$?" The answer depends on the elasticity of substitution as known from Theorem 2.2. The results of the comparative dynamics analysis are summarized in a sensitivity table (Table 3.1) which gives the signs of the partial derivatives of the long run value of a variable under consideration with respect to s, n and δ.

Table 3.1: Sensitivities of the Solow-Swan Model

		s	n	δ
k^*		+	-	-
$(\dot{Y}/Y)^*$		0	+	0
$(\dot{y}/y)^* = (\dot{Y}/Y)^* - \dot{L}/L$		0	0	0
$(Y/L)^*$		+	-	-
w^*		+	-	-
r^*		-	+	+
$\pi(k^*)$ when	$\sigma < 1$	-	+	+
	$\sigma = 1$	0	0	0
	$\sigma > 1$	+	-	-

Golden Rule Path: It was pointed out above that an increase in the saving rate will not affect the long run rate of growth of output. This means that policies to raise the growth rate of either aggregate output or per capita output by stimulating saving, will be ineffective. However, the level of per capita output will be raised by an increase in the saving rate. This is because an increase in the rate of saving will increase k^*. Since per capita output in steady state is $y^* = f(k^*)$, an increase in k^* will result in an increase in the level of y^*. Thus it may be possible to raise the standard of living by adjusting the saving rate even though output may not grow any faster in the long run. If we take per capita consumption (or any monotonically increasing function of it) as an index of the social welfare of the economy, then we can determine the saving rate that will maximize social welfare by maximizing per capita consumption in the steady state. Phelps [8] has called the path corresponding to the maximum per capita consumption the Golden Rule Path which is now a widely accepted name.

Per capita consumption is given by $c = C/L = Y/L - S/L$. But Y/L is $f(k)$ and $S = I = \dot{K} + \delta K$ from (3.2.6) and (3.2.7). Substituting this in the above we get $c = f(k) - (\dot{K} + \delta K)/L = f(k) - k\dot{K}/K - \delta k$. In steady state $\dot{K}/K = n$. Therefore

(3.2.20) $$c^* = f(k^*) - (n + \delta)k^*$$

The necessary condition for maximizing c^* with respect to s is given by

$$\frac{\partial c^*}{\partial s} = [f'(k^*) - (n + \delta)] \frac{\partial k^*}{\partial s} = 0$$

Since $\partial k^*/\partial s > 0$, we have the Golden-rule condition

(3.2.21) $$f'(k^*) - \delta = n$$

The second order condition $\partial^2 c^*/\partial s^2 < 0$ is satisfied because

$$\frac{\partial^2 c^*}{\partial s^2} = [f'(k^*) - (n+\delta)] \frac{\partial k^{*2}}{\partial s^2} + f''(k^*)\left(\frac{\partial k^*}{\partial s}\right)^2$$

The first term vanishes by (3.2.21) and the second term is negative because $f''(k^*)$ is negative.

Equation (3.2.21) states that on the Golden rule path, the net rate of return to capital, which is the marginal product of capital less depreciation, should be equal to the natural rate n. An alternative interpretation is also possible. Equation (3.2.21) and (3.2.14) imply that $f'(k^*) = n + \delta = sf(k^*)/k^*$, from which we get $s = k^*f'(k^*)/f(k^*) = \pi(k^*)$, the share of capital in output. Therefore for per capita consumption to be maximized, the saving rate s should equal the steady state share of capital in output. This condition will be satisfied for the classical saving function, i.e. one in which all returns to capital are reinvested and all returns to labor are consumed. In this case, aggregate saving will be just the rental bill $Kr = Kf'(k)$. The overall saving-income ratio is $s = Kf'(k)/Y = \pi(k)$ which satisfies the Golden-rule condition.

3.2.2 An Example: The Cobb-Douglas Production Function

It would be useful to illustrate some of the results of the previous section with the help of the Cobb-Douglas production function $Y = K^{\alpha}L^{1-\alpha} = Lk^{\alpha}$, $0 < \alpha < 1$. Thus $f(k) = k^{\alpha}$, $w = k^{\alpha}(1-\alpha)$ and $r = \alpha k^{\alpha-1}$. The basic differential equation (3.2.12) then becomes

$$\dot{k} = sk^{\alpha} - (n+\delta)k \tag{3.2.22}$$

Solution to this differential equation is complicated because k^{α} is a non-linear function. However, the differential equation can be transformed into a linear form by means of the transformation $x = k^{1-\alpha}$. Differentiating this with respect to t and substituting for $\dot{k}$ in (3.2.22), $\dot{x} = (1-\alpha)[s - (n+\delta)x]$. It may be recognized that this is of the "variables separable" form (see the Appendix). We can therefore separate the variables and integrate them to get

$$\int \frac{dx}{s - (n+\delta)x} = (1-\alpha)t + \text{constant}$$

The left hand side integrates to $-(1/q)\log(s-qx)$ where $q = n + \delta$.

Multiplying both sides by $-q$ we get $\log(s-qx) = -q(1-\alpha)t$ + constant, or $s - qx$ = const. $e^{-q(1-\alpha)t}$ from which we can solve for x as $x = s/q + Ce^{-q(1-\alpha)t}$, where C is a constant of integration. The capital-labor ratio is then obtained as

$$k(t) = [s/q + Ce^{-q(1-\alpha)t}]^{\frac{1}{1-\alpha}}$$

Since $Y = Lk^{\alpha} = L_o e^{nt} k^{\alpha}$

$$Y(t) = L_o e^{nt}[s/q + Ce^{-q(1-\alpha)t}]^{\frac{\alpha}{1-\alpha}} \tag{3.2.23}$$

This gives the time path of aggregate output. As t tends to infinity, the second term in the square bracket tends to zero because $q(1-\alpha) > 0$. Thus the limiting time path of $Y(t)$ is given by $Y(t) \rightarrow (s/q)^{\alpha/1-\alpha} L_o e^{nt}$. Thus $Y(t)$ grows exponentially at the rate n. In the limit, per capita output will be $(s/q)^{\alpha/1-\alpha}$. The limiting capital-labor ratio is $(s/q)^{1/1-\alpha}$. The time paths of the other variables are obtained by straightforward substitutions.

3.3 Summary

The major result obtained from the Harrod-Domar model is that when capital and labor have to be combined in a fixed proportion to obtain any given level of output, the economy cannot have full employment of both factors, in the long run, unless the warranted rate of growth which is the ratio of the saving rate to the capital-output ratio, equals the natural rate which is the rate of growth of labor force. If the former exceeds the latter, capital stock will grow faster than labor. But since capital and labor have to be used in a fixed proportion, labor will be a bottleneck resulting in excess capacity. On the other hand, if the labor force grows faster, capital will be the limiting factor the consequence being increasing unemployment. There is no automatic mechanism to bring about the equality of the warranted and natural rates. The equality of these two rates can certainly be achieved by specific policies. For example, a less developed country generally has a low saving rate with scarcity of capital and a high rate of growth of population. We can therefore expect the warranted rate to be smaller than the natural rate. The equality can be achieved by any of the following ways: (i) raising the saving rate by taxing income and investing the proceeds, (ii) lowering the rate of growth of population by suitable incentives for family planning and (iii) lowering the capital-output ratio which means using more labor-intensive techniques.

The above mentioned inequality does not arise in the Solow-Swan model because it permits smooth substitutions between capital and labor. Since wages and rents are perfectly flexible, full employment of both factors is possible and in the long run, capital and output will grow at the same rate. Here also the warranted rate, which now depends on the capital intensity, must equal the natural rate. However, there exists a mechanism which spontaneously brings about the equality even if the initial position was not one of equality. If labor force grows more rapidly than the capital stock and is thus relatively plentiful, the wage rate would decline relative to the rents. Firms would then substitute labor for capital and the capital intensity would fall. This would raise the warranted rate. This process will continue until the warranted and natural rates are equal. The mechanism is similar when capital grows faster than labor.

Although the discrepancy between the warranted and natural rates has been eliminated by allowing substitutability between the factors, we are still left with an unhappy result. In the long run, capital, output and labor will all grow at the same rate n, and per capita output will be constant. This rate is independent of the saving rate and therefore policies to raise the long-run growth rate by stimulating saving will be ineffective although the level of per capita consumption can be maximized by adjusting the saving rate to equal the share of capital in output. In the next chapter it will be seen that per capita output can grow over time if there is technical progress. Also another model will be presented in which the long-run growth rate can be raised by increasing the saving rate.

REFERENCES

[1] Allen, R. G. D.: Macro-Economics, St. Martin's Press, 1967.

[2] Domar, Evsey D.: "Expansion and Unemployment," American Economic Review, March 1947.

[3] Goldsmith, Raymond: A Study of Saving in the United States, Princeton, 1955.

[4] Hahn, F. H., and R. C. O. Mathews: "The Theory of Economic Growth: A Survey," Surveys of Economic Theory, Vol. II, St. Martin's Press, 1967.

[5] Harrod, Roy F.: "An Essay in Dynamic Theory," Economic Journal, March 1939.

[6] Harrod, Roy F.: Toward a Dynamic Economics, Macmillan, 1948.

[7] Kuznets, Simon: "Proportion of Capital Formation to National Product," American Economic Review, Papers and Proceedings, May 1952.

[8] Phelps, E. S.: Golden Rules of Economic Growth, W. W. Norton, 1966.

[9] Solow, Robert M.: "A Contribution to the Theory of Economic Growth," Quarterly Journal of Economics, Feb. 1956.

[10] Swan, T. W.: "Economic Growth and Capital Accumulation," Economic Record, Nov. 1956.

[11] Uzawa, H., and J. Stiglitz: Readings in the Modern Theory of Economic Growth, MIT Press, 1969.

[12] Phillips, A. W.: "A Simple Model of Employment, Money and Prices in a Growing Economy," Economica, Nov. 1961.

[13] Phillips, A. W.: "Employment, Inflation and Growth," Economica, Feb. 1962.

[14] Rose, H.: "The Possibility of Warranted Growth," Economic Journal, June 1959.

[15] Jorgenson, D. W.: "On Stability in the Sense of Harrod," Economica, Aug. 1960.

[16] Inada, K.: "On a Two-Sector Model of Economic Growth: Comments and Generalization," Review of Economic Studies, June 1963.

EXERCISES

3.1 Consider the Solow-Swan model with the Cobb-Douglas production function described in Section 3.2.2. Assume that at $t = 0$, the economy is moving along a steady state path with a saving rate s_1. The propensity to save suddenly changes to s_2. Trace the growth path of $Y(t)$ until a new steady state is reached. Show how the rate of growth of output rises (or falls) in the short run but gradually settles down to the natural rate n. Distinguish between the cases $s_1 > s_2$ and $s_1 < s_2$. Obtain the steady state capital output ratio before and after the change.

3.2 Endogenous population growth: It is possible to incorporate a Malthusian variation to the Solow-Swan model (see Hahn and Mathews [4]). Suppose labor force grows at the rate n which is not fixed but is endogenous as given by the relation $n = \alpha(w-\bar{w})$. w is real wage rate, $\bar{w}$ is subsistence wage rate assumed fixed and α is a positive constant. If the current wage rate exceeds the subsistence wage rate, then population would increase. When $w < \bar{w}$ population declines. The constant α is obviously the speed of response to changes in the wage rate. Does a steady state exist in such an economy? What are its properties? Also examine how changes in s, $\bar{w}$ and α would affect crucial variables.

Hint: The long run equilibrium condition is now $sf(k)/k - \delta = \alpha(w-\bar{w})$. As before the left hand side is the warranted rate and is a decreasing function of k. Since the real wage rate is an increasing function of k, the natural rate n is also an increasing function of k. Figure 3.4 represents these relations.

A steady state will generally exist and output will grow, in equilibrium, at the rate n^*. It is interesting to note that when the saving rate is increased n^* is also increased. Thus, unlike the Solow-Swan world, it is now possible to grow faster by raising the overall saving ratio.

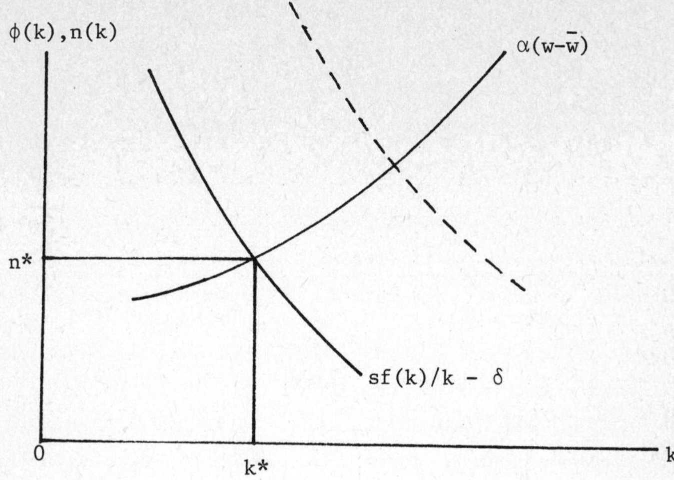

3.3 Suppose in the above example, n responds to per capita income instead of wages, how would the results be affected? Specifically let $n = \psi(y)$ where $y = Y/L$ and $\psi'(y) > 0$.

3.4 Redo exercise 3.3 assuming fixed coefficients in the production function.

3.5 <u>Variable saving ratio</u>: In a Solow-Swan economy assume that the saving rate (s) is not fixed but depends on per capita output (y) and the rate of return to capital (r). How would such an economy behave in the long run? Clearly state (in non-mathematical terms) every assumption made.

<u>Hint</u>: The equilibrium condition is $s(y,r)f(k)/k - \delta = n$.

It is reasonable to assume that the saving rate increases when per capita income rises or when the yield on capital increases. We know that an increase in k decreases $f(k)/k$. An increase in k increases y and therefore raises s. But when k goes up, r is lowered and therefore s goes down. If the yield effect is stronger than the income effect, s will decrease. The warranted rate will then decrease as k goes up and the results will be similar to the Solow-Swan situation. But if, as is more likely, the income effect is stronger, then s and $f(k)/k$ move in opposite directions and the result is ambiguous. Multiple solutions are now possible.

3.6 Assume that the Solow-Swan model has multiple solutions as in Figure 3.2. Examine what happens if some of the solutions coincide, that is, $\phi(k)$ touches the line n instead of crossing it.

3.7 Wage rigidity: Analyze the effects of downward rigidity in real wages in the context of long run growth. More specifically assume that in a Solow-Swan economy workers cannot be paid lower than a minimum ($\bar{w}$) in real terms. Also assume perfect competition and profit maximization. What are the long run consequences of the above behavior? In particular, will there be growth with full employment of factors? If yes, describe the economic mechanism which brings it about. If not, explain what prevents it and suggest policies to achieve full employment and steady growth. Explain how your recommended policies will bring this about.

Hint: Suppose w^* is the equilibrium real wage rate in the unconstrained Solow-Swan case. If $w^* > \bar{w}$, the rigidity is not binding in the long run. The mechanism is the same as described earlier in this chapter. If $w^* < \bar{w}$, then wages cannot fall below $\bar{w}$. Under the marginal productivity conditions firms will operate at $\bar{k}$ which is determined by the equation $w = f(k) - kf'(k) = \bar{w}$. Since $\bar{k} > k^*$, labor will accumulate faster than capital. Since wages cannot fall, there will be unemployment. Mathematically, we add the condition $w = \bar{w}$ which makes the system over-determined. Aggregate output will grow at the rate $sf(\bar{k})/\bar{k} < n$. A possible policy is to raise the saving rate by taxing income and investing it. (Show how this will work and calculate the tax rate in terms of $\bar{k}$ and the known parameters).

3.8 What will happen if the rigidity was in rents rather than wages? Suppose firms will not invest if the real rents fall below $\bar{r}$. How will this alter your conclusions?

3.9 Draw a phase diagram and examine the global stability of Model 2 of Section 3.1.3.

3.10 Unemployment and Wage Adjustments: Suppose that the total supply of labor (L) grows at the rate n. But the demand for labor is N and would depend on the wage rate. Define $k = K/N$ and $x = K/L$. Since the demand and supply may not be equal in the labor market, real wages (w) respond to excess demand or supply according to the relation $\dot{w}/w = h(N-L)/L$, where the speed of adjustment (h) is a fixed positive number. Aggregate output (Y) depends, in the usual neo-classical way, on capital (K) and the employed labor force. Demand for labor is determined by setting the real wage rate equal to the marginal product of employed labor. Demand for capital is determined by the equality of real rents to the marginal product of capital. Capital is assumed to be fully employed and accumulates at the rate $\dot{K} = sY - \delta K$. In the steady state, capital stock and labor demand both grow at the same rate as labor supply.

Answer the following questions assuming alternatively that there is (i) excess demand for labor and (ii) excess supply of labor.

(a) Write down the structural equations.

(b) Does a steady state exist? Is labor fully employed in the steady state?

(c) Draw a phase diagram and analyze the stability of the system. If the phase diagram analysis fails, check for local stability.

(d) How would an increase in the speed of adjustment (h) affect k*, y* and w*?

APPENDIX

DIFFERENTIAL EQUATIONS AND PHASE DIAGRAMS

This appendix surveys some of the techniques of solving differential equations and discusses the use of Phase Diagrams. Only those useful in the theory of economic growth are discussed here. For a more detailed analysis see the references at the end of this section.

A differential equation is a relationship between one or more variables and their derivatives of any order. A differential equation involving several variables and their partial derivatives is known as a partial differential equation and will not be discussed here. Our main concern is with ordinary differential equations which relate a single dependent variable (denoted by x) and its derivatives with respect to another variable (denoted by t). A simple example of this type of differential equation is given by

$$dx/dt = 2t \tag{A.1}$$

The function x(t) given by

$$x(t) = t^2 + 1 \tag{A.2}$$

satisfies the differential equation (A.1) for all values of t. (A.2) is therefore a solution to the differential equation (A.1). The highest derivative in a differential equation determines its order. The highest exponent of the derivatives determines the degree. If this exponent is 1, the differential equation is said to be linear. A linear differential equation of order n has the general form:

$$a_o(t)\frac{d^n x}{dt^n} + a_1(t)\frac{d^{n-1}x}{dt^{n-1}} + \dots\; a_{n-1}(t)\frac{dx}{dt} + a_n(t)x = f(t) \tag{A.3}$$

A natural question that arises is whether a differential equation has a solution and if it does, what can we say about its uniqueness? The question will be answered (without proof) only with respect to a first order non-linear differential equation of the form $\dot{x} = f(x,t)$, where a dot above a variable represents the derivative with respect to t.

Theorem A.1: Consider the differential equation $\dot{x} = f(x,t)$ where $f(x,t)$ is continuous in a certain region R of the x-t plane and where the partial derivative $\partial f/\partial x$ is also continuous.[1] Then for every point (x_o,t_o) in the region R, there exists a solution $x = g(t)$ of the above differential equation satisfying the condition $x_o = g(t_o)$. Moreover this solution is unique.

For proof of this theorem see Pontryagin [5] or Bellman [1].

Let us now examine the ways of solving some simple forms of differential equations which are often encountered in economics.

1. First consider the differential equation

(A.4) $$dx/dt = f(t)$$

where $f(t)$ is a continuous function. This can be solved in a straight forward manner by integrating both sides of the above equation, with respect to t. We then get the general solution to (A.4) as follows:

(A.5) $$x(t) = \int f(t)dt + c$$

where c is a constant of integration. The value of c is arbitrary and each value of c will represent one solution to the differential equation. (A.2) is an example of this kind for the differential equation (A.1). If one of the points on the curve $x(t)$ is known, say $x(t_o) = x_o$, there is a unique curve $x(t)$ passing through this point and satisfying (A.4). This is called a particular solution.

2. A second example, which includes the last as a special case, is the following:

(A.6) $$dx/dt = f(t)g(x)$$

This is called the variables separable case, the reason being that we can separate the variables as follows:

$$\frac{1}{g(x)}\, dx = f(t)dt$$

This can now be integrated as follows:

[1]The assumption on $\partial f/\partial x$ is merely an assumption on f and does not make the equation we are considering a partial differential equation.

(A.7) $$\int \frac{1}{g(x)}\,dx = \int f(t)dt + c$$

from which it may be possible to obtain x(t) explicitly. A special case of this, common in models of economic growth, is obtained by setting g(x) = x and f(t) = λ, a constant. We then get

(A.8) $$\frac{1}{x}\frac{dx}{dt} = \lambda$$

The left hand side is the rate of growth of the variable x with respect to t. This differential equation states that the rate of growth of the variable x is a constant λ. Integrating both sides we obtain log x = gt + c where c is an arbitrary constant. Exponentiation of both sides results in $x(t) = e^c e^{\lambda t}$.

This is a family of exponential curves, one for each value of c. The constant c can be evaluated if we know the value of x at a known value of t. Suppose, for example, it is known that for t = 0, the value of x is x_o (this is called the initial condition) then we obtain $x_o = e^c$. The unique particular solution to the differential equation satisfying the initial condition is then given by the exponential function

(A.9) $$x(t) = x_o e^{\lambda t}$$

In some cases, it may be possible to transform certain non-linear first order differential equations into the variables separable case. An example where such a transformation is possible is given in Section 3.2.2.

3. Another frequently encountered form is the first order linear differential equation

(A.10) $$\dot{x} + f(t)x = g(t)$$

Suppose we can find a variable z(t) such that $\dot{z}/z = f(t)$. Then (A.10) can be rewritten as $\dot{x} + x\dot{z}/z = g(t)$ or $x\dot{z} + z\dot{x} = z(t)g(t)$. The left hand side of the latter is equal to d(xz)/dt. Integrating both sides we get $x(t)z(t) = \int z(t)g(t)dt + c$ where c is a constant of integration. Therefore the solution to (A.10) is given by

(A.11) $$x(t) = \frac{1}{z(t)} \int z(t)g(t)dt + c/z(t)$$

All we need now is z(t). To obtain this, we note that $\dot{z}/z$ can be written as d(log z)/dt = f(t). Integrating this we get log z = $\int f(t)dt$ or

(A.12) $$z(t) = e^{\int f(t)dt}$$

A solution of (A.10) is therefore obtained by first finding z(t) from (A.12) and then using it in (A.11) to obtain x(t). z(t) is called the integration factor.

Stability analysis: In models of economic growth the basic equation of motion describing the behavior of an economy often has the following form:

(A.13) $$dx/dt = \psi(x)$$

where $\psi(x)$ is continuous everywhere. As mentioned earlier, the focus of analysis of growth theory is more on the steady state than on the explicit solution to the differential equation (A.13). A steady state solution to (A.13) is defined as the value of x, denoted by x*, such that $\dot{x} = 0$. In other words, if x takes the value x*, it will have that value for all t. A steady state will exist if we can find an x* such that $\psi(x^*) = 0$. We will not go into the discussion of existence of steady-state solutions to (A.13) but assume that there is at least one such solution. Our interest here is in the behavior of x in the neighborhood of x*.

Let x(t) be a solution to the differential equation (A.13) with an initial condition $x(0) = x_o$. Then a steady state x* given by $\psi(x^*) = 0$, is said to be locally stable if $\lim_{t\to\infty} x(t) = x^*$ in the neighborhood of x*.

We shall now derive the necessary and sufficient condition for local stability of the solution x*. In a neighborhood x*, let $x = x^* + \Delta x$ where Δx is small so that its higher powers can be ignored. Since x* is fixed, $\dot{x} = \dot{\Delta}x$. The differential equation (A.13) then becomes $\dot{\Delta}x = \psi(x^* + \Delta x) = \psi(x^*) + \Delta x\psi'(x^*)$ to a first-order of approximation. But $\psi(x^*) = 0$ and $\psi'(x^*)$ is independent of t. We thus have $\dot{\Delta}x/\Delta x = \psi'(x^*)$, same as (A.8). The solution to this is $\Delta x(t) = \Delta x_o e^{\psi'(x^*)t}$. For local stability x(t) should tend to x* as t becomes indefinitely large; that is, $\underset{t\to\infty}{\text{lt}} \Delta x(t) = 0$. This is possible if and only if $\psi'(x^*) < 0$. Therefore we have the following theorem:

Theorem A.2: Given a differential equation $\dot{x} = \psi(x)$ where $\psi(x)$ is continuous everywhere, a steady state solution x* determined by the equation $\psi(x^*) = 0$ is locally stable if and only if $\psi'(x^*) < 0$. In other words, the $\psi(x)$ curve must intersect the zero axis from above. (See the footnote on page 71.)

Sometimes the differential equation is also written as follows:

(A.14) $$\dot{x}/x = \phi(x)$$

It is easy to show that provided $x^* > 0$, the necessary and sufficient condition for local stability is that $\phi'(x^*) < 0$. A comparison of (A.13) and (A.14) shows that $\psi(x) = x\phi(x)$. Therefore $\psi'(x^*) = x^*\phi'(x^*) + \phi(x^*) = x^*\phi'(x^*)$ since $\phi(x^*) = 0$ in the steady state. Since $x^* > 0$, the necessary and sufficient condition for stability, $\psi'(x^*) < 0$, is equivalent to the condition that $\phi'(x^*) < 0$.

The above result can be represented geometrically. The points of intersection of the curve $\psi(x)$ with the x axis correspond to steady states. Suppose there are three solutions as indicated in Figure A.1. For local stability, $\psi'(x^*) < 0$ for any x* such that $\psi(x^*) = 0$. Thus x_1^* and x_3^* are stable whereas x_2^* is unstable. The arrows in the diagram indicate the direction of movement of x from non-equilibrium points. For example if $x_1^* < x < x_2^*$ then $\dot{x} = \psi(x) < 0$. This means x will decline. Similarly, for $x < x_1^*$, $\dot{x} > 0$ and therefore x will increase. The solution x_1^* is therefore stable. By similar arguments, it is readily shown that x_3^* is stable but x_2^* is not.

In the Solow-Swan model, the basic equation of motion of the economic system is a first-order differential equation in k. In later chapters, we will often encounter a pair of first-order nonlinear differential equations of the form

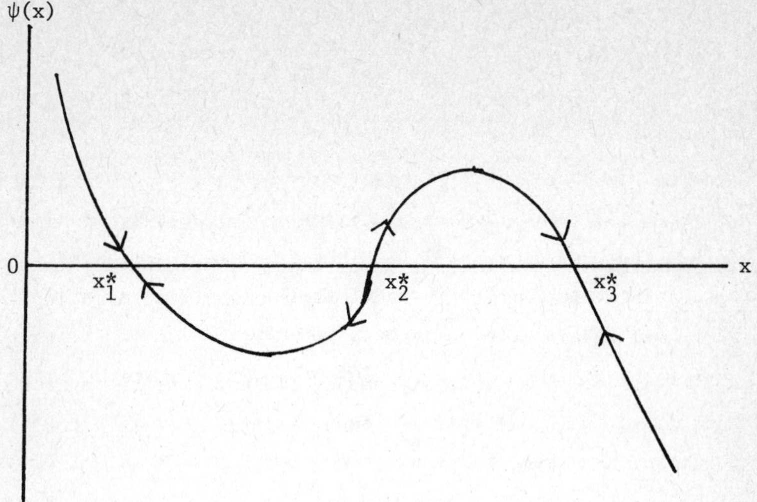

Figure A.1

(A.15) $\dot{k} = P(k,x)$ and $\dot{x} = Q(k,x)$

where the derivatives are taken with respect to the independent variable t. The functions P and Q are assumed to be continuous with continuous first partial derivatives. The equation $P(k,x) = 0$ gives the combinations of x and k such that $\dot{k} = 0$. Similarly, $Q(k,x) = 0$ corresponds to $\dot{x} = 0$. At the intersection of these two curves, say (k^*,x^*), both $\dot{x}$ and $\dot{k}$ are zero. Thus the intersection corresponds to a steady state.

In this section we state the results (without proof) pertaining to the local stability of the steady state (k^*,x^*). More specifically, we state the conditions under which $\underset{t\to\infty}{\mathrm{lt}}\, x(t) = x^*$ and $\underset{t\to\infty}{\mathrm{lt}}\, k(t) = k^*$ when the system initially starts near (k^*,x^*).

Theorem A.3: Let $a_{11} = \partial P/\partial k$, $a_{12} = \partial P/\partial x$, $a_{21} = \partial Q/\partial k$, $a_{22} = \partial Q/\partial x$, $b_1 = -k^*a_{11} - x^*a_{12}$ and $b_2 = -k^*a_{21} - x^*a_{22}$, where the partial derivatives are evaluated at the point (k^*,x^*) given by $P(k^*,x^*) = Q(k^*,x^*) = 0$. Then under quite general conditions the system described by (A.15) will behave in the neighborhood of

(k^*,x^*) as the following linear system:

$$\text{(A.16)}\qquad \begin{aligned} \dot{k} &= b_1 + a_{11}k + a_{12}x \\ \dot{x} &= b_2 + a_{21}k + a_{22}x \end{aligned}$$

(A.16) can be derived from (A.15) by setting $k = k^* + \Delta k$ and $x = x^* + \Delta k$, and taking linear approximations to $P(k,x)$ and $Q(k,x)$ in the neighborhood of (k^*,x^*).[1] Since the linear approximation is valid only in the neighborhood of the steady state solution, the stability analysis is valid only locally.

<u>Theorem A.4</u>: The necessary and sufficient conditions that a solution (k,x) to (A.16) will approach (k^*,x^*), that is $\underset{t\to\infty}{\text{lt}}\, x(t) = x^*$, $\underset{t\to\infty}{\text{lt}}\, k(t) = k^*$, are: $a_{11} + a_{22} < 0$ and $a_{11}a_{22} - a_{12}a_{21} > 0$. The proofs of these theorems are in Bellman [1]. Theorem (A.3) can be extended to the general case of n first-order differential equations in n variables of the type given by (A.15). Similar stability conditions are available for the general case and are discussed in a later section.

<u>Phase Diagrams</u>: A powerful geometric tool for analyzing the stability of a dynamic economic model which is reducible to two first-order differential equations not explicitly involving time (t) is a <u>Phase Diagram</u>.[2] Figure A.1 is an example of a phase diagram for a single differential equation of the form (A.13). The diagram maps the curve $\psi(x)$ and the directional arrows indicate how the variable $x(t)$ will move if it takes on a value other than a steady state x^* given by $\psi(x^*) = 0$.

A similar diagram may be drawn for a system of the type given by (A.15). As mentioned earlier, the steady state (k^*,x^*) is given by the solution to the equations $P(k,x) = Q(k,x) = 0$.

---

[1] We have $\dot{k} = P(k^*{+}\Delta k,\ x^*{+}\Delta x) = P(k^*,x^*) + \Delta k\ a_{11} + \Delta x\ a_{12}$, ignoring higher orders of Δk and Δx. Setting $P(k^*,x^*) = 0$, $\Delta k = k - k^*$, and $\Delta x = x - x^*$, we obtain the first equation in (A.16). The second equation is derived similarly.

[2] An example illustrating the use of a Phase Diagram is given at the end of this Appendix.

These relations can be graphed in two dimensions. If the two curves intersect, then we know that a steady state exists.[1] To illustrate, consider the following two differential equations:

$$\dot{k} = P(k,x) = 10 - 3k + 5x$$
$$\dot{x} = Q(k,x) = 6 + 6k - 12x$$

The equations P = Q = 0 can be solved to give x = -2 + .6k and x = .5 + .5k which can be graphed as in Figure A.2. It is easily shown that the steady state solution is given by $k^* = 25$ and $x^* = 13$. In the manner of Figure A.1 we can draw directional arrows which indicate the forces on k and x when they are not in equilibrium. For example, consider the relation P(k,x) = 0 which says that $\dot{k} = 0$. At any point along this curve evaluate the partial derivative $\partial\dot{k}/\partial x$ or equivalently $\partial P/\partial x$. Suppose this happened to be positive for all k and x along the curve as in the above example. This means that from any point along the curve if k is kept unchanged and x increases, then $\dot{k}$ will take a positive value. Thus the curve representing the equation P(k,x) = 0 divides the k-x plane into two parts. Above and to the left of it, $\dot{k} > 0$ which implies that k will tend to increase. The directional arrows parallel to the k axis in (a) and (b) of Figure A.2 reflect this result.[2] Below the curve $\dot{k} < 0$ and hence k tends to decrease. A similar calculation may be made for the curve represented by Q(k,x) = 0, in order to determine the directional arrows for the movement of x. For example, $\partial\dot{x}/\partial x = -12 < 0$ and the directional arrows for x are as in Figure A.2. The figure drawn in such a manner is a complete phase diagram and may be helpful in answering questions of stability. It is evident from Figure A.2 that from <u>any</u> initial position, not necessarily in the neighborhood of the equilibrium, k and x will ultimately move to the equilibrium point. A system giving rise to such a situation is called

---

[1] Whether or not this is attainable by an economic system is another question.

[2] Sometimes it may be easier to evaluate $\partial\dot{k}/\partial k$ along this curve and draw the arrows based on whether or not it is positive.

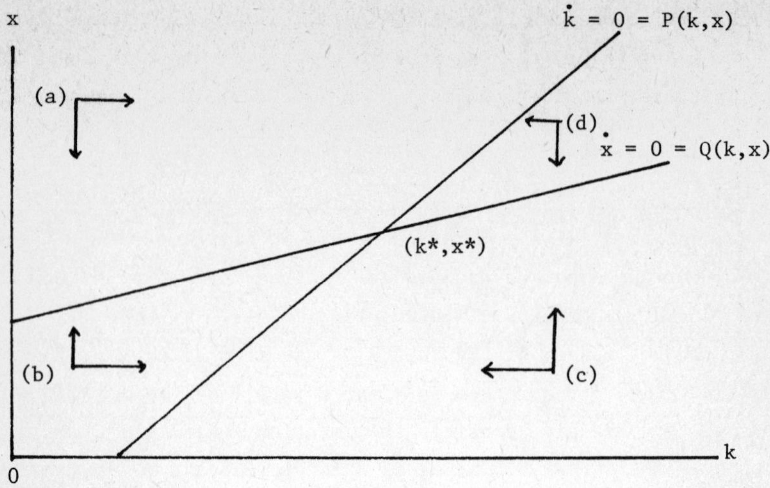

Figure A.2

globally stable. Global stability is not always assured as may be illustrated in the following differential equations:

$$\dot{k} = 1 - x$$
$$\dot{x} = x(k - x - \log x - 1)$$

The $\dot{k} = 0$ equation gives $x = 1$ and the $\dot{x} = 0$ equation gives $k = x + \log x + 1$ which graph as in Figure A.3. Since $\partial\dot{k}/\partial x < 0$ and $\partial\dot{x}/\partial k = x > 0$ for positive values of x, the directional arrows are as in Figure A.3. Global stability cannot be asserted because cyclical behavior is possible. Local stability may be examined by making use of Theorems A.3 and A.4. It is simple to show that $a_{11} = 0$, $a_{12} = -1$, $a_{21} = x^* > 0$ and $a_{22} < 0$. Thus the system is locally stable because both the stability conditions of Theorem A.4 are met. Note, however, that even though there is a unique steady state which is locally stable, global stability may not be assured.

It is also possible to have more than one steady state. Such a possibility is indicated in Figure A.4 in which the middle solution is stable.

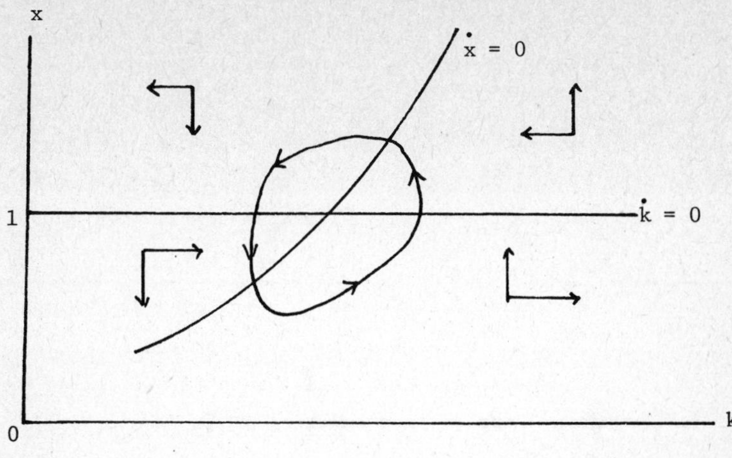

Figure A.3

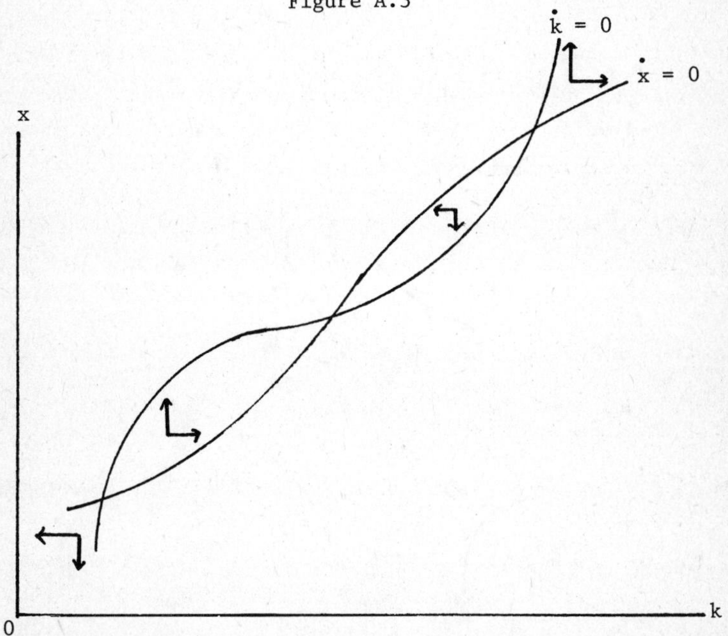

Figure A.4

Figure A.5 is an example of a unique but generally unstable equilibrium. There exists only one possible way in which the equilibrium will be reached. If the initial values of k and x are on the dotted line, then the economy will reach the steady state (k^*,x^*). Otherwise it would move away from the equilibrium. Such a solution is called a Saddle Point. This situation arises when $a_{11}a_{22} - a_{12}a_{21} < 0$.

An Example: We illustrate the use of phase diagrams in analyzing growth models with the help of a model proposed by Phelps [4, pp. 107-116]. Suppose aggregate real output Y(t) is given by the linearly homogeneous production function F(K,L) where K(t) is capital in use and L(t) is labor force. Labor force grows at the rate n; that is, $\dot{L}/L = n$. X(t) is capital in existence and $\dot{X}$ is the amount of saving sY. The economy may have difficulty absorbing the existing capital so that $X(t) \geq K(t)$. The absorption mechanism is given by $\dot{K} = \alpha(X-K)$, where α is a constant parameter $(\alpha > 0)$. Let x and k denote the capital - labor ratios. For

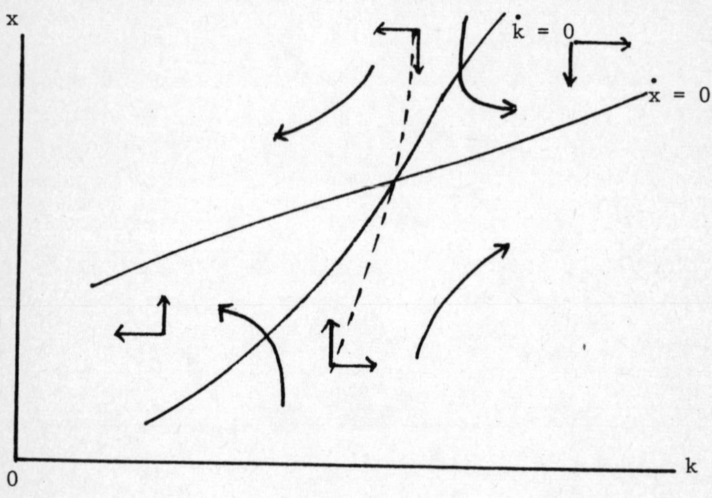

Figure A.5

balanced growth (steady state), capital in existence and capital in use must both grow at the same rate as the labor force.

We shall now analyze the long run behavior of the above model ignoring depreciation. The model may be written as follows:

(A.17) $$Y = F(K,L) = Lf(k)$$

(A.18) $$k \equiv K/L$$

(A.19) $$\dot{L}/L = n$$

(A.20) $$\dot{X} = sY$$

(A.21) $$\dot{K} = \alpha(X-K)$$

(A.22) $$x \equiv X/L$$

There are six endogeneous variables: Y, K, L, X, x, k; and three parameters: n, s, α. The function f(k) is assumed to have neo-classical properties. Logarithmic differentiation of k and the use of (A.19) and (A.21) gives $\dot{k}/k = \dot{K}/K - \dot{L}/L = \alpha(x/k-1) - n$. This gives the basic differential equation in k:

(A.23) $$\dot{k} = \alpha(x-k) - nk \equiv P(k,x)$$

Similarly, logarithmically differentiating (A.22) and using (A.17) and (A.20), we have

(A.24) $$\dot{x} = sf(k) - nx \equiv Q(k,x)$$

By definition, in steady state $\dot{K}/K = \dot{X}/X = \dot{L}/L$ which implies that $\dot{x} = \dot{k} = 0$. We therefore obtain $\alpha(x-k) - nk = 0$ and $sf(k) - nx = 0$. These two equations can be explicitly solved for x as follows:

(A.25) $$x = \left(\frac{\alpha+n}{\alpha}\right)k$$

(A.26) $$x = \frac{sf(k)}{n}$$

Equation (A.25) is simply a straight line through the origin. Assuming neo-classical conditions, (A.26) will map as in Figure (A.6) and a steady state will generally exist.

From (A.23), $\partial\dot{k}/\partial x = \alpha > 0$. This implies that if x is slightly raised above the $\dot{k} = 0$ curve with k unchanged, then $\dot{k}$

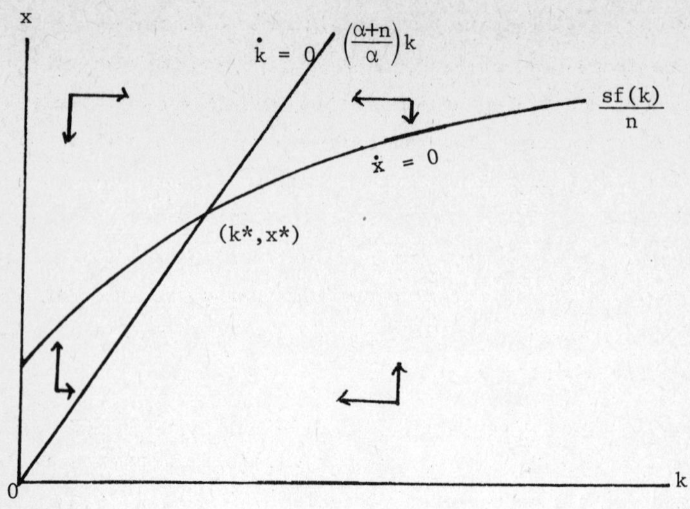

Figure A.6

increases to a positive value. Thus, above the $\dot{k} = 0$ curve $\dot{k} > 0$ which implies that k tends to increase. Below the curve k tends to decrease. The directional arrows parallel to the k-axis in Figure A.6 reflect this result. Similarly, from (A.24) $\partial\dot{x}/\partial x = -n < 0$. Therefore above the $\dot{x} = 0$ curve $\dot{x}$ is negative and x tends to decrease. Below the $\dot{x} = 0$ curve we have the opposite result. The directional arrows parallel to the x-axis indicate this result. Figure A.6 is a complete phase diagram. It is obvious from the phase diagram that no matter where we start initially, we will end up at (k^*,x^*). The system is therefore globally stable.

Changes in the parameters α, n and s shift the $\dot{x} = 0$ and $\dot{k} = 0$ curves. The appropriate sensitivities are thus easy to obtain diagrammatically. The Golden Rule Path is interesting in this model. Aggregate consumption and per capita consumption are derived as follows:

$$C = Y - S = Y - \dot{X}$$

$$C/L = Y/L - \dot{X}/L = f(k) - (\dot{X}/X)(X/L)$$

$$c^* = f(k^*) - nx^*$$

because $\dot{X}/X = n$ in steady state. Using (A.25), we have $c^* = f(k^*) - n[(\alpha+n)/\alpha]k^*$. The necessary condition for the golden rule is that $\partial c^*/\partial s = 0$ which implies $f'(k^*) = n(\alpha+n)/\alpha > n$. The second order condition is also satisfied. In the Solow-Swan model, the golden rule rate of return to capital, $f'(k^*)$, was equal to n whereas here it is larger than n. Since $[(\alpha+n)/\alpha]n = sf(k)/k$ from (A.25) and (A.26), we obtain the relation $f'(k) = sf(k)/k$, or $s = kf'/f = \pi(k)$. Thus for the golden rule path, the share of capital should be the same as the saving rate. This result is the same as in the Solow-Swan model.

General case of n first order differential equations:[1] Consider the following n first order differential equations in the variables $x_1, x_2, \ldots, x_n$:

$$\text{(A.27)} \quad \begin{cases} \dot{x}_1 = f^1(x_1, x_2, \ldots, x_n) \\ \dot{x}_2 = f^2(x_1, x_2, \ldots, x_n) \\ \cdots\cdots\cdots \\ \dot{x}_n = f^n(x_1, x_2, \ldots, x_n) \end{cases}$$

where $\dot{x}_i \equiv dx_i/dt$. The functions f^i are assumed to be continuous with continuous partial derivatives. Note that the functions do not explicitly depend on time. We also assume that the above system has a steady state solution $(x_1^*, x_2^*, \ldots, x_n^*)$ such that $f^i(x_1^*, x_2^*, \ldots, x_n^*) = 0$ for all i. Then proceeding as in Footnone 1 on page 62 it can be shown that the above system will behave in the neighborhood of the steady state as the following linear system:

$$\text{(A.28)} \quad \begin{cases} \dot{x}_1 = b_1 + a_{11}x_1 + a_{12}x_2 + \ldots. + a_{1n}x_n \\ \dot{x}_2 = b_2 + a_{21}x_1 + a_{22}x_2 + \ldots. + a_{2n}x_n \\ \cdots\cdots\cdots \\ \dot{x}_n = b_n + a_{n1}x_1 + a_{n2}x_2 + \ldots. + a_{nn}x_n \end{cases}$$

[1]This section involves a good deal of knowledge of matrices and their properties. The basic references are Gantmacher [3], Bellman [2] and Yaari [8].

where $a_{ij} = (\partial f^i/\partial x_j)^*$ is the partial derivative of f^i with respect to x_j, evaluated at the point $(x_1^*, x_2^*, \ldots, x_n^*)$ and $b_i = - x_1^* a_{i1} - x_2^* a_{i2}, \ldots, - x_n^* a_{in}$. The local stability of (A.27) thus reduces to the question of stability of (A.28) which can be written in the following convenient form using matrix notations:

$$\text{(A.29)} \qquad \dot{x} = Ax + b$$

where

$$x = \begin{bmatrix} x_1 \\ x_2 \\ \vdots \\ x_n \end{bmatrix}, \quad b = \begin{bmatrix} b_1 \\ b_2 \\ \vdots \\ b_n \end{bmatrix}, \quad A = \begin{bmatrix} a_{11} & a_{12} & \cdots & a_{1n} \\ a_{21} & a_{22} & \cdots & a_{2n} \\ \cdots & \cdots & \cdots & \cdots \\ a_{n1} & a_{n2} & \cdots & a_{nn} \end{bmatrix}$$

<u>Theorem A.5</u>: A necessary and sufficient condition that the solution x(t) of the linear system (A.29) converges to x* as $t \to \infty$ is that all the characteristic roots of the matrix A have negative real parts. A proof of this theorem is given in Bellman [2, p. 241].

In a practical situation the computation of the characteristic roots is not easy and therefore a test of stability expressed in terms of the elements of A will be useful. In order to present such a test we need some preliminary steps. Let c_i be the sum of all the ith order principal minors of A. c_i is also called the <u>i^{th} order trace</u>. Thus

$$c_1 = a_{11} + a_{22} + \ldots a_{nn} = \text{trace (A)}$$

$$c_2 = \begin{vmatrix} a_{11} & a_{12} \\ a_{21} & a_{22} \end{vmatrix} + \begin{vmatrix} a_{11} & a_{13} \\ a_{31} & a_{33} \end{vmatrix} + \ldots\ldots$$

$$c_n = |A| = \text{the determinant of A}$$

The characteristic equation $|A - \lambda I| = 0$ is given by $|A - \lambda I| = (-\lambda)^n + c_1(-\lambda)^{n-1} + c_2(-\lambda)^{n-2} \ldots\ c_{n-1}(-\lambda) + c_n - 0$, where λ is a characteristic root of A and I is the nXn identity matrix. Note that the sum of the roots is given by c_1 and the product of the roots is given by $|A|$. Let $\alpha_i = (-1)^i c_i$ be the coefficient of λ^i in the characteristic equation.

Theorem A.6: The characteristic roots of A have negative real parts if and only if all the following conditions are satisfied:

$$\text{(A.30)} \qquad \alpha_1 > 0, \quad \begin{vmatrix} \alpha_1 & 1 \\ \alpha_3 & \alpha_2 \end{vmatrix} > 0, \quad \ldots \quad \begin{vmatrix} \alpha_1 & 1 & 0 & 0 & \cdots & & \\ \alpha_3 & \alpha_2 & \alpha_1 & 1 & 0 & \cdots & \\ \alpha_5 & \alpha_4 & \alpha_3 & \alpha_2 & \alpha_1 & 1 & 0 \cdots \\ \cdots & \cdots & \cdots & \cdots & \cdots & \cdots & \\ \alpha_{2n-1} & \cdots & \cdots & \cdots & \cdots & \cdots & \alpha_n \end{vmatrix} > 0$$

These conditions are known as the Routh-Hurwitz conditions. For more than three differential equations these determinants are difficult to evaluate. When $n = 2$, $\alpha_1 = -\mathrm{tr}(A)$, $\alpha_2 = |A|$ and $\alpha_3 = 0$. Thus the necessary and sufficient conditions are that $\mathrm{tr}(A) = a_{11} + a_{22} < 0$ and $|A| = a_{11}a_{22} - a_{12}a_{21} > 0$, which were the conditions stated in Theorem A.4. It is left as an exercise to the reader to show that for $n = 3$, the corresponding conditions are,

$$\text{(A.31)} \qquad \alpha_1, \alpha_2, \alpha_3 > 0 \quad \text{and} \quad \alpha_1 \alpha_2 > \alpha_3$$

It is interesting to note that $\alpha_1 > 0$ implies that $\mathrm{tr}(A) < 0$ is a necessary condition for stability for any n. Since $\alpha_i = 0$ for $i > n$, the last determinant in (A.30) can be expanded by the last row to give α_n multiplied by the previous determinant which must also be positive. Thus $\alpha_n > 0$ is another necessary condition which implies that $|A|$ must have the sign of $(-1)^n$. In some situations instability may be established by showing that these necessary conditions are violated.

Footnote for Theorem A.2: Strictly speaking, the condition is necessary only for the absence of "first-order instability." For a detailed discussion on this see Samuelson, Foundations of Economic Analysis, Atheneum, 1965, Chapter 10, [6].

REFERENCES

[1] Bellman, R. E.: Stability Theory of Differential Equations, McGraw-Hill, 1953.

[2] Bellman, R. E.: Introduction to Matrix Analysis, McGraw-Hill, 1960.

[3] Gantmacher, F. R.: Matrix Theory, Chelsea Publishing Company, 1959.

[4] Phelps, E. S.: Golden Rules of Economic Growth, W. W. Norton, 1966.

[5] Pontryagin, L. S.: Ordinary Differential Equations, Addison-Wesley, 1962.

[6] Samuelson, P. A.: Foundations of Economic Analysis, Harvard University Press, 1947.

[7] Yamane, T.: Mathematics for Economists, Prentice-Hall, 1962.

[8] Yaari, M. E.: Linear Algebra for Social Sciences, Prentice-Hall, 1971.

CHAPTER 4
TECHNICAL PROGRESS

So far we have considered only two factors which contribute to economic growth -- capital accumulation and growth of the labor force. But growth is possible because of technical changes in the production processes. In fact several studies have found that the observed increases in per capita income cannot be accounted for by capital formation alone. Change in productivity is the major explanation.[1] Technical progress is said to occur if the production function shifts upwards over time; that is, more output can be obtained with the same amounts of labor and capital. Such a shift may be due to innovations, education of the labor force or other factors. In this chapter we study the effects of technical progress on the long run behavior of an economy.

Since output explicitly depends on time, the production function is written as $Y = Q(K,L,t)$ where $Q_t > 0$. As before, the production function will be assumed to be linearly homogenous in capital and labor. Thus $y = Y/L = Q(K,L,t)/L = f(k,t)$. Totally differentiate Q with respect to t and divide the result by Q. We then have

$$\begin{aligned}\frac{\dot{Y}}{Y} &= \left(\frac{KQ_K}{Q}\right)\left(\frac{\dot{K}}{K}\right) + \left(\frac{LQ_L}{Q}\right)\left(\frac{\dot{L}}{L}\right) + \frac{Q_t}{Q} \\ &= \pi(\dot{K}/K) + (1-\pi)(\dot{L}/L) + (Q_t/Q)\end{aligned} \tag{4.1.1}$$

where π is the share of capital in total output. This equation (which can be readily extended to include more inputs) identifies the sources of growth and can be interpreted as follows:

Rate of growth of output = (share of capital) (rate of growth of capital) + (share of labor) (rate of growth of labor) + rate of growth of output attributable to technical change only.

---

[1] An alternative explanation, given by Jorgenson and Griliches [20], is discussed in Section 4.4.

There are several kinds of technical progress. The simplest kind to analyze is _exogenous_ technical change. In this case, technical change is assumed to proceed at rates determined outside the economic system. It is then possible to isolate the effects of changes in technology from those of accumulation of capital and labor. When innovations are induced by existing amounts of resources and the amount of technical progress and its effect on output are determined from within the system, then technical progress is _endogenous_. Clearly, this is the kind most likely to occur in the real world. Technical change is said to have a _bias_ if it is labor-saving or capital-saving and _neutral_ if there is no bias. Precise definitions of these concepts will be given later. In real life, technical changes are incorporated only into new machines. Subsequent innovations generally do not affect the productivity of machines built prior to those inventions. Thus technical change is _embodied_ into newly built machines. If changes in technology affect output independently of the ages of machines, they are said to be _disembodied_. We now take up each of these concepts and discuss in detail their meaning and relevance to long run growth.

4.1 Neutral and Non-neutral Technical Change[1]

Technical progress is _neutral_ if it maintains the balance between capital and labor in a manner to be specified. Otherwise it is biased in favor of one of the factors of production and is either _labor-saving_ or _capital-saving_. Intuitively we can say that an innovation is labor-saving if labor's share in output declines. Similarly, it is capital-saving if capital's share declines which means labor's share increases. If the factor shares are unaffected then the invention is neutral. Thus we can use $\pi(k,t) = k(t)\, f_k(k,t)/f(k,t)$ as a measure for classifying inventions. But which points of the production function, before and after it shifts, do we compare in order to determine the direction

---

[1]Some parts of the analysis of this section are based on the presentation by Hahn and Mathews [16].

of movement of factor shares? Hicks proposed that two points at which the capital-labor ratio is the same be chosen for comparison [18]. An alternative, suggested by Harrod, is to compare two points such that the capital-output ratio is the same [17]. Let us take a closer look at each of these proposals and their implications.

4.1.1 Hicks-neutrality

Technical progress is said to be Hicks-neutral if whenever the capital-labor ratio is constant the rate of technical substitution (R) between capital and labor is also constant. In other words, R is a function of only the capital-labor ratio and is independent of t. This must be true for every capital intensity.

What is the connection between this definition of neturality and the intuitive notion that factor shares will not change? To answer this first note that, due to the linear homogeneity assumption, capital's share π can be rewritten as

$$\pi = \frac{KQ_K}{KQ_K+LQ_L} = \frac{1}{1+(R/k)}$$

Therefore, if k is fixed, π and R have an inverse relation to one another. Neutrality by the above definition leaves R unchanged at points where k is constant, and therefore π is also unchanged. Under the marginal productivity theory, R equals the wage-rental ratio. Therefore Hicks-neutrality leaves relative wages unchanged even though per capita output may be increasing. As mentioned earlier, a labor-saving invention would raise π for a given k. This is possible only if R decreases. Thus technical progress is labor-saving in the Hicksian sense if, for a fixed k, the marginal product of capital is raised by more than that of labor thus lowering relative wages. The opposite is the case if the innovation is capital-saving.

We shall now formalize the above definitions. Let $E_L = Q_{Lt}/Q_L$ and $E_K = Q_{Kt}/Q_K$ where Q_{Lt} and Q_{Kt} are the partial derivatives with respect to t of the respective marginal products. E_L and E_K are thus the rates of increase of the corresponding marginal products. Technical progress is said to be Hicks-neutral if

$E_L = E_K$, labor-saving if $E_L < E_K$ and capital-saving if $E_L > E_K$. Figure 4.1 illustrates these concepts.

f(k,t) is per capita output at time t for a given capital intensity k. The slopes of the tangents at A and B are respectively, the marginal products of capital at time periods 1 and 2. Therefore

$$\left(f_k\right)_{t=1} = \frac{AC}{DC} = \frac{f(k,1)}{DO+k}$$

and hence $DO = [f(k,1) - kf_k]/f_k = MPL/MPK = R(k,1)$.

DO is thus the rate of technical substitution R(k,1). Hicks-neutrality implies that between two time periods if the capital intensity is the same then the rate of technical substitution (and hence relative wages) must be the same. Therefore the two curves should be such that at a given k, the tangents at A and B intersect the k-axis at the same point. This must be true for any k. Technical progress is labor-saving if, for a given capital intensity, the rate of technical substitution decreases. In the diagram, the tangent at B would intersect the k-axis to the right

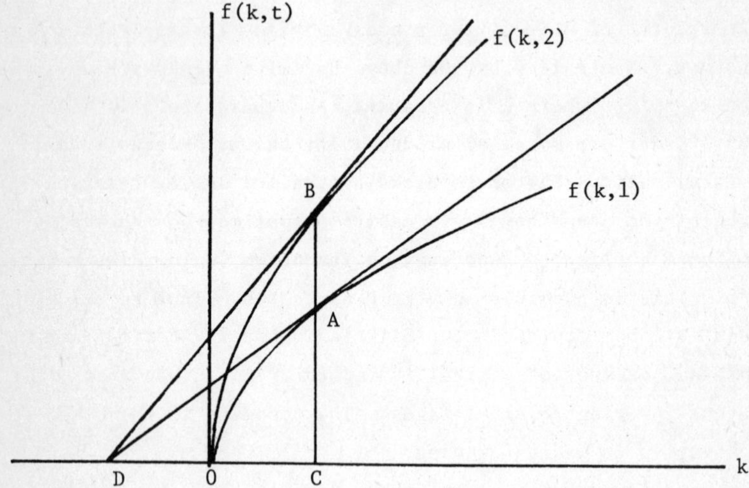

Figure 4.1

of D. Technical progress is capital-saving when the opposite is the case.

<u>Theorem 4.1</u>: Let the production function $Y = Q(K,L,t)$ be continuous with continuous partial derivatives. Also assume that it is linearly homogenous in K and L. Then technical progress is Hicks-neutral if and only if the production function $Q(K,L,t)$ can be rewritten in the form $A(t)\ F(K,L)$.

Thus technical progress can be represented by a simple scale factor which depends on t alone. It is then equivalent to a renumbering of the isoquants.

<u>Proof</u>: When the production function is of the above form, it is easily shown that technical progress is Hicks-neutral. First note that linear homogeneity of Q implies the same of F. The rate of technical substitution is $R = Q_L/Q_K = F_L/F_K$. From Theorem 2.1, if F is homogenous then F_L/F_K is a function of k alone. Thus R is a function of k alone, which implies Hicks neutrality.

To prove that Hicks neutrality implies the above form for the production function we may proceed as follows. From the definition of neutrality, $R = Q_L/Q_K = g(k)$. Logarithmically differentiating this partially with respect to t we obtain $Q_{Lt}/Q_L = Q_{Kt}/Q_K \equiv \alpha(K,L,t)$. Let $\phi(K,L,t) = Q_t/Q$. $\phi(K,L,t)$ can be interpreted as the rate of increase in output attributable to technical change alone. Since Q is linearly homogenous in K and L, $Q(\lambda K,\lambda L,t) = \lambda Q(K,L,t)$ for all positive λ. Partial differentiation of both sides with respect to t gives $Q_t(\lambda K,\lambda L,t) = \lambda Q_t(K,L,t)$. Thus the function Q_t is also linearly homogenous. Therefore the ratio Q_t/Q is homogeneous of degree zero in K and L. It follows from Euler's theorem that $K\phi_K + L\phi_L = 0$. But

$$\phi_K = (QQ_{Kt}-Q_tQ_K)/Q^2 = (\alpha-\phi)Q_K/Q$$

Similarly, $\phi_L = (\alpha-\phi)Q_L/Q$. Therefore, $\alpha - \phi = K\phi_K + L\phi_L = 0$ because $KQ_K + LQ_L = Q$. From this and the expressions for ϕ_K and ϕ_L we obtain the result that $\phi_K = \phi_L = 0$. This implies that $\phi(K,L,t)$ is independent of K and L and may be written as $\psi(t)$; that is, $\partial(\log Q)/\partial t = \psi(t)$. Integrating this partially with respect to t, we obtain $\log Q = \int \psi(t)dt + G(K,L)$. Because the integration is done partially, the second term is a function of K and L rather than an arbitrary constant. Taking exponentials of both sides, Q takes the form $Q(K,L,t) = A(t)\ F(K,L)$. Hence, if technical progress is of the Hicks-neutral type, then the production function is of the above form, thus proving the theorem.

4.1.3 Harrod-neutrality

Technical progress is Harrod-neutral if, whenever the capital-output ratio is unchanged before and after technical progress, then the rate of return to capital (that is, its marginal product) is also unchanged. Equivalently, we can hold capital's rate of return constant and require that its average product (reciprocal of the capital-output ratio) remain the same before and after the technical change. Thus Harrod's definition of neutrality compares two points at which the capital-output ratio is the same, or equivalently the rate of return to capital is the same. Since the capital-output ratio is constant in a steady state, it follows that with Harrod-neutral technical change the distribution of income remains constant in the steady state.

Figure 4.2 illustrates Harrod-neutrality. Select any straight line through the origin giving points A and B on two production functions. These points have the same average product of capital and hence the same capital-output ratio. For neutrality the corresponding marginal products must be the same and therefore the tangents at A and B should be parallel. Between two time periods if the capital-output ratio remains constant but the rate of return to capital is higher in the second period, then capital's share rises and therefore technical progress is labor-saving. If the rate of return to capital is lower, technical change is capital-saving.

Theorem 4.2: Let the production function $Y = Q(K,L,t)$ be continuous with continuous partial derivatives and also linearly homogeneous so that $y = Y/L = f(k,t)$. Furthermore let $f_k > 0$ and $f_{kk} < 0$; that is, capital is always productive but its marginal product is diminishing. Then technical progress is Harrod-neutral

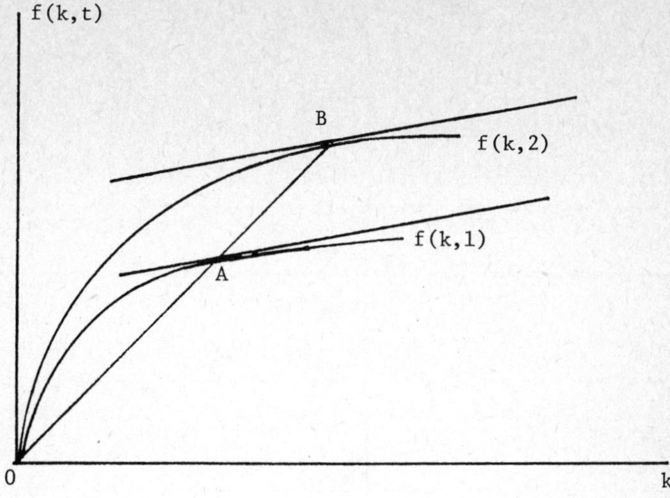

Figure 4.2

<u>if and only if</u> Q can be written in the form Q(K,L,t) = F[K,A(t)L], where A(t) > 0. Because of this property, technical progress of the Harrod-neutral type is also called <u>labor-augmenting</u>.

This proposition was originally proved by Joan Robinson [33]. Harrod-neutrality says that when r, the rate of return to capital is held constant, the average product of capital (APK) remains the same before and after the technical change. At a given level of r there will be an equilibrium capital intensity (say k_1) at which firms operate. Technical progress shifts the average and marginal product (MPK) curves upwards. These curves are shown in Figure 4.3 for two time periods. If the marginal product curve shifts upwards with rents remaining constant, firms would increase their use of capital and capital intensity would rise to a higher level (say k_2). However, if technical progress is neutral, the average product of capital must be unchanged whenever r is unchanged. Therefore AC and DF must be equal as shown in the diagram. Since capital intensity has risen from k_1 to k_2, per capita output must also rise in the same proportion if APK is to remain the same.

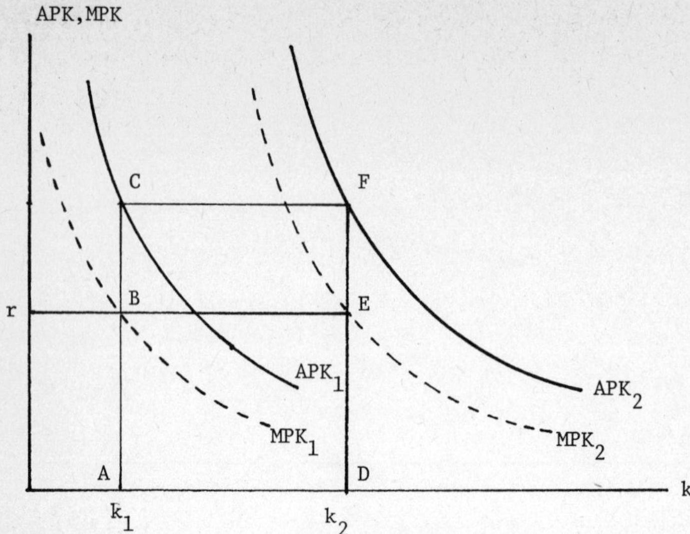

Figure 4.3

Because of constant returns to scale, this is equivalent to raising the labor supply by the same proportion with unchanged technique or for a given labor supply, to an overall increase in the efficiency of labor. Thus Harrod-neutral technical progress takes the form of augmenting labor. In Figure 4.3 if DF were larger than AC, the share of capital would have decreased which implies that technical change was capital-saving.

Uzawa has given a more formal proof of the above proposition which he calls Robinson's Theorem [41]. This proof is given below.[1]

Mathematical proof: Since the production function is linearly homogeneous,

(4.1.2) $$y = f(k,t)$$

We know from Figure 4.2 that $f_k > 0$ and $f_{kk} < 0$ imply that the capital-output ratio x (the reciprocal of the average product of

[1]Readers not interested in the mathematical proof may skip directly to the corollary of the theorem.

capital) is a monotonic increasing function of k. Therefore by the Inverse Function Theorem,[1] k can be written explicitly as a function of x. Substituting for k in (4.1.2) we obtain y in the form $y = f[k(x),t] = \phi(x,t)$. From this we obtain

(4.1.3) $$f_k = \partial y/\partial k = \phi_x \; \partial x/\partial k$$

Differentiating $x = k/y$ partially with respect to k,

(4.1.4) $$\partial x/\partial k = (y-kf_k)/y^2 = (1-xf_k)/\phi$$

Using (4.1.3) and (4.1.4) to solve for f_k, we get

(4.1.5) $$f_k = \phi_x/(\phi+x\phi_x)$$

To prove necessity: Harrod-neutrality implies that if the capital-output ratio is constant then so is the marginal product, that is, f_k is a function of x alone and is independent of t. Let $f_k = \phi_x/(\phi+x\phi_x) = c(x)$. Then, $\phi_x/\phi = c(x)/[1-xc(x)]$ is independent of t. Integrating this partially with respect to x and then taking exponentials of both sides we get

(4.1.6) $$y = \phi(x,t) = A(t)\ \psi(x)$$

Since the integration is done partially with respect to x, we get a function A(t) instead of an arbitrary constant. It is seen from Figure 4.2 that, for a given t, when the capital output ratio x increases so does the average product of labor, y. In other words, $\phi_x > 0$. Therefore, by the Inverse Function Theorem, (4.1.6) can be explicitly solved for x to give

$$x = k/y = \xi[y/A(t)]$$

or

$$\frac{k}{A(t)} = \frac{y}{A(t)}\,\xi\left[\frac{y}{A(t)}\right]$$

---

[1] Let $y = G(x)$ be a continuous and differentiable function such that G(x) is monotonic, i.e. $G'(x) > 0$ for all x, or $G'(x) < 0$ for all x. Then corresponding to each value of y we can find a unique value of x expressed by a relation of the form $x = H(y)$. This function is called the inverse function. For example, if $y = \exp(x)$, the inverse function is $x = \log y$. The function $y = G(x) = x^2$ has no unique inverse because $x = \pm\sqrt{y}$.

Because the relation between them is monotonic, $y/A(t)$ can be written as a function of $k/A(t)$.

(4.1.7) $$\frac{y}{A(t)} = g\left[\frac{k}{A(t)}\right]$$

(4.1.8) Define $F(K,N) \equiv Ng(K/N)$

From (4.1.7), $f(k,t) = y = A(t)g[k/A(t)]$. Therefore, $Q(K,L,t) = Lf(k,t) = LA(t)g[k/A(t)]$.

(4.1.9) Let $N = LA(t)$

Then $Q(K,L,t) = Ng(K/N) = F(K,N) = F[K,LA(t)]$. This proves that when technical change is Hicks-neutral the production function has the special form.

<u>To prove sufficiency</u>: We now must prove that when $Q(K,L,t) = F[K,LAt)]$, technical progress is Harrod-neutral. Define $g(k) = F(k,1)$. We then have $g'(k) > 0$ because $F_K > 0$. Since Q is homogeneous of degree 1,

$$F[K,LA(t)] = LA(t)F[k/A(t),1] = LA(t)g[k/A(t)]$$

or $$y = A(t)g[k/A(t)]$$

Since $xy = k$, this can be rewritten as $y/A(t) = g[xy/A(t)]$. We argued that x and y are monotonically related. Resorting to the Inverse Function Theorem again, $y/A(t)$ can be expressed in terms of x as $y/A(t) = \psi(x)$, i.e. $y = \phi(x,t) = A(t)\psi(x)$. From (4.1.5),

$$f_k = \frac{\phi_x}{\phi+x\phi_x} = \frac{\psi'(x)}{\psi(x)+x\psi'(x)}$$

This means that the marginal product of capital is independent of t and depends only on the capital-output ratio. This is the definition of Harrod-neutrality.

<u>Corollary</u>: Let the production function satisfy the assumptions made in Theorem 4.2. Then technical progress is both Hicks-neutral and Harrod-neutral if and only if the elasticity of substitution between capital and labor is 1. That is, $Q = A(t)K^{\alpha}L^{1-\alpha}$, $0 < \alpha < 1$, $A(t) > 0$.

The detailed proof may be found in Uzawa's paper [41], but an intuitive proof is as follows. Recall that neutrality should leave the share of capital π unchanged. Suppose between two time periods the level of labor remains constant but the levels of capital and output double. Since the capital intensity has doubled, π would change. Since the capital-output ratio is the same, by Harrod-neutrality π should remain constant. The only way π can remain constant when k has changed is when $\partial\pi/\partial k = 0$. This is possible only if the elasticity of substitution is 1 (Theorem 2.2). It is easy to show that a linearly homogeneous production function has elasticity 1 if and only if it is of the Cobb-Douglas form (see exercise 2.4).

<u>Theorem 4.3</u>: Let the production function satisfy the assumptions made in Theorem 4.2. Then a steady state path, in which capital and output grow at the same constant rate (g) and technical progress grows at some constant rate (λ), is possible only if technical progress is of the Harrod-neutral type.*

<u>Proof</u>: From (4.1.1), $f_t/f = \dot{y}/y - \pi\dot{k}/k$. In steady state f_t/f is a constant λ and $\dot{Y}/Y = \dot{K}/K = g$. Therefore $\dot{y}/y = \dot{k}/k = g - n$. Substituting this above we get $\lambda = (1-\pi)(g-n)$. Since g,n and λ are all constant, $\pi(k,t)$ must also be constant. Thus whenever λ and the capital-output ratio are constant, the relative factor shares must also be constant. This implies that technical progress must be Harrod-neutral. In other words, if technical progress is not Harrod-neutral then it is impossible for an economy to stay on a steady state path.

4.1.4 <u>The Solow-Swan Model with Harrod-neutral Technical Progress</u>

We just saw that technical progress must be Harrod-neutral (or equivalently labor-augmenting) for balanced growth to exist. Let us introduce this kind of technical change in the Solow-Swan model and see how the results are altered. The production function can be rewritten as $Y = F(K,N)$ where $N = LA(t)$. N can be interpreted as <u>effective-labor</u> or labor measured in efficiency units. By linear homogeneity, $Y = NF(K/N,1)$. Define k to be equal to K/N, the capital effective-labor ratio. Note that this definition of k is different from the one we have been using so

---

*In other words, Harrod-neutrality is a necessary condition for the existence of a steady state.

far. Henceforth, we will assume that k stands for the capital effective-labor ratio. Under this assumption the production function becomes the same as in (3.2.1) with N replacing L. In steady state, capital and output will grow at the same rate. As argued in the Solow-Swan model this implies that k must be a constant; that is, capital effective-labor ratio is constant in the steady state. Aggregate output will then grow at the same rate as N. $\dot{Y}/Y = \dot{A}/A + \dot{L}/L = \lambda + n$ where $\dot{A}/A$ equals λ. It can be shown that λ is also the rate at which labor productivity is growing (see exercise 4.2). Capital formation is now given by $\dot{K} = sY - \delta K = sNf(k) - \delta K$. It follows from this that $\dot{K}/K = sf(k)/k - \delta$, and hence

$$\dot{k}/k = \dot{K}/K - \dot{N}/N = sf(k)/k - (\lambda+n+\delta)$$

Comparing this with equation (3.2.12), it is evident that all the previous analysis holds if we simply replace n by $(\lambda+n)$ and interpret k as the capital effective-labor ratio rather than the capital-labor ratio. Given this new interpretation Harrod-neutral technical progress behaves like population growth. There is a slight difference in the long run behavior of per capita output and real wages. Since aggregate output grows at the rate $(\lambda+n)$, per capita output grows at the rate λ instead of remaining constant as in the Solow-Swan model. Factor prices are given by the respective marginal products.[1]

$$w = \partial Y/\partial L = A(t)[f(k) - kf'(k)]$$
$$r = \partial Y/\partial K = f'(k)$$

Since k is constant in the steady state, the real rate of return to capital is constant, but real wages rise at the rate λ. The introduction of technical progress thus explains the stylized fact that real wages and per capita output have been rising in advanced economies. It is easy to verify that the relative share of capital is $kf'(k)/f(k)$ which is constant in the steady state because k is constant.

---

[1]Note that real wages are determined by the marginal product of <u>raw</u> labor and not that of <u>effective-labor</u>.

4.1.5 Factor-Augmenting Technical Progress

Production functions which exhibit Hicks-neutrality or Harrod-neutrality are special cases of a class of production functions which exhibit factor-augmenting technical progress. A production function is said to be factor-augmenting if it can be written in the form

$$Y(t) = Q(K,L,t) = F[B(t)K,A(t)L] \tag{4.1.10}$$

If A=B, then technical progress is Hicks-neutral and a constant B is the case of Harrod-neutrality. If A is constant, technical change is purely capital augmenting and is called Solow-neutral. The properties of this case are symmetric to the Harrod-neutral case.

Assuming that B(t) and A(t) grow exponentially at the rates μ and λ respectively, the production function can be rewritten as

$$Y(t) = F[Ke^{\mu t}, Le^{\lambda t}] \tag{4.1.11}$$

As before we will assume that the function F exhibits constant returns to scale. Differentiating (4.1.11) totally with respect to t and dividing the result by Y, we get

$$\frac{\dot{Y}}{Y} = \frac{Ke^{\mu t}F_1}{Y} \cdot \left(\frac{\dot{K}}{K}\right) + \frac{Ke^{\mu t}F_1\mu}{Y} + \frac{Le^{\lambda t}F_2}{Y}\left(\frac{\dot{L}}{L}\right) + \frac{Le^{\lambda t}F_2}{Y} \cdot \lambda$$

Let $\pi = KF_K/Y$ be the share of capital. Since $F_K = F_1e^{\mu t}$, we have $\pi = (Ke^{\mu t}F_1)/Y$. By linear homogeneity, $1 - \pi = (Le^{\lambda t}F_2)/Y$. Using these, we get

$$\frac{\dot{Y}}{Y} = \pi\left(\frac{\dot{K}}{K}\right) + (1-\pi)\left(\frac{\dot{L}}{L}\right) + \pi\mu + (1-\pi)\lambda \tag{4.1.12}$$

The rate of growth of aggregate output is thus expressed as a weighted average of the rates of accumulation of capital and labor plus a weighted average of the rates of factor-augmentation, the weights being the respective factor shares (which will change over time).

Given data on Y,K,L and π, it is possible to estimate the rates of factor augmentation λ and μ. Let

$$(4.1.13) \qquad q_t = \frac{\dot{Y}}{Y} - \pi\left(\frac{\dot{K}}{K}\right) - (1-\pi)\,\frac{\dot{L}}{L}$$

Using this equation (4.1.12) can be written as follows:

$$(4.1.14) \qquad q_t = \lambda + \pi_t(\mu-\lambda)$$

Given time series data on output, capital stock and labor force, a series on q_t can be constructed. We may then estimate λ and μ by regressing q_t on π_t with a constant term. The constant term is an estimate of λ and the sum of the two regression coefficients is an estimate of μ. We may also test whether technical progress is neutral or not with appropriate t-tests. For instance, the hypothesis that $\mu = 0$ implies that technical progress is Harrod-neutral. Hicks-neutrality is tested with the hypothesis $\lambda = \mu$ and Solow neutrality with the hypothesis $\lambda = 0$.

Factor-bias and constancy of shares: With the help of a factor-augmenting production function, we can derive an important proposition in the theory of distribution of factor shares [12]. This is stated in the form of a theorem.

Theorem 4.4: Let the production function be given by (4.1.10) which is assumed to be linearly homogeneous in the two arguments. Also let $\pi = KF_K/Y$ be the relative share of capital $(0 < \pi < 1)$ and σ be the elasticity of substitution. If this share is constant with a rising capital-labor ratio, then technical progress must be labor saving in the Hicksian sense if $\sigma < 1$, Hicks-neutral if $\sigma = 1$ and capital saving if $\sigma > 1$.

Proof: Because of linear homogeneity, $Y = KF_K + LF_L$ from which it follows that

$$(4.1.15) \qquad \frac{\dot{Y}}{Y} = \pi\left(\frac{\dot{K}}{K}\right) + (1-\pi)\left(\frac{\dot{L}}{L}\right) + \pi\left(\frac{\dot{F}_K}{F_K}\right) + (1-\pi)\left(\frac{\dot{F}_L}{F_L}\right)$$

Let $Y = F(KB,LA) = LAf(kB/A)$ where $k = K/L$ is the capital labor ratio. We then have (Exercise 4.11)

$$(4.1.16) \qquad F_K = Bf'$$

$$(4.1.17) \qquad F_L = Af - Bkf'$$

$$R = \frac{F_L}{F_K} = \frac{Af - Bkf'}{Bf'} \tag{4.1.18}$$

$$\sigma = \frac{R}{k}\frac{dk}{dR} = -\frac{f'(Af-Bkf')}{Bkff''} = \frac{-f'A(1-\pi)}{Bkf''} \tag{4.1.19}$$

Differentiating F_K totally with respect to t, we get

$$\frac{\dot{F}_K}{F_K} = \frac{F_{Kt}}{F_K} + \frac{f''}{f'}\frac{B}{A}\dot{k}$$

Using (4.1.19) this becomes

$$\frac{\dot{F}_K}{F_K} = \frac{F_{Kt}}{F_K} - \frac{(1-\pi)}{\sigma}\frac{\dot{k}}{k} \tag{4.1.20}$$

where F_{Kt} is the partial derivative (i.e. keeping K and L unchanged) of F_K with respect to t. Similarly,

$$\frac{\dot{F}_L}{F_L} = \frac{F_{Lt}}{F_{Lt}} + \frac{\pi}{\sigma}\frac{\dot{k}}{k} \tag{4.1.21}$$

Logarithmically differentiating π we get

$$\frac{\dot{\pi}}{\pi} = \frac{\dot{K}}{K} + \frac{\dot{F}_K}{F_K} - \frac{\dot{Y}}{Y}$$

Using (4.1.15), (4.1.20) and (4.1.21) in this and simplifying, we get

$$\frac{\dot{\pi}}{\pi} = (1-\pi)\left[D - \frac{(1-\sigma)}{\sigma}\frac{\dot{k}}{k}\right] \tag{4.1.22}$$

Where $D = (F_{Kt}/F_K) - (F_{Lt}/F_L)$ is the measure of bias discussed in Section 4.1.1. If factor shares are constant then $\dot{\pi} = 0$ and hence

$$D = \frac{1-\sigma}{\sigma}\frac{\dot{k}}{k}$$

It is given that the capital labor ratio is rising, that is $\dot{k} > 0$. Therefore D and $(1-\sigma)$ must have the same sign. In other words, if $\sigma < 1$ then D must be positive which means technical progress must be labor-saving. Similarly, $\sigma > 1$ implies that technical progress is capital-saving. This establishes the theorem.

4.2 Endogenous Technical Progress

In the previous section it was assumed that technical progress was exogenous; that is, the rate of technical change was determined from outside the system. However, in practice this is not so. Technical changes are induced and depend on the amount of resources used in the generation of new innovations. These resources, channelled into education or research, in turn depend on the existing stock of capital, investment, output, etc. Therefore, if a dynamic model of economic behavior is to take into account the technical advancement in production processes, such a model must treat technical progress as induced rather than as exogenous. Here we present three alternative ways of treating innovations as induced. A model proposed by Conlisk [9] assumes that the rate of growth of technical progress depends on the level of per capita income. Arrow's model [2] assumes that the rate of growth of technical change depends on past experience. Thus there is a process of learning by doing. Models proposed by Uzawa [42] and Phelps [31] assume that a part of the labor force is devoted to the generation of technical progress and the remainder to producing the output. In the next few pages these models and their implications are discussed in detail. The models originally proposed by Arrow, Uzawa and Phelps are much more complicated. What we have done here is to capture the underlying ideas and recast them into the simple framework of an aggregate commodity and two factors of production each of which is homogeneous.

4.2.1 Conlisk's model

We first present a model proposed by Conlisk in which the rate of change of technical progress depends on per capita income [9]. An economy with a high per capita income has the resources to spend on education and research which contribute to increases in productivity, whereas a country with low incomes tends to produce its output with inferior technology.

The results of Conlisk's model differ in crucial ways from the Solow-Swan model. First, the long run equilibrium growth rate can be raised by increasing the saving rate. Thus government policy to raise the long run growth rate by increasing the saving rate would now be effective. Second, depreciation of capital has a dampening effect on the equilibrium growth rate. The structural equations of the model are described below.

The production function is now different from the simple neo-classical model and includes technical progress. It was seen in the last section that steady state growth is impossible unless technical progress is Harrod-neutral. Since the interest is on long run balanced growth, it will be assumed that technical progress is indeed Harrod-neutral but that the rate of labor augmentation is endogenous. The assumption of homegeneity of degree one in capital and labor is still retained. The production function thus becomes $Y = F(K,N)$ where $N = LT(t)$, $T(t)$ being the labor augmentation factor. N is to be interpreted as effective-labor. Because of linear homogeneity, the production function can be rewritten as

$$Y = Nf(k) = LTf(k) \tag{4.2.1}$$

$$k = K/LT \tag{4.2.2}$$

k is the capital effective-labor ratio. Technical progress is endogenous and the rate at which labor is augmented is assumed to depend on per capita income. More specifically,

$$\dot{T} = \mu Y/L + \lambda T \quad , \lambda > 0 \tag{4.2.3}$$

The other equations are the same as before. Capital formation is the amount of saving less depreciation and labor force grows at the rate n.[1] Thus

$$\dot{K} = sY - \delta K \tag{4.2.4}$$

$$\dot{L}/L = n \tag{4.2.5}$$

---

[1] Differentiating $N = LT$ we obtain $\dot{N} = L\dot{T} + T\dot{L} = \mu Y + nN$ or equivalently, $\dot{N}/N = \mu Y/N + n$. Thus we can interpret the model in an equivalent way. The rate of growth of effective-labor has two components: an exogenous component depending on n only and an endogenous component depending on the average product of effective-labor. (In the above, λ is assumed as zero for simplicity.)

The saving rate, the rate of depreciation and the population growth rate are all fixed parameters. The endogenous variables of the system are Y,K,L,T and k and are determined by the equations (4.2.1) to (4.2.5). From (4.2.4)

$$\dot{K}/K = sY/K - \delta = sf(k)/k - \delta \tag{4.2.6}$$

Logarithmic differentiation of (4.2.2) with respect to t gives

$$\begin{aligned} \dot{k}/k &= \dot{K}/K - \dot{L}/L - \dot{T}/T \\ &= sf(k)/k - \delta - n - \mu f(k) - \lambda \end{aligned} \tag{4.2.7}$$

The basic differential equation of the system is thus given by

$$\dot{k}/k = sf(k)/k - \mu f(k) - (\lambda+n+\delta) \equiv \psi(k) - (\lambda+n+\delta) \tag{4.2.8}$$

We shall assume that f(k) satisfies the neo-classical conditions; that is, the boundary and interior slope conditions (3.2.16) and (3.2.17). Under these assumptions, f(k) increases with k and f(k)/k decreases with k. Thus $\psi(k)$ is a monotonically decreasing function of k. Also, the average product curve begins at infinity and goes to zero. Therefore $\psi(0) = \infty$ and $\psi(\infty) = -\infty$. Hence, there is a unique solution to the equation $\psi(k) = \lambda + n + \delta$. Since $\psi'(k) < 0$, the system is globally stable. The equilibrium capital intensity k* is given by the equation[1]

$$sf(k^*)/k^* - \delta = \mu f(k^*) + n + \lambda \tag{4.2.9}$$

The left hand side of (4.2.9) is the familiar <u>warranted rate of growth</u>; that is, the rate at which capital stock would grow if there is to be equilibrium in the capital market. The right hand side can be interpreted as the <u>natural rate of growth</u>. It is the rate at which effective-labor is growing. The natural rate is the rate of growth of labor force plus the rate of growth of technology. Since technical progress is endogenous, the rate at which technology is improving depends on the current level of capital intensity. Figure 4.4 represents the two rates of growth. The

---

[1]Note that in the steady state Y and K grow at the same rate. As before this implies that k is constant; that is $\dot{k} = 0$. Thus the capital effective-labor ratio is constant but not the raw capital-labor ratio.

neo-classical assumptions on the production function imply that the warranted rate is a decreasing function of k while the natural rate is an increasing function. The intersection of the two curves gives the equilibrium capital effective-labor ratio k*. The rate of growth of output and capital is

$$g = (\dot{Y}/Y)^* = (\dot{K}/K)^* = sf(k^*)/k^* - \delta = \mu f(k^*) + n + \lambda$$

When long run equilibrium is attained, rents will be constant and wages will rise at the rate $g - n = \mu f(k^*) + \lambda$. The following sensitivities are readily established (exercise 4.3):

$$\frac{\partial g}{\partial s} > 0, \quad \frac{\partial g}{\partial n} > 0, \quad \frac{\partial g}{\partial \mu} > 0, \quad \frac{\partial g}{\partial \delta} < 0$$

$$\frac{\partial k^*}{\partial s} > 0, \quad \frac{\partial k^*}{\partial n} < 0, \quad \frac{\partial k^*}{\partial \mu} < 0, \quad \frac{\partial k^*}{\partial \delta} < 0$$

Three interesting and new conclusions arise in this model. First, when the aggregate saving rate increases, so does the long run rate of growth of output. This did not occur in any of the models discussed earlier. In the simple Solow-Swan model, if the

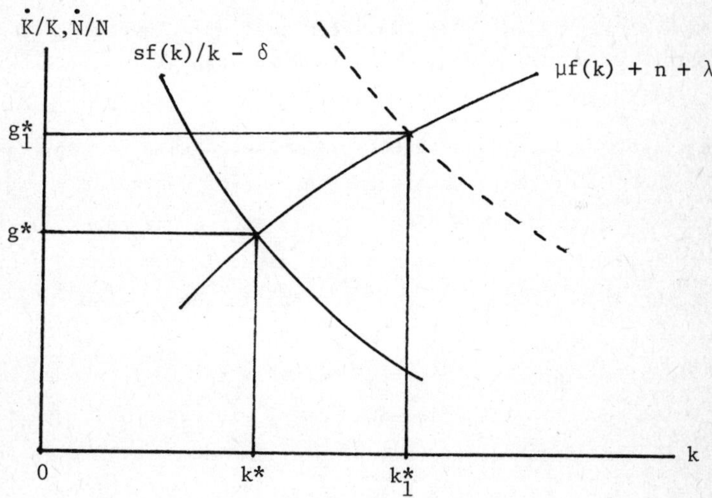

Figure 4.4

saving rate goes up capital stock accumulates faster than the natural rate which is a constant. Thus the warranted rate temporarily rises. However, this will not be sustained in the long run, for capital is now relatively plentiful and therefore rents decline. Firms will then substitute capital for labor thereby raising the capital intensity. This reduces the warranted rate. The process continues until the warranted rate, which rose in the short run, is driven back to the fixed natural rate. The result is that firms operate at a higher equilibrium capital intensity but with no change in the long run rate of growth of output. What makes this result different in the Conlisk model? Unlike in the standard model, the natural rate in the Conlisk model depends on the capital intensity. When the saving rate rises, capital intensity rises as before and the warranted rate, which initially rose, begins to fall. The rise in capital intensity increases f(k) thereby inducing more technological advances which in turn raise the effective-labor force. Thus when the warranted rate is falling, the natural rate, instead of remaining constant as in the standard model, rises. The two rates meet at a level higher than the previous natural rate. Thus, when the saving rate goes up, the long run growth rate increases from g^* to g_1^* in Figure 4.4 and the equilibrium capital intensity increases from k^* to k_1^*.

A second result is that when the rate of depreciation increases (that is, when machines decay faster), the long run growth rate falls, another conclusion not obtained in the standard model. The mechanism is the opposite of the one in the previous paragraph.

The third interesting result pertains to the growth rate of per capita output. The Solow-Swan model with technical progress predicted that in the long run, per capita income will grow at the same exogenous rate as does technology. Thus the observed increases in output per head are explained by technological changes, the source of which is not known. In the Conlisk model we have $(\dot{y}/y)^* = \mu f(k^*) + \lambda$ where y is per capita output. The <u>stylized fact</u> that output per head has increased is explained in this model by a force determined within the model and not by resorting to the assumption of exogeneity of technical progress. Furthermore, an increase in n decreases k* and hence decreases $(\dot{y}/y)^*$. Thus an increase in the population growth rate <u>lowers</u> the equilibrium growth rate of per capita output. This conclusion also is in strong contrast to that obtained in the Solow-Swan model which predicts that changes in the population growth rate will not affect the growth rate of per capita output.

A rough empirical test of the model is possible using cross-country data. From aggregate data for 56 countries, Conlisk has estimated the following relation:

$$g = \alpha_0 + \alpha_1 s + \alpha_2 n$$

g is the <u>average</u> growth rate of real national product during the period 1950-63, s is the average ratio of domestic fixed investment plus change in inventories to the real national product, and n is the average rate of growth of population. The estimated equation is

$$g = \underset{(.009)}{.005} + \underset{(.038)}{.155s} + \underset{(.185)}{.700n} \qquad R^2 = .32 \tag{4.2.10}$$

The numbers in parentheses are the standard errors of the corresponding coefficients. For a cross-section study of this type, a value of .32 for R^2 indicates a reasonably good fit. The ratios of the coefficients of s and n to their standard errors are over 3.75. This means that, according to the data, these coefficients are significantly different from zero and positive. There is thus empirical evidence to indicate that saving rate and population growth rate do positively affect the growth rate of output. Moreover, an increase in n lowers the per capita growth rate (g-n) because $\partial(g-n)/\partial n = -0.3$. This result also was predicted by Conlisk's model. Although Conlisk's model agrees with the above estimated relation, it should be remembered that the data used by him represent only 13 years which cannot be considered long run.

4.2.2 Learning By Doing

The model proposed by Conlisk recognizes the basic fact that innovations cannot be treated as exogenous but are indeed induced. The question is: how is technical change induced? The model in the last section assumes that change in technology is induced by the current level of per capita output. Arrow [2] has argued that "experience" plays a vital role in increasing productivity and cites several examples. If someone has been producing a commodity for a long time, then he learns to produce it more efficiently. For example, the number of man-hours spent in the production of an airframe has been found to decrease with the total number of airframes previously produced [44]. A second example given by Arrow is that the Horndal Iron Works in Sweden observed an average annual increase in productivity of about 2 percent even though there was no new investment for a period of 15 years [27]. This increase in productivity can only be attributed to what Arrow calls learning by doing.

If we admit that experience does contribute to increases in productivity, we are faced with the problem of choosing one or more variables which represent the learning process. Cumulative past output and cumulative past investment are two natural candidates. In this section we take the standard neo-classical model, modify it to take into account this learning process and analyze its long run behavior. The model presented here is a simplified version of Arrow's model. The equations which do not change from previous models are reproduced below.

(4.2.1) $$Y = LTf(k)$$

(4.2.2) $$k = K/LT$$

(4.2.4) $$\dot{K} = sY - \delta K$$

(4.2.5) $$\dot{L}/L = n$$

There are four equations in the five endogenous variables Y,K,L,T and k. One more equation is needed to complete the system. This is accomplished in two alternative ways.

Model 1: In this model the rate at which technical progress takes place is assumed to depend linearly on the rate at which capital stock is growing. More formally,

$$(4.2.11) \qquad \dot{T}/T = \lambda + \alpha\dot{K}/K \qquad \alpha, \lambda > 0$$

The above relation can be derived by the following specification of the technical change factor:

$$(4.2.12) \qquad T = e^{\lambda t}K^{\alpha}$$

Thus the technical change factor depends partly on exogenous factors and partly on the existing capital stock. Logarithmic differentiation of (4.2.12) gives (4.2.11). If $\alpha = 0$ then technical progress is exogenous and grows at a constant rate. Since it is assumed that learning improves productivity, α must be positive.

By now the pattern of analysis is well set. First form the basic differential equation in k. Logarithmic differentiation of (4.2.2) gives

$$\begin{aligned} \dot{k}/k &= \dot{K}/K - \dot{L}/L - \dot{T}/T \\ &= (1-\alpha)\dot{K}/K - (\lambda+n) \end{aligned}$$

from (4.2.5) and (4.2.11). From (4.2.4) and (4.2.1) $\dot{K}/K = sf(k)/k - \delta$. The differential equation in k thus becomes

$$(4.2.13) \qquad \dot{k}/k = \frac{s(1-\alpha)f(k)}{k} - (\lambda+n) - (1-\alpha)\delta$$

The existence of a long run equilibrium depends crucially on whether or not α is less than 1.

Case 1: $\alpha < 1$: If the learning coefficient α is less than 1, the first term of (4.2.13) is a downward sloping curve which has a unique intersection with the horizontal straight line at $\lambda+n+(1-\alpha)\delta$. A unique steady state value k* thus exists and the system is stable. In the steady state, $(\dot{K}/K)^* = (\dot{Y}/Y)^* = g = \dot{L}/L + (\dot{T}/T)^* = n + \lambda + \alpha g$. The growth rate is therefore given by $(\lambda+n)/(1-\alpha)$. In the standard neo-classical model with exogenous technical change, the growth rate is $\lambda+n$. When $\alpha < 1$, Arrow's learning by doing model predicts a higher growth rate in the long run. The higher α, that is, the faster the learning process, the higher is the growth rate. The saving rate, however, is ineffective as an instrument to raise the equilibrium growth rate. Per capita output grows at the rate $(\lambda+n\alpha)/(1-\alpha)$. The implication of this is that an increase in n would increase the rate of growth of per capita output. This result does not seem plausible. In fact, the empirical result obtained by Conlisk indicates that an increase in n will lower the rate of growth of per capita output.

How do factor prices and relative shares behave in such a world? It can be shown that the learning by doing model exhibits increasing returns to scale in capital and labor (exercise 4.5). Aggregate output is given by $F(K, Le^{\lambda t}K^{\alpha})$ after substitution for T from (4.2.12). In the exogenous technical change case, a proportionate rise in capital and labor would increase effective-labor in the same proportion and hence aggregate output would also rise in the same proportion. In Arrow's model the technology factor rises with the level of capital; and therefore effective-labor would increase more than proportionately which implies that aggregate output would rise more than proportionately. Recall from Euler's theorem (2.2.1) that when there is increasing returns to scale, paying factors their marginal product over-exhausts the product. If effective-labor is paid its marginal product f-kf' and capital is paid f'(k), then total product is distributed completely between capital and effective-labor. However, this would create a divergence between the social marginal productivity of capital and its private marginal productivity. This is better seen from the following expressions for the marginal products (see exercise 4.5).

$$(4.2.14) \qquad \begin{cases} \dfrac{\partial Y}{\partial K} = f'(k) + \alpha(f-kf')/k \\[2ex] \dfrac{\partial Y}{\partial L} = T[f-kf'] \end{cases}$$

It is evident that the social marginal product of capital is greater than f'(k). If capital is paid only f'(k), then its indirect effect on output through the learning process is not compensated for. A straightforward way of dealing with this situation is to pay each factor a proportion θ of the corresponding marginal product. θ is determined so as to exhaust the total product. The proportion θ is given by (exercise 4.5)

$$\theta = \frac{f(k)}{f(k) + \alpha(f-kf')} \tag{4.2.15}$$

Since this is a function of k only, it is constant in the steady state, and so is the share of capital in total output. Rents will remain constant and wages will rise at the same rate as T, viz. $(\lambda+\alpha n)/(1-\alpha)$.

Case 2: $\alpha \geq 1$: In this case, the first term of (4.2.13) is either zero or negative making $\dot{k}$ negative. Therefore k steadily declines to zero, and there is no non-trivial steady state solution. We can obtain this result by a straight forward economic argument. If $\alpha \geq 1$, then the technology factor T is rising faster than capital stock. Therefore the natural rate -- the rate of growth of efficient labor -- exceeds the warranted rate. Since efficient labor is now relatively abundant, wages drop relative to rents. Firms will now use more labor thus lowering the capital intensity and raising the warranted rate. But, as can be seen from (4.2.11), the natural rate increases even more (because $\alpha \geq 1$) thus widening the gap between the two rates. The process continues with ever decreasing capital intensity. Thus the learning by doing model has a stable long run equilibrium provided the learning coefficient α does not exceed 1.

Model 2: An alternative learning process is to assume that the technology factor depends on cumulative past output rather than investment. This leads to the following equations:

$$\dot{T}/T = \mu + \beta\dot{X}/X \qquad \mu, \beta > 0 \tag{4.2.16}$$

$$X = \int_{-\infty}^{t} Y(u)du \tag{4.2.17}$$

where X(t) is cumulative past output. (4.2.16) can be obtained by setting $T = e^{\mu t}X^{\beta}$. From the previous model it is clear that the condition $\beta < 1$ is needed. Otherwise a steady state will not exist. Equations (4.2.16) and (4.2.17) now replace (4.2.11). As before,

$$(4.2.18) \qquad \dot{k}/k = \dot{K}/K - \dot{L}/L - \dot{T}/T$$
$$= sf(k)/k - \delta - n - \mu - \beta\dot{X}/X$$
$$= sf(k)/k - (\mu+n+\delta) - \beta\dot{X}/X$$

This equation is difficult to analyze but can be simplified by introducing a new variable x defined as

$$(4.2.19) \qquad x \equiv K/X$$

From (4.2.17), $\dot{X} = Y$. Therefore,

$$(4.2.20) \qquad \frac{\dot{X}}{X} = \frac{Y}{X} = \frac{Y}{K}\frac{K}{X} = xf(k)/k$$

Substituting this in (4.2.18) and rearranging terms,

$$(4.2.21) \qquad \dot{k}/k = \phi(k,x) = (s-\beta x)f(k)/k - (\mu+n+\delta)$$

Logarithmic differentiation of x gives

$$(4.2.22) \qquad \dot{x}/x = \psi(k,x) = \dot{K}/K - \dot{X}/X = (s-x)f(k)/k - \delta$$

where we have made use of (4.2.8) and (4.2.20) in the derivation. (4.2.21) and (4.2.22) are the basic differential equations of the system. We know that in the steady state $\dot{k} = 0$. It will presently be shown that in the steady state $\dot{x}$ is also zero; that is, cumulative output also grows at the same rate as capital. If capital and output grow at the constant rate g, then $K = K_o e^{gt}$ and $Y = Y_o e^{gt}$. We then have

$$X(t) = \int_{-\infty}^{t} Y(u)du = Y_o e^{gt}/g$$

Thus X grows at the same constant rate as capital and output and hence $x = K/X$ is constant. Setting $\dot{k} = 0 = \dot{x}$ in equations (4.2.21) and (4.2.22) and then solving explicitly for x, we get

$$(4.2.23) \qquad x = M(k) = \frac{s}{\beta} - \frac{\mu+n+\delta}{\beta}\frac{k}{f(k)}$$

$$(4.2.24) \qquad x = N(k) = s - \delta k/f(k)$$

In order to examine the existence of a steady state solution, we must first implicitly solve the equation $M(k) = N(k)$ for k. Setting $M(k)$ equal to $N(k)$ and rearranging terms we obtain the following equation:

(4.2.25) $$sf(k^*)/k^* - \delta = (\mu+n)/(1-\beta) > 0$$

Under the neoclassical conditions on the production function there exists a unique k* satisfying the above equation. Next, from (4.2.24) and (4.2.25) we have

$$x^* = \frac{s(\mu+n)}{\mu+n+\delta(1-\beta)} > 0$$

Therefore the steady state solution (k*,x*) is unique and can be attained since both k* and x* are positive. Whether it will be attained from any arbitrary position depends on the stability of the system. Stability can be examined by drawing a phase diagram in the manner indicated in the Appendix to Chapter 3. As a first step towards mapping the curves M(k) and N(k), their slopes are obtained as follows:

$$M'(k) = \frac{-(\mu+n+\delta)}{\beta}\,\frac{f-kf'}{f^2}$$

$$N'(k) = -\delta(f-kf')/f^2$$

Since $f-kf' > 0$ both these slopes are negative for all values of k. Moreover, the absolute value of M'(k) is greater than that of N'(k). This can be shown by evaluating $|M'(k)| - |N'(k)|$ and using the conditions $\beta < 1$ and $f-kf' > 0$. Therefore the M(k) curve is steeper than the N(k) curve. The phase diagram is shown in Figure 4.5. To draw the directional arrows evaluate $\partial\dot{k}/\partial x$ and $\partial\dot{x}/\partial x$.[1] Since $\dot{k} = k\phi(k,x)$ and $\phi(k,x) = 0$ along the M(k) curve,

$$(\partial\dot{k}/\partial x)_{\dot{k}=0} = k\phi_x = -k\beta f(k)/k < 0$$

Therefore, from any point on the M(k) curve, if k is constant and x increased, $\dot{k}$ decreases to a negative value. This means that at all points above the M(k) curve $\dot{k}$ is negative and thus k declines. Below M(k) the opposite is the case. The arrows drawn parallel to the k-axis in Figure 4.5 reflect this result. Similarly, since

[1]The directional arrows may also be drawn by evaluating $\partial\dot{k}/\partial k$ and $\partial\dot{x}/\partial k$. Which of the partial derivatives are chosen is a matter of convenience.

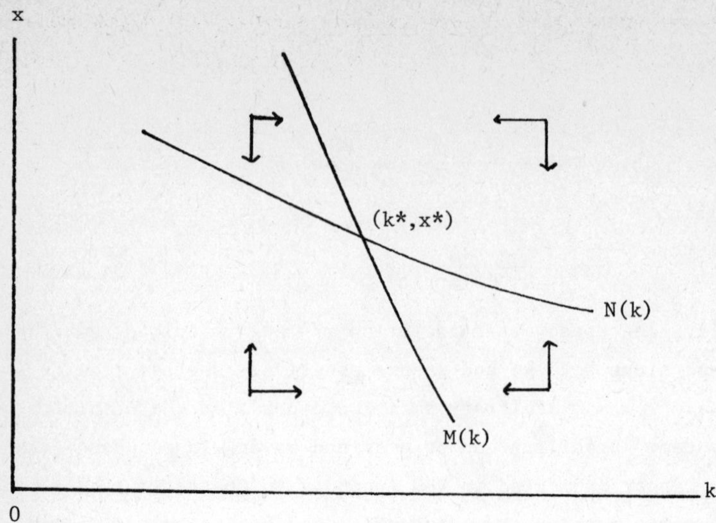

Figure 4.5

$\psi(k,x) = 0$ along the N(k) curve and $\dot{x} = x\psi(k,x)$,

$$(\partial\dot{x}/\partial x)_{\dot{x}=0} = x\psi_x = -xf(k)/k < 0$$

This implies that the directional arrows for movements of x are as given in Figure 4.5. The phase diagram conclusively demonstrates global stability.

In the long run, $(\dot{Y}/Y)^* = (\dot{K}/K)^* = (\dot{X}/X)^* = g$ and k is constant. Logarithmically differentiating (4.2.1) with respect to t and setting $\dot{k} = 0$ we obtain $g = n + \mu + \beta g$.

Therefore $g = (\mu+n)/(1-\beta)$ is the long run growth rate of aggregate output, capital and cumulative output. Per capita output grows at the rate $(\mu+n\beta)/(1-\beta)$. Both of these rates are independent of s and δ. An increase in the learning coefficient β would raise the growth rate. These results are similar to those of model 1. Because T is an integral function of X, there is no easy way to determine factor prices and their shares. However, in the long run $T = X_o^{\beta}e^{(\mu+\beta g)t}$ and is independent of K and L. T behaves as in the Solow-Swan model with exogenous technical change and therefore, equilibrium rents will be constant and wages will rise at the same rate $(\mu+\beta n)/(1-\beta)$ at which per capita output grows.

4.2.3 Uzawa-Phelps Model

In the learning by doing approach the rate of growth of technical change was assumed to depend on cumulative investment or cumulative output. Uzawa and Phelps independently proposed a model in which a part of the labor force is used in the production of technological change [42,31]. Thus there are two sectors; a commodity sector and a second sector which may be called "research and training". In the commodity sector physical output (Y) depends on the stock of capital (K), a portion of the labor force (L_C) used in producing the commodity and Harrod-neutral technical change (T). The production function is thus given by $Y = F(K, L_C T)$. The research and training sector produces changes in technology. The change in technology $(\dot{T})$ depends on the current level of technology (T) and the remaining portion of the labor force engaged in research (L_R). Note that technical change does not depend on investment or the level of capital stock. The technical change equation can be written as $\dot{T} = G(T, L_R)$. The production function and the technical change function are assumed to be linearly homogeneous in the two arguments. The above relations can be simplified by introducing additional notation. Let L be the total labor force, $k = K/(LT)$, $L_R/L = \ell$ and $x = T/L$. k is the capital effective-labor ratio and ℓ is the proportion of total labor force engaged in research. It is assumed that ℓ is a fixed parameter, i.e. the labor allocation to each sector is determined exogenously. Using these definitions, we obtain the following relations:

(4.2.26) $$Y = F(K, L_C T) = (1-\ell)LT\, f[k/(1-\ell)]$$

where $f(k) = F(k,1)$.

(4.2.27) $$\dot{T} = G(T, L_R) = Tg(\ell/x)$$

where $g(z) = G(1,z)$ and $g' > 0$.

(4.2.28) $$k = K/LT$$

(4.2.29) $$\ell = L_R/L$$

(4.2.30) $x = T/L$

(4.2.31) $L = L_C + L_R$

The equations relating to capital formation and growth of labor force are the same as in previous models:

(4.2.4) $\dot{K} = sY - \delta K$

(4.2.5) $\dot{L}/L = n$

The system is comprised of eight structural equations in the eight endogenous variables Y, K, L, T, L_C, L_R, k and x. The parameters are s, n, δ and ℓ. From (4.2.4) and (4.2.26), the rate of growth of capital stock is given by

(4.2.4a) $\dot{K}/K = \frac{s(1-\ell)}{k} f\left[\frac{k}{1-\ell}\right] - \delta$

Logarithmically differentiating k and using (4.2.27) we get

(4.3.32) $\dot{k}/k = \phi(k,x) = \frac{s(1-\ell)}{k} f\left[\frac{k}{1-\ell}\right] - g(\ell/x) - (n+\delta)$

In a similar manner we obtain

(4.2.33) $\dot{x}/x = \psi(x) = g(\ell/x) - n$

Equations (4.2.32) and (4.2.33) are the basic differential equations of the system and we may use the standard technique of analysis. From (4.2.27), $\dot{T}/T = g(\ell/x)$. In the steady state, technical progress takes place at a constant rate by definition. Therefore the left hand side is a constant for all t. This is possible only if x is constant for all t. Thus $\dot{x} = 0$ in steady state and therefore from (4.2.33),

(4.2.34) $g(\ell/x) = n$

Since $g(\ell/x)$ is a decreasing function of x, in general, a unique x* will satisfy the above equation.[1] Using the other steady state condition that $\dot{k} = 0$ we obtain

---

[1]For this, it is sufficient that $g(\ell/x)$ be greater than n for small values of x and less than n for large values of x.

(4.2.35) $$\frac{s(1-\ell)}{k} f\left[\frac{k}{1-\ell}\right] - \delta = 2n$$

The neoclassical conditions on the production function insure that a unique positive k^* exists such that (4.2.35) holds. Thus a unique steady state solution (k^*, x^*) exists. A comparison of equations (4.2.35) and (4.2.4a) shows that $\dot{K}/K = 2n$. Since output and capital grow at the same rate, it follows that the steady state rate of growth of output is 2n and the rate of growth of per capita output is n. Since x is constant in the steady state, $\dot{T}/T = n$. Thus if the research sector uses only labor then we have the peculiar result that technical progress must grow, in the long run, at the same rate as the labor force and that output must grow at the rate 2n. The other implication is that an increase in the rate of growth of labor force will increase the long run per capita income by an equal amount. Conlisk's empirical findings do not support this conclusion.

Factor prices: Because part of the labor force is engaged in generating technical progress, which is not a real commodity, there is no simple mechanism determining factor prices. Maximizing aggregate profits with respect to K, L_C and L_R is difficult because T is a complicated function of L_R. If it is assumed that capital is paid its marginal product which is well defined, the remainder of the output may be allocated to labor. Real rents will then be $r = \partial Y/\partial K = f'[k/(1-\ell)]$, from (4.2.26). Real wages will be determined by the relation $wL = Y - Kr$. This gives the following expression for the wage rate:

$$w = T\left[(1-\ell)f\left(\frac{k}{1-\ell}\right) - kf'\left(\frac{k}{1-\ell}\right)\right]$$

In the steady state k is constant and T grows at the rate n. Therefore rents and factor shares will be constant and wages will rise at the same rate n at which per capita output rises.

Stability analysis: To analyze stability we draw the phase diagram as in the learning by doing model. $\dot{k} = 0$ implies that

$$\phi(k,x) = \frac{s(1-\ell)}{k} f[k/(1-\ell)] - g(\ell/x) - (n+\delta) = 0$$

The slope of this curve at any point is given by $dx/dk = -\phi_k/\phi_x$.

$$\phi_k = s\,\frac{\partial}{\partial k}\left[\frac{f\left(\frac{k}{1-\ell}\right)}{k/(1-\ell)}\right]$$

ϕ_k is negative because the average product of capital is a downward sloping curve. Also, $\phi_x = \ell g'/x^2 > 0$ because $g' > 0$, and hence $dx/dk > 0$. Thus the curve representing the $\dot{k} = 0$ equation is upward sloping as in Figure 4.6. The $\dot{x} = 0$ equation gives $g(\ell/x) = n$. Since the values of x satisfying this equation are independent of k, this relation is represented by a straight line parallel to the k-axis. Since $\phi_k < 0$, below the $\dot{k} = 0$ curve $\dot{k} < 0$ and above it $\dot{k} > 0$. Similarly, since $\psi_x < 0$, $\dot{x}$ is negative above the $\dot{x} = 0$ curve and positive below it. The directional arrows are as in Figure 4.6. It is evident from the phase diagram that the system is globally stable.

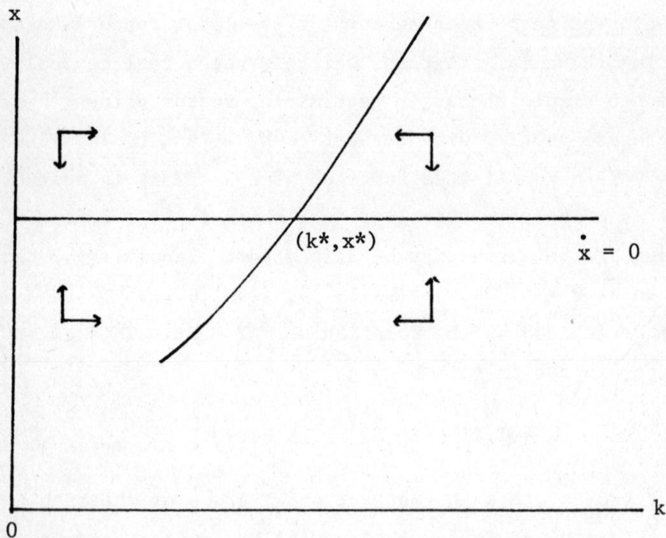

Figure 4.6

4.3 Induced Bias in Technical Change

Models of technical progress proposed by Arrow, Conlisk, Phelps and Uzawa all treat the rate of technical change as induced within the system at a rate determined by one or more characteristics such as per capita income, cumulative past output, investment or the proportion of labor force taking part in research. But all these models share the fundamental weakness of assuming that technical progress is Harrod-neutral and hence is labor augmenting. This assumption is made because otherwise, a balanced growth-path does not exist (Theorem 4.3). The neutrality assumption rules out possible bias in technical change. There is no *a priori* economic reason why technical change need not be labor-saving or capital-saving. In fact, most inventions seem to be labor-saving. Hicks first pointed out that this could be because such inventions come to public attention fairly quickly [18]. Capital-saving improvements in technology (e.g. wireless communications, transistors, integrated circuits, etc.), while they do occur, may not be as visible as labor-saving inventions. As shown in Theorem 4.4, when factor shares are constant over time and the capital-labor ratio is rising, then technical progress will be labor-saving (in the Hicksian sense), if $\sigma < 1$, neutral if $\sigma = 1$ and capital-saving if $\sigma > 1$.

Fellner [13] has argued that in advanced countries in which capital accumulates faster than labor and real wages are rising, firms may anticipate further increases in real wage rates relative to interest rates and choose to move in favor of a labor-saving technology. In addition, market imperfections may generate other distortions to neutralize the effect of the imperfections. For example, distortions in the form of rigidities in the wage rate may cause Keynesian unemployment. Firms may not want to hire workers at such wages but instead favor the installation of labor-saving devices.

Kennedy [23] has introduced an ingenious device called the *innovation possibility frontier* which enables us to determine the direction of bias of an innovation.[1] The frontier provides alternative combinations of rates of capital augmenting and labor augmenting technical change. It is assumed that entrepreneurs will choose that amount of bias which will result in the largest reduction in costs, subject to the innovation possibility frontier. In other words, firms seek to maximize the rate of increase in technical progress subject to the frontier. Drandakis, Phelps and Samuelson [12,34,35] have extended Kennedy's analysis and shown that under certain conditions, a stable steady state path will be achieved and along such a path technical change will be Harrod-neutral. Thus Harrod-neutrality is derived from a more general framework rather than assumed to begin with. To analyze this more formally, assume that the production function is linearly homogeneous and of the factor augmenting form

$$Y(t) = Q(K,L,t) = F[B(t)K, A(t)L] \tag{4.3.1}$$

If $A = B$ then technical progress is Hicks-neutral and a constant B is the case of Harrod-neutrality. If A is a constant, technical change is purely capital augmenting and is called <u>Solow-neutral</u>. Let b denote $\dot{B}/B$ the rate of change of capital augmenting technical progress and a denote $\dot{A}/A$. Firms can choose the rates a and b, but for a given rate of labor augmentation there is a maximum possible rate of capital augmentation. This is given in the form of a frontier exogenously determined by the continuous function $a = \phi(b)$ where $\phi(0) > 0$, $\phi'(b) < 0$, $\phi''(b) < 0$, $a \leq \bar{a}$ and $b \leq \bar{b}$. Such a frontier is presented in Figure 4.7.

The diagram implies that the two kinds of factor augmentation compete with each other. For example, an increase in capital augmentation is possible only with a decrease in labor augmentation. Furthermore, this decrease is at an increasing rate as indicated by the sign of the second derivative of $\phi(b)$. There is no reason to expect that a and b must always be positive. One of them may be negative and therefore the technical change frontier need not

---

[1]Other names used are <u>invention possibility frontier</u> and <u>technical change frontier</u>.

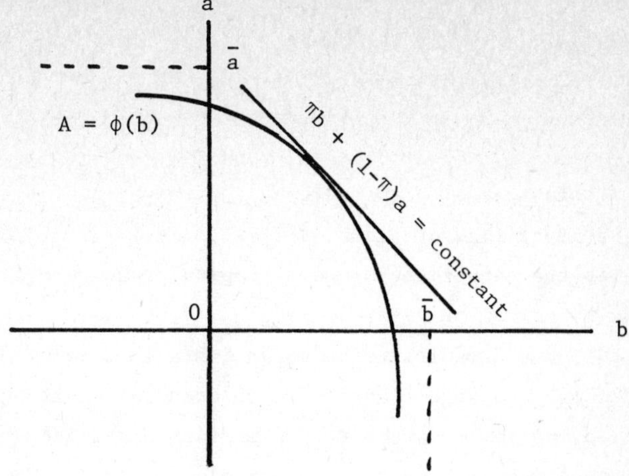

Figure 4.7

be restricted to the positive quadrant.

Partially differentiating (4.3.1) with respect to t and dividing the result by Q, the rate of growth of technical progress is obtained as

(4.3.2) $$Q_t/Q = B'KF_1/Q + A'LF_2/Q$$

where F_1 and F_2 are the partial derivatives of the function F with respect to the first and second arguments respectively. Also, the marginal product of capital is $F_K = BF_1$ and the relative share of capital is $\pi = KF_K/Q = BKF_1/Q$. Applying Euler's theorem to (4.3.1) we get $KBF_1/Q + LAF_2/Q = 1$, or, $LAF_2/Q = 1-\pi$. Using these results in (4.3.2) the following relation is obtained:

(4.3.3) $$q \equiv Q_t/Q = b\pi + a(1-\pi)$$

The overall rate of technical change is thus a linear combination of the rates of factor augmentation. A criterion to use in choosing the amount of bias in technical change is to maximize q (for a given π) subject to the technical change frontier. This maximization would then be carried out at each instant of time. The necessary condition for a maximum is that $\partial q/\partial b = 0$. This gives $\pi + (1-\pi)\phi'(b) = 0$, or

(4.3.4) $\phi'(b) = -\pi/(1-\pi)$

Figure 4.7 illustrates this result by the tangency of the frontier with the straight line of slope $-\pi/(1-\pi)$. It is seen from the diagram that the larger the share of capital, the more capital augmenting technical progress will be.

All the above results refer to an instant of time. To begin with, a technical change frontier which does not shift over time is specified. Given the factor shares, firms maximize the rate of technical progress subject to this frontier. But in a dynamic system, capital intensity and hence factor shares are changing. This means that the levels of a and b chosen at each point of time will change. This can be analyzed by adding other assumptions regarding labor supply and saving behavior. We thus obtain the following system of simultaneous equations:

(4.3.1) $Y = F(BK,AL) = ALf(kB/A)$

(4.3.5) $k = K/L$

(4.3.6) $a = \dot{A}/A$

(4.3.7) $b = \dot{B}/B$

(4.3.8) $a = \phi(b)$

(4.3.9) $\pi = KF_K/Y$

(4.3.10) $\phi'(b) = -\pi/(1-\pi)$

(4.3.11) $\dot{L}/L = n$

(4.3.12) $\dot{K} = sY$

There are nine equations in the nine endogenous variables Y,K,L,A,B,a,b,k, and π. The constant parameters of the system are n and s. For convenience, depreciation has been omitted. In order to examine the steady state and stability properties, we should reduce the system to its basic differential equations. Our convention so far has been to obtain a differential equation in the capital-labor ratio. In this model, however, such a procedure leads to a proof of only local stability. By choosing obscure and algebraically tedious transformations, Drandakis and Phelps [7] are able to prove global stability. In what follows we have recast the analysis by Drandakis and Phelps in our framework. The reader is referred to the papers by Drandakis, Phelps and Samuelson [12,24,25] for more details. Let

(4.3.3) $\quad x \equiv \dot{K}/K$

Using (4.3.12), (4.3.1) and (4.3.5) in this we have $x = sY/K = sAf(kB/A)/k$. Logarithmic differentiation of this with respect to t gives

$$\frac{\dot{x}}{x} = \frac{\dot{A}}{A} - \frac{\dot{k}}{k} + \frac{f'}{f} \cdot \frac{kB}{A}\left(\frac{\dot{k}}{k} + \frac{\dot{B}}{B} - \frac{\dot{A}}{A}\right)$$

$$= a - x + n + \pi(x-n+b-a)$$

because

(4.3.14) $\quad \pi = KF_K/Y = kf'B/(Af).$

As $\phi'(b)$ is monotonic ($\phi'' < 0$), by the Inverse Function Theorem, (4.3.10) can be uniquely solved for as $b = G(\pi)$ with $G'(\pi) > 0$. We therefore get the following differential equation:

(4.3.15) $\quad \dot{x}/x = \pi G(\pi) + (1-\pi)[\phi\{G(\pi)\} - x + n]$

The next step is to obtain a differential equation in π. Logarithmically differentiating (4.3.14).

$$\frac{\dot{\pi}}{\pi} = \frac{\dot{k}}{k} + \frac{\dot{B}}{B} - \frac{\dot{A}}{A} + \left(\frac{f''}{f'} - \frac{f'}{f}\right)\frac{kB}{A}\left(\frac{\dot{k}}{k} + \frac{\dot{B}}{B} - \frac{\dot{A}}{A}\right)$$

$$= (x-n+b-a)\left[1 + \frac{kB}{A}\frac{f''}{f'} - \frac{kBf'}{f}\right]$$

From equation (4.1.19) substitute for f''/f' in terms of σ, the elasticity of substitution between capital and labor. We thus have

(4.3.16) $\quad \dot{\pi}/\pi = -[x-n+G(\pi)-\phi\{G(\pi)\}](1-\pi)(1-\sigma)/\sigma$

Equations (4.3.15) and (4.3.16) completely characterize the dynamic properties of the system.

We shall now establish that a unique steady state exists in which capital stock grows at a constant rate and the share of capital π is constant. Moreover, when a steady state is reached technical change is Harrod-neutral even though this need not be so along the actual path followed by the system. The long run share of capital is independent of the saving rate, the population growth rate, and the elasticity of substitution and depends only on the slope of the technical change frontier at the point where $b = 0$. Capital stock and output grow at the same rate and returns to capital will be constant in long run equilibrium. If the elasticity of substitution between capital and labor is less than 1, then the system is globally stable. To prove all these results, first set $\dot{\pi} = \dot{x} = 0$. We then obtain $x - n + G - \phi(G) = 0 = \pi G + (1-\pi)(\phi-x+n)$. It is easy to see from these that in steady state

(4.3.17) $\quad b^* = G(\pi^*) = 0 \quad$ and $x^* = \phi(0) + n$

where the asterisks denote steady state values. Thus, it is readily seen that along the balanced growth path (if it exists) most of the results stated in the last paragraph hold. We still have to prove that a unique and stable steady state path exists.

Existence: First note that the equations $\dot{\pi} = 0$ and $\dot{x} = 0$ can be explicitly solved for x. From $\dot{\pi} = 0$ we get $x = \phi[G(\pi)] - G(\pi) + n$. The slope of this is $dx/d\pi = \phi'G' - G' < 0$ because $\phi' < 0$ and $G' > 0$, and hence the $\dot{\pi} = 0$ curve is always downward sloping. Also, from Figure 4.7 and equation (4.3.10), as π approaches zero, b approaches $-\infty$. Therefore $G(0) = -\infty$ and $x(0) = \infty$. Similarly, as π approaches 1, $a = \phi(b)$ approaches $-\infty$ and thus $x(1) = -\infty$. It follows therefore that the $\dot{\pi} = 0$ curve starts at $+\infty$ and steadily decreases to $-\infty$.

The equation $\dot{x} = 0$ implies that $x = \pi G(\pi)/(1-\pi) + \phi[G(\pi)] + n$. The slope of this curve is

$$\frac{dx}{d\pi} = \frac{\pi G'}{1-\pi} + \frac{G}{(1-\pi)^2} + \phi' G' = \frac{G(\pi)}{(1-\pi)^2}$$

because $\phi' = -\pi/(1-\pi)$. Thus the slope of the $\dot{x} = 0$ curve depends on the sign of $G(\pi)$. From (4.3.17), $G(\pi^*) = 0$. As $G' > 0$, $G(\pi)$ is negative when $\pi < \pi^*$ and positive when $\pi > \pi^*$. Thus the $\dot{x} = 0$ curve decreases in the range $0 < \pi < \pi^*$, takes the smallest value at π^* (with $x^* = \phi(0) + n > 0$) and thereafter increases. Therefore this curve lies entirely above the π axis and, as is seen from Figure 4.8, yields a unique steady state for which $0 < \pi^* < 1$ and $b^* = 0$ implying Harrod-neutrality.

Stability: To examine the stability we need to draw the directional arrows which indicate the way x and π move when they are not at the long run equilibrium. From (4.3.15),

$$(\partial\dot{x}/\partial x)_{\dot{x}=0} = -x(1-\pi) < 0.$$

This means that from the $\dot{x} = 0$ curve if x is slightly increased, $\dot{x}$ becomes negative and hence x will tend to decrease. Thus above the $\dot{x} = 0$ curve the directional arrows for x will point downward. Below that curve the opposite is the case. From (4.3.16),

$$(\partial\dot{\pi}/\partial x)_{=0} = \pi(1-\pi)(\sigma-1)/\sigma.$$

The directional arrows depend on the magnitude of σ. If $\sigma < 1$ then the above derivative is negative and the directional arrows

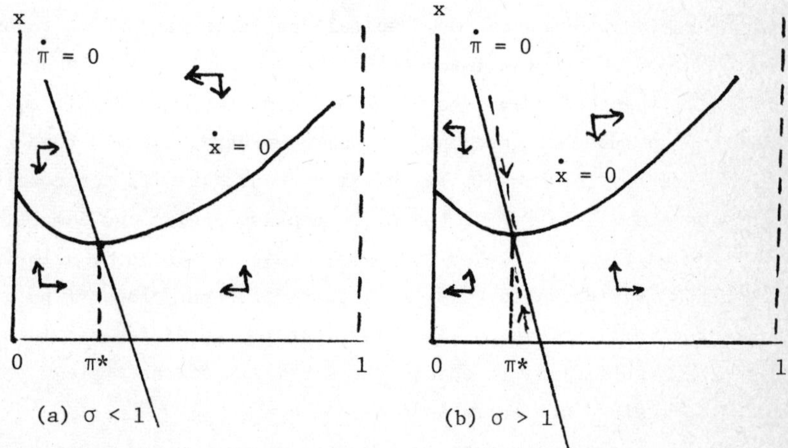

Figure 4.8

will be as in Figure 4.8a. Global stability is hence assured when the elasticity of substitution between capital and labor is less than 1. If $\sigma > 1$, the directional arrows are as in Figure 4.8b implying that the solution is a saddle point (see Figure A.5).

The most interesting aspect of this model is that Harrod-neutrality is derived as a steady state property and need not be assumed initially. This provides a rationale for the widely used assumption of Harrod-neutrality. The model, however, is not without weaknesses. The technical change frontier is exogenously given and does not shift, whereas in the real world we would expect the opportunity locus to be endogenous. For instance, its position might be determined by the amount of resources devoted to a research sector generating the innovations.

Conlisk [10] has extended the above induced bias model to allow for an endogenously determined innovation possibility frontier. He considers two sectors: first a commodity sector producing consumer goods from the given quantities of capital and labor allocated to this sector, and second, a productivity sector producing as joint products, new capital and labor augmenting technical change with the remaining quantities of capital and labor. Technical change is now determined endogenously. Conlisk finds that the optimum bias need not be Harrod-neutral even in the steady state. This result is in strong contrast with the conclusions of the models formulated by Drandakis, Phelps and Samuelson.

Chang [8] has extended the model presented above by allowing a variable saving ratio. Assuming that different proportions of wages and rents are saved, he shows that the condition $\sigma < 1$ is not always sufficient to ensure the stability of the system. His main conclusions are summarized as follows:

(1) A balanced growth path generally exists and technical progress is Harrod-neutral in the steady state.

(2) If $\sigma < 1$ and firms save a greater proportion of their income than workers, a stable steady state growth path can be obtained for most initial conditions.

(3) If $\sigma = 1$, the system is stable irrespective of the saving propensities.

(4) If $\sigma > 1$, the solution is a saddle point. This conclusion is also independent of the saving rates.

4.4 Embodied Technical Progress: Vintage Models

In the Harrod-Domar model, a crucial assumption was that capital and labor must be used in a fixed proportion. These two factors of production were thus complementary and no substitution was possible between them. Neoclassical growth models, on the other hand, assume that capital and labor can be smoothly substituted for each other. Furthermore, in all the concepts of technical progress discussed until now, the age (or *vintage*) of capital equipment did not matter. More specifically, improvements in technology generated increased output with a given stock of capital and labor, regardless of the age of the capital equipment used. It was first argued by Lief Johansen [19] that new ideas are incorporated only in new machines and therefore the efficiency of a machine will depend on its vintage, that is, the year it is installed. He also argued that during the designing stage of a machine several techniques are available to the manufacturer and therefore capital and labor can be substituted for each other at this stage. In this respect the capital-labor ratio is flexible like *putty*. But once the capital equipment is installed, all it needs is operation and maintenance which can be done with a fixed number of workers. Capital intensity is now rigid like clay.[1] There is thus *ex ante* flexibility of factor proportions but *ex post* fixity.

The class of growth models that generated from this line of thinking is known as *vintage growth models* or *embodied technical change models*. In such models the amount of technical change embodied in a machine depends on its vintage. Vintage models, as the one used by Johansen, which assume that factor proportions are variable prior to the installation of capital equipment but fixed

[1] Capital equipment is thus *non-malleable*.

afterwards are referred to as _Putty-Clay_ models. If capital and labor can be smoothly substituted both before and after the installation of a machine but technical progress stops as soon as the equipment is installed, we have a _Putty-Putty_ model. Models of the _Clay-Clay_ type assume fixed coefficients both _ex post_ and and _ex ante_.

As in all the previous models, we will assume that output and labor are homogeneous. However, capital is heterogeneous and each piece of equipment is identified according to the time at which it is first introduced. There is thus no single capital aggregate. Because capital depreciates over time, the amount of capital of vintage v surviving at time t ($t \geq v$) will depend on the original amount of capital introduced at time v and the rate of depreciation. However, machines of other vintages will also be in existence at time t. These machines of various vintages, along with different amounts of labor input per machine, will generate a homogeneous output. Total output is the sum of the outputs from machines of all vintages in use. Of this total, a fixed fraction is consumed and the rest is invested. This investment is the amount of new capital introduced at time t and is labelled accordingly. In Putty-Clay models, the demand for new capital and the corresponding labor requirements at time t, depend on current (and perhaps future) wages and rents. But for capital of earlier vintages, the capital intensity is fixed and does not depend on the wages and rents prevailing at time t. In the Putty-Putty models, the capital-labor requirements of both new and old machines depend on factor prices. In Clay-Clay models, factor proportions are fixed. But in all three types of vintage models, new capital is more productive than old because technical improvements are embodied only into new machines.

4.4.1 A Putty-Clay Model

Many of the results of earlier models carry over to the Putty-Clay models also. For example, the rate of growth of aggregate output is still given by the sum of the growth rate of labor force and the rate of technical progress. In the steady state, per capita income and wages grow at the rate at which technology grows. As in simpler models, the saving rate does not affect these growth rates. A new concept which arises here is the economic life of capital goods; that is, the period for which it is profitable to operate a capital good. It is of interest to analyze the effects of changes in the saving rate and technology on the operating life of capital equipment.

The presentation here is a synthesis of models proposed by Bliss [4], Johansen [19], Kemp and Thanh [21], and Sheshinski [37]. The notation used in vintage models is quite complicated because the output and hence the amounts of labor and capital generating it depend not only on the current time period (t) but also on the vintage (v). Denote the output at time t from capital equipment of vintage v by $Q(v,t)$. In other words, $Q(v,t)$ is the output at time t of machines which were originally installed at time period v ($v \leq t$). Let $K(v,t)$ be the amount of capital equipment of vintage v surviving at time t, and let $L(v,t)$ be the quantity of labor required to work with $K(v,t)$ in order to generate the output $Q(v,t)$. Assume further that all technical progress is Harrod-neutral and exponentially growing. Part of technical progress is assumed to be embodied in new capital and the rest to be disembodied. Embodied technical change affects machines of a given vintage v, but disembodied technical advances affect the efficiency of equipment of all vintages equally.[1] Under the above assumptions we have the following production function:

$$Q(v,t) = F[K(v,t), e^{\alpha v+\beta t}L(v,t)] \tag{4.4.1}$$

α and β are the constant rates of embodied and disembodied technical change respectively. Note that the effect of α stops at time v as soon as the capital equipment is installed. If $\beta = 0$ then all technological advances are embodied. As before, it is postulated that the production function is linearly homogeneous.

---

[1]It will be recognized from this description that all the types of technical changes discussed in the first three sections of this chapter were disembodied.

(4.4.1) then becomes

$$(4.4.2) \qquad Q(v,t) = e^{\alpha v+\beta t}L(v,t)f[k(v,t)]$$

where $f(k) = F(k,1)$ is assumed to have neoclassical properties, and

$$(4.4.3) \qquad k(v,t) = K(v,t)/[e^{\alpha v+\beta t}L(v,t)]$$

$k(v,t)$ is the capital effective-labor ratio of equipment of vintage v surviving at time t.

We now make the assumption that once a piece of equipment is installed, it thereafter needs only a fixed crew to maintain it. Thus the capital intensity of equipment of vintage v remains constant. More specifically,

$$(4.4.4) \qquad k(v,t) = k(v,v)$$

This equation may be rewritten as follows:

$$(4.4.5) \qquad \frac{K(v,t)}{e^{\alpha v+\beta t}L(v,t)} = \frac{K(v,v)}{e^{\alpha v+\beta v}L(v,v)}$$

It is worth pointing out that what is fixed is the number of workers associated with capital of vintage v and <u>measured in efficiency units</u>, and not the raw capital-labor ratio. If $\beta = 0$, that is, if there is no disembodied technical change, this distinction is immaterial because fixity of the capital effective-labor ratio is equivalent to fixity of the capital raw-labor ratio as may be seen by setting $\beta = 0$ in (4.4.5). Another assumption is that capital of all vintages depreciate at the exponential rate δ.[1] Thus

$$(4.4.6) \qquad K(v,t) = K(v,v)e^{-\delta(t-v)}$$

Substituting this in (4.4.5) and rearranging terms, we obtain

$$(4.4.7) \qquad L(v,t) = L(v,v)e^{-(\beta+\delta)(t-v)}$$

The above equation gives the labor requirements at time t for vin-

---

[1]This kind of depreciation, called <u>exponential decay</u>, is chosen because it simplifies the algebra as will be seen presently. For an excellent discussion of different kinds of depreciation see Hahn and Mathews [16].

tage v capital equipment. Using this relation and (4.4.4) in (4.4.2), we get

$$(4.4.8) \qquad Q(v,t) = e^{-\delta t + (\alpha+\beta+\delta)v} L(v,v) f[k(v,v)]$$

Assuming that equipment of all vintages produces the same commodity and that all equipment has the same economic life (θ periods), aggregate output is given by

$$(4.4.9) \qquad Y(t) = \int_{t-\theta}^{t} Q(v,t)dv$$

with the vintage v varying from time period $t-\theta$ to the present time t. The economic life $\theta(t)$ of a machine is the period for which it may be profitably used in production, and is determined endogenously. Specifically, a machine installed at a given time period will be scrapped at the end of θ periods when wages have risen so much that the equipment generates zero profits. We will return to this concept later.

K(t,t) is the amount of capital equipment of vintage t and is therefore the amount of new investment generated at time t. If s is the constant fraction of the total output that is saved, we have the following relation equating saving and investment:

$$(4.4.10) \qquad K(t,t) = sY(t)$$

In order to evaluate the integral on the right hand side of equation (4.4.9) we need to know L(v,v). To obtain this, first assume as we have done in the past, that the total labor force L(t) grows exponentially at the rate n and is therefore given by the following relation:

$$(4.4.11) \qquad L(t) = L_o e^{nt}$$

L(t,t) is the amount of labor working with equipment newly installed at time t. Under the assumption of full employment, this must also be the flow of labor available at time t. This flow has four components. First, the total labor force is growing at the rate n, adding nL(t) workers at time t. Second, some labor is freed because all capital equipment depreciates and *ex post* factor proportions are fixed. The labor thus freed is equal to

$\delta L(t)$. Third, labor productivity increases at the disembodied rate β and thus less workers are required to operate machines. Workers are released at the rate $\beta L(t)$ and they can be employed on new machines. Finally, some labor is freed by the scrapping of equipment exactly θ periods old. The amount of labor available from scrapping is given by the quantity of labor currently associated with equipment installed at time period $t-\theta$. Setting $v = t-\theta$ in (4.4.7), this part of labor is given by $e^{-(\beta+\delta)\theta}L(t-\theta,t-\theta)$. Adding all the four parts of available labor we get

$$(4.4.12) \qquad L(t,t) = (\beta+n+\delta)L_o e^{nt} + L(t-\theta,t-\theta)e^{-(\beta+\delta)\theta}$$

$L(t-\theta,t-\theta)$ can then be obtained as

$$L(t-\theta,t-\theta) = (\beta+n+\delta)L_o e^{n(t-\theta)} + L(t-2\theta,t-2\theta)e^{-(\beta+\delta)\theta}$$

Substituting this in (4.4.12) and proceeding similarly, the expression for $L(t,t)$ becomes

$$L(t,t) = (\beta+n+\delta)L_o e^{nt} + (\beta+n+\delta)L_o \exp[n(t-\theta)-(\beta+\delta)\theta]$$
$$+ (\beta+n+\delta)L_o \exp[n(t-2\theta)-(\beta+\delta)2\theta] + \ldots\ldots$$

Factoring the common terms and simplifying the resulting geometric series we obtain (see exercise 4.6)

$$(4.4.13) \qquad L(t,t) = \frac{(\beta+n+\delta)L_o e^{nt}}{1-e^{-(\beta+n+\delta)\theta}} = \varepsilon(\theta)e^{nt}$$

where

$$\varepsilon(\theta) = \frac{(\beta+n+\delta)L_o}{1-e^{-(\beta+n+\delta)\theta}}$$

This can be substituted in (4.4.8) to give

$$(4.4.14) \qquad Q(v,t) = \varepsilon(\theta)f[k(v,v)]\exp[-\delta t+(\alpha+\beta+n+\delta)v]$$

To evaluate this expression, the explicit form of the function $f(k)$ must be known. The most common form adopted in the literature on vintage models is the Cobb-Douglas production function. However, by focusing on the steady state we can derive the implications of the Putty-Clay model without resorting to a Cobb-Douglas production function. It is assumed that for balanced growth, k must be constant for all v. Substituting for $Q(v,t)$ from (4.4.14) into (4.4.9) and integrating we obtain (see exercise 4.6), for fixed k,

$$Y(t) = \frac{\varepsilon(\theta)f(k)[1-e^{-(g+\delta)\theta}]e^{gt}}{(g+\delta)} \tag{4.4.15}$$

where $g = \alpha+\beta+n$. Since $k(t,t)$ is a constant k in the steady state, from (4.4.3) and (4.4.13),

$$K(t,t) = ke^{(\alpha+\beta)t}L(t,t) = e^{gt}k\varepsilon(\theta)$$

Since $K(t,t)$ is also equal to $sY(t)$, we can solve for $Y(t)$ as

$$Y(t) = (1/s)\varepsilon(\theta)e^{gt}k \tag{4.4.16}$$

Equating (4.4.15) and (4.4.16) the following result is obtained:

$$\frac{sf(k)}{k}\,\frac{1 - e^{-(g+\delta)\theta}}{(g+\delta)} = 1 \tag{4.4.17}$$

Given θ, a steady state will exist if equation (4.4.17) can be solved for k. However, θ is not exogenous and therefore we need another equation between k and θ. This is obtained by alternatively assuming that firms have zero foresight and then perfect foresight.

Case 1: Zero Foresight: Assume that firms have zero foresight which means that they do not look past the current period. Under this assumption, they hire labor up to the point where the marginal product of labor working on current equipment equals the wage rate. Under zero foresight, expected future wages are not considered and future income streams are not discounted. We then have,

$$w(t) = \frac{\partial Q(t,t)}{\partial L(t,t)} = (f-kf')e^{(\alpha+\beta)t} \tag{4.4.18}$$

from (4.4.8) and (4.4.3). Note that at the time of installation of equipment, there is substitutability and therefore the marginal product of labor working on current equipment is well defined. Assuming perfect competition, the same wages are paid to all workers regardless of the vintage of the capital equipment they are working with. The total quasi-rents $P(v,t)$ at time t of equipment of vintage v are,

$$P(v,t) = Q(v,t) - w(t)L(v,t)$$

Since the economic life of all capital equipment is θ periods, all equipment of vintage $t-\theta$ will be scrapped because they earn zero rents. Thus

$$Q(t-\theta,t) = w(t)L(t-\theta,t) \tag{4.4.18a}$$

Using this in (4.4.2) and noting that $k(t-\theta,t) = k$ for all t, we have

$$w(t) = f(k)\exp[(\alpha+\beta)t-\alpha\theta] \tag{4.4.19}$$

Equations (4.4.18) and (4.4.19) imply the following:

$$(f-kf')/f = 1 - \pi(k) = e^{-\alpha\theta} \tag{4.4.20}$$

where $\pi(k) = kf'/f$ and $0 < \pi < 1$. Eliminating θ from (4.4.20) and (4.4.17) we get (see exercise 4.6)

$$A(k) \equiv 1 - \frac{g+\delta}{s}\frac{k}{f(k)} = [1-\pi(k)]^{\frac{g+\delta}{\alpha}} \equiv B(k) \tag{4.4.21}$$

defining $A(k)$ as the left-hand term and $B(k)$ as the right-hand term.

The complete system is specified by the eleven equations (4.4.2), (4.4.3), (4.4.4), (4.4.6), (4.4.7), (4.4.9), (4.4.10), (4.4.11), (4.4.13), (4.4.18), and (4.4.18a), in the eleven unknows $Q(v,t)$, $L(v,t)$, $K(v,t)$, $Y(t)$, $K(t.t)$, $L(t,t)$, $L(t)$, $k(t,t)$, $k(v,t)$, $w(t)$ and $\theta(t)$.

A steady state solution to the Putty-Clay model will exist if equation (4.4.21) can be solved for k. Under the neoclassical assumptions, $f(k)/k$ begins at infinity and declines steadily to zero. Therefore $A(k)$ begins at 1 and decreases monotonically to $-\infty$, as shown in Figure 4.9. By Theorem 2.2 if the elasticity of substitution (σ) between capital and effective-labor is less than 1, then $\pi(k)$ decreases. Therefore $B(k)$ is an upward sloping curve when $\sigma < 1$, constant when $\sigma = 1$ and a downward sloping curve when $\sigma > 1$. A non-trivial solution to the system will exist if

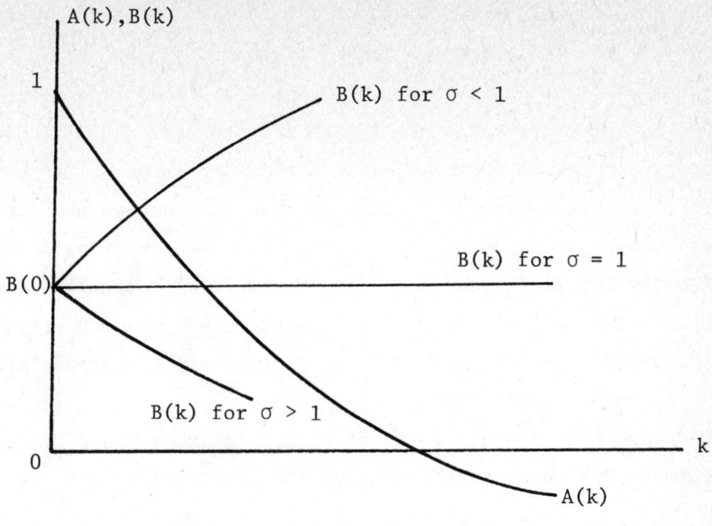

Figure 4.9

$0 < \pi(0) < 1$ and $\sigma \leq 1$ (as for example in the Cobb-Douglas case). It is evident that the solution is unique. Sheshinski [37] has shown that if the elasticity of substitution between capital and effective-labor is not greater than 1, then the system is stable. The proof is complicated and is not reproduced here.

The economic life of a machine is obtained from (4.4.20) as

$$(4.4.22) \qquad \theta = \frac{1}{\alpha} \log\left[\frac{f}{f-kf'}\right] = -\frac{1}{\alpha} \log(1-\pi)$$

The economic life is positively related to π and is independent of the rate of depreciation. If the saving rate increases, the A(k) curve in Figure 4.9 shifts upwards. The equilibrium capital intensity therefore increases as in simpler models. If $\sigma < 1$, then $\pi(k)$ decreases as k increases and therefore from (4.4.22) θ decreases; i.e. as the saving rate increases capital equipment becomes obsolete faster. When $\sigma > 1$, the opposite result occurs; and when $\sigma = 1$, changes in the saving rate do not affect the economic life of a machine. From Figure 4.9 an increase in α lowers the A(k) curve but raises B(k). Therefore the equilibrium capital intensity decreases. If $\sigma \leq 1$, then it is seen from (4.4.22) that an increase in α decreases θ. Thus an increase in the rate of embodied technical change shortens the operating life of capital equipment. Increases in β, n, or δ shift both A(k) and B(k) down. Whether or not k will increase depends on which curve shifts more. The effect of changes in β, n, or δ on k is thus ambiguous. This is true even in the case of a Cobb-Douglas production function. The relative share of labor now depends not only on capital intensity but on the economic life of equipment as well (see exercise 4.8). However, labor's share will be constant in the steady state because k and θ are constant.

The long run rate of growth of aggregate output is given by $g = \alpha+\beta+n$, as is evident from equation (4.4.15). The rate of growth of output is thus given by the rate of increase of the labor force plus the rate at which technical progress (both embodied and disembodied) takes place. Per capita income therefore grows at the same rate $(\alpha+\beta)$ at which labor productivity increases. It is seen from (4.4.18) that wages also grow at this rate. These conclusions are independent of the saving rate and the rate at which capital depreciates, a result obtained in simpler models. The above results are summarized in Table 4.1.

Table 4.1: Sensitivities of the Putty-Clay Model with Zero Foresight

			s	α	β	n	δ
k			+	-	?	?	?
$g = (\dot{Y}/Y)^*$			0	+	+	+	0
$y^* = f(k^*)$			+	-	?	?	?
$(\dot{y}/y)^*$			0	+	+	0	0
		$\sigma < 1$	-	-	?	?	?
θ	for	$\sigma = 1$	0	-	?	?	?
		$\sigma > 1$	+	?	?	?	?

Case 2: Perfect Foresight: If a firm has zero foresight, it does not make any allowance for future increases in wages or discount future earnings. However, if businessmen expect wages to change they will take this into account in arriving at decisions. In hiring labor, they will stop at the point at which an extra worker makes no contribution to the present value of income generated from current investment. We now examine a model in which firms have perfect foresight. Under perfect foresight, firms are assumed to know the wage rate for all t. Both polar assumptions are unrealistic, the truth being somewhere in between. An examination of both extremes will thus give us an idea of the range of conclusions possible.

At a given future $u(u \geq t)$, the total rents received from equipment of current vintage t surviving until time u is given by $Q(t,u) - w(u)L(t,u)$. The discounted present value of this is

$$[Q(t,u) - w(u)L(t,u)]e^{-(u-t)r(t)}$$

where $r(t)$ is the discount rate which equals the market rate of interest at time t if capital markets are perfect. The present value $V(t)$ of the income stream generated from current investment is then

$$V(t) = \int_t^{t+\theta} [Q(t,u) - w(u)L(t,u)]e^{-(u-t)r(t)}du \tag{4.4.23}$$

From (4.4.7) and (4.4.8),

$$L(t,u) = L(t,t)e^{-(\beta+\delta)(u-t)}$$

$$Q(t,u) = Q(t,t)e^{-\delta(u-t)}$$

As in the zero foresight case, we shall restrict ourselves to the balanced growth path. Along this path the wage rate grows at the rate $(\alpha+\beta)$. Thus,

$$w(u) = w(t)e^{(\alpha+\beta)(u-t)}$$

Substituting for $L(t,u)$, $Q(t,u)$ and $w(u)$ into (4.4.23) and integrating with respect to u, the expression for the present value becomes (see exercise 4.9)

$$(4.4.24)\qquad V(t) = Q(t,t)H(\theta,r+\delta) - w(t)L(t,t)H(\theta,r+\delta-\alpha)$$

where $H(\theta,x) \equiv (1-e^{-\theta x})/x$ and it is assumed that $(r+\delta)$ and $(r+\delta-\alpha)$ are non-zero (see exercise 4.7). Firms hire labor to work on current investment so as to maximize $V(t)$ for a given $w(t)$. The condition for this is that

$$(4.4.25)\qquad \frac{\partial V(t)}{\partial L(t,t)} = \frac{\partial Q(t,t)}{\partial L(t,t)} H(\theta,r+\delta) - w(t)H(\theta,r+\delta-\alpha) = 0$$

Comparing the above equation with (4.4.18) note that the current marginal product is equated not to the wage rate but to the discounted wage rate. The condition for the obsolescence of a capital equipment is still valid. Therefore

$$(4.4.19)\qquad w(t) = f(k)\exp[(\alpha+\beta)t - \alpha\theta]$$

Also, from (4.4.18)

$$\frac{\partial Q(t,t)}{\partial L(t,t)} = (f-kf')e^{(\alpha+\beta)t}$$

Substituting these relations in (4.4.25) we obtain the following result which replaces (4.4.20).

$$(4.4.26)\qquad \frac{f-kf'}{f} = \frac{H(\theta,r+\delta-\alpha)}{H(\theta,r+\delta)}\, e^{-\alpha\theta}$$

Equation (4.4.17) carries over to this case also.

$$(4.4.17)\qquad [sf(k)/k]H(\theta,g+\delta) = 1$$

Since we have added a new variable $r(t)$, we need another equation to complete the system. This equation is obtained by noting that in a competitive situation, long run equilibrium is characterized by zero profits. Therefore $V(t)$ = cost of current investment = $K(t,t)$ for all t. Differentiating this with respect to $K(t,t)$ and using (4.4.24) and (4.4.2), we obtain

$$(4.4.27)\qquad 1 = \frac{\partial V(t)}{\partial K(t,t)} = \frac{\partial Q(t,t)}{\partial K(t,t)} H(\theta,r+\delta)$$

$$= f'(k)H(\theta,r+\delta)$$

If the equations (4.4.26), (4.4.17) and (4.4.27) can be solved for the steady state values of k, r and θ, the corresponding values of the other endogenous variables may also be obtained. But explicit solutions are out of reach. We can, however, examine the existence of an equilibrium without explicitly solving the three equations. From (4.4.17),

$$A(k) \equiv 1 - \frac{g+\delta}{s}\frac{k}{f(k)} = e^{-(g+\delta)\theta}$$

From (4.4.26),

$$e^{-\alpha\theta} = [1-\pi(k)]H(\theta,r+\delta)/H(\theta,r+\delta-\alpha)$$

Therefore

$$e^{-(g+\delta)\theta} = [1-\pi(k)]^{\frac{g+\delta}{\alpha}} [H(\theta,r+\delta)/H(\theta,r+\delta-\alpha)]^{\frac{g+\delta}{\alpha}}$$

We thus have the following equation which is similar to (4.4.21).

$$\text{(4.4.21a)} \qquad A(k) = B(k)[H(\theta,r+\delta)/H(\theta,r+\delta-\alpha)]^{\frac{g+\delta}{\alpha}}$$

If $r \to \infty$ this reduces to the zero foresight case. We have shown (Figure 4.9) that A(k) is a decreasing function of k and that the slope of B(k) depends on σ. It is readily seen from (4.4.27) that $H(\theta,r+\delta) = 1/f'(k)$ is an increasing function of k. The slope of the function in square brackets in (4.4.21a) is generally ambiguous. It can be shown that if σ is not greater than 1, then $[H(\theta,r+\delta)/H(\theta,r+\delta-\alpha)]$ is a non-decreasing function of k. The proof is very tedious and is sketched in the papers by Bliss [4, pp. 118-122] and Britto [5]. If $\sigma \leq 1$, B(k) is a non-decreasing function of k. It follows by a similar argument as in the zero foresight case that a unique solution exists. Bliss has also shown that there exists a Golden Rule path along which consumption is maximum. On this path, the rate of return (r) on investment equals the natural rate g. Furthermore, the saving rate is equal to the share of gross profits. As in the zero foresight case, the long run growth rate is $\alpha+\beta+n$ and that of wages is $\alpha+\beta$. Assuming a Cobb-Douglas production function, Kemp and Thanh [21] have shown the following:

(a) Under perfect foresight, the operating life of a machine is longer and the level of output higher than under zero foresight.

If firms have foresight and expect wages to rise they will stop hiring when an extra worker makes no contribution to the present value of earnings from current investment. With lack of foresight firms would hire too much labor and hence equipment would become obsolete sooner.

(b) An increase in the saving rate will lower the rate of interest and increase the operating life of equipment.

(c) An increase in the saving rate will lower labor's share of output.

Physical Durability as an Economic Variable: The concept of the obsolescence of capital equipment discussed in the above vintage models is based on economic considerations only. Britto [6] has studied a perfect foresight putty-clay model in which physical durability of capital equipment is explicitly incorporated. The production function is now specified as $Q(v,t) = F[K(v,t), e^{\alpha v+\beta t}L(v,t), U_v]$ where U_v is the physical lifetime of equipment of vintage v. To the usual assumptions on F, the condition $\partial F/\partial U_v < 0$ is added. This means that if the durability of a machine is to be increased, there is a cost associated with it in the form of a lower rate of output for given amounts of capital and labor used. It follows immediately that, given present value maximization, the operating life of machines is exactly U_v and that quasi-rents cannot fall to zero before that. If quasi-rents did indeed become zero before the time U_v, less durable (physically) equipment could have been constructed which by the assumption $\partial F/\partial U_v < 0$ would have meant higher quasi-rents. Thus durability will never be increased to the point where additional quasi-rents are zero.

4.4.2 A Clay-Clay Model

In this model only one production technique is available both *ex post* and *ex ante*. Technical progress is embodied into new machines but factor proportions are fixed both before and after the installation of a machine. This model is the analogue of the basic Harrod-Domar model and has been extensively analyzed by Solow, Tobin, Von Weisäcker and Yaari [40]. In what follows we have summarized the basic structural equations of the model and the main results without going through all the derivations.

Since the production function has fixed coefficients, it can be written as follows:

$$Q(v,t) = \text{Min}[B(v)K(v,t), A(v)L(v,t)]$$

$A(v)$ and $B(v)$ are exogenously given technology coefficients which depend only on the vintage v, and hence represent embodied technical change. A comparison of this with equation (3.1.1) of the Harrod-Domar model shows that we need $1/B(v)$ units of capital and $1/A(v)$ units of labor to produce each unit of output from equipment of vintage v. Three types of technical progress can be identified. If $B(v)$ is a constant then technical change is purely labor-augmenting or equivalently, Harrod-neutral. If the ratio $A(v)/B(v)$ is constant, we have Hicks-neutral technical change. When $A(v)$ is constant, technical progress is capital-augmenting or Solow-neutral. It is assumed that $A(v)$ and $B(v)$ are increasing functions of v. Under this assumption, transferring one unit of labor from equipment of vintage v to a later vintage would result in a net increase in output. Therefore no machine will be left idle if an older machine is in use. For simplicity, we assume that capital does not depreciate. However, exponential depreciation of the type considered earlier could easily be incorporated into the model. Since capital does not physically depreciate $K(v,t) = K(v,v) = I(v)$, where $I(t) \equiv K(t,t)$ is the investment at time t. Using this relation the production function can be rewritten as follows:

$$Q(v,t) = \text{Min}[B(v)I(v), A(v)L(v,t)] \tag{4.4.28}$$

Because of the fixed coefficient technology, it is possible to calculate the amount of labor required for the level of investment $I(v)$. This is done by equating the two arguments on the right-hand side of (4.4.28). We then have

$$L(v,t) = B(v)I(v)/A(v) \tag{4.4.29}$$

If $\theta(t)$ is the economic life of equipment, then the employment level is given by

$$(4.4.30) \qquad N(t) = \int_{t-\theta}^{t} L(v,t)dv$$

This may or may not equal the supply of labor L(t), given by

$$(4.4.31) \qquad L(t) = L_o e^{nt}$$

Aggregate output from all operating equipment is given by

$$(4.4.32) \qquad Y(t) = \int_{t-\theta}^{t} Q(v,t)dv$$

From this, current investment is obtained as follows:

$$(4.4.33) \qquad I(t) = sY(t)$$

Let N*(t) be the total amount of labor required to staff equipment of all past and current vintages. Thus

$$(4.4.34) \qquad N^*(t) = \int_{-\infty}^{t} L(v,t)dv$$

N*(t) is the maximum possible employment for the given investment history of the economy.

As in the Putty-Clay model, equipment of vintage $t-\theta$ does not earn any quasi-rent. Thus $Q(t-\theta,t) = w(t)L(t-\theta,t)$ where w(t) is the wage rate. Under competition, w(t) is the same for all workers regardless of the vintage of equipment they are working with. Setting $v = t-\theta$ in (4.4.28) and noting that the two arguments on the right-hand side of (4.4.28) are equal because of (4.4.29), we have,[1] $Q(t-\theta,t) = A(t-\theta)L(t-\theta,t)$. Therefore,

$$(4.4.35) \qquad w(t) = A(t-\theta)$$

The quasi-rent is given by the relation $K(v,t)r(v,t) = Q(v,t) - w(t)L(v,t)$. Since $K(v,t) = K(v,v) = I(v)$ and $Q(v,t) = B(v)I(v)$ because the two arguments on the right-hand side of (4.4.28) are equal, we get

$$r(v,t) = B(v) - [w(t)L(v,t)]/I(v)$$

---

[1]Note that the equality of the two arguments does not presuppose full employment. The condition for full employment is specified later.

Using (4.4.29) in the above expression we obtain the following relation for the quasi-rent:

$$(4.4.36) \qquad r(v,t) = \begin{cases} B(v)[1-w(t)/A(v)] & \text{for } v > t-\theta \\ 0 & \text{for } v \leq t-\theta \end{cases}$$

Equations (4.4.28) through (4.4.36) describe the relationships among the ten endogenous variables Y, L, N, I, N*, w, θ, Q(v,t), L(v,t) and r(v,t). We need one more equation to completely determine the system. Solow and others have considered three interesting alternative regimes which the model can represent. Each of these is now described.

1. Labor surplus regime: In this case,

$$(4.4.37a) \qquad N(t) = N^*(t) \leq L(t)$$

Labor supply is growing so fast that even if equipments of all vintages are used, some unemployed labor will still exist. Since labor is in excess supply the wage rate and the marginal product of labor will be zero. Because the wage rate is so low, the economic life will be infinitely large. This can also be seen by setting $N(t) = N^*(t)$ and then noting that $\theta = \infty$. Aggregate output is now limited by capital and

$$Y(t) = \int_{-\infty}^{t} B(v)I(v)dv$$

Differentiating both sides with respect to t, we get $\dot{Y}(t) = B(t)I(t)$. Because $I(t) = sY(t)$, the rate of growth of aggregate output is obtained as $\dot{Y}(t)/Y(t) = sB(t)$. This is the familiar result obtained in the Harrod-Domar model.

2. Full employment regime: The required equation for completing the system is given by the following full employment condition:

$$(4.4.37b) \qquad N(t) = L(t) < N^*(t)$$

Because the labor supply is not adequate to operate equipment of all vintages, some capital is unused. Assuming that technical progress is labor-augmenting (i.e. that B is a constant), Solow and others have obtained the following results for the steady state in this regime:

a) Aggregate output grows at the rate $n+\lambda$ where λ is the rate at which $A(v)$ grows.

b) The wage rate $w(t)$ grows exponentially at the rate λ.

c) The quasi-rent $r(t,t)$ is a constant in the steady state.

d) The economic life of equipment $\theta(t)$ is constant in the long run.

e) An increase in the saving rate reduces θ. This means that machines become obsolete faster.

f) There is a Golden Rule path along which consumption is maximized. On this path, the saving ratio is equal to the share of capital and aggregate output and the rate of return to capital is equal to the growth rate.

All the above results are the same as in the Putty-Clay model with zero foresight. This is not surprising because the fixed coefficient production function is a special case of the general form of a production function with zero elasticity of substitution.

3. Keynesian unemployment regime: This case arises when

$$N(t) < L(t) \leq N^*(t) \tag{4.4.37c}$$

Because demand is insufficient, some labor and a corresponding amount of capital are unemployed. So long as unemployment persists real wages will fall and older machines will then earn positive quasi-rents. As they are brought into operation, employment will rise tending to lower unemployment. Thus for unemployment to exist, some kind of rigidity is necessary in order to prevent the market mechanism from bringing about full employment. For instance, if the real wage is rigid, then unemployment will not cause real wages to fall and hence Keynesian unemployment will prevail. Mathematically, the system is over-determined because there are ten endogenous variables and only nine equations.

Learning by doing: The learning by doing model originally proposed by Arrow [2] and extended by Levhari [26], is a modification of the Clay-Clay model. Arrow assumes that $B(v)$ is a constant and that $A(v) = b[G(v)]^{\alpha}$ where $0 < \alpha < 1$ and

$$G(t) = \int_{-\infty}^{t} K(v,t)dv$$

G(t) cannot be interpreted as aggregate capital because capital is heterogeneous. If machines do not depreciate then G(t) is cumulative investment or the opportunity cost of consumption foregone in the past. The qualitative results are similar to those of the simple version of the model described in section 4.2.2.

4.4.3 The Putty-Putty Case

In the Putty-Putty model originally proposed by Solow [39], there is smooth substitution between labor and capital both before and after the installation of equipment. However, technical progress stops as soon as a given machine is installed. Thus technical progress is embodied into new machines and does not affect machines of earlier vintages. Since the model is basically the same as the simple neoclassical model, the long run results are very similar and therefore not presented here. In the Putty-Clay model there is no *ex post* substitution between capital and labor. Therefore, when wages rise high enough, a machine becomes unprofitable and is scrapped. In the Putty-Putty world an increase in wages would induce substitution towards more capital. In this case quasi-rents never become zero and therefore there is no economic obsolescence but only physical depreciation of capital. In other words, $\theta = \infty$.

The most interesting aspect of this model is the feasibility of defining a capital aggregate even though capital goods are labelled according to their vintages and are therefore heterogeneous. Fisher [15] has shown that if the production function exhibits constant returns to scale and is twice differentiable, then an aggregate capital stock exists if and only if technical change is capital augmenting. Technical progress is capital augmenting (also known as *Solow-neutral*) if the production function can be written as follows:

$$Q(v,t) = F[B(v)K(v,t),L(v,t)]$$

This is analogous to the labor augmenting technical progress of Theorem 4.2. The above relation can be rewritten as follows:

$$Q(v,t) = L(v,t)f[\hat{k}(v,t)]$$

where $\hat{k}(v,t) = B(v)K(v,t)/L(v,t)$ and $f(\hat{k}) = F(\hat{k},1)$. $\hat{k}(v,t)$ may be interpreted as effective-capital labor ratio. The marginal product of labor is $f(\hat{k}) - kf'(\hat{k})$ and is equal to the prevailing wage rate $w(t)$. In a competitive situation labor is paid the same wages regardless of the age of the equipment it is working on. Thus $w = f(\hat{k}) - \hat{k}f'(\hat{k})$.

It was seen in Chapter 2 that the wage rate and capital intensity move in the same direction. When wages increase firms switch to more capital intensive techniques. The relation between the wage rate and capital intensity is therefore monotonic. This can also be seen by differentiating w with respect to k. We then have $dw/dk = - kf''(\hat{k}) > 0$. Therefore, by the <u>Inverse Function Theorem</u>, there is a unique $\hat{k}(v,t)$ corresponding to a given value $w(t)$. $\hat{k}(v,t)$ is then independent of v and can be denoted by $j(t)$. Thus $Q(v,t) = L(v,t)f[j(t)]$. Aggregate output is given by

$$Q(t) = \int_{-\infty}^{t} Q(v,t)dv = f[j(t)]\int_{-\infty}^{t} L(v,t)dv$$

$$= f[j(t)]L(t) = F[j(t)L(t),L(t)]$$

$$= F[J(t),L(t)]$$

where $J(t) = j(t)L(t)$. Thus the aggregate output is a function of labor and $J(t)$ which can be interpreted as <u>aggregate capital</u>. Such a production function is called a <u>Surrogate production function</u>.

4.5 Measurement of Technical Change

In this section we briefly discuss some of the attempts at empirical measurement of technical progress. For detailed surveys of the approach to the theory and measurement of changes in factor productivity, the reader is referred to the recent papers by Nadiri [29], Kennedy and Thirlwall [24] as well as the earlier works by Denison [11], Kendrick [22] and Lave [25]. Only a few selected approaches are presented here.

4.5.1 Simple Arithmetic and Geometric Measures

While there are many ways of measuring total factor productivity, two simple indices commonly used in earlier works are the arithmetic measure by Kendrick [22] and the geometric index by Solow [38]. Both of them assumed that technical change was autonomous and Hicks-neutral so that $Y(t) = A(t)F(K,L)$. It was seen in Section 4.1 that in this case the rate of growth of technical progress can be expressed as follows.

$$\dot{A}/A = \dot{Y}/Y - \pi\dot{K}/K - (1-\pi)\dot{L}/L$$

With time series data on Y, K, L and π one can estimate $\dot{A}/A$. Solow found that over the period 1909-49 per capita income in the U.S. nearly doubled but that only one-eighth of it is attributable to capital accumulation with technical progress accounting for the rest of it. By using the procedure suggested in Section 4.1.5, we can easily extend this to test whether changes in technology are indeed neutral or biased.

Kendrick, on the other hand, used an arithmetic measure. If we assume constant returns to scale and the marginal theory of distribution, we get $Y = A(t)(wL+rK)$. From this, changes in productivity are measured as

$$\frac{\Delta A}{A} = \frac{A_1 - A_0}{A_0} = \frac{Y_1/Y_0}{(WL_1+rK_1)/(WL_0+rK_0)} - 1$$

where the subscript 1 refers to the current period and 0 to the base period. Kendrick's estimates also indicated that technical progress accounted for an overwhelming proportion of the rate of growth in U.S. per capita income.

4.5.2 Measurement with Embodied Technical Change

It will be noted from the above methods that technical change is measured as a residual and will hence include the influence of other variables as well. Suppose, for instance, that another input Z is added so that $Y = BF(K,L,Z)$. The above estimates of factor productivity would then have actually included the contribution to growth in income by the input Z. It is thus clear that a misspecification of the production function in the form of omitted inputs will result in an overestimate of the importance of technological change. Solow argued later [39] that another misspecification is the assumption that productivity changes are disembodied. Making the other extreme assumption that all technical progress is embodied in new capital, he used the following Cobb-Douglas production function to estimate the extent of embodiment of innovations in new capital goods.

$$Y(t) = ae^{\gamma t}L(t)^{\alpha}J(t)^{1-\alpha}$$

where, in the notation used in Section 4.4,

$$Y(t) = \int_{-\infty}^{t} Q(v,t)dv$$

$$L(t) = \int_{-\infty}^{t} L(v,t)dv$$

$$J(t) = \int_{-\infty}^{t} e^{\lambda v}K(v,t)dv$$

$$K(v,t) = K(v,v)e^{-\delta(t-v)}$$

Using these, the production function can be rewritten as

$$Y(t) = ae^{[\gamma-\delta(1-\alpha)]t}L(t)^{\alpha} \int_{-\infty}^{t} e^{(\lambda+\delta)v}K(v,v)dv^{1-\alpha}$$

Because the above equation cannot be readily transformed into a linear relation involving the unknown parameters, their estimation is difficult. Solow, however, was particularly interested in λ, the embodiment coefficient, and hence estimated it with assumed values for α, δ and γ. His conclusion was that the estimated λ using this vintage model was much higher than the corresponding one which assumes that technical progress is fully disembodied. Thus the "residual" attributed to changes in overall productivity is much smaller in a vintage model and hence a greater importance is attributed to capital investment. The method, however, has a serious weakness in that the estimates are very sensitive to the choice of α, δ and γ. In spite of this deficiency, however, it is possible to conclude that a great weight is attached to capital accumulation in the vintage model as compared to the disembodiment hypothesis. The overwhelming importance attributed to the "residual" in the simpler models is therefore not present here.

4.5.3 Growth in Income Attributed to Inputs Only

In estimating changes in factor productivity, Jorgenson and Griliches [20] argued that all technical change can be explained by properly adjusting inputs and outputs to take account of measurement errors in their prices and quantities and also their aggregation. Thus in their approach the residual is negligible. Their method starts with the following national income identity and then derives an index of the rate of growth of factor productivity.

$$\sum_{i=1}^{m} q_i y_i = \sum_{j=1}^{n} p_j x_j$$

where y_i is the quantity of the ith output, q_i is its price, x_j is the quantity of the jth input and p_j is its price. Totally differentiating the above equation by t we can derive the following equation:

$$\Sigma w_i \left[\frac{\dot{q}_i}{q_i} + \frac{\dot{y}_i}{y_i}\right] = \Sigma v_j \left[\frac{\dot{p}_j}{p_j} + \frac{\dot{x}_j}{x_j}\right]$$

where $w_i = q_i y_i/(\Sigma q_i y_i)$ and $v_j = p_j x_j/(\Sigma p_j x_j)$ are the relative value shares of the ith output and jth input respectively. An index of total factor productivity (A) is defined as $A = y/x$ where y is an index of aggregate output determined by the relation $\dot{y}/y = \Sigma w_i \dot{y}_i/y_i$ and x is an index of aggregate input defined from the relation $\dot{x}/x = \Sigma v_j \dot{x}_j/x_j$. These indices are known as "Divisia quantity indices" and yield a measure of the rate of growth of total factor productivity as follows:

$$\dot{A}/A = \Sigma w_i \dot{y}_i/y_i - \Sigma v_j \dot{x}_j/x_j = \Sigma v_j \dot{p}_j/p_j - \Sigma w_i \dot{q}_i/q_i$$

In estimating the above measure, Jorgenson and Griliches first adjust the data, especially that of capital. They argue that capital services rather than capital stock should enter the production function. Thus the flow price of capital services (p_k) is used rather than the asset price (q_k). The various components of capital are also adjusted for biases in investment good deflators. The result of all these adjustments is that during the period 1948-65 the unexplained residual attributed to changes in total factor productivity is estimated at only 0.1 percent per annum. This conclusion evidently depends very much on the nature of adjustments made to the basic data. As pointed out in Nadiri's Survey article, other authors with different kinds of adjustments have found substantially different measures for the residual. The basic conceptual point made by Jorgenson and Griliches, viz. that inputs must be correctly measured and careful attention paid to aggregation biases and appropriateness of price deflators, is quite valid.

4.6 Summary

Technical progress enables entrepreneurs to achieve a higher output with the same amounts of capital and labor. Innovations are labor-saving, capital-saving or neutral accordingly as to whether capital's share in output increases, decreases or is unchanged. Hicks-neutrality requires that if the capital-labor ratio is constant then the marginal rate of substitution between capital and labor must also be constant. This kind of neutrality can be represented by augmenting both capital and labor by the same function of time. Neutrality, as defined by Harrod, requires that whenever the rate of return to capital is unchanged the capital-output ratio must also be unchanged. Harrod-neutrality can be represented by a purely labor augmenting factor. A balanced growth path is not possible unless technical progress is Harrod-neutral.

The main difference between a Solow-Swan world and one with Harrod-neutral technical progress is that in the latter, long run per capita output and real wages grow at the rate at which technical progress is taking place. Thus a model with technical progress can explain the stylized fact that in advanced countries, per capita output has risen steadily.

A major weakness of this approach is that the rate of technical change is specified as exogenously determined, whereas in reality technical change is induced. Several alternative hypotheses have been suggested regarding the manner in which technical change might be induced. Some of these are; (i) the rate of labor augmentation depends on per capita income [Conlisk], (ii) the rate of labor augmentation depends on cumulative past output or investment [Arrow], and (iii) this rate is determined by the amount of labor employed in producing innovations [Uzawa, Phelps]. Richer conclusions are now possible. For instance, in the Conlisk variation, the long run equilibrium growth rate can be increased by raising the saving rate. Also an increasing in the population growth rate will lower that of per capita income.

In spite of their richness, the above approaches are not satisfactory because all of them assume Harrod-neutrality to begin with. There is no reason to expect that innovations will be neutral and not labor-saving or capital-saving. Kennedy's approach is to assume a trade-off frontier between the rates of capital augmentation and labor augmentation and then to maximize technical progress subject to this opportunity locus. It is then possible to show that a unique balanced growth path exists along which technical progress will be Harrod-neutral. If $\sigma < 1$ the system is globally stable [Drandakis, Phelps, Samuelson].

While this approach is a step forward, one may wonder how realistic it is to assume that the trade-off frontier is exogenously given. Conlisk has assumed that the position of the frontier is endogenously determined and shown that in this case the optimum bias need not be Harrod-neutral even in the steady state. Thus the rationale for assuming technical change to be Harrod-neutral disappears if innovations are assumed to have a variable bias determined endogenously.

The embodiment hypothesis, originally proposed by Johansen, led to a different line of thinking in the treatment of innovations. According to this hypothesis, technical progress is embodied only in new machines. Changes in the levels of technology do not affect the productivity of machines of earlier vintages. Another departure to the neoclassical approach, distinct from the embodiement hypothesis but considered along with it, is the assumption of ex post fixity of factor proportions. At the time new capital is introduced, firms consider both current and expected wages and rents in deciding on the optimum production technique. Therefore capital is like putty during this stage. But once the decision is made and new machines are installed, they must be operated in subsequent periods with a fixed coefficient technique. Thus capital becomes like hard-baked clay.

The qualitative implications of the vintage approach are basically similar to models with simpler assumptions about technical progress. But an important contribution of this hypothesis is the concept of economic obsolescence. Since new capital is more productive and wages generally rise, the quasi-rents of older machines decline over time and ultimately reduce to zero. At this point, machines become economically obsolete and are scrapped.

Other variations of the vintage approach include a Putty-Putty technology or a Clay-Clay technology. In the former, there is flexibility of factor proportions both before and after capital is introduced. In this case it is possible to define a capital aggregate, provided technical change is capital-augmenting. In a Clay-Clay world, factor proportions are fixed both ex post and ex ante. Because of this property it is possible to have surplus labor or Keynesian unemployment in such an economy.

When it comes to measuring the change in overall factor productivity, the approaches and hence the conclusions, are as varied as the theoretical models. Assuming technical progress to be disembodied and Hicks-neutral, Solow and Kendrick found that only about one-eighth of the observed rate of growth in per capita income (prior to 1945) can be explained by capital accumulation. If a vintage model (of the Putty-Putty type) is specified as the basic framework, the unexplained portion of the change in total factor productivity is substantially less. Jorgenson and Griliches have completed the circle by pointing out that when inputs are properly adjusted for aggregation biases and appropriate deflators are used, the unexplained portion almost vanishes. Thus all the productivity increases can be explained by appropriately measured inputs.

An overall look at the literature on the theory and measurement of technological change indicates that substantial progress has been made in the understanding of the determinants of changes in factor productivity. The development of vintage models and the technical change frontier are perhaps the most important approaches that have contributed towards a broadening of the spectrum of analysis. On the empirical side, the Jorgenson-Griliches approach of paying a substantial attention to the quality of the data on inputs has been path-breaking, and perhaps even definitive.

REFERENCES

[1] Akerlof, George: "Stability, Marginal Products, Putty and Clay," Essays on the Theory of Optimal Growth, (Ed.) Karl Shell, M.I.T. Press, 1967.

[2] Arrow, Kenneth: "The Economic Implications of Learning by Doing," Review of Economic Studies, June 1962.

[3] Bardhan, P. K.: "Equilibrium Growth in a Model with Economic Obsolescence of Machines," Quarterly Journal of Economics, May 1969.

[4] Bliss, Christopher: "On Putty-Clay," Review of Economic Studies, April 1968.

[5] Britto, R.: "On Putty-Clay: A Comment," Review of Economic Studies, July 1969, pp. 395-398.

[6] Britto, R.: "Durability and Obsolescence in Putty-Clay Models," International Economic Review, October 1970, pp. 455-462.

[7] Britto, R: "Some Recent Developments in the Theory of Economic Growth: An Interpretation," Journal of Economic Literature, Dec. 1973, pp. 1343-1366.

[8] Chang, W. W.: "The Role of Saving in a Growth Model with Induced Inventions," Review of Economics and Statistics, Feb. 1970.

[9] Conlisk, John: "A Modified Neo-classical Growth Model with Endogenous Technical Change," Southern Economic Journal, Oct. 1967.

[10] Conlisk, John: "A Neo-classical Growth Model with Endogenously Positioned Technical Change Frontier," Economic Journal, June 1969.

[11] Denison, E. F.: Why Growth Rates Differ: Postwar Experience in Nine Western Countries, The Brookings Institution, 1967.

[12] Drandakis, E. and E. S. Phelps: "A Model of Induced Invention, Growth and Distribution," Economic Journal, Dec. 1966.

[13] Fellner, W.: "Two Propositions in the Theory of Induced Innovations," Economic Journal, June 1961.

[14] Fellner, W.: "Measures of Technical Progress in the Light of Recent Growth Theories," American Economic Review, Dec. 1967.

[15] Fisher, Franklin: "Embodied Technical Change and the Existence of an Aggregate Capital Stock," Review of Economic Studies, Oct. 1965.

[16] Hahn, F. H., and R. C. O. Mathews: "The Theory of Economic Growth: A Survey," Surveys of Economic Theory, Vol. II, St. Martin's Press, 1967.

[17] Harrod, R. F.: Review of Joan Robinson's Essays in the Theory of Employment, Economic Journal, 1937.

[18] Hicks, J. R.: Theory of Wages, Macmillan and Co., 1963.

[19] Johansen, Lief: "Substitution, Versus Fixed Coefficients in the Theory of Economic Growth: A Synthesis," Econometrica, April 1959.

[20] Jorgenson, D. W. and Z. Griliches: "The Explanation of Productivity Change," Review of Economic Studies, July 1967.

[21] Kemp, Murray and P. C. Thanh: "On a Class of Growth Models," Econometrica, April 1966.

[22] Kendrick, J: Productivity Trends in the United States, Princeton University Press, 1961.

[23] Kennedy, Charles: "Induced Innovation and the Theory of Distribution," Economic Journal, Sept. 1964.

[24] Kennedy, C. and A. P. Thirlwall, "Technical Progress: A Survey," Economic Journal, March 1972, pp. 11-72.

[25] Lave, L: Technological Change: Its Conception and Measurement, Prentice-Hall, 1966.

[26] Levhari, David: "Extensions of Arrow's Learning by Doing," Review of Economic Studies, April 1966.

[27] Lundberg, E.: Produktivitet och räntabilitet, Stockholm: P. A. Norstedt and Söner, 1961.

[28] Mathews, R. C. O.: "The New View of Investment: Comment," Quarterly Journal of Economics, Feb. 1964.

[29] Nadiri, M. I.: "Some Approaches to the Theory and Measurement of Total Factor Productivity: A Survey," Journal of Economic Literature, Dec. 1970.

[30] Phelps, E. S.: "The New View of Investment: A Neo-Classical Analysis," Quarterly Journal of Economics, Nov. 1962.

[31] Phelps, E. S.: Golden Rules of Economic Growth, W. W. Norton and Co., 1966.

[32] Phelps, E. S.: "Substitutions, Fixed Proportions, Growth and Distribution," International Economic Review, Sept. 1963.

[33] Robinson, Joan: "The Classification of Inventions," Review of Economic Studies, 1938.

[34] Samuelson, Paul A.: "A Theory of Induced Innovation Along Kennedy-Weizsäcker Lines," Review of Economics and Statistics, Nov. 1965.

[35] Samuelson, Paul A.: "Rejoinder: Agreements, Disagreements, Doubts and the Case of Harrod-neutral Technical Change," Review of Economics and Statistics, Nov. 1965.

[36] Sato, R.: "The Estimation of Biased Technical Progress and the Production Function," International Economic Review, June 1970.

[37] Sheshinski, E.: "Balanced Growth and Stability in the Johansen Vintage Model," Review of Economic Studies, April 1967.

[38] Solow, R. M.: "Technical Change and the Aggregate Production Function," Review of Economics and Statistics, August 1957.

[39] Solow, R. M.: "Investment and Technical Progress," Mathematical Methods in the Social Sciences, (Eds.) K. J. Arrow, S. Karlin and P. Suppes, Stanford University Press, 1960.

[40] Solow, R.M., James Tobin, C. C. von Weizsäcker and M. Yaari: "Neo-classical Growth with Fixed Proportions," Review of Economic Studies, April 1966.

[41] Uzawa, H.: "Neutral Inventions and the Stability of Growth Equilibrium," Review of Economic Studies, Feb. 1961.

[42] Uzawa, H.: "Optimum Technical Change in an Aggregative Model of Economic Growth," International Economic Review, Jan. 1965.

[43] Vanek, J.: "Toward a More General Theory of Growth with Technological Change," Economic Journal, Dec. 1966.

[44] Wright, T. P.: "Factors Affecting the Cost of Airplanes," Journal of the Aero. Sciences, 1936, pp. 122-128.

EXERCISES

4.1 Analyze the Harrod-Domar model with Harrod-neutral technical change.

4.2 Show that when $Y = F(K,N) = Nf(k)$, where $N = LA(t)$ and $k = K/N$ the capital effective-labor ratio, the expressions for the factor prices and the share of capital in output are the following: $w = F_L = A(t)[f(k) - kf'(k)]$; $r = F_K = f'(k)$; $\pi(k) = kf'(k)/f(k)$. Assuming that $A(t) = e^{\lambda t}$ show that F_{Lt}/F_L, the rate of growth of the marginal product of labor (and hence of wages), is λ. Also prove that the overall rate of growth of technical progress is given by $F_t/F = (1-\pi)\lambda$.

4.3 For the Conlisk model show that the sensitivity table is as given below.

	s	n	λ	δ
k^*	+	-	-	-
$(\dot{Y}/Y)^*$	+	+	+	-
$(\dot{y}/y)^*$	+	-	+	-
$(Y/K)^*$	-	+	+	+
r^*	-	+	+	+

4.4 Investigate the properties of the following Learning by doing model.

$$Y = K^{\beta}N^{1-\beta}$$

$$N = TL$$

$$T = e^{\lambda t}K^{\alpha}$$

Analyze the behavior of factor prices under each of the following alternative assumptions: (i) labor is paid its marginal product and capital is paid the balance, (ii) capital is paid its marginal product and labor is paid the balance.

4.5 Prove (4.2.14) and (4.2.15), noting that T is a function of K also. Also show that $K(\partial Y/\partial K) + L(\partial Y/\partial L) > Y$ which implies that paying factors their respective marginal products would overexhaust the total output.

4.6 Verify equations (4.4.13), (4.4.15) and (4.4.21).

4.7 In the Putty-Clay model with perfect foresight, how would the results be affected if $r + \delta = 0$ or $r + \delta - \alpha = 0$?

4.8 Show that in the Putty-Clay model with zero foresight, the relative share of labor is given by

$$\frac{w(t)\ L(t)}{Y(t)} = \frac{[1-\pi(k)]\ H(\theta,\beta+n+\delta)}{H(\theta,\alpha+\beta+n+\delta)}$$

where $H(\theta,x) \equiv (1-e^{-\theta x})/x$. Thus the share of labor depends not only on capital intensity but on the economic life of equipment as well. Derive a similar result for the perfect foresight case.

4.9 Verify equation (4.4.24).

4.10 Redo the Clay-Clay model incorporating exponential depreciation of capital.

4.11 Verify equations (4.1.16) through (4.1.22).

4.12 Redo the Drandakis-Phelps model of induced bias assuming that the saving ratio is exponentially decreasing, i.e., $s = s_0 e^{-\eta t}$.

CHAPTER 5

MONEY AND ECONOMIC GROWTH

The models we have seen previously are concerned with basically three markets. First, there is a commodity market in which the level of consumption (and hence of saving) depends on the aggregate supply of goods. The supply of goods is determined by a production function relating output to two factors of production, capital and labor. It is assumed that at each instant there is full employment equilibrium represented by the equality of saving and investment. The second market is the capital market. The supply of existing capital is increased by the amount of net investment at any instant. Under the assumption of perfect competition and profit maximization, the marginal product of capital is equal to the real rent on capital. Finally, we have the labor market. The supply of labor grows at an exogenously given constant rate. If there is technical progress, then labor is measured in efficiency units. The demand for labor is determined by setting the marginal product of labor equal to the real wage, another competitive profit maximizing condition. Since wages are also flexible, full employment of labor is assured. We have seen that stable balanced growth is generally possible in an economy operating under the above conditions.

All these models share a major weakness. They completely ignore the role that money plays in determining the pattern of long run growth. The importance of money in carrying out short run stabilization policies is well known from static macro-theory. In a non-monetary economy, capital is the only form in which assets can be accumulated. The introduction of money offers individuals a choice in the composition of total wealth. Both monetary and capital assets can serve as stores of value, thus providing portfolio choices. This throws a different light on the process of accumulation of capital. Saving will no longer equal gross investment because a part of the saving will be held in the form of money. Moreover changes in the price level can no longer be ignored. Price changes affect the real yield on money and therefore alter the portfolio composition thus resulting in different rates of capital accumulation. It is therefore important to examine the effects of the introduction of monetary assets that compete with capital assets.

The first attempt at a systematic analysis of the role of money in determining patterns of growth was by Tobin [23]. Several authors, notably Foley [3], Hahn [6], Levhari and Patinkin [9], Niehans [11], Rose [14], Sidrauski [16,17] and Stein [18,19,20, 21], have since extended Tobin's model. The approaches adopted by these and other economists can be broadly divided into two fundamentally different categories: the _Neo-classical_ and the _Keynes-Wicksell_.

The neo-classical approach [Tobin, Foley and Sidrauski, Levhari and Patinkin] is the one we have adopted in past models. Under this approach, (i) prices adjust instantaneously to maintain equilibrium in all markets and (ii) adequate investment is always forthcoming to offset planned savings. The Keynes-Wicksell approach [Hahn, Rose, Fischer and Stein] is an attempt to integrate growth theory with short run equilibrium analysis. The essential features of the approach are, (i) prices adjust if and only if there is market disequilibrium, and (ii) saving and investment behavior are independently determined and may not always offset each other.

Both the above approaches generally use _outside money_ in their analysis. Money is said to be _outside money_ if it is the liability of a central bank owned by an agency outside the private and corporate sector of the economy. In simple terms, it is the government public debt. Money is said to be _inside money_ if it is the liability of a privately owned banking system. The effect of money on the consumption function may be different depending on whether it is of the inside or outside type. A third type of money is _commodity money_, e.g. gold. This kind of money requires the use of resources in its production. The resources thus used are no longer available for consumption or investment. Niehans [11] has analyzed a model in which a fraction of the stock of money is in the form of gold.

In this chapter, we study several of the models of money and growth. The neo-classical models of Tobin, Sidrauski, Levhari and Patinkin are discussed first. We then consider the Keynes-Wicksell treatment of monetary growth theory.

5.1 Tobin's Model

We first analyze Tobin's model which is the simplest neo-classical growth model with a monetary sector. The following equations are carried over from the basic Solow-Swan model with Harrod-neutral technical change and are unchanged with the addition of a monetary sector:

$$Y = F(K,N) = Nf(k)$$

$$N = Le^{\lambda t} = \text{labor in efficiency units}$$

$$k = K/N \quad \text{the capital effective-labor ratio}$$

$$\dot{L}/L = n$$

$$\dot{K} = I - \delta K$$

$$w = e^{\lambda t}[f(k) - kf'(k)]$$

$$r = f'(k)$$

Now introduce a single monetary asset, called money, with the following properties: (i) it is supplied by the government as a transfer payment and is not a produced commodity, (ii) it is a medium of exchange at a rate determined by the price level and is a store of value, and (iii) it is costless to generate. Let M be the nominal supply of money and P be the aggregate price level. Then M/P represents real balances, that is, the quantity of goods that can be purchased at the existing price level. We shall denote the rate of change of the money supply ($\dot{M}/M$) by μ and the rate of change of the price level ($\dot{P}/P$) by p. Assume that the demand for real balances (denoted by M_d/P) is given by the Liquidity Preference Function M(Y,i) where Y is aggregate output and i is the money rate of interest or equivalently, the opportunity cost of holding money. This opportunity cost is identical to the real rate of return on capital (r) plus the loss through inflation (p) of holding money balances. The money rate of interest is thus given by $i = r + p$.

The liquidity preference function is assumed to be continuous and linearly homogeneous in Y. In other words, if income doubles, the demand for real balances doubles. Then, $M_d/P = Y\, M(1,i) = \beta(i)Y$. Therefore the demand for real balances is proportional to aggregate output and the proportionality factor depends on the money rate of interest. When there is an increase in real rents or the rate of change of the price level, the demand for real balances decreases because the opportunity cost of holding it increases. Therefore, $\beta' < 0$. By dividing both sides of the above relation by K and noting that $Y/K = f(k)/k$ and $i = p + f'(k)$, we have

$$M_d/(PK) \equiv m(k,p) = \beta(i)f(k)/k$$

Money market equilibrium is obtained when the demand for money equals the supply, or $M_d = M$.

Tobin did not use the above approach to derive the demand for real balances. He assumed that the stock of real balances held by a community is proportional to its total wealth. Total wealth is the sum of the stock of capital (K) and the real value of the stock of money (M/P). If a proportion b is held as real balances ($0 < b < 1$), we have $M/P = b(K+M/P)$ or $M/(PK) = b/(1-b) \equiv m$. The proportion b is assumed to depend on the capital intensity and the rate of inflation and therefore $m = m(k,p)$.[1] The stronger assumption that $m = \beta f(k)/k$ was not made by Tobin but is added here because it simplifies the algebra without changing the qualitative implications of Tobin's conclusions.

Under the above framework, the disposable income of the economy will not be the same as the aggregate output of goods. Furthermore, saving and investment will not be equal in equilibrium because a part of the saving will be held in the form of money and

---

[1]For convenience we will sometimes use the terms <u>inflation</u> and <u>monetary expansion</u> in place of p and μ respectively. But the arguments apply equally well to deflation and contraction.

will not be invested in capital assets. The real disposable income of the economy is equal to aggregate output (Y) plus the real value of transfer payments made (in the form of paper money) by the government at each instant ($\dot{M}/P$) less the loss in the real value of existing cash balances caused by a price increase (pM/P).[1] Disposable real income (Y_d) is therefore given by $Y + (\mu-p)(M/P)$. Another way of obtaining the second term is to differentiate M/P with respect to t and thus obtain the value of the change in real balances due to changes in the money supply and the price level. Assuming a constant saving income ratio, aggregate saving is given by $S = sY_d = sY + s(\mu-p)(M/P)$. As mentioned earlier, not all of this saving can be used for gross investment. The change in the real value of money given by $(\mu-p)(M/P)$ cannot be held in the form of physical assets and must be held as cash balances. Therefore total investment for the purpose of capital accumulation will be saving less the above value and gives the relation $I = S - (\mu-p)(M/P)$. This equation may also be obtained in another way. Real consumption (C) is given by real disposable income multiplied by (1-s). Since gross investment is aggregate output less physical consumption, $I = Y-C$. Therefore,

$$I = Y - (1-s)Y - (1-s)(\mu-p)(M/P) = sY + s(M/P)(\mu-p) - (M/P)(\mu-p)$$

Since the first two terms represent aggregate saving, the stated relation between saving and investment is readily obtained. We now have the basic set of equations needed to analyze the long run properties of the system. Gathering all the above equations and rearranging them according to markets, we obtain the following system of simultaneous equations:

(5.1.1) Production function $\begin{cases} Y = Nf(k) \\ k \equiv K/N \end{cases}$

(5.1.2)

---

[1] If prices decrease, there are capital gains but the expression is the same with p taking on a negative value. Also, depreciation of capital may be subtracted from Y_d but this has not been done here for simplicity. (See Exercise 5.10).

$$
\text{Commodity market}
\begin{cases}
S = sY_d & (5.1.3)\\
Y_d = Y + (M/P)(\mu - p) & (5.1.4)\\
I = S - (M/P)(\mu - p) & (5.1.5)
\end{cases}
$$

$$
\text{Capital market}
\begin{cases}
\dot{K} = I - \delta K & (5.1.6)\\
r = f'(k) & (5.1.7)
\end{cases}
$$

$$
\text{Labor market}
\begin{cases}
\dot{L}/L = n & (5.1.8)\\
N = Le^{\lambda t}, \quad g = \lambda + n & (5.1.9)\\
w = e^{\lambda t}[f(k) - kf'(k)] & (5.1.10)
\end{cases}
$$

$$
\text{Money market}
\begin{cases}
\frac{M}{PK} = m(k,p) = \beta(i)f(k)/k \quad \beta'(i) < 0 & (5.1.11)\\
i = r + p & (5.1.12)\\
\dot{M}/M = \mu & (5.1.13)\\
\dot{P}/P = p & (5.1.14)
\end{cases}
$$

There are 14 structural equations in the 13 endogenous variables Y, Y_d, K, L, N, S, I, M, P, w, r, i and k. We need one more endogenous variable to complete the system. If the central banking authority exogenously controls the rate of growth of the money supply, then μ can be treated as a policy parameter. In that case the rate of change of the price level p will be endogenous. On the other hand, if price stability is the goal (i.e. $p = 0$) then μ cannot be predetermined and will be endogenous. This implies that the central bank will make instantaneous adjustments in μ. Note that μ and p cannot both be parameters because then the system would be overdetermined.

Basic differential equations: Before considering the above two cases, we shall reduce the system to two basic differential equations in k and p.[1] Let s_o be the investment-output ratio.

---

[1] Other variables can be chosen in which to reduce the system. For example, k and $x = M/(PL)$ or k and $m = M/(PK)$.

From (5.1.3), (5.1.4) and (5.1.5) we have

(5.1.15) $\qquad s_o(k,\mu,p) = I/Y = s - \beta(r+p)(\mu-p)(1-s)$

From (5.1.6), the rate of growth of capital stock is

$$\dot{K}/K = s_o Y/K - \delta = s_o f(k)/k - \delta$$

Since $\dot{k}/k = \dot{K}/K - g$ where $g \equiv \lambda + n$, we obtain the following differential equation in k:

(5.1.16) $\qquad \dot{k}/k = s_o(k,\mu,p)f(k)/k - (g+\delta)$

The form of this equation is identical to that for $\dot{k}/k$ in the Solow-Swan model. The difference is that the investment rate s_o is not constant but depends on the rate of monetary expansion, the rate of inflation and on the capital intensity. To obtain the differential equation in p, first differentiate (5.1.11) logarithmically with respect to t and use the definitions of μ and p. This gives

(5.1.17) $\qquad \mu - p - \dot{K}/K = \frac{1}{m}\frac{\partial m}{\partial k}\dot{k} + \frac{1}{m}\frac{\partial m}{\partial p}\dot{p}$

In order to simplify this expression we define two elasticities. Let η be the partial elasticity of demand for real balances with respect to the capital stock and ε be the partial elasticity of demand for real balances with respect to the money rate of interest, both of which depending on k and p. Thus

(5.1.18) $\qquad \eta(k,p) = \frac{K}{(M/P)}\frac{\partial(M/P)}{\partial K} = \frac{1}{m}\frac{\partial(Km)}{\partial K} = 1 + \frac{k}{m}\frac{\partial m}{\partial k}$

(5.1.19) $\qquad \varepsilon(k,p) = -\frac{i}{(M/P)}\frac{\partial(M/P)}{\partial i} = -\frac{i}{m}\frac{\partial m}{\partial i} = -\frac{i\beta'}{\beta} = -\frac{i}{m}\frac{\partial m}{\partial p}$

An increase in the money rate of interest lowers the demand for real balances and therefore ε will be positive. A number of empirical studies (see [16] for a summary of them) have shown that $\varepsilon < 1$, that is, the demand for real balances with respect to the money rate of interest is inelastic. An increase in the capital stock lowers rents. Since capital assets are now less attractive, demand for real balances will rise and therefore we can assume that η is positive. In fact, under Tobin's assumption that the aggregate holding of real balances is in proportion to total wealth, it can be shown that $\eta > 1$. Since $m(k,p) = b/(1-b)$, we have $m_k/m = b_k/[b(1-b)]$. An increase in k lowers real rent and hence increases the proportion of wealth held in monetary assets. Second, an increase in k increases real income and hence increases b through the transactions motive. Thus $b_k > 0$ implying that $m_k > 0$. It follows that $\eta > 1$. The demand for real balances with respect to the capital stock is thus elastic. Using the expressions for the elasticities in (5.1.17), we obtain

$$\mu - p - (\dot{k}/k+g) = (\eta-1)\dot{k}/k - \varepsilon\dot{p}/i$$

Solving for $\dot{p}$, the following differential equation in p is obtained:

$$\text{(5.1.20)} \qquad \dot{p} = (i/\varepsilon)[p - \mu + g + \eta\,\dot{k}/k]$$

Equations (5.1.16) and (5.1.20) constitute the basic differential equations in k and p. Two cases will be examined: a stable price level and price flexibility.

5.1.1 A Stable Price Level

By using an appropriate monetary policy, the government may maintain a stable price level for all t, if such is its goal. In order to achieve full employment and price stability, the government must create a deficit of proper magnitude every instant (i.e. treat μ as endogenous). In this case a unique steady state path exists and the system is stable. The steady state capital intensity, however, is lower than the corresponding capital intensity in the Solow-Swan (SS) model. In the SS model, the Golden Rule condition for maximizing long run per capita consumption was that the saving ratio must equal the share of profits in output. In the Tobin model the optimum saving rate is larger than the share of capital. These results may be obtained by proceeding as follows:

The assumption of price stability implies that $p = 0$ for all t. Therefore from (5.1.20),

$$\text{(5.1.20a)} \qquad \mu = g + \eta(k)\dot{k}/k$$

Thus for full employment and price stability the rate of monetary expansion cannot be set at an arbitrary level but must be continuously varied according to (5.1.20a). The needed rate of monetary expansion is given by the natural rate g plus or minus a correction factor which is the product of the rate of growth of capital intensity and the partial elasticity of demand for real balances with respect to the capital stock. In this case we can reduce the system to a single differential equation in k. Substituting for s_o from (5.1.15) and μ from (5.1.20a) and then solving for $\dot{k}/k$, we obtain

$$(5.1.16a) \qquad \frac{\dot{k}}{k} = \frac{A(k)}{B(k)} \equiv \frac{s_o(k,g,0)a(k) - (g+\delta)}{1 + (1-s)\eta\beta a(k)}$$

where $a(k) = f(k)/k$ is the average product of capital and $s_o(k,g,0)$ is given by

$$(5.1.15a) \qquad s_o(k,g,0) = s - (1-s)g\beta(r)$$

Since $\dot{k} = 0$ in the steady state, it follows from (5.1.20a) that $\mu^* = g = (\dot{K}/K)^*$. This means that the stock of capital and the nominal money supply must both grow, in the long run, at the same rate g. This is because when k is constant and p = 0, the money rate of interest must be constant. Therefore from (5.1.11), real balances per unit of capital must also be constant. Thus along the balanced growth path the government must continuously create a deficit ($\dot{M}$) equal to the product of the existing stock of money and the natural rate g.

To examine whether a balanced growth exists, set $\dot{k} = 0$, $p = 0$ and $\mu = g$ in (5.1.16). This yields the following equation:

$$(5.1.21) \qquad s_o(k,g,0)f(k)/k = (g+\delta)$$

Since the production function has neo-classical properties, the average product of capital f(k)/k is a montonic function decreasing from infinity to zero. To make economic sense the gross investment rate s_o must be greater than zero and less than 1.[1]

[1] If real balances are too large then, aggregate output may not be large enough to satisfy consumption demand. For example, let Y = 100, $\dot{M}$ = 200, P = 2 and s = 1/5. Then C = 160 > Y. s_o will then have a negative value. To avoid this situation we need the conditions $s > (1-s)(\mu-p)\beta(i)$.

Assuming this, an economically feasible steady state solution with positive k* will exist. If $s_o(k,g,0)$ is a monotonically decreasing function of k then so is $s_o(k,g,0)f(k)/k$ and a unique balanced growth will exist. Differentiating (5.1.15a) with respect to k, we obtain $\partial s_o/\partial k = -(1-s)g\beta'f'' < 0$ because $\beta' < 0$ and $f'' < 0$. Therefore $s_o f(k)/k$ is a strictly decreasing function of k. This establishes the uniqueness of the balanced growth path.

How does the steady state value k* obtained in this model compare with that in the SS model? To answer this, note that the second term of equation (5.1.15a) is negative implying that $s_o < s$. In the SS model the steady state condition was $sf(k)/k = g + \delta$. It is therefore evident from Figure 5.1 that in the Tobin model with price stability ($T : p = 0$), the equilibrium capital intensity (k_2^*) will be lower than the k_1^* corresponding to the SS model without a monetary sector. This result is intuitively obvious. If disposable income increases without an increase in real output, consumption will increase at the expense of investment. The introduction of a monetary asset is thus equivalent to an overall

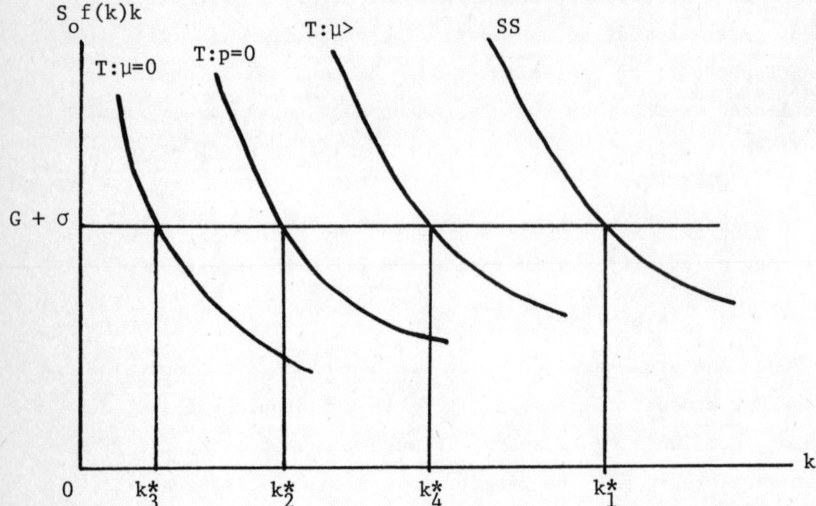

Figure 5.1

reduction in the investment rate. We have seen in the SS model that a lowering of the investment rate will decrease the equilibrium capital intensity.

Although the introduction of money does lower k^* and hence decreases the long run per capita income as compared to a barter economy, it does not immediately follow that the latter economy is therefore preferable. Even in a one-commodity world several types of exchanges must take place. First, labor must exchange its services for the commodity. Second, firms must borrow capital from workers some of whom may be employed by other firms. Third, if households' expenditures are made more or less continuously over time but their income is received at discrete points of time, there is a need for inventory holding. All these impose transaction costs which will greatly be reduced if a common medium of exchange exists. Thus it doesn't make much sense to compare a barter economy with a monetary economy. It is more meaningful to ask what happens if the stock of money and its rate of change alters as a result of government policy. This question is examined in Section 5.1.2.

Golden Rule: A reduction in the long run capital intensity also leads to a reduction in the per capita output $f(k^*)$. However, maximizing per capita consumption will give rise to the same maximum per capita consumption as in the SS model. Since effective-labor N is independent of the saving rate, maximizing C/L is equivalent to maximizing C/N. We have

$$C/N = Y/N - I/N = f(k) - (\dot{K}+\delta K)/N$$

In the steady state this reduces to $c^* = f(k^*) - (g+\delta)k^*$. The necessary condition for a maximum is that $f'(k^*) = g + \delta$, the same as in the SS model. Thus the Golden Rule rate of return to capital, net of depreciation, is equal to the natural rate of growth. Since the k^* satisfying the equation $f'(k^*) = g + \delta$ is unique, the corresponding c^* will be the same in both the Tobin and Solow-Swan models. Therefore as long as the government pursues appropriate policies to set the saving rate equal to the Golden Rule rate, there is no loss in per capita consumption at its maximum, due to the introduction of a monetary asset. However, this saving rate will be higher than that in the SS model. To establish this, note that in steady state $s_o^* f(k^*)/k^* = g + \delta$. For Golden Rule, $g + \delta = f'(k^*)$. We therefore have $s_o^* = \pi^*$; that is, the share of capital is equal to the investment rate. The above condition implies the following two equations:

$$\pi^* = s_o^* = s - (1-s)g\beta(r^*)$$

$$s_{opt} = \pi^*(1+g\beta^*/\pi^*)/(1+g\beta^*)$$

Since $\pi < 1$, $s_{opt} > \pi^*$. Since π^* is the optimum saving rate for the SS model, we have the result that the optimum saving rate is larger in the Tobin model than in the SS model. This can also be seen from Figure 5.1. Assume that the SS economy is on the golden rule path. If the saving rate is the same in the Tobin and SS models then k^* will be lower in the former model. Only a rise in the saving rate of the monetary model will yield the same k^* as in the SS model.

The long run growth rate is g as in the SS model. The effects of changes in the parameters g, s and δ on the equilibrium capital intensity k^* are also similar. Since k_2^* is smaller than k_1^*. equilibrium rents will be higher in the monetary model.

Stability analysis: We shall now show that Tobin's model with price stability is stable. Recall from the Appendix to Chapter 3 (A.14) that the sufficient condition for a steady state solution to be stable is that $[\partial(\dot{k}/k)/\partial k]^* < 0$. We have,

$$\left(\frac{\partial(\dot{k}/k)}{\partial k}\right)^* = \frac{A'(k^*)}{B(k^*)}$$

because $A(k^*) = 0$. Since $B(k^*) > 0$, the necessary and sufficient condition becomes $A'(k^*) < 0$. We showed earlier that $\partial s_o/\partial k < 0$. Also $a(k)$ is a decreasing function of k. Therefore $A'(k) < 0$ and hence the stability condition is satisfied. Therefore, when prices are fixed by appropriate monetary policy, a unique and stable balanced growth path exists.

It is possible to give an economic argument for the stability in this case. Suppose capital stock accumulates faster than labor (expressed in efficiency units). Then because capital is relatively plentiful, rents will fall. Firms will substitute capital for labor and use a more capital intensive technique. Since the average product of capital then declines, investment per unit of capital will decrease. Moreover, when capital intensity rises and rents fall, demand for real balances per unit of capital will increase (because $\partial m/\partial k > 0$). The portfolio composition therefore moves in favor of monetary assets and away from capital assets. This further reduces investment and therefore the rate of accumulation of capital falls. This process will continue as long as the capital stock grows faster than g. Ultimately capital accumulation slows to the rate g and balanced growth is achieved. The mechanism is similar when effective-labor grows faster than capital.

5.1.2 Flexible Price Level

If the rate of monetary expansion μ is a policy instrument under the exogenous control of the central banking authority, prices will be variable (i.e. p is endogenous). We will then have a determinate system with 14 equations and 14 unknowns. When prices are flexible, a unique steady state still exists but the system is no longer stable. In the steady state, capital intensity will be constant ($\dot{k} = 0$) and prices will change at a constant rate ($\dot{p} = 0$). Therefore from (5.1.20)

(5.1.22) $$p^* = \mu - g$$

If the government expands the money supply at a rate higher than the natural rate g, then there will be inflation in the long run and if $\mu < g$, there will be deflation. In order to maintain long run price stability, monetary expansion must proceed at the natural rate.

The condition for steady state is still the same as that implied by equation (5.1.21), but the expression for the investment rate is slightly different. We have

(5.1.15b) $$s_o(k,\mu,\mu-g) = s - (1-s)g\beta(r+\mu-g)$$

The only change from the stable price level case is that the investment rate is different.

Suppose μ, which is now exogenous and under government control, is set at zero; that is, the government holds the money supply constant. The equilibrium money rate of interest will then be $r - g$ and is smaller than in the fixed price case. Therefore from (5.1.15b) the overall investment rate in the flexible price case ($\mu = 0$) will be smaller than the investment rate in the fixed price case ($\mu = g$). Economically, the lower investment in the flexible price case with $\mu = 0$ is due to the lower opportunity cost for holding money (and hence an increased demand for money). The equilibrium situation is pictured in Figure 5.1 ($T : \mu = 0$). The long run capital intensity (k_3^*) is lower than both k_1^* and k_2^*. It is obvious that when $\mu = 0$, the golden rule saving rate is even higher than in the fixed price case.

If, however, the rate of monetary expansion is larger than the natural rate g then the money rate of interest $r + \mu - g$ is greater than r. Then the investment rate in the flexible price case is higher than the case when prices are constant. The corresponding steady state solution (k_4^*) will be higher than k_2^*. The implication from this model is that when μ is greater than g thereby inducing inflation at the rate $\mu - g$, the long run capital intensity and hence per capita income will be higher than when monetary expansion is smaller than the natural rate. If the rate of inflation is so large that the demand for real balances is reduced to zero, then the Solow-Swan situation will prevail. However, under no circumstances can the equilibrium capital intensity in this money model be higher than the equilibrium k^* in the Solow-Swan model.

Neutrality of money: There has been considerable attention in the literature on the neutrality of money. Money is said to be neutral if monetary changes do not affect the equilibrium capital intensity and other real variables of the system. The only effect will be a change in the price level. However, we must distinguish between two ways of influencing the money supply. First, there may be a change in the absolute quantity of the money supply with no change in the rate of its expansion. It is seen from (5.1.15b) that the investment rate does not depend directly on M. Thus money is neutral in this sense. For example, if the money supply doubles and thereafter increases at the same rate μ, then after an adjustment period the same long run equilibrium will be attained with the same value of p*, k* and m* but with the absolute price level doubled. The second way of influencing the money supply is by changing the rate of monetary expansion μ. It is clear from (5.1.15b) that changes in μ will not be neutral. We have $\partial s_o/\partial\mu = -(1-s)g\beta' > 0$ since $\beta' < 0$. An increase in μ would therefore shift the curve $s_o a(k)$ upwards resulting in a higher k*; that is, $\partial k^*/\partial\mu > 0$. The effects of changes in μ on the other variables in the system are easily obtained and are presented in Table 5.1 (Exercise 5.1).

Stability analysis: In order to analyze the stability of the equilibrium (p*,k*) refer to theorems A.3 and A.4 of the appendix to Chapter 3. The first step is to calculate the partial derivatives of $\dot{k}$ and $\dot{p}$ with respect to k and p in the neighborhood of

Table 5.1: Sensitivities for Tobin's Model

		s	μ	n	λ	δ
k*		+	+	-	-	-
$(\dot{Y}/Y)^*$		0	0	+	+	0
$(\dot{y}/y)^*$		0	0	0	+	0
y*		+	+	-	-	-
w*		+	+	-	-	-
r*		-	-	+	+	+
$\pi(k^*)$ for	$\sigma < 1$	-	-	+	+	+
	$\sigma = 1$	0	0	0	0	0
	$\sigma > 1$	+	+	-	-	-
p*		0	+	-	-	0

the equilibrium. Since $\dot{k} = k(\dot{k}/k)$, we have

$$a_{11} = \left(\frac{\partial \dot{k}}{\partial k}\right)^* = \left(\frac{\partial(\dot{k}/k)}{\partial k}\right)^* k^*$$

The second term vanishes because $\dot{k} = 0$ at $k = k^*$. Differentiating $\dot{k}/k$ in (5.1.16) partially with respect to k and p and setting $\mu - p = g$ we obtain:

$$a_{11} = k^*[s_o^* a'(k^*) + a^* \partial s_o/\partial k] < 0$$

since $a'(k) < 0$ and from the last section $\partial s_o/\partial k < 0$. Also

$$a_{12} = \left(\frac{\partial \dot{k}}{\partial p}\right)^* = k\left(\frac{\partial(\dot{k}/k)}{\partial p}\right)^* = k^* a(k^*)\left(\frac{\partial s_o}{\partial p}\right)^*$$

$$= k^* a(k^*)(1-s)(\beta^* - g\beta') > 0$$

using equation (5.1.15). The slope of the $\dot{k} = 0$ curve in the neighborhood of (p^*, k^*) is $(\partial k/\partial p)^*_{\dot{k}=0} = -a_{12}/a_{11} > 0$. The $\dot{k} = 0$ curve is therefore upward sloping in the neighborhood of the equilibrium as shown in Figure 5.2. Proceeding similarly, we obtain from (5.1.20)

$$a_{21} = (\partial \dot{p}/\partial k)^* = i^* \eta^* a_{11}/(\varepsilon^* k^*) < 0$$

$$a_{22} = \left(\frac{\partial \dot{p}}{\partial p}\right)^* = \frac{i^*}{\varepsilon^*}\left[1 + \frac{\eta^* a_{12}}{k^*}\right] > 0$$

The slope of the $\dot{p} = 0$ curve is also positive and is given by

$$\left(\frac{dk}{dp}\right)^*_{\dot{p}=0} = \frac{-a_{22}}{a_{21}} = -\left(\frac{k^* + \eta^* a_{12}}{\eta^* a_{11}}\right)$$

$$= -\frac{k^*}{\eta^* a_{11}} + \left(\frac{dk}{dp}\right)^*_{\dot{k}=0} > \left(\frac{dk}{dp}\right)^*_{\dot{k}=0} \quad \text{since } a_{11} < 0$$

It follows that in the neighborhood of the equilibrium both the $\dot{p} = 0$ and $\dot{k} = 0$ curves are upward sloping and the $\dot{p} = 0$ curve has a higher slope than the $\dot{k} = 0$ curve. Recall from Theorems A.3 and A.4 that the necessary and sufficient conditions for local stability are $a_{11} + a_{22} < 0$ and $a_{11}a_{22} - a_{21}a_{12} > 0$. Since $a_{11} < 0$ and $a_{22} > 0$, the sign of $a_{11} + a_{22}$ is indeterminate. We have shown that the $\dot{p} = 0$ curve has a higher slope than the $\dot{k} = 0$ curve.

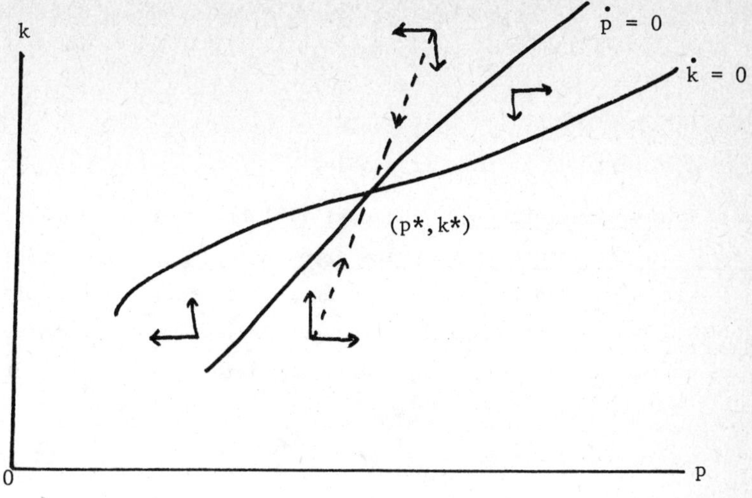

Figure 5.2

Therefore $-a_{22}/a_{21} > -a_{12}/a_{11}$. Since $a_{11} < 0$ and $a_{21} < 0$, $a_{11}a_{22} - a_{21}a_{22} < 0$. Thus the second condition for stability is violated and the system is generally unstable with a saddle point. This result may also be obtained with the help of the phase diagram presented in Figure 5.2.

Since $a_{11} < 0$, as k is increased slightly from any point along the $\dot{k} = 0$ curve, $\dot{k}$ decreases to a negative value. Therefore for all points above the $\dot{k} = 0$ curve, the directional arrows for k will point downward. Below the curve we have the opposite result. Similarly since $a_{21} < 0$, as k is increased from any point along the $\dot{p} = 0$ curve, p decreases to a negative value. Therefore at all points above the $\dot{p} = 0$ curve, the directional arrow for p will point to the left. These directional arrows are drawn in Figure 5.2 and it is evident that the steady state is a saddle point.[1] Only if the initial values of k and p lie along the dotted line will the system converge to the steady state. Thus Tobin's mone-

[1]See also Figure A.5 of the appendix to Chapter 3.

tary model with flexible prices is generally characterized by saddle point instability. Given this instability, the sensitivity analysis done earlier is questionable. However, we shall presently show that the sensitivity table 5.1 holds provided the model is suitably modified to make it stable.

Price expectations: Sidrauski [17] has modified the above model to take into account price expectations. p is now interpreted as expected rate of change in prices and will generally differ from the actual rate of change, $\dot{P}/P$. Consumers modify their expectations according to the following adaptive expectations rule:

$$\dot{p} = \alpha(\dot{P}/P-p) \qquad \alpha > 0$$

When the actual rate of price change is below expectations, people revise their expectations downward. α is the speed of adjustment and is assumed to be constant. The rate of money expansion (μ) is now exogenously determined. The procedure for analysis is exactly the same with the above equation replacing (5.1.14). The differential equation in k is the same as (5.1.16). The differential equation for p now becomes

$$\text{(5.1.20a)} \qquad \dot{p} = \frac{\alpha}{(\alpha\varepsilon/i-1)}\,[p - \mu + g + \eta\,\dot{k}/k]$$

The steady state conditions and hence the sensitivities are the same as in Tobin's model (see exercise 5.3). The stability properties are, however, different. The $\dot{k} = 0$ and the $\dot{p} = 0$ curves will again be as in Figure 5.2. However, the directional arrows for the $\dot{p} = 0$ curve depend on the speed of adjustment (α). If $\alpha > i^*/\varepsilon^*$ then $(\partial\dot{p}/\partial k)^* < 0$ and hence the directional arrows will be as in Figure 5.2 implying that the steady state is a saddle point as in Tobin's model (in which $\alpha \to \infty$). If the speed of adjustment is less than i^*/ε^* the phase diagram will be as in Figure 5.3. Thus the system will be stable provided individuals are sluggish in revising their expectations (i.e. $\alpha < i^*/\varepsilon^*$). Note that in this case, the sensitivity table 5.1 is valid.

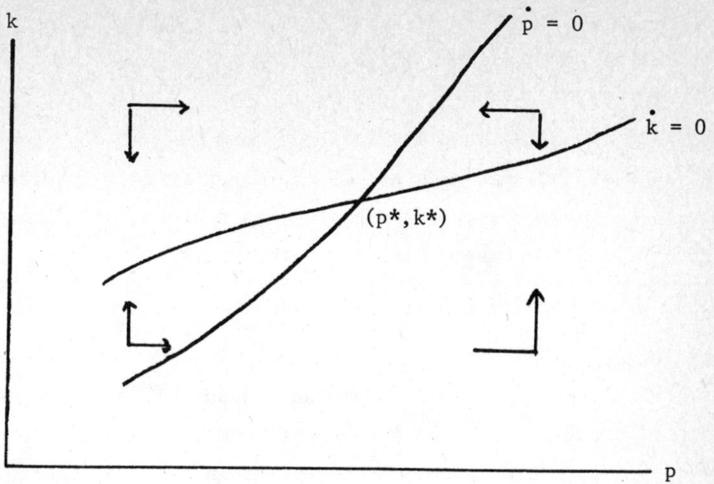

Figure 5.3

5.2 Money as a Consumer Good

It was pointed out earlier that although a monetary economy has a lower long run capital intensity than that of the Solow-Swan barter economy, the existence of transaction costs provides a powerful motive for holding money. Levhari and Patinkin (LP) argue that any rationale for holding money ought to interpret money balances either as a consumer good or as a producer good [9]. We shall consider the first case here. If money is treated as a consumer good then people derive utility from their money holdings. The interpretation is not that people derive utility directly from holding money but that money provides utility by offering protection against uncertainties that especially arise because expected expenditure and income may not coincide. The holding of money in the interim period between wage payments provides some security and hence the consumer indirectly derives utility from money balances. One can also argue that money holdings provide utility by enabling individuals to consume more in a future period by restricting present consumption.

Under the Levhari-Patinkin interpretation, the cost to the community of holding money balances should be included in disposable income just as the cost of holding a commodity is included in disposable income. We have already seen that the opportunity cost of holding a unit of money is the money rate of interest $i = r + p$. The total cost, to the economy as a whole, of holding real balances is Mi/P. Disposable income therefore becomes[1]

(5.2.4) $$Y_d = Y + (M/P)(\mu-p) + Mi/P$$

which replaces (5.1.4).

All the other assumptions are unchanged. Thus the only effect of treating money as a consumer good is to alter the definition of disposable income which results in a correspondingly altered consumption function. The analysis is therefore similar to those of previous models, but there is one important difference in the conclusions. Unlike the Tobin model, it is now theoretically possible to have a higher equilibrium capital intensity than in the simple SS model. This proposition and its empirical feasibility are examined below.

The investment-output ratio now has the following form:

(5.2.15) $$s_1(k,\mu,p) = s - \beta(i)(\mu-p)(1-s) + si\beta(i)$$

Since the procedure is similar, we simply write down the basic differential equations in k and p without derivation.

(5.2.16) $$\dot{k}/k = s_1(k,\mu,p)f(k)/k - (g+\delta)$$

(5.2.20) $$\dot{p} = (i/\varepsilon)[p-\mu+g+\eta\dot{k}/k]$$

The $\dot{p}$ equation has the same form as before but in the $\dot{k}$ equation, s_o is replaced by s_1. In steady state, $\dot{p} = \dot{k} = 0$. Therefore we have the following equilibrium conditions: $s_1(k,g,0)a(k) = g + \delta$ and $\mu - p = g$ where

(5.2.15a) $$s_1(k,g,0) = s - \beta(i)g(1-s) + si\beta(i)$$
$$= s_o(k,g,0) + si\beta(i)$$

---

[1]The numbering of the equations in this section is not continuous but is designed to match the numbers of the corresponding equations in the previous section.

Differentiating (5.2.15a) with respect to k, we have (see exercise 5.4)

$$\partial s_1/\partial k = \partial s_o/\partial k + s(1-\varepsilon)\beta f'' < 0$$

because $\partial s_o/\partial k < 0$, $\varepsilon < 1$ and $f'' < 0$. Therefore a unique steady state exists.

In the SS model the overall investment ratio is s. In Tobin's model the investment-output ratio is less than s because of the presence of the negative second term in (5.1.15), thus resulting in a smaller capital intensity than in the SS model. However, a comparison of (5.1.15) with (5.2.15) shows that the investment-output ratio in the LP model is higher than the corresponding ratio in the Tobin model because of the third term in (5.2.15). Thus the equilibrium k* in the LP model will be higher than the corresponding k* in the Tobin model. This is true irrespective of whether prices are constant or variable.

Will the LP model yield a higher long run capital intensity than the Solow-Swan model? It is evident from (5.2.15a) that the necessary and sufficient condition for s_1 to be larger than s is $si^* > g(1-s)$. Therefore, in order to obtain a higher capital intensity than in the Solow-Swan model it is necessary and sufficient that $i^* > g(1-s)/s$. In other words, if the equilibrium money rate of interest is greater than $g(1-s)/s$ then a higher k* is theoretically possible. The empirical feasibility of this condition obviously depends on the values of g, s and i*. For most countries the gross saving ratio will probably not exceed 25 percent. The natural rate g is the rate of growth of labor force plus the rate of growth of technical progress and is the long run rate of growth of output. Table 5.2 gives the minimum money rate of interest necessary to satisfy the condition $s_1 > s$, for alternative values of g and s. It is found that, to achieve a larger capital intensity, the minimum money rate of interest is generally high except when the saving rate is large and g is relatively small. However, as we saw in the last chapter, Conlisk has shown using cross-country data that the higher the saving rate the higher the growth rate. If we assume that the labor force grows at an

Table 5.2: Minimum Money Rate of Interest for Alternative Values of g and s

g	s	min i*
.02	.10	.18
(.038)	(.10)	(.34)
.04	.10	.36
.06	.10	.54
.02	.15	.11
.04	.15	.23
(.046)	(.15)	(.26)
.06	.15	.34
.02	.20	.08
.04	.20	.16
(.054)	(.20)	(.22)
.06	.20	.24
.04	.25	.12
.06	.25	.18
(.062)	(.25)	(.19)

annual rate of 2.5 percent and estimate g for s = .10, .15, .20 and .25, we obtain the values presented in parentheses in Table 5.2.[1] It is evident that the lower bound for the money rate of interest is unrealistically large and can be attained only with a large rate of inflation. The empirical plausibility of obtaining a higher k* in the LP model is therefore questionable. However, even if the k* for the LP model is smaller than the Solow-Swan k*, individuals are not necessarily worse off because they now derive utility from money balances as well as from phsyical consumption.

The stability results of this model are similar to those of the Tobin model and will only be sketched. As before, we must distinguish between constant and variable prices.

---

[1]Recall from the last chapter that the estimated relation obtained by Conlisk is: $g = .005 + .155s + .700n$.

5.2.1 Constant Prices

In this case $p = 0$ for all t.[1] Proceeding as in the Tobin model we obtain the following equation:

$$\frac{\dot{k}}{k} \equiv \frac{A(k)}{B(k)} = \frac{s_1(k,g,0)a(k) - (g+\delta)}{1 + (1-s)\eta\beta a(k)} \tag{5.2.16a}$$

As in the last section, the necessary and sufficient condition for stability is $A'(k) < 0$.

$$A'(k^*) = s_1^* a'(k^*) + a^* \partial s_1 / \partial k$$

Since the average product of capital is a downward sloping curve, $a'(k) < 0$. It is shown earlier that $\partial s_1/\partial k < 0$. Therefore $A'(k^*) < 0$ which implies that the LP economy is stable if the price level is held constant by the instantaneous adjustment of the rate of change of the money supply.

It is fairly easy to show that $\partial k^*/\partial s > 0$ and $\partial k^*/\partial g < 0$ (exercise 5.1). These results are the same as in the SS model. Since the rate of growth of money supply is endogenous, the question of neutrality of money does not arise.

5.2.2 Variable Price Level

When the rate of monetary expansion is exogenously controlled by monetary authorities, money market equilibrium will be achieved through fluctuating prices. Since $\dot{k} = \dot{p} = 0$ in the steady state, we have the familiar result $p^* = \mu - g$. The other equilibrium condition is

$$s_1(k,\mu,\mu-g)a(k) = g + \delta \qquad \text{where}$$

$$s_1(k,\mu,\mu-g) = s - g(1-s)\beta(r+\mu-g) + s(r+\mu-g)\beta(r+\mu-g) \tag{5.2.15b}$$

The qualitative results of this situation are similar to the flexible price case of Tobin's model. The expressions for the partial derivatives a_{ij} $(i,j = 1,2)$, are similar with s_1 substituted for s_o (see exercise 5.6). The phase diagram will be as in

---

[1]Levhari and Patinkin did not assume that $p = 0$ but that $p = p_o$. Since price stability is feasible within the framework of the model, we will assume that $p = 0$.

Figure 5.2 indicating that the steady state solution is a saddle point. The results regarding the non-neutrality of money are also the same and the sensitivities are as in Table 5.1.

To summarize, the treatment of money as a consumer good does not substantially alter the qualitative results of Tobin's model. Although in theory a steady state with a higher k^* than in the Solow-Swan model is possible, its empirical plausibility is questionable.

Variable saving ratio: So far we have assumed that the saving ratio is constant. Levhari and Patinkin assume that $s = s(r,p)$. If the capital intensity increases, real rents fall. A fall in the yield on capital will lower the saving rate. Therefore $\partial s/\partial k < 0$. Since the overall investment rate s_1 is positively related to s (see equation 5.2.15a), it follows that $\partial s_1/\partial k < 0$. An increase in the rate of inflation will tend to increase current consumption and therefore $\partial s/\partial p < 0$. However, the sign of $\partial s_1/\partial p$ is ambiguous (exercise 5.5). Using these results, Ramanathan [12,13] has shown that even if the saving function is of this general form, the system is unstable. Assuming a still more general savings function, $s = s(r,p,y)$ with $\partial s/\partial y > 0$, he has shown that stability is impossible unless increases in p (for a fixed k) substantially reduce the saving rate s. An increase in p (with k constant) leads to a reduction in the real value of existing balances and hence of disposable income. Since output per unit of capital (or labor) is unchanged, consumption will decline, and saving will therefore increase. On the other hand, an increase in p will reduce the rate of saving and hence reduce the level of saving. The net effect is ambiguous and is a matter for empirical determination.

5.3 Money as a Producer Good

In the last section consumers were assumed to derive utility from holdings of money because money offers protection against uncertainty. In such a situation monetary expansion causes a shift in consumption patterns. An alternative approach, also adopted by Levhari and Patinkin [9], is to assume that individuals derive utility only from the consumption of commodities and that money is essentially held by firms because it enables them to obtain a larger bundle of goods. For example, the availability of credit makes it possible to generate more output. Money is thus a Producer good. A simple way of treating money under this assumption is to assume that real balances enter directly into the production function. Production depends on fixed capital K as well as working capital M/P. The production function is written as $Y = F(K,N,M/P)$. Real balances therefore constitute a third factor of production. Monetary expansion now causes shifts in production patterns. It is assumed that the production function is linearly homogeneous in all the arguments, that is, when capital stock, effective-labor and real balances are all increased proportionately, output is increased by the same proportion. Because of this property the production function can be written as $Y = NF[K/N,1,M/(PN)] = Nf(k,m)$ where $k = K/N$ and $m = M/PN$. When money is treated as a producer good, people do not derive utility directly from money holdings and therefore the opportunity cost of holding money is not to be included in disposable income (see exercise 5.9). The expression for disposable income is then the same as in Tobin's model -- $Y + (\mu-p)(M/P)$.

The demand for money is no longer given by 5.1.11 but is now determined by marginal conditions. Firms will use capital and labor at levels determined by equating their marginal products to the corresponding factor prices. In a similar manner, firms will use money at a level determined by equating the marginal product of money to the money rate of interest. In equilibrium, the real rate of return to capital is the money rate of interest less the rate of price change. The above results and other assumptions regarding saving and investment behavior are summarized in the following equations:

(5.3.1)	Production function	$Y = Nf(k,m)$
(5.3.2)		$k \equiv K/N$
(5.3.3)	Commodity market	$S = sY_d$
(5.3.4)		$Y_d = Y + (\mu - p)(M/P)$
(5.3.5)		$I = S - (\mu - p)(M/P)$
(5.3.6)	Capital market	$\dot{K} = I - \delta K$
(5.3.7)		$r = f_k \equiv \partial f/\partial k$
(5.3.8)	Labor market	$\dot{L}/L = n$
(5.3.9)		$N = Le^{\lambda t}$
(5.3.10)		$w = e^{\lambda t}[f - kf_k - mf_m]$
(5.3.11)	Money market	$i = \partial Y/\partial(M/P) = f_m \equiv \partial f/\partial m$
(5.3.12)		$i = r + p$
(5.3.13)		$\dot{M}/M = \mu$
(5.3.14)		$\dot{P}/P = p$
(5.3.15)		$m \equiv M/(PN)$

We have 15 equations in the 15 endogenous variables $Y, Y_d, K, N, L, S, I, M, P, w, r, i, m, k, \mu$ or p. As before, only μ or p can be treated as a parameter but not both. Ignoring this point for the time being we can derive the basic differential equations in k and m. From (5.3.3), (5.3.4), (5.3.5) and (5.3.6) the rate of accumulation of capital is given by

$$\dot{K}/K = sY/K - (M/PK)(\mu - p)(1-s) - \delta$$

Using (5.3.1), the definitions of k and m, and noting that $\dot{k}/k = \dot{K}/K - g$ the following differential equation in k is obtained:

$$\dot{k}/k = sf(k,m)/k - (m/k)(\mu - p)(1-s) - g - \delta \tag{5.3.16}$$

Logarithmically differentiating (5.3.15) with respect to t

(5.3.17) $\dot{m}/m = \mu - p - g$

In steady state $\dot{k} = \dot{m} = 0$. We thus have the familiar result that in steady state $\mu - p = g$. Substituting this in (5.3.16) and setting $\dot{k} = 0$, we obtain the following equation involving k and m:

(5.3.18) $\phi(k,m) \equiv sf(k,m) - m(1-s)g - gk = 0$

In order to obtain a steady state solution, we need another equation in k and m. This may be obtained in one of two ways. If price stability is the goal and μ is accordingly instantaneously adjusted, we have $p = 0$, and our second equation is

(5.3.19) $\psi(k,m) = f_m - f_k = 0$

Steady state values of k and m may be obtained by jointly solving equations (5.3.18) and (5.3.19). If prices are variable and μ is exogenous, then our second equation is

(5.3.19a) $\mu - f_m + f_k = g$

In this case, equilibrium solutions are obtained by solving (5.3.18) and (5.3.19a). It is interesting to note that since the production function is linearly homogeneous and k^* and m^* are constant in the steady state, the long run growth rate is still g.

The question of monetary neutrality may be examined by differentiating (5.3.18) and (5.3.19a) partially with respect to μ and solving for $\partial k^*/\partial\mu$. We have,

(5.3.20) $\partial k^*/\partial\mu = [sf_m-(1-s)g]/\Delta$

(5.3.21) $\partial m^*/\partial\mu = (g-sf_k)/\Delta$ where

(5.3.22) $\Delta = (sf_k-g)(f_{km}-f_{mm}) - (f_{kk}-f_{km})[sf_m-(1-s)g]$

Under the assumption of diminishing marginal returns $f_{mm} < 0$ and $f_{kk} < 0$. If we also assume that factors are <u>co-operant</u>, that is, the marginal product of a factor increases whenever the level of another factor increases, then $f_{km} = f_{mk} > 0$. Even these assumptions are not adequate to determine the signs of the above partial derivatives. However, Harkness [7] has shown that if the system is assumed to be stable, the above signs become determinate.

This can be proved by proceeding as follows.

Let $a_{11} = (\partial\dot{k}/\partial k)^*$, $a_{12} = (\partial\dot{k}/\partial m)^*$, $a_{13} = (\partial\dot{k}/\partial p)^*$, etc. Then

$$a_{11} = sf_k^* - g \qquad a_{12} = sf_m^* - g(1-s)$$

$$a_{13} = m^*(1-s) \qquad a_{21} = 0$$

$$a_{22} = 0 \qquad a_{23} = -m^*$$

$$a_{31} = f_{kk} - f_{km} \qquad a_{32} = f_{km} - f_{mm}$$

$$a_{33} = 1$$

a_{31}, a_{32} and a_{33} are the partial derivatives of the equation in p given by $p - f_m + f_k = 0$, obtained from (5.3.11) and (5.3.12). Recall from the Appendix to Chapter 3 that a necessary condition for local stability is that the determinant of the a_{ij}'s must be negative. It can be shown that the determinant is $-m^*\Delta$. Thus a necessary condition for stability is that $\Delta > 0$. Additional algebraic manipulations are needed to determine the signs of $\partial k^*/\partial\mu$ and $\partial m^*/\partial\mu$. Note that in equilibrium, per capita disposable income is $y_d = f(k,m) + gm$. As the production function is linearly homogeneous, by Euler's theorem, $f(k,m) = w + mf_m + kf_k$ where w is the real wage rate. Using these two relations and (5.3.19a) we get $y_d = w + m\mu + f_k(k+m)$. From (5.3.18) $g = sy_d/(k+m)$. Thus

$$sf_k - g = sf_k - sy_d/(k+m) = -s(w+m\mu)/(k+m) < 0 \tag{5.3.23}$$

This, together with the stability condition $\Delta > 0$ implies that $\partial m^*/\partial\mu > 0$. It is seen from (5.3.23) and (5.3.22) that $sf_m - (1-s)g$ must be positive as otherwise Δ will be negative. Therefore from (5.3.20) it follows that $\partial k^*/\partial\mu > 0$ also. Therefore, under the assumption of stability, an increase in the rate of monetary expansion will increase the long run capital-labor ratio and per capita real cash balances. If, as in the earlier models, stability does not hold, the above conclusions are not justified. However, as pointed out earlier, the comparative dynamics exercise is meaningless from the point of view of policy unless stability is assured.

5.4 The Keynes-Wicksell Approach

The models discussed in the earlier sections follow the neo-classical approach in which markets are always in equilibrium and investment is also equal to saving. In recent years a number of economists (Stein [18], Rose [14], Hahn [6], Nagatani [10], Hadjimichalakis [4,5], Fischer [2], to name a few) have questioned both assumptions. They argued that prices will change if and only if there is market disequilibrium. Furthermore, this disequilibrium may come about because of independently determined saving and investment behavior (hence the name Keynes-Wicksell). They found that if the above modifications are introduced into the neo-classical model, the conclusion that an increase in the rate of monetary expansion will raise long run capital intensity, is no longer certain. In this section we present the detailed analysis of a Keynes-Wicksell (KW) model which is a modification of Tobin's model.[1] Several other variations are possible and are discussed in the exercises at the end of the chapter. The first four equations of the KW model are the same as in Section 5.1. Unlike the neo-classical model, investment behavior is determined independently. It is assumed that investment demand per unit of capital is a function of the capital intensity (k), the money rate of interest (i) and the rate of inflation (p). Thus $I/K = I(k,p,i)$. Another distinctive feature of the KW approach is that prices change if and only if there is excess demand or supply. More specifically, the rate of price change is assumed to be proportional to the excess supply of money. We therefore have,

$$p = h[M/(PK) - m(k,p)] \qquad h > 0$$

Because of the budget constraint, an excess supply of real balances implies an equal amount of excess demand for goods and vice versa.[2] Excess demand in the commodity market is investment

---

[1]For a very detailed and thorough examination of the KW model and its relation to the neo-classical model see Stein [21].

[2]The bond market is not explicitly considered here because it is always assumed to be in equilibrium.

(I) less desired physical saving which is total desired saving (S) minus that part of total saving held as monetary assets $[(M/P)(\mu-p)]$.[1] Hence

$$(M/PK) - m(k,p) = I/K - S/K + (M/PK)(\mu-p)$$

When planned saving and investment are unequal what is ex post investment? One can argue that it is the minimum of I and physical savings. But this assumes that the plans of either firms or workers are frustrated. It is quite possible that some investment plans are realized and some consumption plans are realized. In this case ex post investment will lie between ex ante investment and desired saving. A simple way, adopted by Stein, of incorporating this is to assume that ex post investment (which is equal to capital accumulation) is a linear combination of investment demand and desired savings. Thus

$$\dot{K} = bI + (1-b)[S - (M/P)(\mu-p)] - \delta K \qquad 0 \leq b \leq 1$$

If b = 0 then consumption plans are realized and if b = 1, investment plans are fully realized. By adding the other equations of the model, the complete structural equations of the KW model are written below.

(5.4.1) Production function $Y = Nf(k)$

(5.4.2) $k = K/N$

(5.4.3) Commodity market $S = sY_d$

(5.4.4) $Y_d = Y + (M/P)(\mu-p)$

(5.4.5) $I/K = I(k,p,i)$

(5.4.6) Capital market $\dot{K} = bI + (1-b)[S-(M/P)(\mu-p)] - \delta K$

(5.4.7) $r = f'(k)$

[1]Note that this is also equivalent to C + I - Y, as was seen in deriving equation (5.1.5). Also see the next section regarding some conceptual problems with this equation.

(5.4.8) Labor market $\dot{L}/L = n$

(5.4.9) $N = Le^{\lambda t}, \quad g = \lambda + n$

(5.4.10) $w = e^{\lambda t}[f(k)-kf'(k)]$

(5.4.11) Money market $\frac{M}{PK} - m(k,p) = \frac{I}{K} - \frac{S}{K} + \frac{M}{PK}(\mu-p)$

(5.4.12) $p = h[M/(PK)-m(k,p)]$

(5.4.13) $\dot{M}/M = \mu$

(5.4.14) $\dot{P}/P = p$

As in the earlier models the long run properties of the above model can be analyzed by reducing the system to two differential equations. Substituting for I from (5.4.11) into (5.4.6) and noting that $\dot{K}/K = \dot{k}/k + g$, we get

$$\dot{k}/k = bp/h + S/K - (M/PK)(\mu-p) - (g+\delta)$$

Using (5.4.3), (5.4.4) and (5.4.1) in the above relation and observing from (5.4.12) that $M/PK = p/h + m$, we obtain the following differential equation in k:

(5.4.15) $$\dot{k}/k = bp/h + sf(k)/k - (1-s)(p/h+m)(\mu-p) - (g+\delta)$$

Differentiate (5.4.12) with respect to t.

$$\dot{p} = h(M/PK)(\mu-p-\dot{K}/K) - hm_k\dot{k} - hm_p\dot{p}$$

Solving for p, substituting for M/PK and proceeding as for (5.1.20) we get

(5.4.16) $$\dot{p} = \frac{p + hm}{1 + hm_p}\left[\mu - p - g - \left(\frac{p+hm\eta}{p+hm}\right)\left(\frac{\dot{k}}{k}\right)\right]$$

Equations (5.4.15) and (5.4.16) constitute the basic differential equations of the KW system. Steady state solutions are, as before, obtained by setting $\dot{k} = \dot{p} = 0$. The equilibrium conditions are thus given by

(5.4.17) $$p^* = \mu - g$$

(5.4.18) $$b(\mu-g)/h + sa(k^*) - (1-s)g[(\mu-g)/h+m^*)] - (g+\delta) = 0$$

where $a(k) = f(k)/k$.

The first question to examine is that of monetary neutrality with respect to the rate of change of the money supply. We have,

$$(5.4.19) \qquad \frac{\partial k^*}{\partial \mu} = \frac{-b/h + (1-s)g(1/h+m_p^*)}{sa'(k^*) - (1-s)gm_k^*}$$

The denominator is negative because $a'(k) < 0$ and $m_k > 0$. However, the sign of the numerator is generally ambiguous. Recall that in the neo-classical approach, $\partial k^*/\partial\mu$ was unambiguously positive. This conclusion is no longer valid. The direction of change will also depend on the speed of adjustment (h) and the degree of realization (b) of consumption and investment plans. For instance, if the speed of adjustment is greater than $-1/m_p^*$, that is, when $1/h + m_p^*$ is negative, $\partial k^*/\partial\mu > 0$ regardless of the value of b. Similarly, if $b \geq (1-s)g$ then also $\partial k^*/\partial\mu > 0$ irrespective of the value of h. Therefore for large speeds of adjustment or if investment plans are mostly realized (i.e. b is large) then an increase in the rate of monetary expansion will unambiguously increase the equilibrium capital intensity. If, however, both the adjustment speed and b are small, $\partial k^*/\partial\mu$ can indeed become negative. For example, if $b = 0$ (i.e. consumption plans are fully realized) and $h < -1/m_p^*$ then $\partial k^*/\partial\mu < 0$. As a general result we have the following statement:

$$(5.4.20) \qquad \partial k^*/\partial\mu \gtreqless 0 \quad \text{according as} \quad h(1-s)gm_p^* \lesseqgtr b - (1-s)g$$

It was pointed out earlier that b is a measure of the degree to which savings or investment plans are realized. The higher b the greater the degree to which investment plans are realized. It will therefore be of interest to examine the effects of changes in b on the long run capital intensity. From (5.4.18), we have

$$\frac{\partial k^*}{\partial b} = \frac{\mu/h}{-sa'(k^*) + (1-s)gm_k^*}$$

Since $m_k > 0$ and $a'(k) < 0$, $\partial k^*/\partial b > 0$ which means the greater the degree to which investment plans are realized, the higher the long run capital intensity.

Stability property: To examine the question of stability we need the partial derivatives of $\dot{k}$ and $\dot{p}$ with respect to k and p, evaluated at k*. We have,

$$a_{11}/k^* = (\partial\dot{k}/\partial k)^* = s(k^*f'-f^*)/k^{*2} - (1-s)gm_k^* < 0$$

$$a_{12}/k^* = (\partial\dot{k}/\partial p)^* = b/h + (1-s)(m^*-gm_p^*) + (p^*-g)/h$$

$$a_{21} = \left(\frac{\partial\dot{p}}{\partial k}\right)^* = -\left(\frac{p^*+hm^*\eta^*}{1+hm_p^*}\right)\frac{a_{11}}{k^*}$$

$$a_{22} = \left(\frac{\partial\dot{p}}{\partial p}\right)^* = -\left(\frac{p^*+hm^*\eta^*}{1+hm_p^*}\right)\frac{a_{12}}{k^*} - \left(\frac{p^*+hm^*}{1+hm_p^*}\right)$$

Therefore

$$\frac{a_{22}}{a_{21}} = \frac{a_{12}}{a_{11}} + \left(\frac{p+hm^*}{p+hm^*\eta^*}\right)\frac{k^*}{a_{11}}$$

It follows that

$$\Delta = a_{11}a_{22} - a_{12}a_{21} = -(p^*+hm^*)a_{11}/(1+hm_p^*)$$

Since $m + (p/h) = M/(PK) > 0$, $p^* + hm^* > 0$ which, together with the condition $\eta^* > 0$, implies that $p^* + hm^*\eta^* > 0$. Therefore a necessary condition for stability is given by $a_{11}/[m_p^* + (1/h)] < 0$. Since $a_{11} < 0$, the necessary condition becomes $1+hm_p^* > 0$ or $h < -1/m_p^*$. Thus a necessary condition for stability is that the speed of adjustment in the money market be small, that is, prices must respond slowly to excess demand or supply. Note that as $h \to \infty$ the adjustment tends to be instantaneous (and reduces to the neo-classical case) and the model becomes unstable. In other words, if the prices adjust too quickly to market disequilibrium, the situation becomes destabilizing.

The condition $h < -1/m_p^*$ will not assure stability because it is only necessary. If, in addition, $a_{12} > 0$ then stability will be achieved. It is easy to see from the above expressions that under these two conditions, $a_{11} + a_{22} < 0$ and $\Delta > 0$ and therefore the system is stable. An interesting but somewhat strong sufficient condition to make a_{12} positive is $\mu \geq 2g$, i.e. if the rate of monetary expansion is at least twice the natural rate and the adjustment speed is small then the system will be stable, irrespective of the values of b and s. A much weaker sufficient condition is $\mu \geq 2g - b/(1-s)$ or equivalently, $b \geq (1-s)(2g-\mu)$. If b is large this condition is easily satisfied. For instance even if g = .08 and s = .05, the above inequality will be satisfied if b exceeds .16. For g = .04 and s = .10, b need be larger than only .072.

It is interesting to note that if $h < -1/m_p^*$, $b \geq (1-s)g$ and $g \leq \mu$ then the system is stable and furthermore $\partial k^*/\partial\mu > 0$. On the other hand, if $h < -1/m_p^*$, $b = 0$ and $\mu \geq 2g$ then the system is stable but $\partial k^*/\partial\mu < 0$. Thus widely differing conclusions are possible depending on the values of the parameters b, s, g and μ.

5.5 A Synthesis of Neo-classical and Keynes-Wicksell Models[1]

We now present a synthesis of the two kinds of monetary growth models discussed earlier. In carrying out this synthesis, we eliminate two conceptual drawbacks suffered by the KW model. First, the steady state condition $\mu - g = p^* = h[M^*/P^*K^* - m^*]$ implies that unless $\mu = g$ there will be, even in the long run, a persistent disequilibrium. If, as is often the case, $\mu > g$ there will be a permanent excess demand with individuals continuously frustrated in their desire to buy goods, an obviously undesirable feature in the steady state. Second, the condition (5.4.11) which states that excess demand in the money market equals the excess supply in the goods market is not quite appropriate because the left-hand side refers to the _stock_ of money and its demand whereas the right-hand side represents the _flow_ of goods. The proper specification would be to relate the asset demands in the capital, money and bond markets to their respective supply. This can be achieved by making the simplifying assumption that the bond market is always in equilibrium. In this case we can solve for the money rate of interest as $i = B(k,p,x)$ where $x \equiv M/(PK)$ is real balances per unit of capital. An increase in the capital intensity, _ceteris paribus_, has two effects. First, income rises and hence the demand for bonds goes down when wealth is held constant (be-

---

[1] The presentation in this section is adopted from Fischer [2] and Stein [21, Ch. 5].

cause demand for money will go up). Secondly, an increase in k reduces the yield on capital and therefore through the substitution effect increases the demand for bonds and hence reduces the nominal interest rate. It is assumed that the substitution effect dominates the income effect implying that $\partial B/\partial k < 0$. An increase in real balances will increase the demand for bonds (through wealth effect) and hence reduce their yield, that is $\partial B/\partial x < 0$. An increase in the expected inflation rate will drive up the nominal interest rate and hence $\partial B/\partial p > 0$.

Aside from the above modification, the determination of the price level is also specified differently. In the following synthesized model, we present only the equations that are different from those in Section 5.4.

(5.5.11) $\quad i = B(k,p,x)$

(5.5.12) $\quad \dot{P}/P = p + h[I/K - S/K + (M/PK)(\mu-p)]$

(5.5.14) $\quad \dot{p} = \alpha(\dot{P}/P-p)$

(5.5.15) $\quad x \equiv M/(PK)$

The variable p is now interpreted as the <u>expected</u> rate of price change whereas the <u>actual</u> price change is denoted by $\dot{P}/P$. Equation (5.5.14) is simply the adaptive expectation rule used in Section 5.1. Equation (5.5.12) states that the actual rate of inflation is equal to the expected rate plus a factor proportional to the excess demand in the goods market. It will be seen that persistant excess demand (or supply) will no longer exist in the steady state. From (5.4.6),

$$\dot{K} = b[I - S + (M/P)(\mu-p)] + S - (M/P)(\mu-p) - \delta k$$

Using (5.5.12), (5.5.14), (5.4.3) and (5.4.4) in this we can derive the following differential equation in k.

(5.5.16) $\quad \dot{k}/k = b\dot{p}/(\alpha h) + sf(k)/k - (1-s)x(\mu-p) - (g+\delta)$

Logarithmically differentiating (5.5.15) and using (5.5.14) we get

(5.5.17) $\quad \dot{x}/x = \mu - p - g - \dot{p}/\alpha - \dot{k}/k$

From (5.5.12) and (5.5.14) we obtain

(5.5.18) $\dot{p}/(\alpha h) = I(k,p,i) - sf(k)/k + (1-s)x(\mu-p)$

The system is thus reduced to three basic differential equations. Setting $\dot{k} = \dot{x} = \dot{p} = 0$ for the steady state we have $(\dot{P}/P)^* = p^* = \mu - g$, and the conditions

(5.5.19) $sa(k^*) - (1-s)x^*g - (g+\delta) = 0$

(5.5.20) $I(k^*,p^*,i^*) - sa(k^*) + (1-s)x^*g = 0$

or equivalently,

$$I(k^*,p^*,i^*) - (g+\delta) = 0$$

(5.5.21) $i^* = B(k^*,p^*,x^*)$

It is readily seen that because $(\dot{P}/P)^* = p^*$ in the long run, equation (5.5.12) implies that the disequilibrium disappears in the steady state. To examine the long run impact of an increase in the rate of growth of money supply, differentiate the steady state equations with respect to μ. We get the pair of equations

$$\begin{bmatrix} sa'(k^*) & -g(1-s) \\ (I_k^*+I_i^*B_k^*) & I_i^*B_x^* \end{bmatrix} \begin{pmatrix} \partial k^*/\partial\mu \\ \partial x^*/\partial\mu \end{pmatrix} = \begin{pmatrix} 0 \\ -I_p^*-I_i^*B_p^* \end{pmatrix}$$

The explicit solutions are as follows.

$$\partial k^*/\partial\mu = -g(1-s)(I_p^*+I_i^*B_p^*)/\Delta$$

$$\partial x^*/\partial\mu = -sa'(k^*)(I_p^*+I_i^*B_p^*)/\Delta$$

where

$$\Delta = sa'(k^*)I_i^*B_x^* + g(1-s)(I_k^*+I_i^*B_k^*)$$

Earlier we made the assumptions that $B_k < 0$, $B_x < 0$ and $B_p > 0$. An increase in k will reduce the real yield to capital and hence reduce investment, that is, $I_k < 0$. If the expected rate of price change increases, we can expect investment to rise also and hence $I_p > 0$. If the nominal interest rate rises then bonds are more attractive assets and therefore $I_i < 0$. Even with the above assumptions, the signs of the above derivations are generally ambiguous without additional assumptions regarding the relative magnitudes of some of the terms.

The assumption that the system is stable is also not adequate to remove the ambiguity. Under very restrictive additional assumptions, such as the specification that $I(k,p,i) = n + r + p - i$, that the assets are gross-substitutes, slow adjustment speeds, etc., Fischer and Stein have shown that the neo-classical results $\partial k^*/\partial \mu > 0$ and $\partial x^*/\partial \mu < 0$ hold in this synthesized model also.

5.6 Summary

Monetary growth theory is concerned with the role of monetary policy in a growing economy. Money serves both as a store of value and as a medium of exchange. The presence of a monetary asset offers some choice in the portfolio composition of individuals. Since a part of total savings will be in the form of real balances, capital accumulation will be affected by changes in money supply. Changes in the price level will also affect the rate of accumulation of capital partly through a change in the money rate of interest and partly through a change in the real value of the existing stock of money.

Under Tobin's framework, the introduction of a monetary sector lowers the long run equilibrium capital intensity as compared to a non-monetary economy. Consequently, per capita income is also lowered. However, by setting the saving rate equal to its optimum golden rule value, a monetary economy can attain the same maximum per capita consumption as a "real" economy. If there is a monetary sector, the optimum saving rate will be larger than the equilibrium share of capital and hence larger than the optimum saving rate of a Solow-Swan economy. As long as there is no disutility attached to a higher saving rate, this difference in the optimum saving rates should not matter. In both models, the golden rule real rate of return to capital, net of depreciation, is the same as the natural rate of growth.

If the central banking authority maintains price stability by suitable monetary policies, a unique and stable balanced growth path exists. Along this path the rate of monetary expansion μ must equal the natural rate g. A unique steady state exists even if prices are variable and μ is exogenously controlled. But this situation is generally characterized by saddle point instability. Monetary expansion will not be neutral in the sense that an increase in the rate of growth of money supply will increase long run capital intensity and hence affect all real variables in the system. If $\mu > g$, we have an inflationary situation in which the equilibrium capital intensity and hence per capita output and real wages are higher than in the price stability case ($\mu = g$). The implication is that in order to raise real per capita output the government must pursue an inflationary monetary policy. However, per capita output can be raised to the level of a barter economy only if the rate of monetary expansion and the resulting inflation are so large that demand for money is reduced to zero.

Levhari and Patinkin argue that any rationale for holding money ought to interpret real balances either as a consumer good or as a producer good. Money is a consumer good if it enters into individuals' utility functions. In this case, the opportunity cost of holding money must be included in disposable income just as the opportunity cost of holding a commodity is included in disposable income. The disposable income and hence the consumption function are thus different from Tobin's definition. In an economy in which individuals treat money as a consumer good, it is theoretically possible to attain an equilibrium per capita output higher than in a non-monetary economy. However, it is easy to show that for this result to be empirically feasible the money rate of interest must be unrealistically large.

Another approach adopted by Levhari and Patinkin is to say that individuals derive utility only from commodities and that the they hold money because it enables them to generate more output. For example, the availability of credit enables enterpreneurs to produce more. Under this approach money is treated as a producer good and changes in the money supply will cause shifts in production patterns. The demand for money is determined by marginal conditions in the same way that the demand for capital and labor are determined. The question of monetary neutrality is generally indeterminate in this model. If, however, stability is assumed then an increase in the rate of monetary expansion will increase the equilibrium capital-labor ratio and per capita real cash balances.

When the rate of monetary expansion is exogenous and prices fluctuate to maintain full employment equilibrium, all the neo-classical monetary models exhibit general instability. By introducing an adaptive expectations rule for expected changes in prices, Sidrauski has shown that if individuals are sluggish in adjusting their expectations (that is, have a low speed of adjustment), then Tobin's model is likely to be stable. A similar result may be obtained for the Levhari-Patinkin model also.

The neo-classical money models discussed in the earlier paragraphs have been extended by Stein, Rose, Nagatani, Fischer, etc. to allow for disequilibrium in the markets. This approach, commonly known as the Keynes-Wicksell approach, radically differs from the neo-classical approach in two respects. First, saving and investment are independently determined and hence need not be equal at a given point of time. Second, prices change if and only if there is disequilibrium in the commodity and money markets. If these modifications are made, the direction of change in capital intensity as a result of an increase in the rate of monetary expansion is ambiguous. Widely differing conclusions are now possible.

One of the unhappy conclusions of the Keynes-Wicksell model is the chronic disequilibrium which would persist even in the steady state. Consumers and works would thus be continuously frustrated. Fischer and Stein have synthesized the two approaches into a single model in which this disequilibrium disappears in the long run. However, the indeterminacy of the effect of monetary policy on the long run capital intensity still persists unless strong assumptions are made in which case the neo-classical results hold in the synthesized model also.

REFERENCES

[1] Davidson, Paul: "Money, Portfolio Balance, Capital Accumulation and Economic Growth," Econometrica, April 1968.

[2] Fischer, S.: "Keynes-Wicksell and Neo-Classical Models of Money and Growth," American Economic Review, Dec. 1972, pp. 880-890.

[3] Foley, D. K., and M. Sidrauski: Monetary and Fiscal Policy in a Growing Economy, New York, 1971.

[4] Hadjimichalakis, M.: "Money, Expectations and Dynamics--An Alternative View," International Economic Review, Oct. 1971, pp. 381-401.

[5] Hadjimichalakis, M.: "Equilibrium and Disequilibrium Growth With Money--The Tobin Models," Review of Economic Studies, Oct. 1971, pp. 457-479.

[6] Hahn, F. H.: "On Money and Growth," Journal of Money, Credit and Banking, May 1969, 1, pp. 172-187. (This entire issue is devoted to monetary growth theory.)

[7] Harkness, J.: "The Role of Money in a Simple Growth Model: Comment," American Economic Review, March 1972, 62, pp. 177-179.

[8] Johnson, H. G.: "The Neo-classical One-sector Growth Model: A Geometrical Exposition and Extension to a Monetary Economy," Economica, Aug. 1966.

[9] Levhari, D., and D. Patinkin: "The Role of Money in a Simple Growth Model," American Economic Review, Sept. 1968, 58, pp. 714-753.

[10] Nagatani, K.: "A Monetary Growth Model With Variable Unemployment," Journal of Money, Credit and Banking, May 1969, pp. 188-206.

[11] Niehans, J.: "Efficient Monetary and Fiscal Policies in Balanced Growth," Journal of Money, Credit and Banking, May 1969, 1, pp. 228-251.

[12] Ramanathan, R.: "The Role of Money in a Simple Growth Model: Comment," American Economic Review, March 1972, 62.

[13] Ramanathan, R.: "A General Framework for Analyzing the Stability of Monetary Growth Models," Discussion Paper No. 72-9, UCSD Department of Economics, 1972.

[14] Rose, H.: "Unemployment in a Theory of Growth," International Economic Review, September 1966, 7, pp. 260-282.

[15] Shell, K., M. Sidrauski and J. E. Stiglitz: "Capital Gains, Income and Saving," Review of Economic Studies, Jan. 1969.

[16] Sidrauski, M.: "Rational Choice and Patterns of Growth in a Monetary Economy," American Economic Review (Proceedings), May 1967.

[17] Sidrauski, M.: "Inflation and Economic Growth," Journal of Political Economy, Dec. 1967, 75, pp. 796-810.

[18] Stein, J. L.: "Money and Capacity Growth," Journal of Political Economy, Oct. 1966, 74, pp. 451-465.

[19] Stein, J. L.: "Neoclassical and Keynes-Wicksell Monetary Growth Models," Journal of Money, Credit and Banking, May 1969, 1, pp. 153-171.

[20] Stein, J. L.: "Monetary Growth Theory in Perspective," American Economic Review, March 1970, 60, pp. 85-106.

[21] Stein, J. L.: Money and Capacity Growth, Columbia University Press, 1971.

[22] Teigen, R.: "Demand and Supply Functions in the United States: Some Structural Estimates," Econometrica, Oct. 1964, 32, pp. 476-509.

[23] Tobin, J.: "Money and Economic Growth," Econometrica, Oct. 1965, 33, pp. 671-684.

[24] Villanneva, D. P.: "A Neo-Classical Monetary Growth Model With Independent Saving and Investment Functions," Journal of Money, Credit and Banking, Nov. 1971, pp. 750-759.

EXERCISES

5.1 Verify the sensitivity table 5.1. Are the results different for the LP model?

5.2 Redo the analysis of the money models assuming that of the total money supply M, a fixed proportion is outside money and the remainder is inside money.

5.3 For the Sidrauski model with price expectations, obtain the sensitivities of changes in the expectations coefficient α.

5.4 Using equation (5.2.15a) and the conditions $\beta' < 0$, $\varepsilon < 1$ and $f'' < 0$, show that $\partial s_1/\partial k < 0$.

5.5 Prove the result in exercise 5.4 under the assumption that the saving rate $s = s(r,p)$ where $s_r < 0$ and $s_p < 0$. Show also that the sign of $\partial s_1/\partial p$ is ambiguous.

5.6 Show that the LP model with flexible prices is unstable even under the assumption that $s = s(r,p)$. Is this result the same for the Tobin model also?

5.7 How would the conclusions of the money models be affected if consumption was proportional to wealth where the proportionality factor depends on k and p?

5.8 Suppose workers save a proportion s_w out of their disposable income, firms save a proportion s_c of their income and let workers hold a fixed proportion of the total money supply. Analyze the monetary models of Tobin, Levhari, Patinkin and Sidrauski under the above saving behavior.

5.9 Assume that of the total money supply M, a portion M_1 is treated as a consumer good and the remainder M_2 is treated a as a producer good. Construct a monetary growth model incorporating the modification and analyze its implications.

5.10 The definition of disposable income used in all the models was that $Y_d = Y + (\mu-p)M/P$. No allowance is thus made for loss in income due to depreciation. Redo the models under the modification that disposable income is given by $Y + (\mu-p)M/P - \delta K$.

CHAPTER 6

NEO-CLASSICAL MODELS WITH TWO INCOME CLASSES

In this chapter we relax the neo-classical assumption that the aggregate saving ratio is a constant and treat the two income groups separately. The classical savings function assumes that wage earners do not save and that capital owners (we will call them firms for simplicity) do not consume but reinvest all their income. A more general assumption adopted by Kaldor [4] and followed up by Pasinetti [6] and others, is to assume that wage earners save a proportion s_w and that firms save a different proportion s_c of their respective incomes.[1] We thus have two classes of income receivers, workers and firms, receiving different incomes and saving different proportions of their incomes. Several studies have estimated short run consumption functions with cross-section data and shown that firms save on average a higher proportion of their income than workers at the same level of income.[2] Firms have strong needs for investment funds which are expected to yield high returns. They therefore plow back a good part of profits into the business which results in a higher saving-income ratio. While the empirical results are based on short run consumption functions, the motives for additional saving by entrepreneurs are powerful even in the long run. It is therefore of considerable interest to study growth models which assume different saving rates for the two classes of income receivers.

We now analyze the Solow-Swan model with this more general assumption about saving behavior. Money markets are first excluded but are introduced in Section 6.3. All the other assumptions are the same as before. Even under this simple extension, the results are not straightforward. It will be seen that the long run behavior of the model crucially depends on the values of the saving rates.

---

[1] Kaldor and Pasinetti did not use the marginal productivity assumption in their analysis, nor did they assume that investment is determined by saving behavior rather than independently. Their approach is discussed in the next chapter.

[2] For a survey of these studies see Ferber [3].

6.1 Different Saving Propensities for Workers and Firms

The model consists of the following self-explanatory equations:

$$Y = NF(k)$$
$$k \equiv K/N$$
$$N = Le^{\lambda t}$$
$$\dot{L}/L = n$$
$$\dot{K} = S - \delta K$$

There are five equations in the six unknowns Y,K,N,L,S and k. In the Solow-Swan model the system was completed by adding the savings relation $S = sY$. But since wage earners and entrepreneurs save at different rates, the expression for saving will be different in this model. The total income of firms (rental bill) is $Kf'(k)$. Since they save a proportion s_c of this, their saving is $s_c KF'(k)$. Workers receive the balance $Y-Kf'$ and save s_w of it. Thus their saving is $(Y-Kf')s_w$ giving total saving as

$$S = s_c Kf' + (Y-Kf')s_w$$

Capital formation, which is the same as net investment, is therefore

$$\dot{K} = S - \delta K = s_c Kf' + (Y-Kf')s_w - \delta K$$

Dividing by K we obtain the rate of growth of capital stock (warranted rate) as

$$\dot{K}/K = \phi(k) \equiv s_c f' + s_w(Y/K-f') - \delta$$

Using the relation $Y/K = f(k)/k$ and rearranging the terms, this becomes

(6.1.1) $$\dot{K}/K = \phi(k) \equiv s_w f/k + (s_c-s_w)f' - \delta$$

The above equation can also be written as follows:

(6.1.2) $$\dot{K}/K = s(k)f(k)/k - \delta \equiv \phi(k)$$

where

(6.1.3) $$s(k) = s_c \pi(k) + s_w[1-\pi(k)]$$

Equation (6.1.2) is similar to the one obtained in the Solow-Swan model but the overall saving ratio is no longer a constant but a function of the capital-labor ratio. Except in very special cases, s(k) will be strictly greater than zero but less than 1 (see exercise 6.1). Therefore the behavior of $\phi(k)$ at 0 and ∞ is the same as that of $f(k)/k$ and $\phi(0) = \infty$, $\phi(\infty) = -\delta$. By the continuity of $\phi(k)$, a k^* must exist such that $\phi(k^*) = g \equiv \lambda + n$. The uniqueness of the steady state depends on the relative magnitudes of s_c and s_w.

Case 1: $s_c \geq s_w$: If, in addition to the neo-classical conditions, the saving income ratio of firms is at least as great as that of workers, then there exists a unique solution which is also stable. Since $s_c = s_w$ is the Solow-Swan case, we need consider only $s_c > s_w$. As pointed out earlier, there is substantial empirical justification for this assumption. Differentiating $\phi(k)$ we get

$$(6.1.4) \qquad \phi'(k) = s_w(kf'-f)/k^2 + (s_c-s_w)f'' < 0$$

because $f'' < 0$ and $f-kf' > 0$. Therefore $\phi(k)$ is monotonically decreasing and hence a unique solution exists. The system is also stable because $\phi'(k^*) < 0$. Thus the neo-classical conditions together with the assumption $s_c \geq s_w$ generate a unique and stable steady-state path.

Case 2: $s_c < s_w$: If wage earners save a larger proportion of income than firms (empirically this is not a plausible case), the neo-classical conditions are no longer adequate to guarantee uniqueness. The sign of $\phi'(k)$ is ambiguous since the second term of (6.1.4) is now positive while the first term is still negative. Multiple equilibria are now possible as in Figure 3.2. Those solustions for which $\phi'(k^*) < 0$ will be stable.

If, in addition to the condition that $s_c < s_w$, the elasticity of substitution (σ) is not less than one, then a unique stable solution exists. If $\sigma = 1$, the share of capital is constant and therefore s is a constant. Since $f(k)/k$ is downward sloping, so is $\phi(k)$ and hence uniqueness is assured. If σ is greater than 1, then an increase in k increases capital's share, that is, the income distribution moves in favor of firms (Theorem 2.2). When $s_c < s_w$ firms consume a greater proportion of their income which is now higher. This means the overall saving rate will decline as k increases.[1] $\phi(k)$ is therefore a downward sloping curve. Uniqueness is thus assured in this case also. If $\sigma < 1$, $\pi(k)$ decreases as k increases and the overall saving rate will rise. But since $f(k)/k$ declines, the net effect on the warranted rate of growth is ambiguous. More than one solution is possible if $s_c < s_w$ and the elasticity of substitution between capital and labor is less than one.

An increase in the saving rate of either firms or workers would raise aggregate saving and therefore increase net investment. We would therefore expect the long run capital intensity to increase. That this is so is easily seen from (6.1.1). An increase in s_c or s_w will increase the warranted rate. The $\phi(k)$ curve (assumed monotonic) would shift upwards and therefore intersect the straight line g at a higher capital intensity. Similarly, an increase in the rate of growth of labor force or the rate of depreciation would lower the steady state capital intensity. These results are very similar to those of the Solow-Swan model.

6.2 Wage Earners Receiving Dividend Income Also

In the analysis of the previous section, the saving-income ratio was assumed different for workers and firms. In particular, workers were assumed to save a positive proportion of their income. However, all the returns from capital went to the firms. This gives rise to some conceptual difficulties. If workers save a positive amount, the resulting increase in capital should obviously belong to workers and any returns on their capital (call them dividends for convenience) should go to them. Since this was not done in the last section, the validity of the analysis is

---

[1]Another way of seeing this is to note that $s'(k) = (s_c - s_w)\pi'(k)$. If $\sigma > 1$, then $\pi'(k) > 0$. This implies that when $s_c < s_w$, $s'(k) < 0$.

questionable. This point was originally pointed out by Pasinetti [6]. He argued that a more realistic assumption would be to let workers have a share in the capital stock and receive any income generated from it. Thus there will be, as before, two classes of income receivers: workers and firms. Firms own K_c of the capital stock, receive dividend income amounting to $K_c r$ and save a proportion s_c of this. Workers own K_w of the capital stock, receive both wage and dividend income amounting to $Y-K_c r$ (total income less that paid to firms) and save at the rate s_w.

In this section we analyze the long run properties of a model which incorporates the Pasinetti saving behavior described above. Samuelson and Modigliani [9] have carried out a detailed analysis of the model but the approach taken here is somewhat different.[1] The structural equations of the model and the main results are described in Section 6.2.1. The complete details of the analysis are presented in 6.2.2.

6.2.1 The Pasinetti-Samuelson-Modigliani Model

The production function is the same as before. Therefore

(6.2.1) $$Y = Nf(k)$$

(6.2.2) $$k \equiv K/N$$

The following equations refer to the commodity market:

(6.2.3) $$S = S_c + S_w$$

(6.2.4) $$S_c = s_c K_c r$$

(6.2.5) $$S_w = s_w(Y-K_c r)$$

S, S_c and S_w are respectively, total saving, saving of owners of capital and saving of workers. K_c is the amount of capital owned by firms, and r is the rate of return to capital. For simplicity, we will ignore depreciation in the analysis. The capital market equations are then given by:

(6.2.6) $$\dot{K}_c = S_c$$

---

[1] The presentation here follows that of Conlisk and Ramanathan [2].

(6.2.7) $\dot{K}_w = S_w$

(6.2.8) $K = K_c + K_w$

(6.2.9) $r = f'(k)$

(6.2.10) $x \equiv K_c/K \qquad 0 \leq x \leq 1$

K_w is the stock of capital owned by workers, K is total capital, and x is the proportion of capital held by firms. Equations (6.2.6) and (6.2.7) state that the saving of a given class goes into increasing its stock of capital. The labor market equations are the same as encountered previously.

(6.2.11) $L = L_o e^{nt}$

(6.2.12) $w = [f(k) - kf'(k)]e^{\lambda t}$

(6.2.13) $N = Le^{\lambda t}$ = effective-labor

The model consists of 13 simultaneous equations in the 13 endogenous variables $Y,N,K,L,S,S_c,S_w,K_c,K_w,k,x,w$ and r. The known parameters of the system are λ,n,s_c and s_w.

<u>Basic differential equations</u>: Unlike the model of the previous section, it is not possible to reduce the structural equations to a first order differential equation in the capital effective-labor ratio. However, the system can be reduced to two first order differential equations. Several choices of variables are possible for this purpose.[1] Samuelson and Modigliani analyzed the system in terms of the three variables k, $k_c = K_c/N$ and $k_w = K_w/N$. It is more convenient to use k and $x = K_c/K$, and additional results can be obtained. Equations (6.2.4), (6.2.5), (6.2.6), (6.2.7) and (6.2.9) imply that

(6.2.14) $\dot{K}_c = s_c K_c f'(k)$

(6.2.15) $\dot{K}_w = s_w(Y-K_c f')$

Differentiating (6.2.8) with respect to t and using (6.2.14) and (6.2.15), we get $\dot{K} = s_c K_c f' + s_w(Y-K_c f')$. Dividing both sides by

---

[1]For a discussion of the choice of variables see Conlisk and Ramanathan [2].

K and using the relations (6.2.10), (6.2.1) and (6.2.2) we obtain the following:

(6.2.16) $$\dot{K}/K = (s_c - s_w)xf'(k) + s_w f(k)/k$$

Logarithmic differentiation of (6.2.2) gives $\dot{k}/k = \dot{K}/K - g$. It follows from this and (6.2.16) that

(6.2.17) $$\dot{k}/k \equiv \phi(k,x) = (s_c - s_w)xf'(k) + s_w f(k)/k - g$$

Given the capital intensity and the proportion of capital owned by firms, the rate of change of the capital intensity is given by the above equation. To obtain a similar equation in x, logarithmically differentiate (6.2.10) with respect to t. We then have, $\dot{x}/x = \dot{K}_c/K_c - \dot{K}/K$. Using (6.2.14) and (6.2.16) we get

(6.2.18) $$\dot{x}/x \equiv \psi(k,x) = s_c f' - [(s_c - s_w)xf' + s_w f/k]$$

Relations (6.2.17) and (6.2.18) are the basic equations of motion of the system. We know that in the steady state $\dot{k} = 0$. Setting (6.2.17) to zero and solving the resulting equation explicitly for x we obtain (for $s_c \neq s_w$)

(6.2.19) $$x = M(k) = \frac{g - s_w f/k}{(s_c - s_w)f'}$$

For a given value of k, the function M(k) determines the unique value of x such that $\dot{k} = 0$, that is, there is no tendency for k to change. But this situation may not prevail forever because of (6.2.18).

We will now show that in the steady state $\dot{x} = 0$, that is, x must also be constant. The general definition of a steady state is that all the variables in the system grow exponentially at constant rates, some of which may be zero. Under this definition, $\dot{K}_c/K_c = g_c$ and $\dot{K}_w/K_w = g_w$ where g_c and g_w are constants. It follows that $\dot{K} = K_c g_c + K_w g_w$. Dividing by K and setting $x = K_c/K$, we get $\dot{K}/K = xg_c + (1-x)g_w$. In the steady state $\dot{K}/K$ is a constant <u>for all t</u>. Since g_c and g_w are constant, x must also be constant as otherwise $\dot{K}/K$ will not be constant. Therefore $\dot{x} = 0$ in the steady state. Setting (6.2.18) to zero and solving for x we obtain the relation

$$(6.2.20) \qquad x = N(k) = \frac{s_c f' - s_w f/k}{(s_c - s_w) f'} = \frac{s_c \pi - s_w}{(s_c - s_w)\pi}$$

where $\pi = kf'/f$, the share of capital in output. For a given capital intensity, the N(k) curve gives the unique value of x such that $\dot{x} = 0$. At a point of intersection of these two curves, $\dot{x} = \dot{k} = 0$. Thus a point of intersection, call it (k^*, x^*), corresponds to a steady state. "Will the two curves intersect at a unique point and if so, is the intersection attainable? Will the system spontaneously move towards (k^*, x^*)?" To answer these questions a considerable amount of algebraic manipulation is required. The details of the analysis are given in the next section. The rest of this section summarizes the results.

The graphs of the two curves M(k) and N(k) intersect at a unique point determined by the following equations:

$$(6.2.21) \qquad s_c f'(k^*) = g$$

$$(6.2.22) \qquad x^* = \frac{s_c \pi(k^*) - s_w}{(s_c - s_w)\pi(k^*)}$$

The first equation is a straightforward manipulation of the equilibrium condition $M(k^*) = N(k^*)$ and under the neo-classical conditions, determines k^* uniquely. The second equation which gives x^* uniquely as a function of k^* is simply the definition of the equilibrium condition $x^* = N(k^*)$. But it is not certain whether x^* is attainable. Since x is the ratio of firms' capital to the total stock of capital, it must lie between 0 and 1. But there is no guarantee that x^* will also lie in that interval. The graphs of M(k) and N(k) will either intersect in the positive first quadrant with $0 < x^* < 1$ or not. Call the first the Passinetti Case and the second the Solow-Swan Case.

Pasinetti case: In this case $0 < x^* < 1$. It is easily shown that the condition $x^* < 1$ implies that $s_c > s_w$.[1] This, together with the condition $x^* > 0$ implies that $s_c \pi(k^*) > s_w$ as may be seen

[1] From (6.2.22), $1-x^* = s_w(1-\pi)/(s_c-s_w)\pi$. Since the numerator is positive, the denominator must also be positive to have $x^* < 1$.

from (6.2.22). This is a necessary condition for the existence of the Pasinetti case. But, as Samuelson and Modigliani point out, its empirical plausibility is doubtful. For example, if the share of capital is one-fourth and firms save 20 percent of their income, then the above inequality will not be satisfied for s_w any higher than .05, a low figure. Figure 6.1 presents a range of reasonable values for s_c and s_w. The region ABCD represents the range $.1 \leq s_c \leq .33$, $.05 \leq s_w \leq .15$. The darkened area gives the Pasinetti case for $\pi \leq .25$. It is evident that only a very small set of combinations of s_c, s_w and π give rise to the Pasinetti case.

If the condition $s_c\pi(k^*) > s_w$ is satisfied, a unique steady state with positive values of both k* and x* will exist. "Will the system move towards this equilibrium if it is initially not there?" The answer is that, provided the elasticity of substitution between capital and labor is not less than 1, the system is globally stable. If $\sigma < 1$, only local stability is assured. These results are proved in the next section.

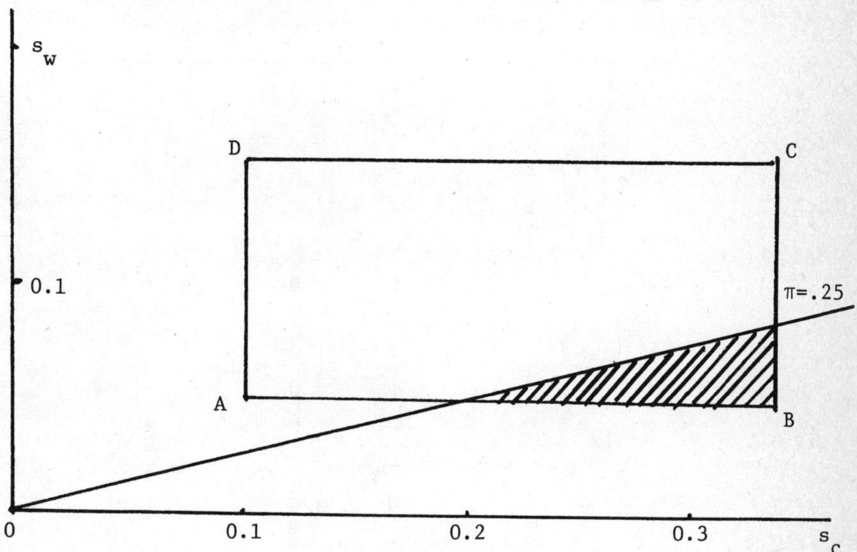

Figure 6.1

The effects on k^* and x^* of changes in the parameters g, s_c and s_w may be analyzed by partially differentiating (6.2.21) and (6.2.22) with respect to each parameter and solving for the corresponding partial derivatives. The sensitivity table thus obtained is presented in Table 6.1 (see exercise 6.3). It is seen from the sensitivity table that workers' propensity to save affects only the proportion of total capital stock held by them. Moreover, the equilibrium rate of return to capital is independent of s_w and also, as we shall see, the form of the production function. Samuelson and Modigliani called this result the Passinetti Paradox. A careful look at equation (6.2.14) shows that the above result is a consequence of our basic assumptions rather than any special mechanism. From (6.2.14), $\dot{K}_c/K_c = s_c r$. In steady state $\dot{K}_c/K_c = \dot{K}/K = g$. Therefore $r = g/s_c$. Since we have not made use of the other equations, this result is perfectly general and is valid for any kind of production possibilities.

Table 6.1: Sensitivities of the Pasinetti Case

		s_c	s_w	g
k^*		+	0	-
x^* when	$\sigma < 1$	?	-	+
	$\sigma = 1$	+	-	0
	$\sigma > 1$	+	-	-
$(\dot{Y}/Y)^*$		0	0	+
$(\dot{y}/y)^*$		0	0	+ if λ increases
$(Y/L)^*$		+	0	-
w^*		+	0	-
r^*		-	0	+
$\pi(k^*)$ when	$\sigma < 1$	-	0	+
	$\sigma = 1$	0	0	0
	$\sigma > 1$	+	0	-

By proceeding exactly as in the Solow-Swan model, we can also obtain the golden rule condition. Although per capita consumption depends on k, since k* is independent of s_w, s_w is useless as an instrument to maximize long run per capita consumption. Maximization of per capita consumption with respect to s_c gives the condition $f'(k^*) = g$. From this and (6.2.21) it is evident that $s_c = 1$. In other words, regardless of the value of s_w, the golden rule path will be attained if firms save all of their income.

Solow-Swan case: This case arises when the condition $s_c \pi(k^*) > s_w$ is not satisfied and is so called because the economy will ultimately behave as in the Solow-Swan model. Since the proportion of capital stock (x) held by firms cannot be negative or exceed 1, the intersection point (k^*, x^*) cannot be attained in the Solow-Swan case. "Where will the economy go in such a situation?" The answer is symmetric (or dual) to the Pasinetti paradox and is stated below:

Dual result: If $s_c \pi(k^*) \leq s_w$ where $s_c f'(k^*) = g$, then k^{**} given by the equation $s_w f(k^{**})/k^{**} = g$ is the unique and globally stable steady-state value of the capital effective-labor ratio. k^{**} and hence $(Y/K)^{**}$, y^{**}, w^{**}, r^{**} and $\pi(k^{**})$ are all now independent of s_c. The average product of capital, $(Y/K)^{**}$, is also independent of the form of the production function. In the long run $x \to 0$, all the capital stock will be owned by one group and we revert to the Solow-Swan world. It is interesting to note that it is the workers who will ultimately own all the capital (Marxism in reverse!). The above results are independent of the elasticity of substitution between capital and labor.

Since k^{**} is independent of s_c, s_c is ineffective as an instrument in attaining the golden rule path. Maximizing per capita consumption in the steady state with respect to s_w we obtain the condition $f'(k^{**}) = g$. Since $g = s_w f(k^{**})/k^{**}$, the optimum saving rate for workers is given by

$$s_w = k^{**}f'(k^{**})/k^{**} = \pi(k^{**})$$

Thus, for golden rule, the workers' saving rate must be the same as the equilibrium share of capital. Firms' saving rate may take any value. In both the Pasinetti and Solow-Swan cases, the golden rule rate of return to capital equals the natural rate g.

6.2.2 Stability Properties of the Model[1]

In this section we carry out a detailed analysis of the long run behavior of the Pasinetti model. As a first step it is necessary to obtain the derivatives of the functions M(k) and N(k). These derivatives are:

$$M'(k) = \frac{s_w f'(f-kf')/k^2 - f''(g-s_w f/k)}{(s_c-s_w)f'^2} \tag{6.2.23}$$

$$N'(k) = \frac{s_w f'(f-kf')/k^2 + f'' s_w f/k}{(s_c-s_w)f'^2} \tag{6.2.24}$$

using the first part of (6.2.20) and

$$N'(k) = \frac{s_w \pi'(k)}{(s_c-s_w)\pi^2} \tag{6.2.25}$$

using the second part of (6.2.20).

Pasinetti case: It was seen earlier that this case arises when $s_c > s_w$ and $s_c\pi(k^*) > s_w$. From the first condition it follows that the denominators of M'(k) and N'(k) are positive. Under the neo-classical conditions we know that $f-kf' > 0$. Therefore the first term of the numerator of M'(k) is positive. Also $x \geq 0$ and therefore M(k) is defined only for the values of k for which $g > s_w f/k$. From this and the condition $f'' < 0$ it follows that $M'(k) > 0$. A comparison of M'(k) and N'(k) shows that since $f'' < 0$, $M'(k) > N'(k)$. Also using equation (2.9) of Chapter 2, we obtain

$$N'(k) \gtreqless 0 \quad \text{according as } \sigma \gtreqless 1$$

---

[1]This section may be omitted by anyone not interested in the details of the analysis.

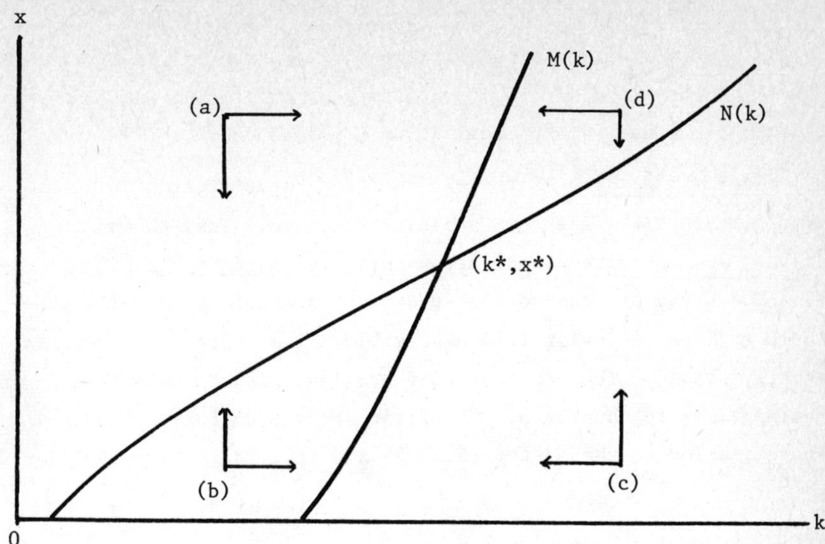

Figure 6.2

Case 1: $\sigma \geq 1$: If the elasticity of substitution between capital and labor is greater than one (the conclusions are the same for $\sigma = 1$) the above slope conditions imply that M(k) and N(k) will graph as in Figure 6.2.

In order to find out which way the economic system will move from a non-equilibrium position, we need to determine the directions of movement of k and x. To examine this first obtain the partial derivative $\partial\dot{k}/\partial x$ at a point along the M(k) curve.[1] From (6.2.17), $\dot{k} = k\phi(k,x)$ and therefore $\partial\dot{k}/\partial x = k\phi_x + \phi = k\phi_x$, because $\phi = 0$ along the M(k) curve. We have $\phi_x = (s_c - s_w)f' > 0$. Therefore above and to the left of M(k), k will tend to increase. The directional arrows drawn parallel to the k-axis in regions (a) and (b) in Figure 6.2 reflect this result. Below M(k) we have the opposite result. In a similar manner, from (6.2.18), $\partial\dot{x}/\partial x = x\psi_x = -x(s_c - s_w)f' < 0$. The directional arrows for x implied by

[1] See the section on phase diagrams and the example in the Appendix to Chapter 3.

this are also presented in Figure 6.2. The phase diagram demonstrates conclusively the global stability of the (k*,x*) equilibrium. To summarize, in the Pasinetti case there is a unique globally stable steady state equilibrium provided $\sigma \geq 1$.

<u>Case 2: $\sigma < 1$</u>: If the elasticity of substitution is less than 1, then N(k) is a downward sloping curve. Thus the phase diagram and the directional arrows will be as in Figure 6.3.

The phase diagram no longer demonstrates global stability because cyclical behavior is now possible. The system, however, is locally stable. The procedure for proving this was described in the Appendix to Chapter 3. The first step is to form a linear approximation to the system (6.2.17) and (6.2.18). This is given by:

$$\begin{aligned} \dot{k} &= b_1 + a_{11}k + a_{12}x \\ \dot{x} &= b_2 + a_{21}k + a_{22}x \end{aligned} \tag{6.2.26}$$

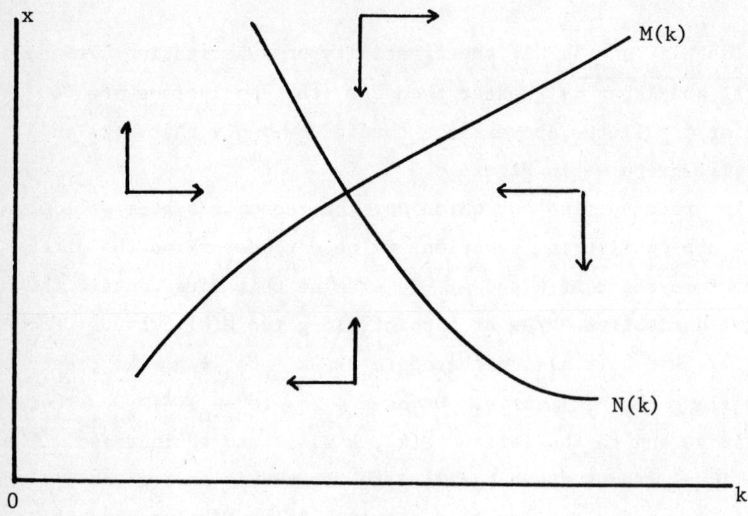

Figure 6.3

where a_{ij}'s are the partial derivatives of $\dot{k}$ and $\dot{x}$ evaluated at (k^*,x^*). The differential equations (6.2.17) and (6.2.18) may be rewritten as follows:

$$\dot{k} = k\phi(k,x) \quad \text{and} \quad \dot{x} = x\psi(k,x)$$

$$a_{11} = \left(\frac{\partial\dot{k}}{\partial k}\right)^* = k^*\phi_k^* + \phi^* = k^*\phi_k^*$$

because the second term is zero at (k^*,x^*).

$$a_{11} = k^*[(s_c-s_w)x^*f'' + s_w(k^*f'-f)/k^{*2}] < 0$$

because $s_c > s_w$, $f'' < 0$ and $f-k^*f' > 0$.

$$a_{12} = \left(\frac{\partial\dot{k}}{\partial x}\right)^* = k^*\phi_x^* = k^*(s_c-s_w)f' > 0$$

$$a_{21} = \left(\frac{\partial\dot{x}}{\partial k}\right)^* = x^*\psi_k^*$$

$$= x^*[s_cf'' - (s_c-s_w)x^*f'' - s_w(k^*f'-f)/k^{*2}]$$

$$a_{22} = \left(\frac{\partial\dot{x}}{\partial x}\right)^* = \psi^* + x^*\psi_x^* = x^*\psi_x^*$$

because the first term is zero at (k^*,x^*)

$$= -\ x^*(s_c-s_w)f' < 0$$

From Theorem A.4 the necessary and sufficient condition that a solution to (6.2.26) will approach (k^*,x^*) as $t \to \infty$ is that $a_{11} + a_{22} < 0$ and $a_{11}a_{22} - a_{12}a_{21} > 0$. It is easy to see that $a_{11} < 0$, $a_{22} < 0$ and hence $a_{11} + a_{22} < 0$. Also,

$$a_{11}a_{22} - a_{12}a_{21} = -k^*x^*(s_c-s_w)f's_cf'' > 0$$

Therefore the system given by (6.2.17) and (6.2.18) is locally stable.

In the above case ($\sigma < 1$) there is a unique steady state which is locally stable but its global stability is not assured. It should be noted from this that uniqueness and local stability need not imply global stability.

Solow-Swan case: This case arises when the condition $s_c\pi(k^*) > s_w$ is not satisfied. There are two sub-cases: (1) $s_c > s_w$ and

(2) $s_c \leq s_w$. Only case (1) is considered here. See exercise 6.5 for hints on case (2).

$s_c > s_w$: Let k** be the capital intensity satisfying the following relation:

$$s_w f(k^{**})/k^{**} = g \tag{6.2.27}$$

The M(k) curve intersects the k-axis at k**. To the right of k**, $g > s_w f/k$ and from (6.2.23) M'(k) is positive. Hence M(k) is upward sloping starting from k**. Because $s_c > s_w$ and $s_c \pi(k^*) \leq s_w$ for this case, $x^* \leq 0$ as may be seen from (6.2.22). This means that the curves M(k) and N(k) intersect below the k-axis (the conclusions are the same for $x^* = 0$). Also, $M'(k) > N'(k)$ to the right of k**. But the N(k) curve may be upward or downward sloping depending on the elasticity of substitution between capital and labor. The three possibilities are shown in Figure 6.4. The directional arrows are derived in the manner indicated earlier.

The phase diagram demonstrates that from any initial position, $k \to k^{**}$. Thus k** is the globally stable long run capital intensity. All the capital is ultimately owned by one of the two classes and we are back in the Solow-Swan world. By proceeding similarly, the above result can be established for case (2) also (see exercise 6.5). Thus, in the Solow-Swan case, all diagrams demonstrated conclusively the global stability of k** with $x \to 0$.

6.3 The Pasinetti Paradox in a Two-Class Monetary Growth Model[1]

In this section we extend the two-class model of economic growth by incorporating a monetary sector (see Ramanathan [8]). The introduction of a monetary asset that competes with a capital asset substantially alters not only the behavioral characteristics of an economic system but the long-run implications as well. For instance, the standard two-class model with capital owners (or firms) and workers (or households), the proportion of capital held by each group is endogenously determined. If a monetary asset exists, then firms and households will not only save different pro-

[1] A condensed version of this section appeared in Ramanathan [8].

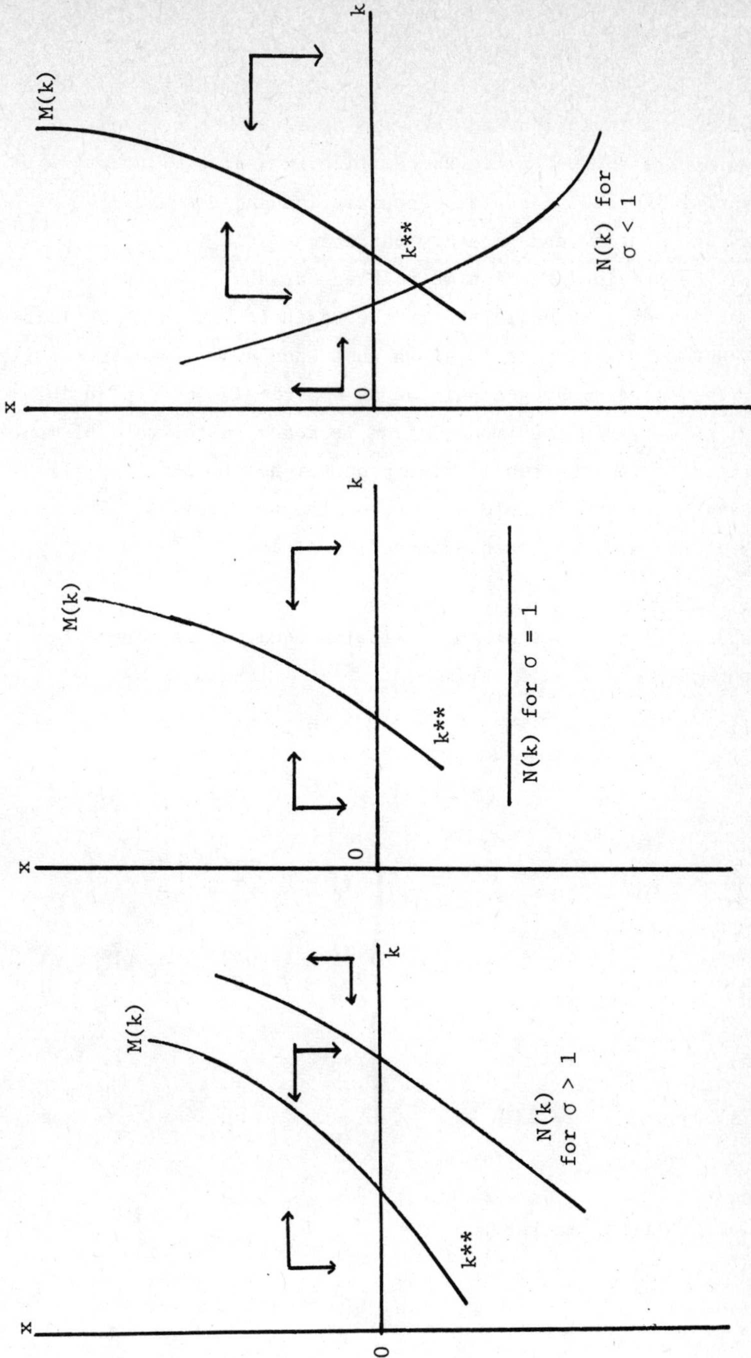

Figure 6.4

portions of their respective incomes and earn dividend income on capital assets but also have different demands for money. The two groups will thus respond differently in terms of money demand to changes in the inflation rate or rate of return to capital. This in turn alters the portfolio composition in a dissimilar way with substantial impacts on capital accumulation and the balanced growth path of real and monetary variables.

In the previous section we pointed out that the empirical plausibility of the condition for the Pasinetti Paradox is limited. In the present section it is shown that when a monetary sector is added, the corresponding condition is empirically more plausible. We also investigate the impact of an increase in the rate of monetary expansion on the equilibrium proportions of total capital stock and money supply held by each of the two classes. The stability of the model is then examined.

6.3.1 The Model

The model consists of the following equations arranged by markets:

Production function

$$Y = Lf(k) \tag{6.3.1}$$

$$k = K/L \tag{6.3.2}$$

Goods market

$$Y_c = K_c r + \frac{M_c}{P}\left(\frac{\dot{M}_c}{M_c} - \pi\right) \tag{6.3.3}$$

$$Y_w = Y - K_c r + \frac{M_w}{P}\left(\frac{\dot{M}_w}{M_w} - \pi\right) \tag{6.3.4}$$

$$S_c = s_c Y_c \tag{6.3.5}$$

$$S_w = s_w Y_w \tag{6.3.6}$$

Labor market

$$\dot{L}/L = n \tag{6.3.7}$$

$$w = f(k) - kf'(k) \tag{6.3.8}$$

Capital market

$$K = K_c + K_w \tag{6.3.9}$$

$$x = K_c/K \tag{6.3.10}$$

$$r = f'(k) \tag{6.3.11}$$

$$\dot{K}_c = S_c - \frac{M_c}{P}\left(\frac{\dot{M}_c}{M_c} - \pi\right) \tag{6.3.12}$$

$$\dot{K}_w = S_w - \frac{M_w}{P}\left(\frac{\dot{M}_w}{M_w} - \pi\right) \tag{6.3.13}$$

Money market

$$\dot{M}/M = \mu \tag{6.3.14}$$

$$\dot{P}/P = \pi \tag{6.3.15}$$

$$M = M_c + M_w \tag{6.3.16}$$

$$z = M_c/M \tag{6.3.17}$$

$$M_c/(PK_c) = \alpha(k,\pi) \tag{6.3.18}$$

$$M_w/(PK_w) = \beta(k,\pi) \tag{6.3.19}$$

As the demand for real balances will be different for each of the two classes, $\alpha \not\equiv \beta$ in equations (6.3.10) and (6.3.11). Because of the presence of a monetary sector, the incomes of the two classes (equations (6.3.3) and (6.3.4) must include the respective shares of the real value of new monetary transfer payments ($\dot{M}/P$) less the proportional loss of current monetary holdings through inflation ($M\pi/P$). Similarly, capital accumulation of each class is given by savings less the above net change in the real value of money balances. The proportion of wealth held in the form of real balances will be a decreasing function of the rate of inflation. Thus $\alpha_\pi < 0$ and $\beta_\pi < 0$, the suffixes denoting the partial derivatives wherever unambiguous. An increase in the capital-labor ratio, _cateris paribus_, reduces the yield on capital and also increases income and hence would increase the demand for money. Therefore, α_k and β_k will both be positive. Following the standard two-class model, it is assumed that firms save a fixed fraction s_c ($0 < s_c < 1$) of their disposable income and that the saving rate for workers is s_w ($0 < s_w \leq s_c$). Equations (6.3.1) through (6.3.19) completely determine the time paths of the nineteen endogenous variables, Y, Y_c, Y_w, L, K, K_c, K_w, S_c, S_w, M, M_c, M_w, P, k, π, w, r, x and z.

6.3.2 Basic Differential Equations

The above system can be reduced to four differential equations in the variables k, x, π and z. Differentiating (6.3.17) logarithmically with respect to t we get

$$\dot{M}_c/M_c = \mu + \dot{z}/z \tag{6.3.20}$$

From this and (6.3.16),

$$\dot{M}_w/M_w = \mu - \dot{z}/(1-z) \tag{6.3.21}$$

In equation (6.3.12) substitute for S_c from (6.3.5), $\dot{M}_c/M_c$ from (6.3.20) and use (6.3.3) to give

$$\dot{K}_c = s_cK_cf'(k) - (1-s_c)(M_c/P)(\mu-\pi+\dot{z}/z) \tag{6.3.12a}$$

Proceeding similarly,

$$\dot{K}_w = s_wLf(k) - s_wK_cf'(k) - (1-s_w)\frac{M_w}{P}\left(\mu - \pi - \frac{\dot{z}}{1-z}\right) \tag{6.3.13a}$$

Thus

$$\dot{K} = s_wLF(k) + (s_c-s_w)K_cf'(k) - (1-s_c)(M_c/P)(\mu-\pi+\dot{z}/z) - (1-s_w)\frac{M_w}{P}\left(\mu - \pi - \frac{\dot{z}}{1-z}\right) \tag{6.3.22}$$

Noting that $\dot{k}/k = \dot{K}/K - n$, we get the following differential equation in k.

$$\dot{k}/k = s_wf(k)/k + (s_c-s_w)xf'(k) - (1-s_c)x\alpha(k,\pi)(\mu-\pi+\dot{z}/z) - (1-s_w)(1-x)\beta(k,\pi)\left(\mu - \pi - \frac{\dot{z}}{1-z}\right) - n \tag{6.3.23}$$

Differentiating (6.3.10) with respect to t and using (6.3.12a) we obtain the differential equation in x as

$$\dot{x}/x = s_cf'(k) - (1-s_c)\alpha(k,\pi)(\mu-\pi+\dot{z}/z) - \dot{k}/k - n \tag{6.3.24}$$

Logarithmic differentiation of (6.3.18) gives

$$\dot{M}_c/M_c = \pi + \dot{K}_c/K_c + \alpha_k\dot{k}/\alpha + \alpha_\pi\dot{\pi}/\alpha$$

Using (6.3.20) and the logarithmic derivative of (6.3.10) we get the following differential equation in π.

$$\alpha_\pi\dot{\pi}/\alpha = (\mu-\pi-n) + \dot{z}/z - \dot{x}/x - \left(1 + \frac{k\alpha_k}{\alpha}\right)\dot{k}/k \tag{6.3.25}$$

By proceeding similarly with respect to M_w we get a differential equation in z.

$$\frac{\dot{z}}{1-z} = (\mu-\pi-n) + \frac{\dot{x}}{1-x} - \left(1 + \frac{k\beta_k}{\beta}\right)\frac{\dot{k}}{k} - \frac{\beta_\pi}{\beta}\dot{\pi} \tag{6.3.26}$$

Equations (6.3.23) through (6.3.26) form the basic differential equations of the system.

6.3.3 Steady-state Properties

In the steady state $\dot{k} = \dot{x} = \dot{\pi} = \dot{z} = 0$. Using these conditions, the long run solutions (denoted by an asterisk) for k, π and x are given by the following equations.

$$\pi^* = \mu - n \tag{6.3.27}$$

$$s_c f'(k^*) - (1-s_c)\alpha^* n - n = 0 \tag{6.3.28}$$

$$s_w f(k^*)/k^* + (s_c-s_w)x^* f'(k^*) - (1-s_c)x^*\alpha^* n - (1-s_w)(1-x^*)\beta^* n - n = 0 \tag{6.3.29}$$

From (6.3.28) we have

$$r^* = f'(k^*) = n[1 + (1-s_c)\alpha^*(k^*,\mu-n)]/s_c \tag{6.3.30}$$

As in the Pasinetti-Samuelson-Modigliani (PSM) non-monetary two-class model (which is a special case of this with α and $\beta = 0$), the long run interest rate (i.e., the real return to capital) is independent of the workers' saving rate and the form of the production function. An additional result we obtain in this model is that workers' demand for real balances has no effect whatsoever on the equilibrium capital intensity or interest rate. As compared to the PSM model, the long run interest rate is higher here. Equivalently, the equilibrium capital intensity is lower. This result is easily rationalized. The availability of a monetary asset which competes with the capital asset draws funds away from capital accumulation thus resulting in a lower capital-labor ratio and a higher yield on capital holdings.

Equation (6.3.29) can be solved explicitly for x^*, the proportion of total capital held by firms in the long run situation. Using (6.3.28) we get

$$(6.3.31) \qquad x^* = \frac{s_c f'(k^*) - s_w f(k^*)/k^* + (1-s_w)\beta^* n - (1-s_c)\alpha^* n}{(s_c - s_w) f'(k^*) + (1-s_w)\beta^* n - (1-s_c)\alpha^* n}$$

An explicit solution for z^*, the proportion of money held by firms, is also readily obtained. From (6.3.18) and (6.3.19) we have $\alpha/\beta = (M_c K_w)/(M_w K_c)$. Using (6.3.10) and (6.3.17) and solving for z we get

$$(6.3.32) \qquad z^* = \frac{\alpha^* x^*}{\alpha^* x^* + \beta^*(1-x^*)}$$

If $0 \leq x^* \leq 1$, then it is clear that $0 \leq z^* \leq 1$. It would therefore be of interest to examine the conditions under which x^* will lie between 0 and 1.

It was pointed out earlier that empirical studies indicate that $s_c > s_w$. Firms expect a high return to investment and hence would tend to save a higher fraction of income than workers. It can also be argued that firms have better portfolio management than workers. They hire professional money managers and are likely to be more invested in capital assets. This implies that they will have a tendency to hold a smaller proportion of their wealth in the form of non-productive real balances. Thus $\beta > \alpha$, although the degree to which β exceeds α would depend on the rate of inflation and the yield on capital. Throughout the rest of the section we assume the above two inequalities. It follows from the two conditions that the denominator of (6.3.31) is positive. It is also easily verified that $x^* < 1$, but there is no assurance that $x^* > 0$. In fact, as we showed earlier, $s_c \rho(k) > s_w$ is a necessary condition for this to hold, where $\rho(k) = kf'(k)/f(k)$ is the relative share of capital in total output.[1] In this model also a

[1] Note that we have changed the notation to ρ in order to avoid confusion because π is now the rate of growth of prices.

similar condition is necessary for x^* to be positive, but it will be presently shown that in contrast to the PSM model, the new condition is empirically more plausible.

Since the denominator of (6.3.31) is positive (given $s_c > s_w$ and $\beta > \alpha$), $x^* > 0$ if and only if the numerator of (6.3.31) is also positive. That is,

$$x^* \left\{ \begin{matrix} > \\ = \\ < \end{matrix} \right. 0 \quad \text{according as} \quad s_c f' - s_w f/k + (1-s_w)\beta^* n - (1-s_c)\alpha^* n \left\{ \begin{matrix} > \\ = \\ < \end{matrix} \right. 0$$

Substituting for n from equation (6.3.28) into the above and simplifying we get the following modified inequality for x^* to be positive.

$$s_c \rho(k^*) > s_w \left\{ \frac{1 + \alpha(1-s_c)}{1 + \beta(1-s_w)} \right\} \tag{6.3.33}$$

Since $\beta(1-s_w) > \alpha(1-s_c)$ by assumption, the above inequality is more plausible than the PSM condition $s_c \rho(k^*) > s_w$, for reasonable values of the parameters. For example, let $s_c = 1/6$, $s_w = 1/20$, $\alpha = 1/20$, $\beta = 1/10$ and $\rho = 3/10$. This gives $x^* = 0$ for the PSM model but results in a positive x^* in the monetary model. Another example is $s_c = 2/11$, $s_w = 1/20$, $\rho = 1/4$, $\alpha = 1/20$, $\beta = 1/6$. For these values the PSM condition $s_c \rho > s_w$ is not satisfied but the modified inequality is satisfied. It should be pointed out, however, that although the modified condition is more plausible, the range of possible values for which inequality (6.3.33) holds does not increase substantially as compared to the PSM model. As before, we shall call the case in which inequality (6.3.33) holds, the <u>Pasinetti case</u> and the opposite situation the <u>Solow-Swan case</u>. We first analyze the Pasinetti case in detail.

6.3.4 Sensitivity Analysis for the Pasinetti Case

We now compute the sensitivities of changes in the values of the parameters and compare the results with the non-monetary two-class PSM model as well as other monetary models. As in the PSM model, $\partial k^*/\partial s_w = 0 = \partial r^*/\partial s_w$. The sensitivities of k^* with respect to changes in n, s_c and μ are given below.

(6.3.34) $$\frac{\partial k^*}{\partial n} = \frac{-1 - (1-s_c)(\alpha^* - n\alpha^*_\pi)}{(1-s_c)n\alpha^*_k - s_c f''} < 0$$

(6.3.35) $$\frac{\partial k^*}{\partial s_c} = \frac{\alpha^* n + f'(k^*)}{(1-s_c)n\alpha^*_k - s_c f''} > 0$$

(6.3.36) $$\frac{\partial k^*}{\partial \mu} = \frac{-(1-s_c)n\alpha^*_\pi}{(1-s_c)n\alpha^*_k - s_c f''} > 0$$

The sensitivities of n and s_c for the PSM model may be obtained by setting α, β and all their partial derivatives to zero. The direction of change is the same as in the PSM model. Similarly, the effect of expanding the money supply at a faster rate results in an increase in the equilibrium capital intensity. This result is consistent with all neoclassical monetary growth models. It would be of considerable interest to further extend this model along Keynes-Wicksell lines, but this is not undertaken here (exercise 6.7).

Although the direction of change is the same as in the PSM model, as one would expect, the magnitudes are different. It is interesting to note, however, that none of the three sensitivities presented above depend on β or its derivatives in any form. Thus workers' demand for real balances has no effect on the magnitude of these sensitivities. The only role played by the households' asset demand function is to affect the equilibrium proportion of capital held by each group as well as the fraction of total money stock that is held by each of the two classes, as is evident from equations (6.3.31) and (6.3.32).

Substituting for n from (6.3.28) into (6.3.31) and using the relation $\rho(k) = kf'(k)/f(k)$, we obtain the following expression for the long run proportion of capital held by firms.

(6.3.37) $$x^* = \frac{s_c[1 + \beta^*(1-s_w)] - s_w[1 + \alpha^*(1-s_c)]/\rho^*}{s_c[1 + \beta^*(1-s_w)] - s_w[1 + \alpha^*(1-s_c)]}$$

The denominator of x^* is positive because $s_c > s_w$ and $\beta > \alpha$. The numerator is positive because of the inequality (6.3.33). The corresponding expression for the PSM model is $x^*_{PSM} = (s_c - s_w/\rho)/(s_c - s_w)$. The sensitivities of x* in the PSM model depend mainly on the elasticity of substitution between capital and labor. In the modified model, they depend in addition on the asset demand functions of capitalists as well as workers. It would be of interest to examine the nature of the effect of changes in the rate of monetary expansion on the proportions of capital and money held by each of the two classes.

Denote x* by N/D where N and D are respectively the numerator and denominator of (6.3.37). Then

$$\frac{1}{x^*}\frac{\partial x^*}{\partial \mu} = \frac{1}{N}\frac{\partial N}{\partial \mu} - \frac{1}{D}\frac{\partial D}{\partial \mu}$$

After a considerable amount of algebraic manipulation, it can be shown that a set of sufficient conditions for $\partial x^*/\partial\mu$ to be negative is the following:

(a) elasticity of substitution between capital and labor is less than 1

(6.3.38) (b) $(1-s_c)[1+(1-s_w)\beta^*]\alpha^*_k > (1-s_w)[1+(1-s_c)\alpha^*]\beta^*_k$

(c) $(1-s_c)]1+(1-s_w)\beta^*]\alpha^*_\pi > (1-s_w)[1+(1-s_c)\alpha^*]\alpha^*_\pi$

(d) inequality (6.3.33) to be satisfied

If the first three inequalities are reversed, then $\partial x^*/\partial\mu$ will be positive. Thus an expansionary monetary policy could mean a decrease or increase in the proportion of capital held by firms depending on the magnitudes of s_c, s_w, α^*, β^*, α^*_k, β^*_k, α^*_π and β^*_π. The effect on z*, the proportion of money held by firms, is also similarly ambiguous.

6.3.5 Stability of the Pasinetti Case

It was proved in the previous section that global stability will be achieved provided the elasticity of substitution between capital and labor is not less than one. It will be presently shown that in the extended model with a monetary sector, even this condition will not assure global stability. Stronger conditions are required. Although the system with four differential equations can be reduced to three by eliminating z and $\dot{z}$, the Routh-Hurwitz conditions are still quite complicated. We therefore restrict ourselves to the special case in which the monetary authorities continuously adjust μ, the rate of monetary expansion, to maintain a stable price level. Thus $\pi = \dot{\pi} = 0$ for all time periods. The sensitivities will be the same as before with $\pi^* = \mu - n$ replaced by zero in all the expressions. The system can then be reduced to the following two differential equations.

$$b_{11}\dot{k}/k + b_{12}\dot{x}/x = c_1$$
$$b_{21}\dot{k}/k + b_{22}\dot{x}/x = c_2$$

where

$$b_{11} = 1 + (1-s_c)x\alpha(1 + \frac{k\alpha_k}{\alpha}) + (1-s_w)(1-x)\beta(1 + \frac{k\beta_k}{\beta}) > 0$$
$$b_{12} = (1-s_c)x\alpha - (1-s_w)\beta x < 0$$
$$b_{21} = 1 + (1-s_c)\alpha(1 + \frac{k\alpha_k}{\alpha}) > 0$$
$$b_{22} = 1 + (1-s_c)\alpha > 0$$
$$c_1 = s_w f/k + (s_c - s_w)xf' - (1-s_c)x\alpha n - (1-s_w)(1-x)\beta n$$
$$c_2 = s_c f' - (1-s_c)\alpha n - n$$

Let

$$c_{1k} = \partial c_1/\partial k, \quad c_{1x} = \partial c_1/\partial x, \text{ etc.}$$

Then

$$c_{1k} = s_w(kf'-f)/k^2 + (s_c - s_w)xf''$$
$$- (1-s_c)x\alpha_k n - (1-s_w)(1-x)\beta_k n < 0$$
$$c_{2k} = s_c f'' - (1-s_c)n\alpha_k < 0$$
$$c_{1x} = (s_c - s_w)f' - (1-s_c)\alpha n + (1-s_w)\beta n > 0$$
$$c_{2x} = 0$$

Also let $a_{11} = (\partial\dot{k}/\partial k)^*$, $a_{12} = (\partial\dot{k}/\partial x)^*$, etc., all of which are evaluated at the steady state. Then the necessary and sufficient conditions for local stability are $a_{11} + a_{22} < 0$ and $a_{11}a_{22} - a_{12}a_{21} > 0$. We have $a_{11} = k^*(b_{22}c_{1k} - b_{12}c_{2k})/\Delta$, where $\Delta =$

$b_{11}b_{22} - b_{12}b_{21}$. It is easily verified that a_{11} is negative and Δ is positive. Similarly

$$a_{12} = k^* b_{22} c_{1x}/\Delta > 0$$

$$a_{21} = x^*(-b_{21}c_{1k}+b_{11}c_{2k})/\Delta$$

$$a_{22} = x^* b_{21} c_{1x}/\Delta < 0$$

Therefore $a_{11} + a_{22} < 0$ satisfying the first stability condition. It also follows that

$$(6.3.39) \qquad -\frac{a_{11}}{a_{12}} = -\frac{c_{1k}}{c_{1x}} + \frac{b_{12}}{b_{22}} \cdot \frac{c_{2k}}{c_{1x}}$$

$$(6.3.40) \qquad -\frac{a_{21}}{a_{22}} = -\frac{c_{1k}}{c_{1x}} + \frac{b_{11}}{b_{21}} \cdot \frac{c_{2k}}{c_{1x}}$$

Subtracting (6.3.39) from (6.3.40) and rearranging terms we get

$$a_{11}a_{22} - a_{21}a_{22} = \frac{a_{12}a_{22}c_{2k}\Delta}{b_{21}b_{22}c_{1x}} > 0$$

thus proving local stability of the Pasinetti case. What can we say about global stability? Note that $-a_{11}/a_{12}$ is the slope of the curve representing the relation $\dot{k} = 0$, which is positive because $a_{11} < 0$ and $a_{12} > 0$. Thus the $\dot{k} = 0$ curve is upward sloping. However, $-a_{21}/a_{22}$ which is the slope of the $\dot{x} = 0$ relation has an ambiguous sign because of the indeterminacy of the sign of a_{21}. If a_{21} is positive, then this will also be upward sloping but with a smaller slope than $\dot{k} = 0$ because

$$-\frac{a_{21}}{a_{22}} = -\frac{a_{11}}{a_{12}} + \frac{\Delta}{b_{21}b_{22}} \cdot \frac{c_{2k}}{c_{1x}}$$

and the second term on the right is negative. In this case, the phase diagram will be as in Figure 6.5a. The directional arrows indicate the direction of movement of k and x from initial points not on the steady state. The phase diagram conclusively demonstrates global stability <u>provided $a_{21} > 0$</u>. If $a_{21} < 0$, then $\dot{x} = 0$ is downward sloping as in Figure 6.5b. Cyclical behavior is now possible but local stability is assured. There is no straight-

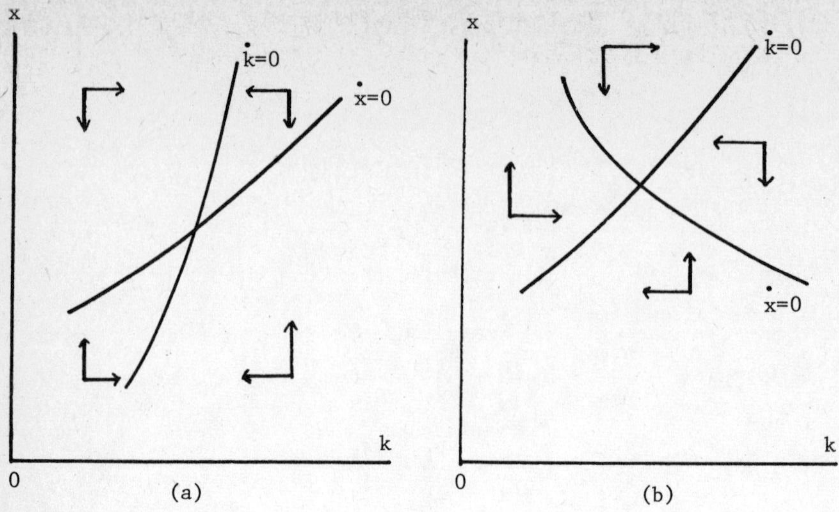

Figure 6.5

forward interpretation for this stability condition. Specific assumptions on the elasticity of substitution between capital and labor do not assure this condition.

6.3.6 The Solow-Swan Case

If inequality (6.3.33) is reversed, then $x^* < 0$, and hence the steady state will not be attained. Where will the economy end up in this situation? The $\dot{k} = 0$ curve would still be upward sloping. The $\dot{x} = 0$ curve would be upward sloping only if $a_{21} > 0$. But since the intersection gives a negative x^*, the phase diagram will be as in Figure 6.6a. If $a_{21} < 0$, the phase diagram will be as in Figure 6.6b. Both diagrams demonstrate global stability, but the economy will ultimately reach k^{**} (with $x = 0$) where k^{**} is given by setting $x = 0$ in the $\dot{k} = 0$ relation. Thus

$$s_w f(k^{**})/k^{**} = (1-s_w)\beta(k^{**},0)n + n \tag{6.3.41}$$

This corresponds to the dual theorem that Samuelson and Modigliani derived. Now the long run capital-labor ratio is independent of the firms' saving rate and asset demand function.

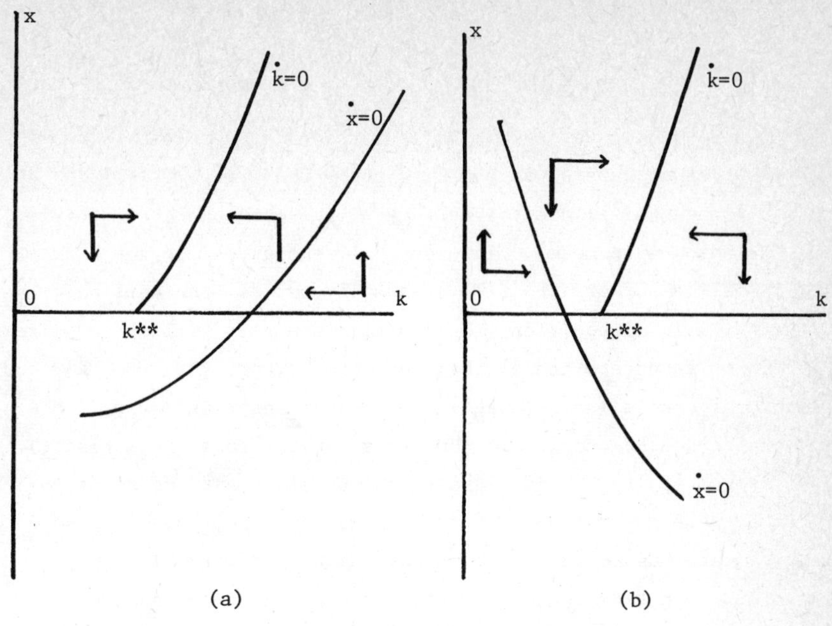

Figure 6.6

Since $\beta > 0$, the steady state k** will be smaller than that in the PSM model. Other results may similarly be derived.

6.4 Summary

Many of the results of the Solow-Swan model carry over to an economy in which workers own a share of capital and also receive dividend income. Balanced growth between these two groups, with each owning a positive share of capital, is possible provided the equilibrium capital intensity, k*, obtained from the relation $s_c f'(k^*) = n$, satisfies the inequality $s_c \pi(k^*) > s_w$ (the Passinetti case). If, in addition, the elasticity of substitution between capital and labor is not less than 1, then balanced growth will be achieved from any initial position. If $\sigma < 1$, only local stability is assured. In the Pasinetti case, the equilibrium capital intensity, per capita output, real wages, real rents and factor shares are all unaffected by any change in the workers' saving rate. Furthermore, equilibrium rents are also independent of the form of the production function (Pasinetti paradox). The effects of changes in s_c are the same as in the Solow-Swan model. To achieve golden rule in such an economy, firms must save all of their income.

If s_c, s_w and k^* do not satisfy the above inequality (the Solow-Swan case), it is impossible for both groups to have positive shares of capital in the long run. One group will ultimately own all the capital and the economy will become one characterized by the Solow-Swan model. Interestingly enough, since $x = K_c/K \rightarrow 0$, it is the workers who will eventually own all the capital. From any initial position, the capital intensity will converge to k^{**} which is determined by the equation $s_w f(k^{**})/k^{**} = n$. k^{**} and hence per capita income, wages, rents and factor shares will now be unaffected by changes in the firms' saving rate (Dual result). The above results are independent of the elasticity of substitution between capital and labor. For golden rule, the workers' saving rate must be the same as the share of capital in output.

Of a monetary sector is introduced in the two-class model, many of the results substantially change. First, the necessary condition for the Pasinetti case is now empirically more plausible. Secondly, workers' demand for real balances has no effect on the equilibrium capital intensity or the interest rate. Although local stability is assured, global stability requires conditions much stronger than the elasticity condition imposed in the non-monetary model.

REFERENCES

[1] Britto, R.: "A Study in Equilibrium Dynamics in Two Types of Growing Economies," Economic Journal, Sept. 1968.

[2] Conlisk, John and R. Ramanathan: "Expedient Choice of Transforms in Phase-Diagramming," Review of Economic Studies, July 1970.

[3] Ferber, Robert: "Research on Household Behavior," American Economic Review, March 1962.

[4] Kaldor, Nicholas: "Alternative Theories of Distribution," Review of Economic Studies, 1955-56.

[5] Meade, James: "The Outcome of the Pasinetti Process -- a Note," Economic Journal, March 1966.

[6] Pasinetti, Luigi: "Rate of Profit and Income Distribution in Relation to Economic Growth," Review of Economic Studies, Oct. 1962.

[7] Pasinetti, Luigi: "The Rate of Profit in a Growing Economy -- a Reply," Economic Journal, March 1966.

[8] Ramanathan, R.: "The Pasinetti-Paradox in a Two-class Monetary Growth Model," Journal of Monetary Economics, July 1976.

[9] Samuelson, Paul and Franco Modigliani: "The Pasinetti Paradox in Neo-classical and More General Models," Review of Economic Studies, Oct. 1966. See also the comments, in the same issue, by Pasinetti, Robinson and Kaldor.

EXERCISES

6.1 a) In the model presented in section 6.1 show that if $s_w = 0$, then the steady state is given by the equation $s_c f'(k) = g$. Does a unique stable solution exist?

b) Show that if $s_c = 0$, the steady state condition becomes $s_w[1-\pi(k)]f(k)/k = g$. Does a steady state exist and if so, is it stable? Hint: If $\pi(0) < 1$, a stable steady state exists. But if $\pi(0) = 1$, existence is not guaranteed. (assume a constant elasticity of substitution production function and examine when this case can be ruled out.)

6.2 Assume that aggregate supply is given by a neo-classical production with two factors -- capital and labor. Labor grows at an exogenously given rate. Firms own all the capital stock. Income distribution is determined by the marginal productivity theory. Suppose now the government levies a proportional tax, at the non-negative rate t, on earnings of workers as well as firms and invests all of the revenue. Assume for simplicity that revenue collection is a costless affair. Workers consume all their disposable income and firms save a proportion s of their disposable income. Capital depreciates at the proportionate rate δ.

a) Examine the long run equilibrium of an economy operating under the above rules. Clearly state in non-mathematical terms any additional assumptions you make.

b) Argue intuitively (that is, without making use of diagrams or equations) how an increase in the tax rate would affect the equilibrium level of per capita output and its rate of growth.

c) Suppose you are a policy maker and want to set the tax rate such that golden rule is attained. What is the optimum tax rate? Is it feasible, that is, does it lie between 0 and 1? If firms save all of their disposable income, what will be the optimum tax rate?

6.3 By taking partial derivatives of (6.2.21) and (6.2.22) alternatively with respect to s_c, s_w and g, verify the sensitivity table 6.1.

6.4 Prove the results in equations (6.2.23), (6.2.24) and (6.2.25).

6.5 In the Solow-Swan case of the Pasinetti model show that k** is the stable long run capital intensity even when $s_c \leq s_w$. <u>Hints</u>: When $s_c < s_w$, the slope of M'(k) is ambiguous. But it can be shown that M'(k**) < 0. First prove the following results which involve a considerable amount of work:

$x^* > 1$

$N(k) > 1$ for all k

If $\pi(0) = 0$ then $M(0) = N(0) = \infty$

If $\pi(0) \neq 0$ then $M(0) = \dfrac{s_w}{(s_w - s_c)\pi(0)} > 1$

$M(0) \geq N(0)$

Therefore the M(k) curve begins above the N(k) curve and above the line x = 1. Now map the M(k) and N(k) curves distinguishing between the cases $\sigma \geq 1$ and $\sigma < 1$. Then draw the directional arrows appropriately and establish the desired result.

6.6 Redo the Pasinetti model using the transform variables k and $z = K_c/K_w$ ($z \geq 0$) instead of x. (See Conlisk and Ramanathan [2].)

6.7 Incorporate the features of the Keynes-Wicksell model discussed in the last chapter into the two-class monetary growth model.

6.8 Carry out a complete stability analysis of the two-class monetary model in the case when $\pi \neq 0$ for all periods, that is, where μ is exogenous.

CHAPTER 7

CAMBRIDGE GROWTH MODELS

For the past two decades, a group of distinguished economists on the faculty of the University of Cambridge in England have severely criticized the approaches to the theory of economic growth used by the neo-classical school. Almost all the growth models discussed until now adopt the neo-classical approach. Salient features of that approach are the concept of an aggregate capital stock, smooth and well-behaved production functions, marginal productivity theory of income distribution, no independent investment function and full or near-full employment assumed. The Cambridge School (Nicholas Kaldor, Joan Robinson, Luigi Pasinetti, etc.), on the other hand, prefers to work with fixed coefficients or an activity analysis approach to production, independently determined investment function, factor prices not determined by marginal products, different propensities to save for workers and firms, and full employment not necessarily attained automatically. Some of the objections of the Cambridge critics have been taken into account in recent works by neo-classicists. For instance, the Keynes-Wicksell approach, discussed in Chapter 5, retains most of the features of the neo-classical models but considers saving and investment behavior as being determined independently. Vintage models relax, at least partly, the concept of a homogeneous capital stock. In the last chapter we explored in detail the properties of neo-classical models using the Kaldor-Pasinetti assumption of two income classes with different propensities to save. In the present chapter we explore some of the alternative approaches adopted by the Cambridge economists and examine their implications. For an excellent treatment of the Cambridge controversy, the reader is referred to Wan's book [15 , Ch. 3].

7.1 A Simple Kaldorian Model

Although the Cambridge economists criticized several aspects of the neo-classical models, in their own models they did not take account of all those criticisms simultaneously. For example, Kaldor's 1956 model [5] retained the assumption of full employment and treated investment as being determined by the level of savings rather than independently. He used the fixed coefficients production function

$$(7.1.1) \qquad Y = \mathrm{Min}(K/\alpha, L/\beta)$$

As in the last chapter, there are two classes of income receivers, workers and firms. The total wage bill is denoted by W and firms' profits by P. Thus

$$(7.1.2) \qquad Y = W + P$$

Workers are assumed to save a fixed fraction s_w of their income and firms save a proportion s_c ($\neq s_w$) out of profits. Total savings are thus given by

$$(7.1.3) \qquad S = s_c P + s_w W$$

If depreciation is ignored and all savings go into investment and capital accumulation, we have

$$(7.1.4) \qquad I = S$$

$$(7.1.5) \qquad \dot{K} = I$$

Define r to be the rate of return to capital.

$$(7.1.6) \qquad r = P/K$$

As before, the labor supply (measured in efficiency units to allow for neutral technical progress) grows at the exogenous rate n.

$$(7.1.7) \qquad \dot{L}/L = n$$

The assumption of full employment implies that

$$(7.1.8) \qquad K/\alpha = L/\beta$$

The above equations completely determine the eight endogenous variables Y,K,L,S,I,P,W and r. It will be readily apparent that this model is nothing but the Harrod-Domar (HD) model with two classes of income receivers and different saving propensities. Recall that in the basic HD model steady state was impossible unless the warranted rate, which was the ratio of the saving rate to the capital-output ratio, was equal to the rate of growth of the labor force. In the Kaldor model also a similar condition is necessary but it is less restrictive. The rate of accumulation of capital is easily shown to be the following.

(7.1.9) $\dot{K}/K = s_c P/K + s_w(Y-P)/K = s_w/\alpha + r(s_c - s_w)$

The steady state condition is $\dot{K}/K = n$, that is,

(7.1.10) $s_w/\alpha + r(s_c - s_w) = n$

which implies that

(7.1.11) $r = \dfrac{n - s_w/\alpha}{s_c - s_w}$

(7.1.12) $\pi = Kr/Y = \alpha r = (\alpha n - s_w)/(s_c - s_w)$

In order for this steady state to be feasible, we must have $0 \le \pi \le 1$. If $s_c > s_w$, then the following inequality is a necessary and sufficient condition for a meaningful steady state.

(7.1.13) $s_w/\alpha \le n \le s_c/\alpha$

It will be recalled that in the HD model with $s_c = s_w = s$, this condition reduced to $s/\alpha = n$ which is not likely to hold except by coincidence. As the above inequality is less restrictive, a steady state is more likely to be achieved. For example, let $s_c = 1/6$, $s_w = 1/12$ and $\alpha = 2.5$, then $1/30 \le n \le 1/15$ is likely to hold (remember that n includes technical progress). Other similar examples are easy to construct.

Although the long run equilibrium in the Kaldor model is more likely to be attained than that in the HD model, there is no inherent mechanism that automatically moves the economy towards the unique steady state in which the share of capital is given by (7.1.12) or, equivalently, the return to capital is fixed as in (7.1.11). The government has to adjust the income distribution to the value consistent with the steady state. As an illustration, suppose the government taxes a fraction t of all income and invests it. We then have

$$\dot{K} = I = s_c P(1-t) + s_w(1-t)(Y-P) + tY$$

It follows that

$$\dot{K}/K = s_w(1-t)/\alpha + (s_c - s_w)(1-t)r + t/\alpha$$

In the steady state this must equal n. Solving for the tax rate we obtain

$$t = \frac{n - s_w/\alpha - (s_c - s_w)r}{(1-s_w)/\alpha - (s_c - s_w)r} \tag{7.1.14}$$

For a better understanding of this relation, it can be rewritten as follows, after noting that $\alpha r = \pi$, the relative share of capital.

$$t = \frac{(\alpha n - s_w)/(s_c - s_w) - \pi}{(1-s_w)/(s_c - s_w) - \pi} \tag{7.1.14a}$$

It is easy to verify that when $s_c > s_w$ the denominator is always positive. Also the inequality $s_w \leq n \leq s_c$ assumed earlier assures that t is not larger than 1 in absolute value. However, it can be negative because the income distribution may be such that the share of capital may be greater than $(\alpha n - s_w)/(s_c - s_w)$ making the numerator of (7.1.14a) negative. If that happens, the policy prescription is a subsidy rather than a tax, but the mechanism by which a subsidy can be given is ambiguous in this model. If we allow for substitutability between capital and labor, this delimma is eliminated and automatic mechanisms exist which push the economy towards the steady state without government intervention. Such a model is explored in the next section.

7.2 A Neo-Keynesian Model with Pasinetti Saving Behavior[1]

We now incorporate a neo-classical production function but assume that investment behavior is determined independently from saving behavior. Aggregate output (Y), is as before given by the linearly homogeneous production function $F(K,L) = Lf(k)$. Labor force grows exponentially at the constant rate n. Firms own K_c of the capital stock and receive an income of $K_c r$ where r is the real rate of return to capital. Out of this they save a fixed fraction s_c. Their demand for investment per unit of capital is given by the Keynesian function $I(x,r)$, where $x(=K_c/K)$ is the fraction of total capital owned by them. The investment demand function is

---

[1]This section is taken from Ramanathan [8].

assumed to be continuous and differentiable in x and r. Workers own the remainder of the capital stock (K_w) and receive dividend income amounting to $K_w r$, in addition to all the wage income wL, where w is the real wage rate. Wages as well as rents on capital are assumed to be flexible so as to assure full employment of both factors at all periods of time. These factor prices need not, however, equal the respective marginal products. Workers' saving-income ratio is $s_w (\leq s_c)$. The goods market is also assumed to be cleared at each instant of time implying that investment demand equals total saving. Capital is assumed to depreciate exponentially at the rate δ. The structural equations representing the model just described are stated below.

(7.2.1) $$Y = Lf(k)$$

(7.2.2) $$k = K/L$$

(7.2.3) $$K = K_c + K_w$$

(7.2.4) $$x = K_c/K$$

(7.2.5) $$\dot{K}_c = s_c K_c r - \delta K_c$$

(7.2.6) $$\dot{K}_w = s_w(Y - K_c r) - \delta K_w$$

(7.2.7) $$I/K = I(x,r)$$

(7.2.8) $$\dot{K} = I - \delta K$$

(7.2.9) $$\dot{L}/L = n$$

(7.2.10) $$Y = wL + Kr$$

The investment demand function needs further exploration. If the yield on capital increases or the fraction of total capital owned by firms goes up, then firms' profits will also rise thus increasing the demand for investment. Therefore I_x and I_r will both be positive. The reasonableness of this assumption will be readily apparent if we make the simplifying assumption that investment demand is a fixed fraction (λ) of firms' profits. Thus $I = \lambda K_c r$, or equivalently, $I/K = I(x,r) = \lambda xr$. For the present we retain this particular formulation of the investment function because it yields powerful results, but consider the more general version later. For the system to be economically meaningful, λ must be greater than s_c as may be seen from the derivation $\lambda xr = I/K = s_c xr + s_w(Y-K_c r)/K$, or equivalently, $(\lambda-s_c)xr = s_w(Y-K_c r)/K$. If λ is less than s_c then it follows that $Y - K_c r$, which is workers' total income, must be negative which is impossible. Therefore we will henceforth make the assumption that $\lambda > s_c$.

The rate of growth of the total stock of capital can be seen to be the following.

$$\dot{K}/K = \lambda xr - \delta = s_w a(k) + (s_c-s_w)xr - \delta \tag{7.2.11}$$

where $a(k) = f(k)/k$ is the average product of capital. The above equation can be solved for r as

$$r(x,k) = \frac{s_w a(k)}{(\lambda-s_c+s_w)x} \tag{7.2.12}$$

As we have not made any assumption about steady state, equation (7.2.12) holds at all time periods and follows from the condition for the static clearence of the goods market. It is evident that $\partial r/\partial x$ and $\partial r/\partial k$ are both negative. A similar derivation is possible for the wage rate. We have

$$w(x,k) = f(k) - kr(x,k) = \frac{[(\lambda-s_c)x-s_w(1-x)]f(k)}{(\lambda-s_c+s_w)x} \tag{7.2.13}$$

7.2.2 Steady State Properties

The long run properties of this model can be obtained by first reducing the system to two differential equations, one in k and one in x. From equation (7.2.11) and the relation $\dot{k}/k = \dot{K}/K - n$, we get

$$\dot{k}/k = \phi(k) \equiv \frac{\lambda s_w a(k)}{\lambda-s_c+s_w} - (n+\delta) \tag{7.2.14}$$

Balanced growth is attained when $\dot{k} = 0$ which gives

$$\frac{\lambda s_w a(k)}{\lambda-s_c+s_w} = n + \delta \tag{7.2.15}$$

Under the neo-classical conditions on f(k) and the added assumption that $\lambda > s_c$, there is a unique capital intensity k* satisfying (7.2.15). How does the proportion of capital owned by firms behave over time? To answer this we need a differential equation in x. This is given by

(7.2.16) $\dot{x}/x = \dot{K}_c/K_c - \dot{K}/K = (s_c-\lambda x)r = \dfrac{(s_c-\lambda x)s_w a(k)}{(\lambda-s_c+s_w)x}$

In the long run, $\dot{x}$ is also equal to zero which implies from equation (7.2.16) that $s_c - \lambda x = 0$. Denoting steady state values by an asterisk we note that the equilibrium ratio of the stock of capital owned by firms to the total capital stock is

(7.2.17) $x^* = s_c/\lambda$

The long run rate of return to capital is given by

(7.2.18) $r^* = (n+\delta)/s_c$

We argued earlier that $\lambda > s_c$, from which we note that x* is less than 1. Thus a unique and feasible value of x* exists. Furthermore it depends entirely on the behavior of firms, as represented by λ and s_c, and is independent of the workers' saving propensity, the rate of growth of the labor force and the depreciation rate. This conclusion is in strong contrast to the result obtained in the neo-classical version of this model discussed in the last chapter. It will be recalled that two cases arose in that model. The first case was the so called <u>Pasinetti Paradox</u> which states that, in the long run, the yield on capital (r*) is independent of the workers' saving propensity and the form of the production function (as is seen from equation (7.2.18)). As we have stressed before, this is no paradox but a direct consequence of an assumption built into the model (see equation (7.2.5)). In steady state, $\dot{K}_c/K_c = \dot{K}/K = n$ and therefore $r^* = (n+\delta)/s_c$, regardless of how the rest of the model was specified. The interesting feature of their model as pointed out by Samuelson and Modigliani, was that the Pasinetti Paradox is not always attainable. Only if the condition $s_c\pi(k^+) > s_w$ (where $\pi(k) = kf'(k)/f(k)$ is the relative share of capital in output and k^+ is the steady state capital intensity in their model as determined by the equation $s_c f'(k^+) = n + \delta$) was satisfied did the Paradox hold. Otherwise the economy will tend toward a <u>dual state</u> in which the equilibrium capital intensity, denoted by k**, satisfies the equation $s_w f(k^{**}/k^*) = n + \delta$, and x converges to zero, that is, workers own all the capital. The Samuelson-Modigliani paper also questioned the empirical plausibility of the above condition and argued that the dual result is more likely to hold. In our modified neo-Keynesian model also $r^* = (n+\delta)/s_c$ but there is no dual result and no similar condition need be satisfied for the Pasinetti Paradox to arise. The economy will ultimately reach that equilibrium. In other words, the steady state characterized by equations (7.2.15), (7.2.17) and (7.2.18) is globally stable. This will be formally demonstrated presently.

7.2.3 Stability Analysis

The set of all points (k,x) such that $\dot{k} = 0$ is given by equation (7.2.15) which is independent of x. Similarly $\dot{x} = 0$ whenever $s_c - \lambda x = 0$, regardless of the value of k. Therefore the curves representing the relations $\dot{k} = 0$ and $\dot{x} = 0$ in a phase diagram are vertical and horizontal respectively, as shown in Figure 7.1. Also, $\partial\dot{k}/\partial k < 0$ at any point on the $\dot{k} = 0$ line and $\partial\dot{x}/\partial x < 0$ at all points on the $\dot{x} = 0$ line. This implies that the directional arrows representing the movement over time of a point (k,x) not on either of the two straight lines are as in Figure 7.1. The phase diagram conclusively demonstrates that the Pasinetti Paradox situation is the unique globally stable long run equilibrium and that no dual result arises. The stability of the model can also be argued intuitively. Suppose capital accumulates faster than labor. Rents will then fall and hence firms will be induced to substitute capital for labor thus raising the capital intensity. Saving as well as investment demand per unit of capital will therefore decrease thus slowing down the rate of accumulation of capital. This process will continue until that rate equals n. The mechanism is the reverse when labor grows faster than capital. With regard to x, the fraction of total capital owned by firms, suppose K_c grows faster than K. Assume for simplicity that k is already in steady state. This increase in x implies a rise in investment demand. When equilibrium is restored in the goods market, the

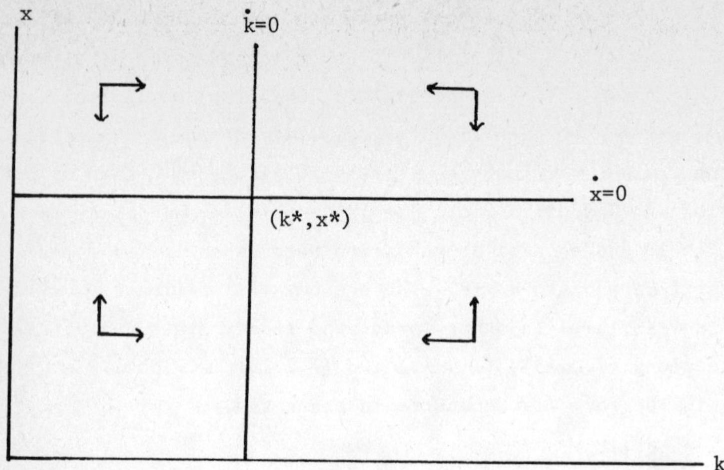

Figure 7.1

rate of return to capital (r) would have decreased, as is evident from equation (7.2.12). But $s_c r - \delta = \dot{K}_c/K_c$ and hence a fall in rents implies a reduction in the rate of growth of K_c. This reduction will persist as long as x is higher than the equilibrium value. Eventually, K_c will grow at the same rate as K and L. Thus balanced growth is restored automatically.

7.2.4 Long Run Effects of Changes in Parameters

By noting the nature of the shifts of $\phi(k)$ in equation (7.2.14) with respect to changes in the parameters s_c, s_w, n, δ and λ, and using equations (7.2.15) and (7.2.18), the sensitivities presented in Table 7.1 are easy to establish. They can also be derived from intuitive arguments. Suppose λ increases. This implies that, _cateris paribus_, investment demand will temporarily rise. The yield on capital will consequently fall and the return to labor rise. If capital owners save a higher fraction of their income than workers (as is confirmed by most empirical studies), the above decrease in firms' income and corresponding increase in labor income would result in a decrease in the overall savings.

Table 1: Long Run Effects of Changes in Parameters

	s_c	s_w	n	δ	λ
k*	+	+	-	-	+ when $s_c < s_w$; - when $s_c > s_w$
x*	+	0	0	0	-
r*	-	0	+	+	0

A + means the effect is in the same direction (e.g. $\partial k^*/\partial s_c > 0$), a - implies that the effect is in the opposite direction and zero means no effect.

This, combined with an ultimate fall in investment demand (due to a lower r), implies that capital stock would tend to grow slower and hence, in the long run, firms will use a technology with a lower capital intensity. Therefore a higher λ will result in a lower k* when $s_c > s_w$. If either of the savings propensities increases, then the overall savings go up accompanied by an increase in the return to capital. Investment demand will then rise to match the increased savings and hence capital accumulation will tend to be at a faster rate. The long run effect of this is to raise the capital intensity k*. Other sensitivities can be argued similarly.

7.2.5 A General Investment Demand Function

The reader would have already noted that many of the results which are in strong contrast to the neo-classical two-class model of Pasinetti, Samuelson and Modigliani, arise because of the specific choice of the investment demand function. We now turn our attention to the more general formulation that $I/K = I(x,r)$ where I_x and I_r are both positive. Equation (7.2.11) now becomes

$$\dot{K}/K = I(x,r) - \delta = s_w a(k) + (s_c - s_w)xr - \delta \tag{7.2.11a}$$

The goods market equilibrium condition determining r, for given k and x, is

(7.2.12a) $I(x,r) = s_w a(k) + (s_c - s_w)xr$

The differential equations for k and x are, respectively,

(7.2.14a) $\dot{k}/k = I(x,r) - (n+\delta)$

(7.2.16a) $\dot{x}/x = s_c r - \dot{k}/k - (n+\delta) = s_c r - I(x,r)$

Because r cannot be explicitly solved in terms of x and k, as was conveniently possible earlier, equations (7.2.14a) and (7.2.16a) do not completely determine the time paths of x and k. We have to add the equation (7.2.12a) also. Assuming that it can be solved uniquely for r as a function r(x,k) we note that equations (7.2.14a) and (7.2.16a) completely characterize the dynamic properties of the model when r(x,k) is substituted for r. The steady state conditions now become

$$I(x^*,r^*) = s_w a(k^*) + (s_c - s_w)x^*r^*$$
$$I(x^*,r^*) = n + \delta$$
$$s_c r^* = n + \delta$$

which can be rewritten as follows.

(7.2.15a) $s_w a(k^*) = [s_w x^* + s_c(1-x^*)](n+\delta)/s_c$

(7.2.17a) $I[x^*,(n+\delta)/s_c] = n + \delta$

(7.2.18) $r^* = (n+\delta)/s_c$

As is expected, the equilibrium value of r* is still the same. However, k* and x* can no longer be determined in the straightforward manner possible earlier. The steady state value of x can be obtained by solving equation (7.2.17a). But without additional assumptions on the investment demand function there is no assurance that such a solution will even exist nor that it will be attainable, because the value of x* satisfying equation (7.2.17a) may not be in the range (0,1), thus giving rise to the possibility of the dual result obtained by Samuelson and Modigliani.

We argued earlier that it is reasonable to assume that $\partial I/\partial x > 0$ for all x, $0 \leq x \leq 1$. For the solution to be economically meaningful, the wage rate should be non-negative, that is, w(x,k)

> 0 for all x and k such that $k > 0$ and $0 \leq x \leq 1$. Under the marginal productivity theory, this condition is assured because $w = f(k) - kf'(k) > 0$ by the neo-classical properties of f(k). In the neo-Keynesian case that assurance is no longer there. We therefore require that $f(k) - kr(x,k) > 0$. Since the static condition (7.2.12a) must also be satisfied, the above condition becomes,

$$(7.2.20) \qquad I(x,r) \geq r[s_c x + s_w(1-x)]$$

This condition must be satisfied in particular at $x = 1$ and $r^* = (n+\delta)/s_c$ which means $I[1,(n+\delta)/s_c] \geq n + \delta$. A steady state is assured if we also assume that $I[0,(n+\delta)/s_c] < (n+\delta)$. Thus a set of sufficient conditions for the existence and uniqueness of a steady state in the Pasinetti-Paradox case is

$$(7.2.21) \qquad \begin{array}{ll} \text{(a)} & I[0,(n+\delta)/s_c] \leq n + \delta \\ \text{(b)} & \text{Wage rate} \geq 0 \quad \forall\, x,k : 0 \leq x \leq 1,\ k > 0 \\ \text{(c)} & I_x > 0 \quad \forall\, x,k : 0 \leq x \leq 1,\ k > 0 \end{array}$$

It is clear that because I(x,r) is continuous with $I_x > 0$, there must exist a unique value of x with $0 \leq x^* \leq 1$, such that $I[x^*,(n+\delta)/s_c] = n + \delta$. Note that, unlike the neo-classical Pasinetti model, the crucial condition in our model which is (7.2.21a) does not depend on the equilibrium capital intensity. Instead, the investment demand function is restricted to the class that satisfies (7.2.21). Furthermore, (7.2.21a) is not a strong condition because when $x = 0$, $I[0,(n+\delta)/s_c]$ is likely to be zero and will therefore satisfy (7.2.21a). It follows therefore that as long as the investment demand function is restricted to the class that satisfies the economically justifiable conditions (7.2.21), there exists a unique long run equilibrium which is attainable. There is thus no dual result even in the case of a general investment function.

7.2.6 Comparative Dynamics of the General Case

We now examine the effects of changes in the parameters of the model on the equilibrium values of the capital intensity and the ratio of total capital owned by firms. It is evident from equation (7.2.17a) that x* is independent of workers' saving-income ratio. This result also is different from that of the neo-classical two-class model. An increase in s_c would increase x* because $\partial x^*/\partial s_c = r^*I_r^*/(s_c I_x^*) > 0$ since I_r and I_x are positive by assumption. What will be the effect of changing n or δ on x*? Partial differentiation of (7.2.17a) with respect to n or δ gives

$$\partial x^*/\partial n = \partial x^*/\partial \delta = (1-I_r^*/s_c)/I_x^* = (1-\eta^*)/I_x^*$$

where $\eta = rI_r/I$ is the partial elasticity of investment demand with respect to the rate of return to capital. Because $I_x > 0$,

$$\frac{\partial x^*}{\partial n} \gtreqless 0 \quad \text{according as } \eta^* \lesseqgtr 1$$

When $I/K = \lambda xr$, $\partial x^*/\partial n = 0$, because $\eta = 1$. In the neo-classical two-class model, $\partial x^*/\partial n$ depended on the elasticity of substitution between capital and labor. In our model, the degree of factor substitutability plays no role in the determination of the equilibrium value of the fraction of total capital owned by firms. Instead, the partial elasticity of demand for investment with respect to the yield on capital plays a key role not only in the long run effects on x* but also those on k*. The sensitivities for k* are given below.

$$\frac{\partial k^*}{\partial n} = \frac{\partial k^*}{\partial \delta} = \frac{(n+\delta)(\eta^*-1)(s_c-s_w) + I_x^*[s_w x^* + s_c(1-x^*)]}{s_c s_w I_x^* a'(k^*)} \tag{7.2.22}$$

where a'(k) is the derivative of a(k) and is negative.

$$\frac{\partial k^*}{\partial s_w} = \frac{-s_c r^*(1-x^*)}{s_w^2 a'(k^*)} \tag{7.2.23}$$

$$\frac{\partial k^*}{\partial s_c} = \frac{r^*[1-x^*-(s_c-s_w)\partial x^*/\partial s_c] - s_w a^*/s_c}{s_w a'(k^*)} \tag{7.2.24}$$

From the neo-classical conditions on the production function, $a'(k) < 0$. Therefore, $\partial x^*/\partial s_w > 0$ unambiguously. But the other sensitivities are not so clear-cut. If $\eta^* \geq 1$ and $s_c \geq s_w$ then $\partial k^*/\partial n < 0$, which is the standard neo-classical result. But if $\eta^* < 1$ and $s_c > s_w$, then the numerator of $\partial k^*/\partial n$ can become negative making $\partial k^*/\partial n > 0$. Similarly, $\partial k^*/\partial s_c$ can become negative but the elasticity η^* is irrelevant there. Thus results contrary to those encountered in neo-classical models are now possible.

It is possible to argue that because I = S at each instant of time, η must be ≥ 1 at least for large k. Consider a point in time, with (k,x) given. Then the savings schedule $s_w a(k) + (s_c - s_w)xr$ must have a positive intercept and will graph as in Figure 7.2. The investment line presumably has a zero intercept. Therefore for a unique r, the investment schedule must be steeper than the savings schedule for all (k,x).[1] Thus $I_r(x,r) > (s_c - s_w)x$, for all x. Using the short-run equilibrium condition $I(x,r) = s_w a(k) + (s_c - s_w)xr$, this inequality can be rewritten as follows.

$$rI_r(x,r) > I(x,r) - s_w a(k) \quad \forall\ k,x$$

Equivalently, we have

$$\eta > 1 - (s_w a/I) \quad \forall\ k,x$$

As $k \to \infty$, $a(k) \to 0$ and hence $\eta \geq 1$ in the limit. We will sometimes impose the somewhat stronger condition that $\eta \geq 1$ for all k and x. For example, with this condition, we have $\partial k^*/\partial n < 0$ which is the neo-classical result.

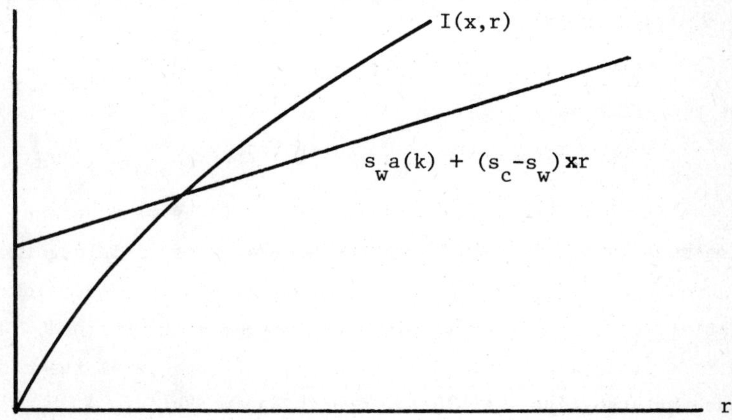

Figure 7.2

[1] I am indebted to John Conlisk for bringing this to my attention.

7.2.7 Stability of the General Model

The sensitivities just discussed are not meaningful unless the model is stable. We now investigate the stability properties of this case. Let $a_{11} = (\partial\dot{k}/\partial k)^*$, $a_{12} = (\partial\dot{k}/\partial x)^*$, $a_{21} = (\partial\dot{x}/\partial k)^*$ and $a_{22} = (\partial\dot{x}/\partial x)^*$, be the partial derivatives of $\dot{k}$ and $\dot{x}$ with respect to k and x respectively, evaluated at the steady state.

$$a_{11} = k^*I_r^*r_k^*; \qquad a_{12} = k^*(I_x^*+I_r^*r_x^*)$$

$$a_{21} = x^*(s_c-I_r^*)r_k^*; \qquad a_{22} = x^*(s_c r_x^*-I_x^*-I_r^*r_x^*)$$

$$a_{11}a_{22} - a_{21}a_{12} = -s_c k^*x^*I_x^*r_k^*$$

where $r_x = \partial r/\partial x$ and $r_k = \partial r/\partial k$, which can be obtained from equation (7.2.12a) as follows.

$$r_k = \frac{s_w a'(k)}{I_r-(s_c-s_w)x} \tag{7.2.25}$$

$$r_x = \frac{(s_c-s_w)r-I_x}{I_r-(s_c-s_w)x} \tag{7.2.26}$$

The denominator of both the above equations is positive because we argued earlier that $I_r > (s_c-s_w)x$. Also, the numerator of r_k is negative. Therefore $r_k < 0$ unambiguously. The numerator of r_x can be rewritten as

$$(s_c-s_w)r - I_x = [I-xI_x-s_w xa(k)]/x = [I(1-\varepsilon)-s_w xa(k)]/x$$

where $\varepsilon = xI_x/I$ is the partial elasticity of investment demand with respect to x. If $\varepsilon \geq 1$ then the numerator of r_x is negative. Therefore, $r_x < 0$ provided $\varepsilon \geq 1$. If this elasticity condition is not satisfied, the sign of r_x might be ambiguous or reversed. Because $r_k < 0$, $a_{11}a_{22} - a_{21}a_{12} > 0$ thus satisfying one of the conditions for stability. The other condition is that $a_{11} + a_{22} < 0$. We readily see that a_{11} is negative. But a_{22} can be of either sign in general. However, from (7.2.26)

$$I_r r_x + I_x = (s_c-s_w)(r+xr_x) = (s_c-s_w)r(1-\theta)$$

where $\theta = -xr_x/r$ is the elasticity of r with respect to x. If $\theta \leq 1$ and $\varepsilon \geq 1$ then $r_x < 0$ and $I_x + I_r r_x > 0$ thus implying that

$a_{22} < 0$. Therefore a set of sufficient conditions for stability is that $\varepsilon \geq 1$ and $\theta \leq 1$. An alternative set of sufficient conditions are $\eta \geq 1$ and $r_x \geq 0$. We note then that $a_{22} = s_c r_x^*(1-\eta^*)x^* - I_x^* x^*$ which is negative.

If the above elasticity conditions are not met for ε and θ or for η and r_x, a_{22} may be positive. If this destabilizing effect is weak, $a_{11} + a_{22}$ might still be negative thus assuring stability. But if a_{22} has a large enough positive value, the model may be unstable. a_{22} is the rate of change in x when x is slightly increased from the steady state value. a_{11} is the corresponding rate of change for k when it is slightly increased from k*. Thus stability is assured if in absolute value, rate of change of k is larger than that of x in the neighborhood of the equilibrium.

7.2.8 Summary

The major conclusions arrived at with the neo-Keynesian model analyzed here may be summarized as follows.

a) If the investment demand is such that it rises with x, is zero when x = 0, and gives rise to an equilibrium wage rate that is positive at each instant, then a unique steady state exists which is attainable with $0 < x^* < 1$. Unlike the neo-classical two-class model, there is no dual result here.

b) In contrast to the neo-classical model the degree of factor substitutability has no role in the determination of x*. In the long run, x* is independent of workers' saving propensity. If investment demand is a fixed fraction of firms' income, then x* is independent of n and δ also.

c) The partial elasticity of demand for investment with respect to the yield on capital plays a significant role in the long run effects of n and δ on x* and k*.

d) In the special case when investment demand is proportional to firms' income, a globally stable long run equilibrium exists. In the general case, stability is assured if any one of the following sets of conditions is satisfied.

(i) $\varepsilon = xI_x/I \geq 1$ and $\theta = -xr_x/r \leq 1$

(iii) $\eta = rI_r/r \geq 1$ and $r_x \geq 0$

(iii) the rate of change of k is larger in absolute value than that of x in the neighborhood of the equilibrium.

Thus several of the results are in strong contrast to those of the neo-classical two-class model.

7.3 The Technical Progress Function

Another variant of the neo-Keynesian model was introduced by Kaldor and Mirrlees in 1962 [6]. The chief differences in their formulation are a specific form of the investment demand function and a replacement of the production function with a Technical Progress Function. In a production function, the level of output is determined by the levels of capital and labor. A technical progress function, on the other hand, relates the rate of growth of per capita output to that of the capital-labor ratio. Thus $\dot{y}/y = g(\dot{k}/k)$, where y is per capita output and k is the capital-labor ratio. It is assumed that $g(0) > 0$, $g'(\cdot) > 0$ and $g''(\cdot) \leq 0$. The first assumption states that even if the capital intensity is unchanged, per capita output will grow. This corresponds to neutral technical progress. The second and third assumptions imply that if capital intensity grows faster, then per capita output will also grow faster but at a decreasing rate. This corresponds to the diminishing marginal productivity assumption. Other assumptions will be added later as needed. The above function cannot generally be integrated to give a production function (see Black [1]), except when $g(\cdot)$ is linear, in which case the production function has the Cobb-Douglas form.

The investment demand function is specified in a manner different from that in the last section. Let $X(t)$ be the desired level of capital at time t. Then the desired capital-output ratio is assumed to depend linearly on the rate of return to capital. Therefore, $X/Y = I(r)$.[1] In equilibrium, desired capital is equal to the actual level of capital, that is, $X(t) = K(t)$ for all t. The remaining equations of the model are unchanged. The complete

---

[1]Kaldor and Mirlees did not use this investment function but derived one from a vintage model. To capture the essence of their model we have used a simpler formulation.

model is specified below.

(7.3.1) $\dot{y}/y = g(\dot{k}/k)$

(7.3.2) $y = Y/L$

(7.3.3) $k = K/L$

(7.3.4) $Y = W + P$

(7.3.5) $r = P/K$

(7.3.6) $w = W/L$

(7.3.7) $X/Y = I(r)$

(7.3.8) $S = sY$

(7.3.9) $\dot{K} = S - \delta K$

(7.3.10) $K = X$

(7.3.11) $L = L_o e^{nt}$

(7.3.12) $x = Y/K$

Here also the marginal productivity of income distribution is not invoked. The model can be reduced to a single differential equation in x. We have, $\dot{x}/x = \dot{Y}/Y - \dot{K}/K = \dot{y}/y - \dot{k}/k = g(\dot{k}/k) - \dot{k}/k$. From equation (7.3.9), $\dot{k}/k = sx - (n+\delta)$. Therefore we have the following differential equation.

(7.3.13) $\dot{x}/x = \phi(x) \equiv g[sx-(n+\delta)] - [sx-(n+\delta)]$

Steady state is attained when $\dot{x} = 0$, that is, when x satisfies the following equation.

(7.3.14) $g[sx-(n+\delta)] = sx - (n+\delta)$

This equation is of the form $g(z) = z$ and will have a solution if, in addition to the conditions $g(0) > 0$, $g'(z) > 0$ and $g''(z) < 0$, we add the stipulation that $g'(z) < 1$ for some $z > 0$. Then the g(z) function will graph as in Figure 7.3. There are two points z_1^* and z_2^* such that $g(z^*) = z^*$. The corresponding values for x are $x_i^* = (n+\delta+z_i^*)/s$. It is clear that there exists at least one meaningful solution. If $n+\delta+z_1^* > 0$, there will be two solutions as in Figure 7.4. Because the stability condition is that the $\phi(x)$ curve must intersect the x-axis from above (see Chapter 3, Theorem A.2 in the Appendix), x_2^* is a stable solution but x_1^* is unstable. Global stability is hence not assured. If, however, $x_1^* < 0$, there is a unique steady state which is globally stable.

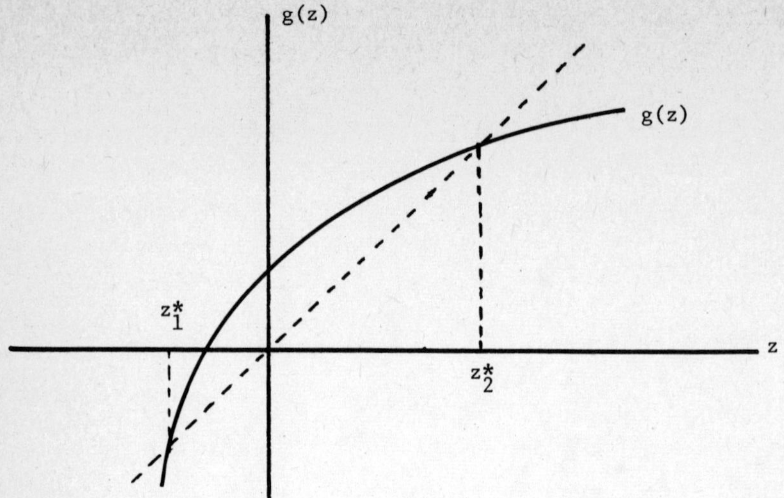

Figure 7.3

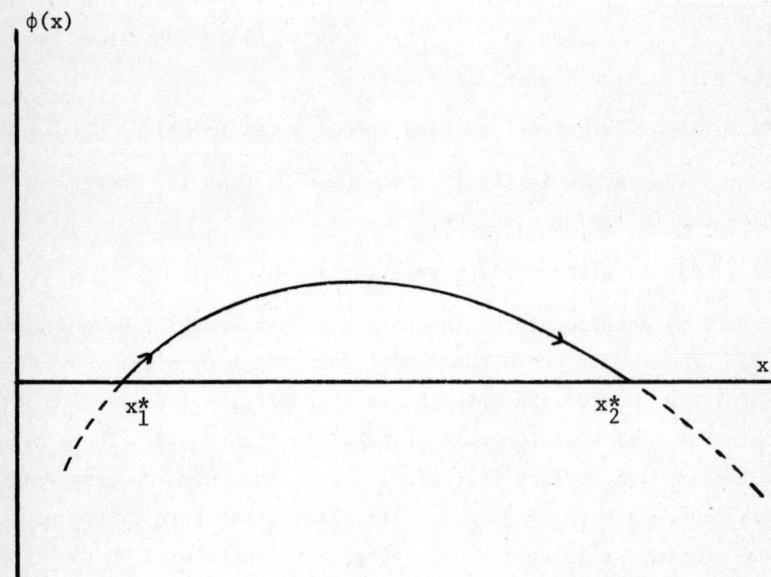

Figure 7.4

Because of the ambiguity in uniqueness, not all of the sensitivities to changes in the parameters are meaningful in this model. It will be noted, however, that the steady state values of x and k do not depend on the form of the desired investment function. Any function would serve the purpose because its only role is the determination of r, the real yield on capital, which is constant in the steady state. The rate of growth of per capita output is $(\dot{y}/y)^* = g(\dot{k}/k)^* = z^*$. This depends only on the form of the function g(z) and is independent of the parameters s, n, δ, or of the form of I(r).

Simple extensions to this model are easy to carry out and are suggested in the exercises at the end of this chapter.

7.4 Robinson's Criticisms

Another severe critic of the neo-classical school (besides Kaldor) is Mrs. Joan Robinson [9,10,11]. Unlike Kaldor, who is willing to use the concept of an aggregate capital, Mrs. Robinson denies that heterogeneous capital goods can be aggregated into a single measure of capital. Furthermore, whereas Kaldor postulates a definite relationship between investment and the rate of profit, Mrs. Robinson believes that investment decisions depend on a variety of factors not all of which are quantifiable. They are subsumed under the term animal spirits and includes such things as willingness to take a risk, experiences with past investment decisions, government policies etc. Like Kaldor she vehemently opposes the aggregate production function and the marginal productivity theory of income distribution but prefers an activity analysis approach to production, arguing that firms work in reality with a "book of who's who of blue prints."

In this book, we have not attempted to reformulate Mrs. Robinson's models in the standard framework we have been using all along for two reasons. First, many of her models are not closed and hence the determination of several variables is open to question. Because of this feature, it is not possible to derive growth paths explicitly. Secondly, almost all her arguments are verbal and due to her insistence on incorporation of realistic phenomena such as imperfect financial markets, monopoly power, wage bargaining etc., make quantification difficult. Admittedly, this does not do full justice to Mrs. Robinson's criticisms. The reader is referred to an excellent summary of Mrs. Robinson's (and Kaldor's as well) criticisms, in Wan [15], who has also recast her arguments into formal models and has critically examined her results. For other summaries of the controversy, but at a less technical level, see Jones [4] and Hamberg [3].

7.5 Summary

The controversy between the neo-classical school of thought, with which most of this book is concerned, and the Cambridge theory of growth and distribution has resulted in one of the liveliest of debates in economics. Although several models exist which have mixed the two approaches, two essential differences exist between the two schools. The Cambridge critics (Mrs. Robinson being the most vocal among them) insist that the aggregate production function is a nebulous concept because it uses a capital aggregate which is impossible to construct. They also oppose the marginal theory of income distribution on the ground that first it assumes perfect competition which is non-existent and furthermore, if technology is discrete marginal products are not well defined. Another significant difference is the independence of investment decisions from saving behavior. But, as we have seen in the Keynes-Wicksell models of Chapter 5, neo-classical formulations can readily accommodate the above Keynesian feature. We showed similarly in Section 7.2 that a production function with an independent investment function can lead to meaningful balanced growth paths without resorting to the marginal productivity theory. The results are, however, substantially different from those obtained from purely neo-classical models. As to which one is better, it is more a matter of empirical testing rather than one of theoretical superiority.

The issue of existence of a capital aggregate and an associated production function is one that the neo-classicists cannot easily duck. The necessary and sufficient conditions for the existence of such an aggregate measure are quite stringent and are not likely to be fully met. Most neo-classical economists acknowledge the conceptual problems associated with that concept but they would defend it as Solow did (see [13]); "in my mind it is either an illuminating parable, or else a mere device for handling data, to be used so long as it gives good empirical results and to be abandoned as soon as it doesn't, or as soon as something better comes along." Whether the "neo-classical parables" are valid or not depends on the use to which they are put and on whether the results obtained from them are useful in understanding long run growth behavior of an economy. We encourage the reader to study the Cambridge economists' criticisms carefully and make up his/her own mind.

REFERENCES

[1] Black, J., "The Technical Progress Function and the Production Function," Economica, 1962, pp. 166-70.

[2] Conlisk, John and R. Ramanathan, "Expedient Choice of Transforms in Phase Diagrams," Review of Economic Studies 36 (1), 1970, pp. 77-88.

[3] Hamberg, Daniel, Models of Economic Growth, Harper & Row, 1971.

[4] Jones, Hywel G., An Introduction to Modern Theories of Economic Growth, McGraw-Hill, 1976.

[5] Kaldor, Nicholas, "Alternative Theories of Distribution," Review of Economic Studies 23 (2), 1956, pp. 83-100.

[6] Kaldor, Nicholas and A. Mirrlees, "A New Model of Economic Growth," Review of Economic Studies 29 (3), 1962, pp. 174-92.

[7] Pasinetti, Luigi, "Rate of Profit and Income Distribution in Relation to Economic Growth," Review of Economic Studies 29 (4), 1962, pp. 267-79.

[8] Ramanathan, Ramu, "Investment Demand, Pasinetti Saving Behavior and Equilibrium Growth," Discussion Paper 78-4, UCSD Department of Economics, 1978.

[9] Robinson, Joan, "The Production Function and the Theory of Capital," Review of Economic Studies, 1953-4, pp. 81-106.

[10] Robinson, Joan, Essay in the Theory of Economic Growth, McMillan and Co., 1962.

[11] Robinson, Joan, The Accumulation of Capital, McMillan and Co., 1969.

[12] Samuelson, Paul and F. Modigliani, "The Pasinetti Paradox in Neo-classical and More General Models," Review of Economic Studies 33 (4), 1966, pp. 269-301.

[13] Solow, Robert, "Review of Capital and Growth," American Economic Review, Dec. 1966, pp. 1257-1260.

[14] Stein, Jerome, Money and Capacity Growth, Columbia University Press, New York, 1971.

[15] Wan, Henry, Economic Growth, Harcourt, Brace and Jovanovich, 1971.

EXERCISES

7.1 In Kaldor's simple model, consider other kinds of tax schemes, such as taxing profits and turning it over to labor or vice versa.

7.2 Verify the sensitivity table 7.2.

7.3 Redo the model in Section 7.1 with depreciation.

7.4 Analyze the model in Section 7.2 by assuming that λ is not exogenous but a function of k, that is, $\lambda(k)$. Compare this with earlier results.

7.5 In the model with technical progress function, assume that these are two income classes with different savings propensities.

CHAPTER 8

THE SPEED OF ADJUSTMENT IN GROWTH MODELS

Until now, the focus of our analysis has been on the existence of the balanced growth path and its properties. However, it is of considerable interest to consider the question: How long will it take an economic system to reach a balanced growth path? For example, suppose that a given economy is already in long run equilibrium growth. Now let the government increase the overall saving rate by appropriate fiscal measures. We know that (see exercise 3.1) the effect of this is to raise the growth rate initially but eventually the growth rate will move back to the natural rate. How long will it take to achieve nearly complete adjustment, if the values of the parameters of the system are known? What are the policy implications of the length of the adjustment period? If the adjustment period is very long, then an increase in the growth rate resulting from a higher saving rate will continue for a long time. On the other hand, if the fiscal policy goal is to raise the equilibrium level of per capita income, a small adjustment time is more desirable. If the model adjusts to equilibrium faster than the parameters are likely to change, then there is a strong justification for assuming the parameters to be constant. If adjustment is slow, the limiting behavior of the model is not very relevant because the values of the parameters would have changed in the interim period. It is therefore essential to know the adjustment time for a given model of economic growth. In this chapter, we take a broad spectrum of growth models and compare their speeds of adjustment.

8.1 The Solow-Swan Model

The first attempt at calculating adjustment times for growth models was made by Ryuzo Sato [5,6]. Assuming a Cobb-Douglas production function with constant returns to scale, he has obtained the speed of adjustment for the following Solow-Swan model with Harrod-neutral technical progress:

(8.1.1) $$Y = aK^{\alpha}(Le^{\lambda t})^{1-\alpha}$$

(8.1.2) $\dot{K} = sY - \delta K$

(8.1.3) $\dot{L}/L = n$

By following the same procedure as in Chapter 3, Section 3.2.2, we can obtain the rate of growth of output as follows:

$$(8.1.4) \qquad \dot{Y}/Y = \alpha\left[\frac{1}{g+\delta} + \frac{C}{sa}\, e^{-(1-\alpha)(g+\delta)t}\right]^{-1} + (1-\alpha)g - \alpha\delta$$

where $g = \lambda+n$ is the limiting rate of growth of aggregate output. Setting $t = 0$ in (8.1.4) and denoting the initial rate of growth by g_o, we obtain the constant C as

$$\frac{C}{sa} = \frac{g - g_o}{(g+\delta)[g_o-g+\alpha(g+\delta)]}$$

Therefore the aggregate growth rate g_t is given by

$$(8.1.5) \qquad g_t \equiv \dot{Y}/Y = \frac{\alpha(g+\delta)}{1 + \left[\dfrac{g - g_o}{(g_o-g)+\alpha(g+\delta)}\right] e^{-(1-\alpha)(g+\delta)t}} + g(1-\alpha) - \alpha\delta$$

The Sato papers analyze the speed of adjustment in terms of p_t, the adjustment ratio, defined as

(8.1.6) $p_t = (g_t-g_o)/(g-g_o)$

From an initial growth rate of g_o the economy moves towards g, the limiting growth rate, and at any time t has a growth rate g_t. Thus a high p_t implies that most of the adjustment has taken place. Substituting (8.1.6) in (8.1.5) we can solve explicitly for t as a function of p_t and the known parameters of the system.

$$(8.1.7) \qquad t = \frac{1}{(1-\alpha)(g+\delta)} \log\left[1 + \frac{\alpha p_t/(1-p_t)}{\alpha + \dfrac{g_o - g}{g + \delta}}\right]$$

Table 8.1 gives the adjustment time (in years) for $\alpha = .4$ and $.8$, $\delta = .04$, $g = .03$ and for various values of p_t. The typical range of values assumed for α is from .25 to .4. But, as argued by Conlisk [2], if human capital is included in K, then α is likely to be much higher, perhaps as high as 0.8. In almost all neo-classical growth models labor is assumed to accumulate at an exogenous rate whereas capital accumulates at an endogenously determined rate. Since investment in human capital diverts resources from other uses, it is endogenous and should logically be part of K which implies that α should be larger. If this is the case, the speed of adjustment is very small as seen from Table 8.1. It will take 115 to 193 years for 90 percent adjustment if $\alpha = .8$. Thus the limiting behavior of the Solow-Swan model is not particularly relevant because of the slow speed of adjustment.

How will a change in the parameters affect the adjustment time (see exercise 8.1)? A comparison of Tables 8.1 and 8.2 (especially for $g_o = .10$) indicates that an increase in the natural rate g lowers the adjustment time but not substantially. The following conclusions are easy to obtain from (8.1.7) and Tables 8.1, 8.2 and 8.3:

(i) The higher the initial growth rate the smaller the adjustment time.

(ii) If capital depreciates faster, then the adjustment time is reduced.

(iii) An increase in the share of capital α increases the adjustment period.

The above results can be substantiated by intuitive reasoning. We have seen that in most growth models the limiting growth rate is $\lambda + n$. Thus the exogenous labor input (measured in efficiency units) bottlenecks the growth rate. If capital depreciates slower or if the share of capital is larger, then firms can substitute capital for labor and thus evade the bottleneck for longer periods of time.

It is evident from the above analysis that a variety of alternative values for the parameters yield high adjustment periods. Without explicitly assuming a Cobb-Douglas production function but under the assumption that technical progress is factor-augmenting, A. B. Atkinson [1] has shown that the adjustment time is large. He has also shown that the higher the elasticity of substitution (σ) the larger the adjustment period. Since a larger value for σ implies greater substitutability of capital for labor, firms can

Table 8.1

ADJUSTMENT TIME (IN YEARS) FOR THE SOLOW-SWAN MODEL

(g = .03 and δ = .04)

p_t	$g_o - g < 0$		$g_o - g > 0$	
	g_o = .01	g_o = .025	g_o = .10	g_o = .035
.90	83(193)	59(171)	30(115)	51(159)
.75	58(124)	37(104)	15(61)	30(95)
.50	36(67)	19(53)	6(26)	15(47)

Note: The figures in parentheses are for α = .8 and those outside the parentheses are for α = .4.

Table 8.2

ADJUSTMENT TIME (IN YEARS) FOR THE SOLOW-SWAN MODEL

(g = .05 and δ = .04)

p_t	$g_o - g < 0$	$g_o - g > 0$	
	g_o = .045	g_o = .10	g_o = .055
.90	45(132)	29(102)	41(125)
.75	28(80)	15(57)	24(74)
.50	14(41)	6(26)	12(37)

Note: The figures in parentheses are for α = .8 and those outside the parentheses are for α = .4.

Table 8.3

ADJUSTMENT TIME (IN YEARS) FOR THE SOLOW-SWAN MODEL

($g = .05$ and $\delta = .07$)

p_t	$g_o - g < 0$		$g_o - g > 0$	
	$g_o = .01$	$g_o = .045$	$g_o = .10$	$g_o = .055$
.90	56(117)	33(98)	23(81)	31(94)
.75	41(76)	20(59)	13(45)	18(56)
.50	27(42)	10	6(21)	9(28)

delay the labor bottleneck. This immediately raises the question whether most growth models share this property or whether more realistic assumptions will reduce the adjustment time. In the next few sections we discuss the speed of adjustment of other growth models which are more sophisticated.

8.2 A Model with Unemployment

Conlisk [2] has extended the above model to include increasing returns to scale and unemployment by adding a few Keynesian equations to Sato's model. He shows that the adjustment time is reduced to a third of the previous estimates. Since the analysis is complicated we restrict ourselves to a discussion of the structural equations of the model and its main results.

The production function has the Cobb-Douglas form but with an increasing return to scale. We thus have

(8.2.1) $$Y = [a\ e^{\lambda t}\ K^{\alpha}\ L^{1-\alpha}]^{\beta}$$

where K and L are the amounts of capital and labor actually used and may differ from the available supply. Y is therefore the actual output. Denoting the full employment levels of capital and labor respectively by $\tilde{K}$ and $\tilde{L}$, potential output $\tilde{Y}$ is given by

(8.2.2) $$\tilde{Y} = [a\, e^{\lambda t} \tilde{K}^{\alpha} \tilde{L}^{1-\alpha}]^{\beta}$$

It is assumed that when the economy is fully employed, the saving income ratio is constant but when there is unemployment, the saving income ratio depends on the rate of unemployment u. More specifically,

(8.2.3) $$\tilde{S}/\tilde{Y} = a_o$$

(8.2.4) $$S/Y = a_o(1-u)^a \qquad a_o,\ a > 0$$

Investment demand (I) expressed as a ratio to potential saving ($\tilde{S}$) is determined by the effective rate of return to capital. Since the total return to capital is Kr, the effective rate of return is $Kr/\tilde{K}$. Thus

(8.2.5) $$I/\tilde{S} = b_o(Kr/\tilde{K})^b \qquad b > 0$$

Since desired saving must equal desired investment, we have the following equilibrium condition:

(8.2.6) $$I = S$$

The above level of investment adds to the potential stock of capital $\tilde{K}$ but only a fraction (1-u) of the potential stock of capital will be in actual use. Thus

(8.2.7) $$\dot{\tilde{K}} = I - \delta\tilde{K}$$

(8.2.8) $$K = (1-u)\tilde{K}$$

Because the production function exhibits increasing returns to scale, paying each factor its marginal product will overexhaust the total product. A simple income distribution is to pay each factor the proportion $1/\beta$ of its marginal product so as to exactly distribute the total product. Thus

(8.2.9) $$r = \frac{1}{\beta}\frac{\partial Y}{\partial K}$$

The potential supply of labor is assumed to grow at the exogenous rate n.

(8.2.10) $$\tilde{L} = \tilde{L}_o e^{nt}$$

Assuming that the rate of unemployment (u) is the same for both factors (somewhat unrealistic but a useful simplification), we obtain

(8.2.11) $L = (1-u)\tilde{L}$

The wage rate is given by

(8.2.12) $w = \frac{1}{\beta}\frac{\partial Y}{\partial L}$

Equations (8.2.1) through (8.2.12) completely specify the system for the determination of the 12 endogenous variables $Y,\tilde{Y},K,\tilde{K},L,\tilde{L},S,\tilde{S},I,w,r$ and u. Using annual data for the United States for the period 1929-59, excluding six war years, Conlisk has estimated the parameter a to be 3.84 and b to be 1.36. Table 8.4 presents the adjustment time for $\beta = 1.1$, $\delta = .04$ and $g = .03$. A comparison of Tables 8.1 and 8.4 shows that for $\alpha = .4$ the adjustment time in the unemployment model is one-third of the same for the Sato model. For $\alpha = .8$ the adjustment period is halved by the unemployment model. It is therefore evident that the introduction of unemployment and increasing returns to scale substantially increases the speed of adjustment making limiting behavior much more relevant.

Table 8.4

ADJUSTMENT TIME (IN YEARS) FOR THE UNEMPLOYMENT MODEL

($g = .03$ and $\delta = .04$)

p_t	$g_o - g < 0$		$g_o - g > 0$	
	$g_o = .01$	$g_o = .025$	$g_o = .10$	$g_o = .035$
.90	28(107)	21(96)	11(67)	19(90)
.75	20(68)	13(58)	6(35)	11(54)
.50	12(37)	7(30)	2(15)	5(26)

Note: The figures in parentheses are for $\alpha = .8$ and those outside the parentheses are for $\alpha = .4$.

8.3 Other Models

Kazuo Sato [7] has extended Ryuzo Sato's model by incorporating embodied technical change and exponential depreciation of capital. He shows that for g - .04, a - 1/2, δ = .08 and n = .01 to .03, the adjustment period for the vintage model is 25 to 37.5 percent of that for the Sato model. A.B. Atkinson [1] has also calculated the adjustment period for the Shell-Stiglitz [8] vintage model with two types of capital and shown that the period of adjustment is substantially smaller than that of the simple Solow-Swan model. Gapinski [9] too uses a vintage model with a CES production technology at the design stage but a fixed coefficient technology, ex post. He shows that the greater the elasticity of substitution, the slower is the adjustment. Using a two-sector growth model with fixed coefficients, Ramanathan [3] has shown that for a variety of choice of parameters, the adjustment period is only 2 to 5 years, a conclusion in strong contrast to most other models. However, in a later paper Ramanathan [4] relaxed the fixed coefficients assumption and used the CES production function. He showed that if elasticity of substitution (σ) is not small in both sectors then the adjustment time can be very large. Thus $\sigma = 0$ is a very crucial assumption. All these provide further evidence that the speed of adjustment is very sensitive to the specification of the model.

REFERENCES

[1] Atkinson, A. B.: "The Timescale of Economic Models: How Long is the Long Run?", Review of Economic Studies, April 1969.

[2] Conlisk, John: "Unemployment in a Neo-classical Growth Model - The Effect on Speed of Adjustment," Economic Journal, September 1966.

[3] Ramanathan, R.: "Adjustment Time in the Two-Sector Growth Model with Fixed Coefficients," Economic Journal, December 1973.

[4] Ramanathan, R.: "The Elasticity of Substitution and the Speed of Convergence in Growth Models," Economic Journal, September 1975.

[5] Sato, Ryuzo: "Fiscal Policy in a Neo-classical Growth Model - An Analysis of the Time Required for Equilibrating Adjustment," Review of Economic Studies, February 1963.

[6] Sato, Ryuzo: "The Harrod-Domar Model Versus the Neo-classical Growth Model," Economic Journal, June 1964.

[7] Sato, Kazuo: "On the Adjustment Time in Neo-classical Growth Models," Review of Economic Studies, July 1966.

[8] Shell, Carl and Joseph Stiglitz: "The Allocation of Investment in a Dynamic Economy," Quarterly Journal of Economics, November 1967.

[9] Gapinski, James H.: "Steady Growth, Policy Stocks and Speed of Adjustment under Embodiment and Putty-Clay," Journal of Macroeconomics, Spring 1981, pp. 147-176.

[10] Satro, Ryuzo: "Adjustment Time and Economic Growth Revisited," Journal of Macroeconomics, Summer 1980, pp. 239-246.

EXERCISES

8.1 Another approach to the speed of adjustment issue is to note that the slope of the $\dot{k}/k$ curve (see Figure 3.3) at the equilibrium capital intensity k* is a measure of the adjustment speed. The steeper the slope is, the faster k* is likely to be reached. For example, for the Solow-Swan model,

$$\frac{\dot{k}}{k} = s\,\frac{f(k)}{k} - (\lambda+n+\delta)$$

a. Show that the absolute value of the slope of the above curve at k* is given by

$$V \equiv \left|\frac{d}{dk}\,(\dot{k}/k)\right|^{*} = (\lambda+n+\delta)\,[1-\pi(k^{*})]/k^{*}$$

where $\pi(k)$ is the share of capital.

b. Using the above expression, show that an increase in λ, n or δ will reduce the adjustment period whenever the elasticity of substitution σ is not less than 1.

c. Examine the effect of an increase in the saving rate.

CHAPTER 9
OPTIMAL GROWTH

In all the models discussed so far, the saving and consumption behavior were basically determined at each point in time without any regard to the question of whether a given economy would be willing to save more in one period and invest it so that a larger output may be obtained in the next period and hence a larger consumption. The saving rate s is often a given parameter which can be altered by appropriate fiscal policy. We did attempt to find the "optimum" value of s by maximizing the per capita consumption level <u>in the steady state</u>. Thus among all possible steady state paths, we chose the Golden Rule path for which consumption per capita in the steady state was the highest. In models of optimal growth the saving or consumption behavior is not simply given but is chosen so as to maximize an <u>inter-temporal</u> objective function (that is, one defined over several periods) rather than one defined only in the steady state. More specifically, an entire consumption path c(t) is chosen, from among alternative consumption paths see (Figure 9.1) such that an objective function of the form W[c(t),t] is maximized over a given horizon [0,T], subject to appropriate constraints.

In this chapter, we present an introduction to optimal growth models. Only a basic model is presented here. Detailed proofs are not given and may be found in Wan [5] or Burmeister and Dobel [1]. Additional models may be found in Shell [4].

9.1 Inter-temporal Optimization

Let u(c) be a utility function (twice differentiable) assumed to depend only on the amount c, the level of per capita consumption. Note that u doesn't explicitly depend on t. The welfare function that is maximized as part of the social choice problem of selecting an optimum consumption path is as follows.

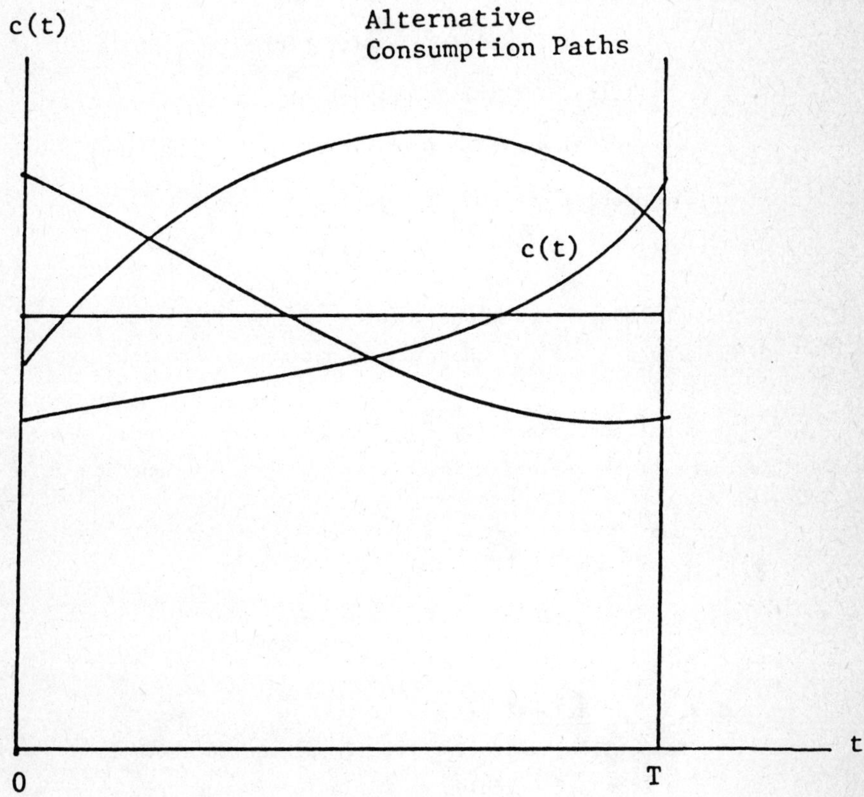

Figure 9.1

$$(9.1) \qquad V = W[c(t),t] = \int_0^T e^{-\rho t} u[c(t)]dt$$

W will be readily recognized as an inter-temporal utility function. ρ is the discount rate (≥ 0). Thus future consumption levels are valued less depending on how far from the present they are valued at. We now impose additional assumptions relevant to a neo-classical growth model. Output is given, as usual, by a linearly homogeneous production function satisfying the Inada conditions. Consumption equals output less net saving (or equivalently investment). Thus

$$(9.2) \qquad \begin{aligned} c(t) &= C(t)/L(t) = f[k(t)] - S(t)/L(t) \\ &= f[k(t)] - [\dot{K}(t) + \delta K(t)]/L(t) \\ &= f[k(t)] - \dot{k}(t) - (n+\delta)k(t) \end{aligned}$$

The social choice problem can now be formally stated as follows.

$$\underset{k(t)}{\text{Max}}\ W[f\{k(t)\} - \dot{k}(t) - (n+\delta)k(t),t]$$

subject to the "boundary conditions" $k(0) = k_0$ and $k(T) = k_T$. Note that the original goal of choosing an optimum consumption path has been transformed to that of choosing an optimum capital intensity $k(0)$. The terminal condition $k(T) = k_T$ can be relaxed as will be seen later. In terms of the specific inter-temporal utility function we get

$$(9.3) \qquad \begin{aligned} V &= \int_0^T e^{-\rho t} u[f\{k(t)\} - \dot{k}(t) - (n+\delta)k(t)]dt \\ &\equiv \int_0^T F[k(t),\dot{k}(t),t]dt \qquad \text{defining } F[\cdot]\ . \end{aligned}$$

9.1.1 Calculus of Variations

The inter-temporal optimization problem presented above is a special case of a standard Calculus of Variations procedure, which may be stated as follows:

$$(9.4) \qquad \underset{k(t)}{\text{Max}}\ V = \int_0^T F(k,\dot{k},t)dt$$

subject to the constraint that k(0) and k(T) are given. The function F is assumed to be twice differentiable and k(t) is also differentiable. In our case, we maximize the social welfare V with respect to the time path of capital intensity. The condition that F must be twice differentiable translates into the assumption that the utility function is twice differentiable. This approach to the problem was originally used by Ramsey [3]. Figure 9.2 illustrates this inter-temporal optimization problem. Each choice of a time path in 9.2.a determines a curve $F(k,\dot{k},t)$ in 9.2.b , associated with which there is a welfare index V. The problem is to choose k(t) so as to maximize the area under the curve in 9.2.b .

Euler-Lagrange Theorem: This theorem gives the necessary condition for an interior optimum as

$$(9.5) \qquad \frac{\partial F}{\partial k} = \frac{d}{dt}\left(\frac{\partial F}{\partial \dot{k}}\right) \qquad \forall\ t \in [0,T]$$

For a proof of this see Wan's book pp. 406-411. We shall only apply it in the growth context.

$$\frac{\partial F}{\partial k} = e^{-\rho t}u'(c)[f'(k) - (n+\delta)]$$

$$\frac{\partial F}{\partial \dot{k}} = -e^{-\rho t}u'(c)$$

The necessary condition for an interior maximum is thus

$$e^{-\rho t}u'(c)[f'(k) - (n+\delta)] = \frac{d}{dt}[-e^{-\rho t}u'(c)]$$

$$= -e^{\rho t}\dot{u}'(c) + \rho e^{-\rho t}u'(c)$$

where $\dot{u}'$ is the time derivative of u'(c) which is the marginal utility of consumption. By cancelling $e^{-\rho t}$ and bringing the u terms to one side we get

$$(9.6) \qquad \frac{\dot{u}'[c(t)]}{u'[c(t)]} = \frac{u''(c)\dot{c}}{u'(c)} = \rho + n + \delta - f'[k(t)]$$

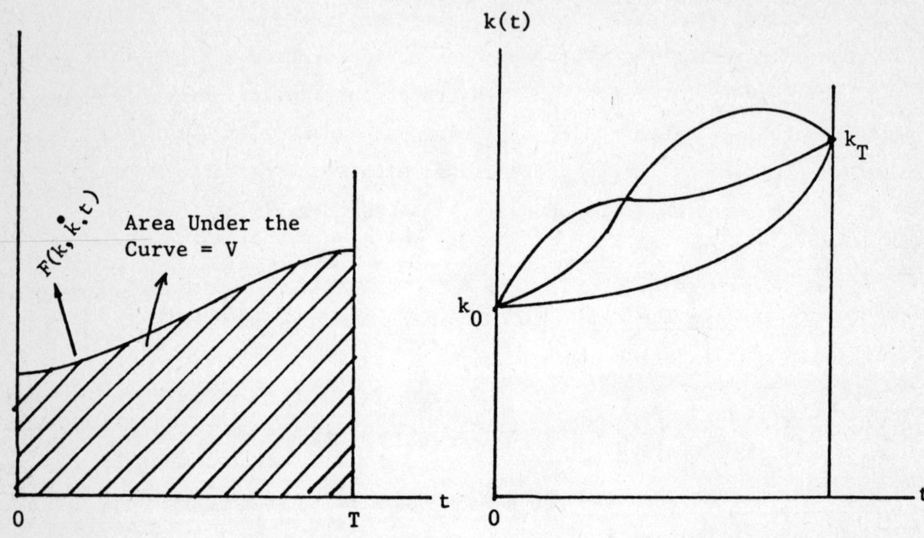

Figure 9.2

To examine the above equation further, denote $u'[c(t)]$ by $q(t)$. Note that $q(t)$ is the marginal utility of consumption and can be interpreted as the shadow price of consumption in "utils" at time t. Its present value is

$$(9.7) \qquad p(t) \equiv e^{-\rho t} q(t) = e^{-\rho t} u'[c(t)]$$

Using this in the Euler equation we get

$$(9.8) \qquad \dot{p}/p = n + \delta - f'[k(t)]$$

which can be solved as follows.

$$(9.9) \qquad p(t) = p(0) \exp\left[\int_0^t \{n+\delta-f'[k(t)]\}dt\right]$$

or equivalently,

$$(9.10) \quad p(0) = p(t) \exp\left[\int_0^t (f'-n-\delta)dt\right]$$

Before exploring the above results further, we shall consider an alternative approach to the issue of inter-temporal optimization.

9.1.2 Optimal Control Theory

The calculus of variations problem is also equivalent, in most cases, to the optimal control problem originally solved by Pontryagin [2]. Let $k(t)$ be a variable characterizing the state of a system. Let $x(t)$ be the variable whose time path is to be chosen optimally. $k(t)$ is called the "state" variable and $x(t)$ the "control" variable. The system is also characterized by an equation of motion, called the "transitional equation," of the form $\dot{k}(t) = \phi[k(t),x(t),t]$. The objective function to be maximized is of the form $G(k,x,t)$. The optimal control problem is stated as follows:

$$\max_{x(t)} \int_0^T G[k(t),x(t),t]dt$$

subject to

(9.11) $\dot{k}(t) = \phi[k(t),x(t),t]$

(9.12) $k(0) = k_0$ and $k(T) = k_T$

The last two boundary conditions are called "transversality conditions" which can be relaxed and will also pay an important role when the time horizon is infinite, i.e. $T \to \infty$.

A Theorem on the Maximum Principle: This theorem states that, if the function $x^*(t)$ solves the above optimal control problem, there exists a function of t, called $\lambda(t)$, satisfying the following conditions.

(9.13) $x^*(t)$ also maximizes

$$H[k(t),x(t),\lambda(t),t] = G[k(t),x(t),t] + \lambda(t)\phi[k(t),x(t),t]$$

and hence $\partial H/\partial x = 0$ for an interior solution. Also,

(9.14) $\dot{\lambda}(t) = -\partial H/\partial k \Big|_{x(t) = x^*(t)}$

(9.15) $\lambda(T) \geq 0,\ \lambda(T) \cdot x(T) = 0$

This theorem can actually be stated more generally for a problem with multi-dimensional state and control variables. We will not prove this but only apply it.

The function H is called the "Hamiltonian" and $\lambda(t)$ is called the "dual" variable. It will be recognized that λ is similar to the Lagrangian multiplier of the static optimization problem subject to constraints. The calculus of variations approach fails when the solution is at the boundary of the space of feasible solutions, but the control theoretic approach does not.

Let us now apply the maximum principle to the problem of choosing the optimum consumption path. The Hamiltonian is now (with $x \equiv c$)

$$H = e^{-\rho t}u[c(t)] + \lambda(t)[f[k(t)] - c(t) - (n+\delta)k(t)]$$

For an interior solution, a necessary condition is $\partial H/\partial c = 0$. This implies that

$$e^{-\rho t}u'[c(t)] - \lambda(t) = 0 \quad \text{or}$$

(9.16) $$\lambda(t) = e^{-\rho t}u'[c(t)]$$

Thus the dual variable $\lambda(t)$ is nothing but the discounted present value of the marginal utility of consumption, which we earlier denoted by $p(t)$ [see equation (9.7)].

The condition 9.14 gives

$$\dot{\lambda}(t) \equiv \dot{p}(t) = - p(t)[f'[k(t)] - (n+\delta)]$$

or $$\dot{p}(t)/p(t) = n + \delta - f'[k(t)]$$

which is the same as equation (9.8). Thus both the calculus of variations approach and the control theoretic approach give identical results in this model.

9.2 Economic Interpretations

It is possible to give a variety of economic interpretations to the results obtained so far. First consider a special case. Suppose that $\rho = 0$ and that we are already in the steady state, that is, $k(t) = k^*$ and $c(t) = c^*$. The left-hand side of (9.6) is then zero. It follows that $n + \delta = f'(k^*)$. Recall that this was the Golden Rule condition, which when combined with the steady state condition $sf(k^*)/k^* = n + \delta$, gave $s^* = k^*f'(k^*)/f(k^*) = \pi(k^*)$, the share of capital. Thus the Golden Rule is a special case of the optimum rule.

Note that $p(0) = u'[c(0)]$ and is equal to the extra utility derived from an extra unit of consumption initially (at $t = 0$). Suppose that instead of consuming it you had invested it until the time t and let it compound continuously, what would you have? The "net" marginal product of capital after deducting depreciation is $f'(k) - \delta$. Thus one unit of addition to capital (rather than to consumption) will produce $f'(k) - \delta$ extra units of output at a given instant. When compounded continuously, we get at time t, $\exp [\int_0^t (f'(k)-\delta)dt]$. But in the meantime population has grown by a multiple of e^{nt}. Therefore, on a per capita basis the gain in output by saving and investing rather than by consuming it is $\exp [\int_0^t [f'(k)-n-\delta]dt]$. The marginal utility when this output is consumed is $p(t)$ times that because, on the margin, $p(t)$ is the extra utility per unit of consumption. Thus the Euler equation can be given the following economic interpretation. The marginal utility of consumption at time 0 is equated to the marginal utility of the consumption derived (in present value terms) by sacrificing consumption initially and investing it to produce additional output in the future.

Another interesting question that arises is "under what conditions will consumption increase (or decrease)?" This can also be answered by looking at the Euler equation. Note that $f'[k(t)]$ is the rent on capital $r(t)$. The present value of the rental, net of depreciation, is $r(t) - \delta - \rho = f'[k(t)] - \rho - \delta$. If this exceeds n, the rate of growth of population, then $\dot{u}[c(t)]$ is < 0, under the assumption that $u'(c) > 0$. If we also assume diminishing marginal utility, $u''(c) < 0$, which implies that when $\dot{u}' < 0$, consumption must rise, because $\dot{u} = u''c$. Thus

$$\dot{c}(t)\left\{ \begin{matrix} \geq \\ = \\ < \end{matrix} \right. 0 \quad \text{according as } r - \delta - \rho \left\{ \begin{matrix} \geq \\ = \\ < \end{matrix} \right. n$$

If the net rental rate exceeds n, the consumption path will be rising. This can also be seen by looking at the time path of $p(t)$.

When $r - \delta - \rho = n$ at first and then goes up, the marginal utility $p(t)$ goes down and hence $c(t)$ will increase. Another way of looking at it is as follows. If $r - \delta - \rho - n$ rises, a unit of consumption sacrificed today produces more output and hence future consumption will go up, that is, $c(t)$ will go up.

Yet another interpretation is possible. Recall the golden rule condition $r^* - \delta = f'(k^*) - \delta = n$ which said that the net return on capital should equal n. The Euler equation gives a generalization of that condition. We can rewrite the Euler equation as $f'(k) - \delta + (\dot{p}/p) = n$. The left-hand side has the extra term $(\dot{p}/p)$ which is the rate of change of marginal utility. Therefore the net yield to capital plus that to utility should equal the rate of growth of population.

9.3 Phase Diagram Analysis

The optimal trajectory must satisfy the following differential equations in k and c:

$$(9.17)\qquad \dot{k} = f[k(t)] - (n+\delta)k(t) - c(t)$$

$$= g[k(t)] - c(t) \qquad \text{defining } g(k). \text{ Also}$$

$$u''\dot{c}/u' = \rho + n + \delta - f'[k(t)]$$

which can also be written as

$$(9.18)\qquad \dot{c} = u'(c)[\rho-g'(k)]/u''(c)$$

$$(9.19)\qquad k(0) = k_0,\quad k(T) = k_T$$

If equation (9.17) is differentiated with respect to t and c substituted from (9.18), we get a second order differential equation in k. Solution of the differential equation requires two boundary conditions, and hence the need for the transversality conditions (9.19). If the t argument is suppressed, you will note that (9.17) and (9.18) constitute a familiar pair of differential equations and are amendable to Phase Diagram analysis. The condition $\dot{c} = 0$ implies that $g'(k) = \rho$ or $f'(k) = n + \delta + \rho$ which is the well-known Golden Rule condition for $\rho \neq 0$. If $f(k)$ has the neo-classical properties, a unique k^* such that $\dot{c} = 0$ exists. Thus $\dot{c} = 0$ implies a vertical line in the Phase Diagram (see Figure 9.3).

The condition $\dot{k} = 0$ implies $c = g(k)$. $\partial c/\partial k = g'(k) = f'(k) - (n+\delta) = 0$ at $\bar{k}$ say. Because $f'' < 0$, $\bar{k} > k^*$. If $k < \bar{k}$ then $g'(k) > 0$ and if $k > \bar{k}$ then $g'(k) < 0$. Therefore $g(k)$ increases until $k = \bar{k}$ is reached and thereafter decreases. The slope of $g(k)$ at $k^* = g'(k^*) = \rho$. If $\rho = 0$, that is, if the future is not discounted, then $\bar{k} = k^*$. It is readily seen that the concavity of f and u assures an interior value of (k^*,c^*). Let us now draw the directional arrows. From (9.18), $\partial\dot{c}/\partial k = -(u'/u'')g'' < 0$, because $u' > 0$, u'', $g'' < 0$. Therefore from the $\dot{c} = 0$ relation if k increases, c becomes negative and hence c decreases. The arrows for c are therefore as in the diagram. From (9.18), $\partial\dot{k}/\partial c < 0$ unambiguously. Therefore above the $\dot{k} = 0$ curve k decreases implying the arrows drawn. It is obvious that the steady state is a saddle point.

9.3.1 The Transversality Conditions

Until now we have not made any use of the boundary conditions. Note that each solution to the Euler equation corresponds to an optimum trajectory. Thus the planner who carries out the optimization procedure has to specify the initial and terminal conditions. Several possibilities arise.

Case 1: $k_0 < k_T \leq k^*$ (equivalent to $k_T < k_0 \leq k^*$): Figure 9.4 depicts this case. Per capita consumption will monotonically increase whereas k(t) might increase at first and then decrease. The dotted lines are two possible paths. Note that the steady state path is not feasible unless $k_T = k^*$.

<u>Case 2: $k^* \leq k_0 < k_T$ (similar to $k_T < k_0$):</u> The dotted lines in Figure 9.5 are again the feasible paths. As in Case 1 steady state is not feasible. In fact, all finite horizon problems rule out the steady state unless k* is on the boundary.

<u>Case 3: $k_0 < k^* < k_T$:</u> Note from Figure 9.6 that c(t) cannot be above the g(k) curve as otherwise k_T cannot be attained.

<u>Case 4: $k_T < k^* < k_0$:</u> In this case c(t) cannot be below the g(k) curve (Figure 9.7).

<u>The Infinite Horizon Case</u>: If the planning horizon is infinite, several modifications are needed. The terminal transversality condition is replaced by the condition $\underset{t\to\infty}{\mathrm{lt}}\, k(t) = k^*$. In other words, the steady state is attained in the long run. Secondly the integral $\int_0^\infty e^{-\rho t} u[c(t)d]dt$ must converge for which either u[c] must be bounded from above (i.e. satiation) and ρ must be positive, or f[k(t)] is bounded above and (ρ > 0).

If f and u are concave functions with either of them bounded above, then there is at most one optimal trajectory that satisfies the Euler equation and the new transversality condition.

The proof of this is on pages 306-307 of Wan's book. Figure 9.3 makes this clear. The dotted line is the only time path that will attain the steady state in the long run. Furthermore, any arbitrary (k_0, c_0) cannot assure that (k^*, c^*) will eventually be attained. For a given k_0, c_0 must be such as to put the system on the dotted line.

The more general statement of the Transversality condition is:

$$\underset{t\to\infty}{\mathrm{lt}} \left(\frac{\partial F}{\partial k}\right) k(t) = 0$$

in the Variational form and $\underset{t\to\infty}{\mathrm{lt}}\, p(t)k(t) = 0$ in the Control Theory form. The alternative condition implies that if $f'(k) \neq n + \delta + \rho$ then $\underset{t\to\infty}{\mathrm{lt}}\, k(t) = 0$, that is, the economy eventually eats away its capital.

The infinite horizon case raises a whole host of problems which are discussed very well in Wan's book, page 273.

Existence: The issue of existence is not trivial because some models may give rise to the first-order conditions which have no solution. In general, if W is bounded above, existence is not difficult. See Wan pp. 308-312 on this issue.

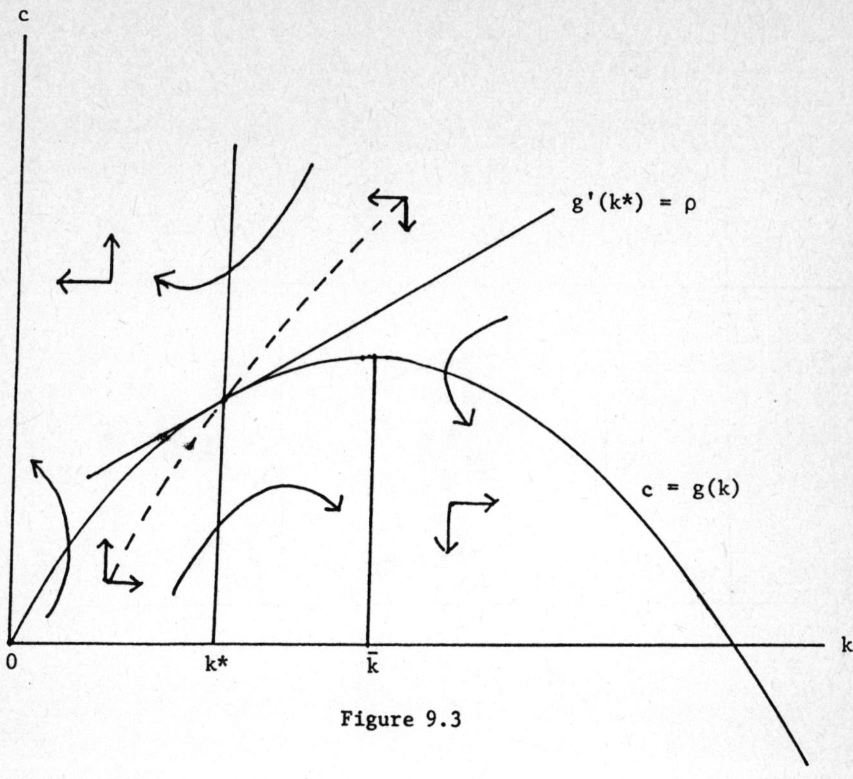

Figure 9.3

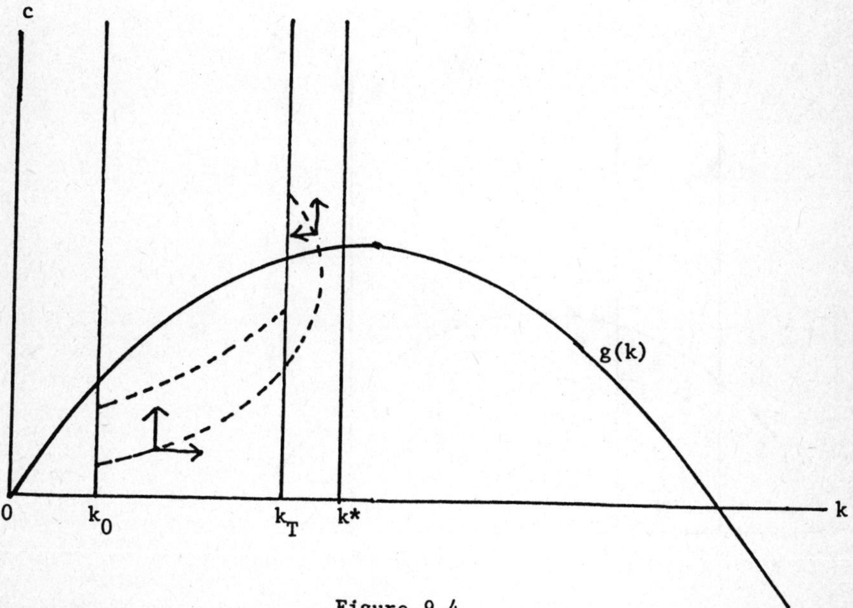

Figure 9.4

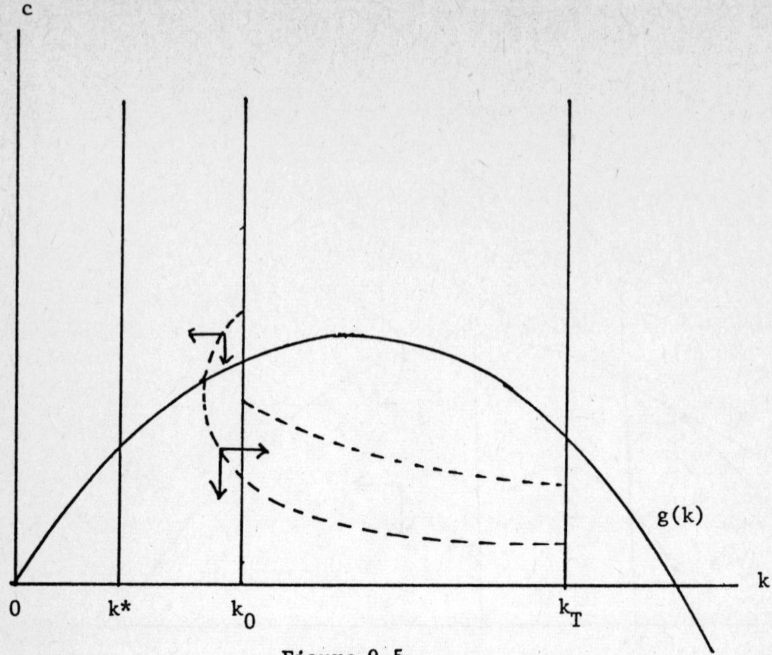

Figure 9.5

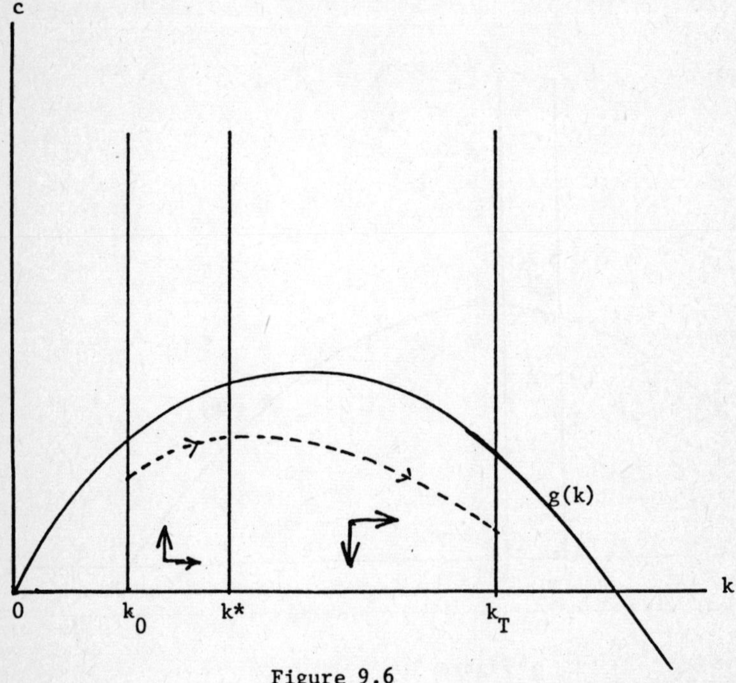

Figure 9.6

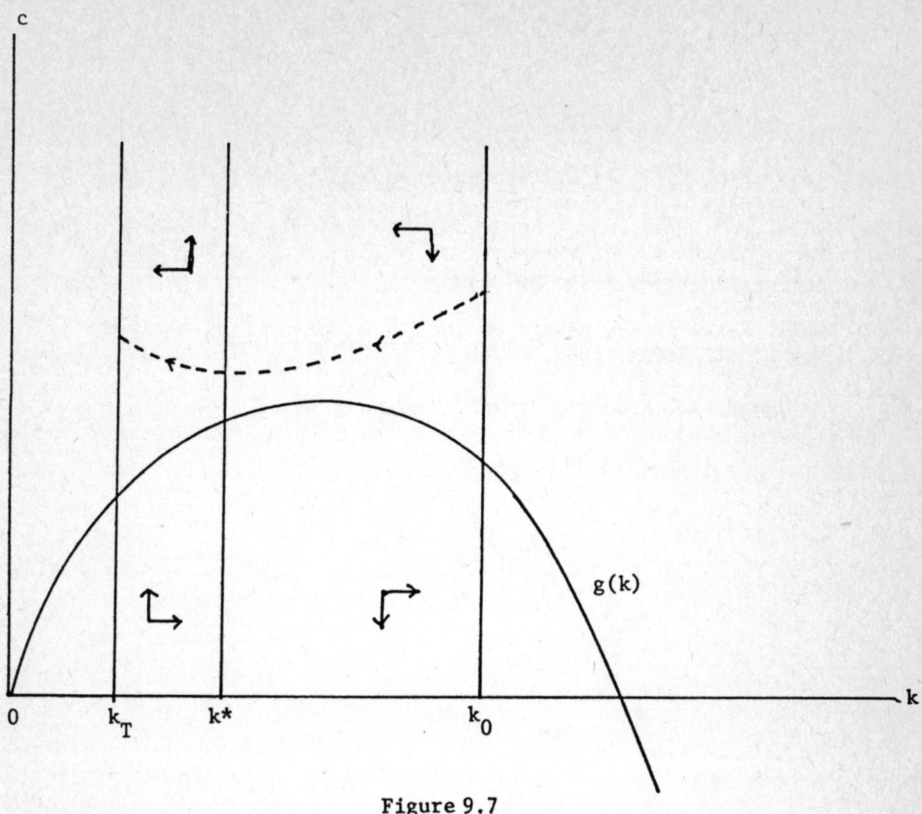

Figure 9.7

REFERENCES

[1] Burmeister, Edwin and A.R. Dobell, _Mathematical Theories of Economic Growth_, Mac Millan, 1970.

[2] Pontryagin, L.S., _et al_, _The Mathematical Theory of Optimal Processes_, Interscience Publishers, 1962.

[3] Ramsey, Frank P., "A Mathematical Theory of Living," _Economic Journal_, Vol. 38, 1928, pp. 543-549.

[4] Shell, Karl, (Ed.), _Essays on the Theory of Optimal Economic Growth_, MIT Press, 1967.

[5] Wan, Henry Y., Economic Growth, Harcourt, Brace, Jovanovich, 1971.

EXERCISES

9.1. Consider a Solow-Swan growth model with capital-labor ratio k and (per worker) production function f(k). Two approaches for setting a desirable saving level yield different conclusions about the long-run equilibrium saving rate, call it s.

(a) The golden-rule approach. Set s so that k obeys $f'(k) = n + \delta$, where n is the population growth rate and δ is the depreciation rate.

(b) The optimal-growth approach. Set s so that k obeys $f'(k) = n + \delta + \rho$, where ρ is a social discount rate.

Answer the following two questions.

(i) State the "golden-rule" optimization problem which $f'(k) = n + \delta$ solves. Then state the "optimal-growth" optimization problem which $f'(k) = n + \delta + \rho$ solves.

(ii) Which approach (golden-rule or optimal-growth) yields a larger value of k in the long run? Explain in terms of economic intuition why the differing assumptions of the two approaches lead to the difference in result.

9.2. The Planning Commission of a county decides to choose a consumption plan c(t) so as to maximize

$$W = \int_0^T e^{-\rho t} U[c(t) - \bar{c}]\, dt$$

subject to the conditions ($\rho > 0$ and $\bar{c}$ is fixed for all t)

$$\dot{k}(t) = f\{k(t)\} - nk(t) - c(t)$$

$$k(0) = k_0 \text{ and } k(T) = k_T,$$

where $U(\cdot)$ is a utility function such that $U(0) = 0$, $U' > 0$ and $U'' < 0$.

a. Provide an intuitive interpretation for the utility function $U(\cdot)$.

b. From the optimality conditions, derive the differential equations in k(t) and c(t).

c. Draw the phase diagram for the case $k_0 < k_T < k^*$ and trace the optimal path (k,c) in the diagram. Does the plan call for increasing/decreasing k(t) and c(t) over time?

CHAPTER 10

TWO SECTOR GROWTH MODELS

In this and the next chapters, we consider models in which the economy consists of two types of commodities, consumption goods and investment (or capital) goods. It will be recalled that in a single good economy, the commodity served both consumption and investment needs. In practice, however, it will be more appropriate to treat the production and demand for the two types of commodities separately. We first review the static two-sector, two-factor model and derive many propositions which will be useful in discussing open economy models. Issues on dynamic behavior of these models are then explored.

10.1 The Static Two-Sector Model

As stated above, there are now two kinds of goods, each produced by capital and labor. One of the goods will be labelled "consumption goods" and the other "capital or investment goods". The commodities will be distinct in the sense that all consumption goods will, by definition, be fully consumed. Similarly, all investment goods will be fully saved and invested to add to the existing stock of capital. There is thus no saving of consumption goods and no consumption of investment goods.

10.1.1 The Supply Side

The supply of the two goods are given by the neo-classical production functions

(10.1.1) $$Y_i = F_i(K_i, L_i) = L_i f_i(k_i) \qquad i=1,2$$

where

(10.1.2) $$k_i = K_i/L_i$$

Per capita output is

(10.1.3) $$y_i = Y_i/L = \ell_i f_i(k_i)$$

(10.1.4) $$\ell_i = L_i/L$$

L is total labor. Full employment of both factors implies the following two equations.

(10.1.5) $K = K_1 + K_2$

(10.1.6) $L = L_1 + L_2$

Dividing these two equations by L and using (10.1.2) and (10.1.4) we get

(10.1.7) $k = k_1 \ell_1 + k_2 \ell_2$

(10.1.8) $1 = \ell_1 + \ell_2$

Let P_i be the prices of the two commodities, p their ratio $(=P_1/P_2)$ with good 2 as the numeraire , r be the rate of return to capital, W be the nominal wage rate, and w be the wage-rental ratio. We also assume that consumption goods are labelled 2 and investment goods are labelled 1. Perfect competition, full flexibility of all prices and profit maximization yield the following equations.

(10.1.9) $r = P_i f_i'$

(10.1.10) $W = P_i(f_i - k_i f_i')$

(10.1.11) $w = W/r = (f_i/f'_i) - k_i$

(10.1.12) $p = P_1/P_2 = f'_2/f_1'$

Given the overall capital-labor ratio (k) and the wage rental ratio w, the above 14 equations uniquely determine the 14 unknowns $p, y_1, y_2, k_1, k_2, \ell_1, \ell_2, Y_1, Y_2, K_1, K_2, L_1, L_2$ and W. It will be useful to present a graphical summary of the above results. Figure 10.1 presents the average product of labor in each industry $f_i(k_i)$ in terms of the capital intensity k_i. By proceeding as we did in Chapter 2, it is easily verified that when w - OX , the corresponding k_i is OA. We thus have $k_i(w)$ as the capital intensities that correspond to efficient allocation of the factors. It is readily

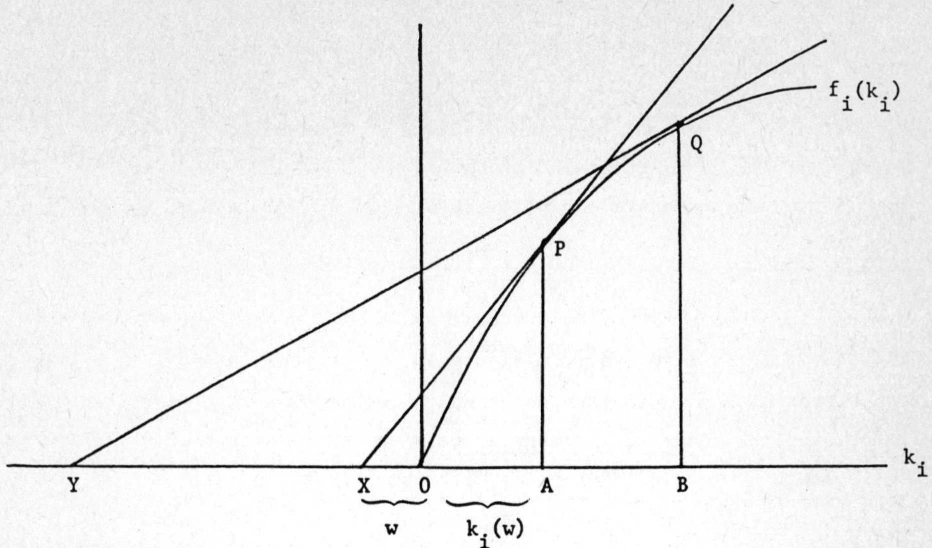

Figure 10.1

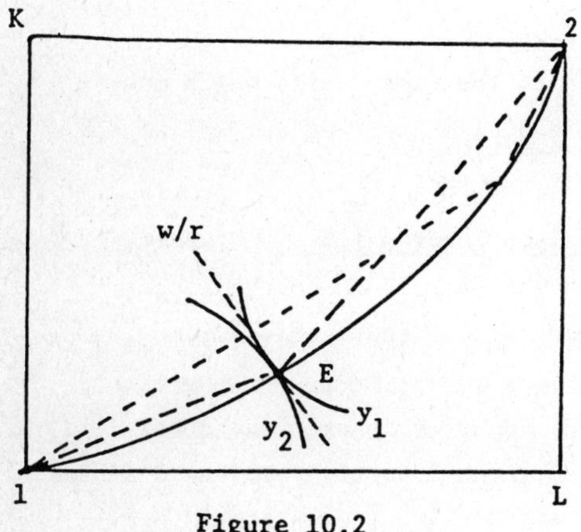

Figure 10.2

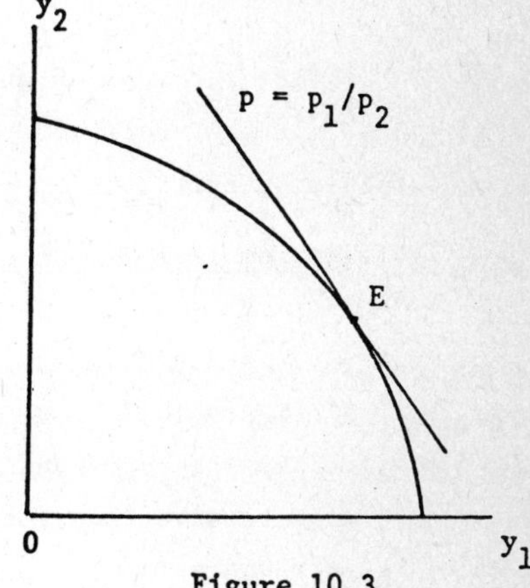

Figure 10.3

seen that as w increases, k_i also increases. Figure 10.2 represents the well-known Edgeworth-Box diagram. The contract curve is the locus of efficient allocations and corresponds to tangency points of isoquants. The common slopes of these isoquants at these tangency points are the wage-rental ratios.

Given a fixed overall capital labor ratio k, a fixed w, and the neoclassical conditions on the production functions, there exists a unique point E on the contract curve which is a point of efficiency. The capital intensities $k_i(w)$ as well as the per capita output levels $y_i(w)$ are also determined from Figure 10.2. The combinations of y_1 and y_2 corresponding to each point on the contract curve determine the production-possibility frontier represented in Figure 10.3. For the point E to be a production equilibrium, the price ratio p must be the slope of the tangent to the production possibility frontier at E. This determines p(w). Equations (10.1.7) and (10.1.8) then determine ℓ_1 and ℓ_2. From all of these, the remaining variables are readily determined.

It will be noted that there is a one-to-one correspondence between w and p. Given w, a unique p will be determined that makes the supply side completely efficient. Equivalently, given p, there exists a unique w that will maintain production efficiency.

Before turning our attention to the demand side which makes possible the overall determination of w and p, let us explore the supply side further.

Theorem 10.1 (Stolper-Samuelson Theorem [12]: An increase in the price of a commodity increases the return to the factor used more intensively in the production of that commodity.

In Figure 10.2 $k_2 > k_1$ at every point of the contract curve. Thus the consumption goods industry is everywhere more capital intensive than the capital goods industry. In the U.S. and in many industralized countries, this is a reasonable assumption. Suppose the price of investment goods rises. Then from Figure 10.3,

y_1 will increase. We see from Figure 10.2 that, when $k_2 > k_1$, this corresponds to a higher wage rental ratio. Also from equation (10.1.10) nominal wages will also rise, thus proving the theorem.[1] The above theorem is widely used in international trade theory, to derive the impact of increased import tariffs on domestic wage and rental rates.

Theorem 4.2 (Rybczyniski's Theorem [9] : For a fixed p , an increase in the supply of a given factor expands the output ot the industry using that factor more intensively, and contracts the output of the other industry.

To illustrate, suppose the supply of labor increases with no change in K and p. Then because labor is used more intensively in the investment goods industry, y_1 will increase and y_2 will decrease. This is depicted in Figure 10.4. Suppose L increases to L'. Because the price ratio p remains unchanged, the capital intensities will also be unchanged. The new equilibrium will thus be at E' on the same ray as 1E with 2'E' being parallel to 2E. It is obvious that the output of 1 at E' is larger than that at E. Similarly, the output of 2 at E' is smaller than that at E. This proves the theorem.[1]

10.1.2 The Demand Side and Overall Static Equilibrium

We are now ready to explore the demand side of the model. When combined with the supply side discussed above, we obtain the complete static equilibrium. Let y be the total per capita output (a GNP measure per capita) in terms of consumption goods. Then

$$y = py_1 + y_2 \tag{10.1.13}$$

Let s_r be the saving rate of capital owners and s_w that of workers. The overall per capita saving is therefore

$$S/L = s_r kf_2' + (y-kf_2' \; s_w = s_w \, y + (s_r-s_w)kf_2' \tag{10.1.14}$$

---

[1] For an algebraic proof of the theorem see Kemp [8, pp. 16-18].

[2] For an algebraic proof of this theorem, see Kemp [8, pp. 14-16].

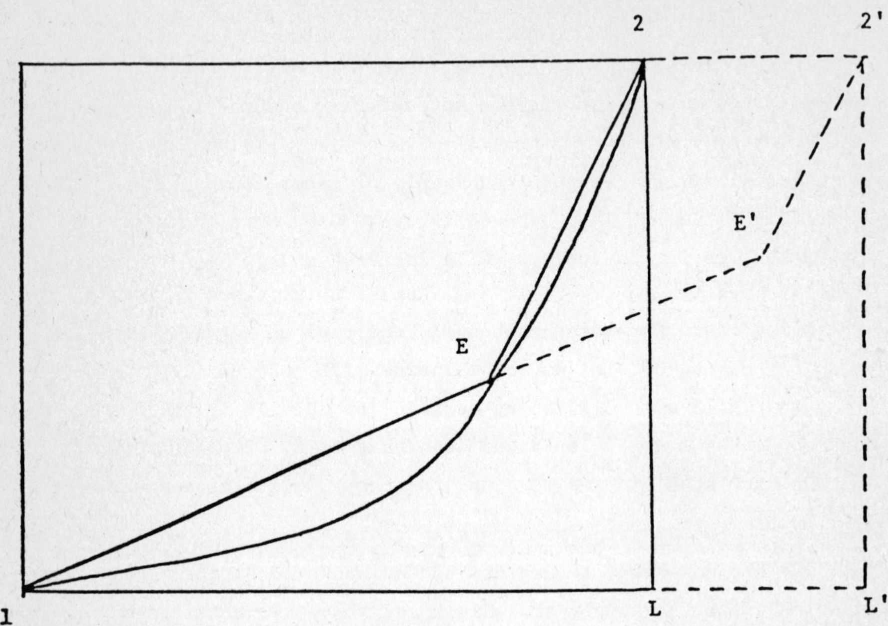

Figure 10.4

In equilibrium, saving must equal investment. Equivalently, S/L is the per capita demand for investment goods which, in equilibrium, must equal per capita supply of such goods. We thus have the market clearing condition,

$$py_1 = s_w y + (s_r - s_w)kf'_2 \tag{10.1.15}$$

or equivalently, using equation (10.1.13),

$$(1-s_w)py_1 = s_w y_2 + (s_r - s_w)kf'_2 \tag{10.1.16}$$

Using all the equations presented above, it can be shown that (see Inada [4], p.124)

$$k = \frac{k_1k_2 + [(1-s_w)k_2 + s_wk_1]w}{s_rk_2 + (1-s_r)k_1 + w} \equiv \psi(w) \tag{10.1.17}$$

Under the neo-classical conditions $f'_i(0) = \infty$, $f'_i(\infty) = 0$, $f'_i(k_i) > 0$, and $f''_i(k_i) < 0$, it is easy to show that $k_i(0) = 0$ and $k_i(\infty) = \infty$. In (10.1.17) the numerator is quadratic in k_i and w whereas the denominator is linear. Therefore it is evident that $\lim_{w\to 0} \psi(w) = 0$ and $\lim_{w\to\infty} \psi(w) = \infty$. $\psi(w)$ will graph as in Figure 10.5 and $\psi(w) = k$ has at least one solution in w. Two questions arise; how can we rule out multiple solutions? Will ℓ_i be positive at the equilibrium w? It is easily verified from (10.1.7) and (10.1.8) that

$$\ell = \frac{k - k_2}{k_1 - k_2} \qquad \ell_2 = \frac{k_1 - k}{k_1 - k_2}$$

Substituting for k from (10.1.17) we get

$$\ell_1 = \frac{s_rk_2 + s_ww}{s_rk_2 + (1-s_r)k_1 + w}$$

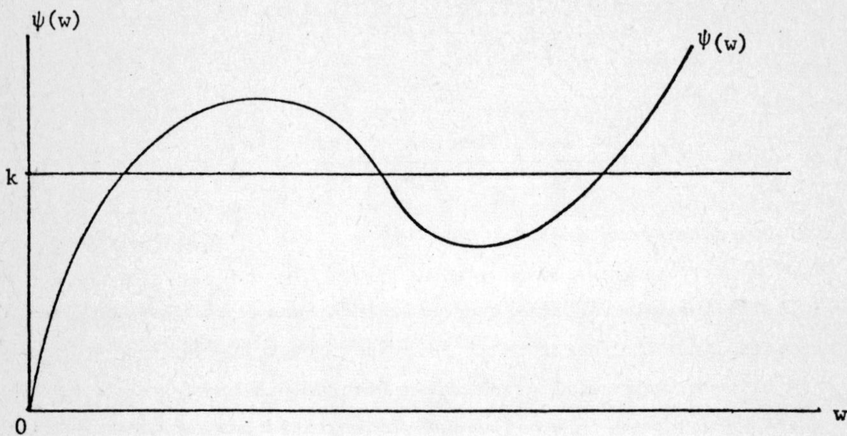

Figure 10.5

$$\ell_2 = \frac{(1-s_r)k_1 + (1-s_w)w}{s_r k_2 + (1-s_r)k_1 + w}$$

Thus ℓ_1, $\ell_2 > 0$ and all solutions are positive. A unique solution will be obtained if it can be shown that $\psi(w)$ is monotonically increasing. But $\psi(w)$ is monotonic only under special circumstances.

10.1.3 Sufficient Conditions for a Unique Solution in the Static Model

Inada has shown [June 1963 p.124: there is a typographical error in the expression for $\psi'(w)$] that

(10.1.18)
$$\psi'(w) = \Big\{(k_2-k_1)\ [(s_r-s_w)k_1 + s_r(1-s_w)(k_2-k_1)] + (k_2+w)(s_w+s_r k_2)k_1' + (k_1+w)\ (1-s_r)k_1 + (1-s_w)w\ k_2'\Big\} \div s_r k_2 + [(1-s_r)k_1 + w]^2$$

a. $s_w = s_r$: If $s_w = s_r = s$, all terms are non-negative and one is positive. Thus $\psi'(w) > 0$. This is the result obtained in Uzawa II. The economic reasoning behind this is given below.

It was argued earlier that as w increases both industries will switch to relatively more capital, increasing both capital intensities. If $s_r = s_w = s$, (10.1.13) and (10.1.14) imply that

(10.1.18)
$$p \cdot y_1/y_2 = s/1-s$$

First let $k_1 > k_2$. Since the second industry is more labor intensive, an increase in w will increase its price relatively more. Therefore p will go down. From (10.1.17) y_1 will increase relative to y_2. But since industry 1 is more capital intensive and both industries increase their capital intensities, the overall capital will go up relative to overall labor. But $k = \psi(w)$ and hence $\psi(w)$ will increase when w increases.

When $k_1 < k_2$, p goes up and y_1/y_2 goes down. But when w increases both capital intensities still increase. Now since y_2

goes up relative to y_1 and is more capital intensive, the overall capital labor ratio will again go up. Thus $\psi'(w) > 0$ in both cases.

b. $k_1 = k_2$: In this case, it is obvious from (10.1.16) that $\psi'(w) > 0$.

c. $k_2 > k_1$ and $s_r \geq s_w$: In this case $(k_2-k_1)(s_r-s_w) \geqq 0$. Therefore from (10.1.16) it follows that $\psi'(w) > 0$. This is Uzawa's famous result for the case $s_r = 1$ and $s_w = 0$, and may be stated as

Theorem 4.3: If the consumption goods industry is more capital intensive and capital saved everything and workers consumed everything, then there exists a unique static equilibrium.

d. $k_1 > k_2$ and $s_r < s_w$: This case is obvious because $(k_1-k_2)(s_w-s_r) > 0$.

e. $\sigma_1 + \sigma_2 > 1$: σ_1 is the elasticity of substitution between capital and labor and is given by

$$\sigma_i = \frac{w}{k_i}\frac{dk_i}{dw} = \frac{wk_i}{k_i}$$

After a considerable amount of algebra, it can be shown that

$$\text{(10.1.19)} \qquad \psi'(w) = \frac{\psi'(w)}{w} \cdot \frac{A}{B \cdot C} \quad \text{where}$$

$$A = k_1k_2w[(s_w+s_r)(\sigma_1+\sigma_2-1) + 2\sigma_2(1-s_w-s_r) + 2s_ws_r]$$

$$+ (1-s_r)k_1^2(\sigma_2k_2+ws_w) + s_rk_2^2[\sigma_1k_1 + w(1-s_w)]$$

$$+ w^2[\sigma_1s_wk_1 + \sigma_2(1-s_w)k_2]$$

$$B = k_1k_2 + w[s_wk_1 + k_2(1-s_w)]$$

$$C = (1-s_r)k_1 + s_rk_2 + w$$

Since $\psi(w)$, B and C are positive, $\sigma_1 + \sigma_2 \geq 1$ implies that A and hence $\psi'(w)$ is positive.

10.2 The Dynamic Two-Sector Model

We now add the conditions for capital accumulation and growth of labor force.

(10.2.1) $\dot{K} = Y_1 - \delta K$

(10.2.2) $\dot{L}/L = n$

Since $k = k/L$, $\dot{k}/k = \dot{K}/K - n$ which reduces to

(10.2.3) $\frac{\dot{k}}{k} = \frac{Y_1}{k} - (\delta+n) = \frac{Y_1}{k} - (\delta+n)$

Substituting for y_1 from (10.1.15) we get

$$\frac{\dot{k}}{k} = \frac{s_w y}{pk} + \frac{(s_r - s_w) f_2'}{p} - (\delta+n)$$

Since the total product is distributed between labor and capital,

$$y = rk + W = r(k+w) = (k+w)pf_1'$$

Substituting this in the above expression and since $f_2' = pf_1'$ it follows that

(10.2.4)
$$\begin{aligned}\frac{\dot{k}}{k} &= s_w f_1' \frac{(k+w)}{k} + (s_r - s_w) f_1' - (\delta+n) \\ &= \frac{f_1'}{k}(ws_w + ks_r) - (\delta+n) \\ &= \phi(w) - (\delta+n) \quad \text{defining } \phi(w)\end{aligned}$$

It can be shown that

(10.2.5) $\frac{1}{\phi(w)} \frac{\partial\phi}{\partial w} = \frac{s_w k_1 - s_r k}{(w+k_1)(ws_w + ks_r)} - \frac{ws_w k'}{k(ws_w + ks_r)}$

Remember that in the dynamic model k is also a variable and is a function of w. Because $k' = \chi'(w) > 0$, if $(k_2 - k_1)(s_r - s_w) > 0$ then $\lim_{w\to 0} \Phi(w) = \infty$ and $\lim_{w\to\infty} \phi(w) = 0$. Thus there exists at least one equilibrium w^* such that

(10.2.6) $\phi(w^*) = \delta + n$

This is a steady state w* and results in corresponding values for k^*, k_i^* etc. Since the existence of a steady state path is established, the next question to explore is the stability of the equilibrium.

10.3 Stability of the Long-run Equilibrium

a. $k_2 > k_1$ and $s_r \geq s_w$: This is the condition satisfied by Uzawa's I and II models. The first condition, viz. that the consumption goods sector is more capital intensive than the investment goods sector, is very crucial in these models. The second condition is satisfied if everybody saves the same proportion of income or if consumers do not save and firms do not consume.

It is evident from the expression for ℓ_1 that if $k_2 > k_1$ then $k > k_1$. This together with $s_r \geq s_w$, implies that $s_r k > s_w k_1$. Using this in (10.1.22) we get $\partial\phi/\partial w < 0$. Thus in this case, $\phi(w)$ is monotonic decreasing and we showed earlier that $\psi(w)$ is monotonic increasing. The phase diagram will look like Figure 10.6.
It is easily verified that this is a stable equilibrium.

b. $k_2 < k_1$ and $s_r < s_w$: We know that $\psi(w)$ is still monotonic increasing. Also $\psi(w)$ starts at ∞ and ends at zero. Therefore a solution exists. But $\phi(w)$ may not be monotonic and so multiple solutions are possible as in Figure 10.7.
For stability $\phi(w)$ has to intersect $\delta + n$ from above. Therefore k_1^* and k_3^* are stable and k_2^* is unstable. Since the outermost intersections are always stable, we have global stability of the system.

c. ϕ is monotonic but ψ is not: In this case, the phase diagram is as in Figure 10.8.

Let k* correspond to w* on the ψ curve. If k* intersects $\psi(w)$ along OA or DE there is no problem because we get a unique stable equilibrium. If $k_A < k < k_B$ then three w's are possible and therefore three values for $\phi(w)$. Since the sign of $\dot{k}$ may be positive for one w and negative for another, it is ambiguous as to which way k will move. Inada assumes that $\dot{k}$ is determined in such a way as to preserve continuity of k (as well as that of w

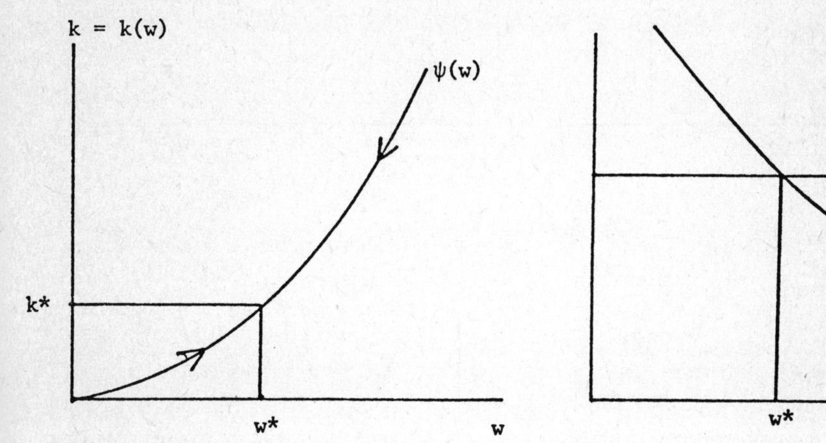

Figure 10.6

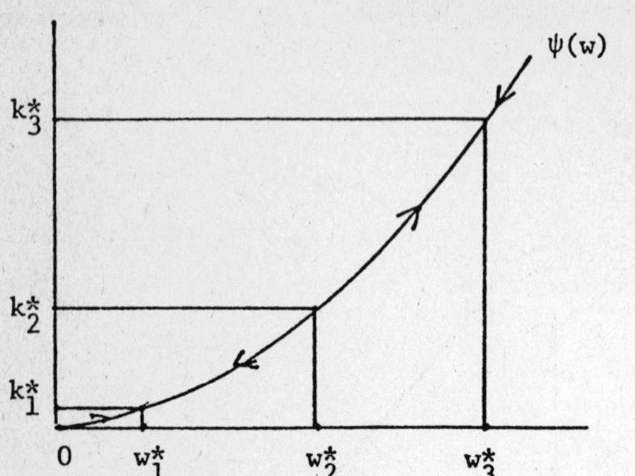

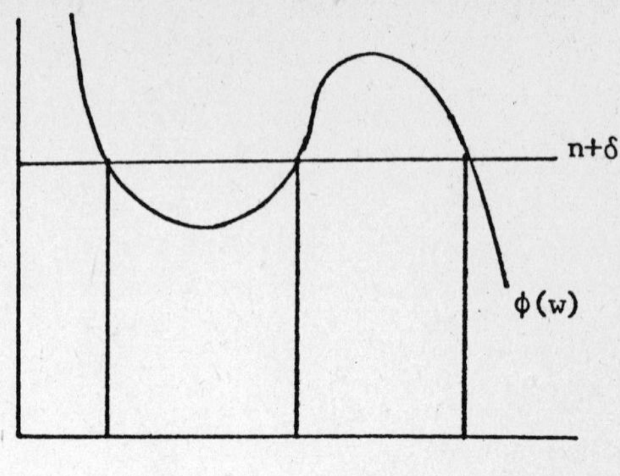

Figure 10.7

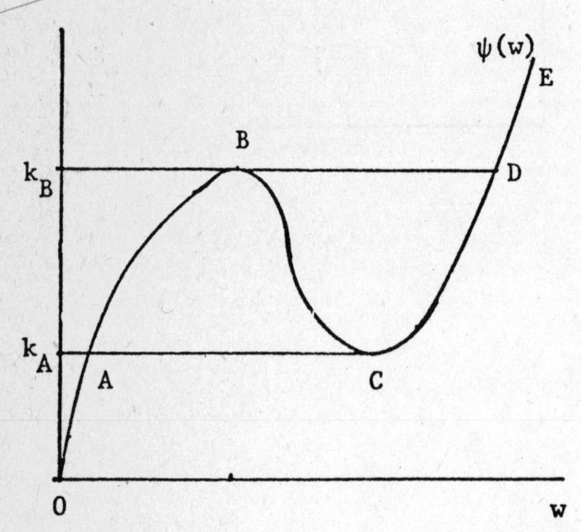

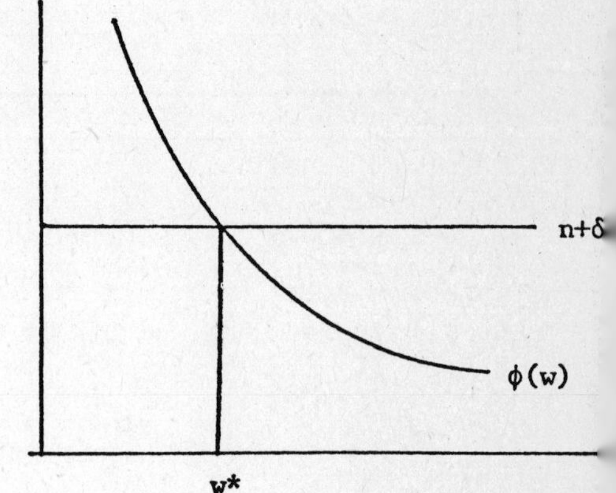

Figure 10.8

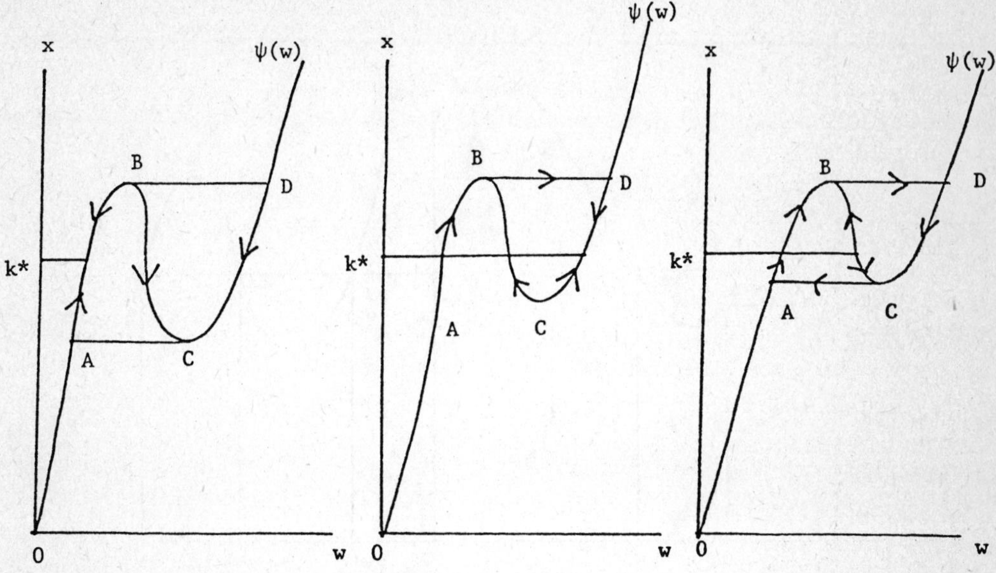

Figure 10.9

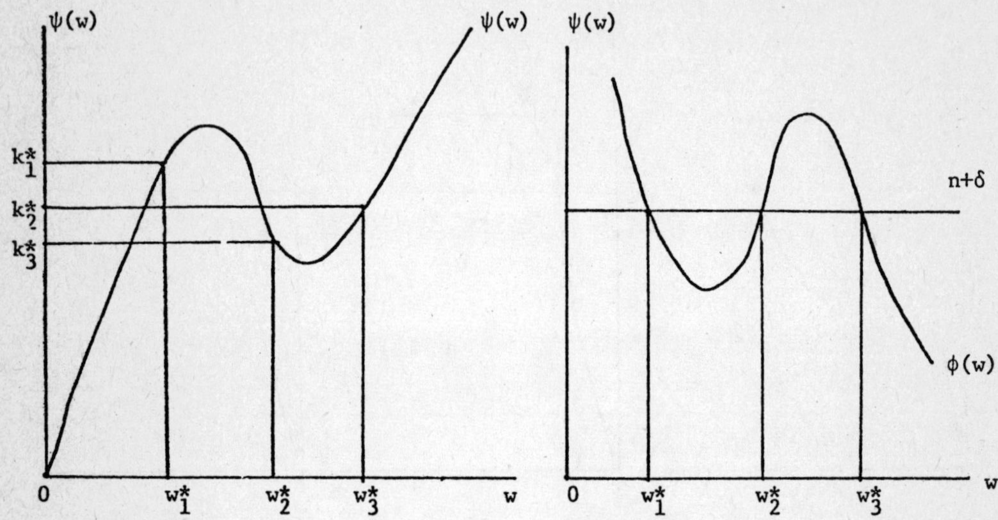

Figure 10.10

whenever possible). Three subcases arise depending on whether (k^*,w^*) is in AB, BC or CD. The phase diagram in Figure 10.9 indicates the directional arrows for these cases.

A solution in AB is stable under the continuity assumption. If the initial (k_o,w_o) was in BC or CE we move towards C (because of continuity) and then jump to A and then move to P. Thus wherever we start P is ultimately reached. In a similar manner the solution P in CD can be shown to be stable. But if the intersection is in BC, we can never get to P unless we happened to be there initially. Wherever we start, we will keep going round and round in the direction ABDC never reaching P. Thus this is a perpetual cycle.

d. Both ϕ and ψ are non-monotonic: If ϕ and ψ are non-monotonic, Inada's continuity assumption ensures stability of all equilibria and hence global stability. The case of interest is when the intersections are as in Figure 10.10.

Because the signs for k are as indicated in the right diagram, the directional arrows are as drawn in the left diagram. It is evident that all the equilibria are stable.

Conclusion: We have thus shown that under the continuity assumption, there is global stability (in general) in all but one case; exception: case d when (k^*,w^*) is in the BC segment of the $\psi(w)$ curve.

10.4 Extension to the Case of Variable Savings Ratio

Inada's June 1964 article extends the above analysis to the case where the saving ratio varies with income. The two factors are now assumed to save the same proportion s out of income. As a first step, we shall obtain certain preliminary results with reference to the static model.

Differentiating (10.1.9) with respect to w, we obtain

$$\frac{dk_i}{dw} = \frac{-(f_i')^2}{f_i f_i''} > 0 \qquad (10.4.1)$$

Logarithmic differentation of (10.1.10) gives

$$\frac{1}{p}\frac{\partial p}{\partial w} = \frac{f_2''k_2'}{f_2'} - \frac{f_1''k_1'}{f_1'}$$

Using (10.4.1) and (10.1.9) in this, we get

$$\frac{1}{p}\frac{\partial p}{\partial w} = \frac{k_2-k_1}{(k_1+w)(k_2+w)} \tag{10.4.2}$$

It was seen earlier that

$$y = pf_1'(k+w) = f_2'(k+w)$$

Logarithmic differentiation of this gives

$$\frac{1}{y}\frac{\partial y}{\partial w} = \frac{f_2''k'_2}{f_2'} + \frac{1}{k+w}$$

Using (10.4.1) and (10.1.9) we get

$$\frac{1}{y}\frac{\partial y}{\partial w} = \frac{k_2-k}{(k+w)(k_2+w)} \tag{10.4.3}$$

If $k_2 > k_1$, i.e., if consumption goods are more capital intensive than investment goods, then $k_2 > k$ and hence $\partial p/\partial w > 0$, $\partial y/\partial w > 0$. In other words, as labor becomes relatively more expensive than capital, then the capital good, which uses relatively more labor, becomes more expensive and the gross national product per capita also increases. In the special case when firms save everything and workers consume everything, Uzawa [13] (June 1962) has shown that the higher the wage-rental ratio the larger the amount of new capital. If the capital intensity inequality is reversed, the conclusions are also reversed.

Consider for the moment that s is fixed and does not depend on income. Then it can be shown that [Uzawa p.110]

$$\frac{\partial w}{\partial s} = \left[\frac{1}{k_1+w} - \frac{1}{k_2+w}\right] \div \left[\frac{s(1+k_1')}{(k_1+w)^2} + \frac{(1-s)(1+k_2')}{(k_2+w)^2} - \frac{1}{(k+w)^2}\right]$$

It should be noted that k_i depends on s also. Uzawa also shows that under the capital intensity condition ($k_2 > k_1$), both numerator and denominator are positive. Thus the equilibrium wage-rental ratio increases as the average propensity to save increases.

Now replace the fixed saving coefficient by the assumption

(10.4.4) $\quad s = g(y) \quad \text{where } g'(y) > 0 \text{ and } 0 < g < 1$

The general equilibrium in the static model with a given k is determined as below. Fix the value of s. Then given k we know from Section 10.1 that w is uniquely determined, call it w(k,s). By the same argument k_1, k_2, p and y are all determined as functions of w(k,s). Let y be written y[w(k,s),k]. Since g(y) is the saving ratio, we have

(10.4.5) $\quad s = g[y[w(k,x),k]]$

If s can be uniquely determined from (10.4.5) then with a given k we will have unique values for w, k_i, p and y. Define

(10.4.6) $\quad \theta(s) = s - g[y(w,k)]$

Then

(10.4.7) $\quad \frac{d\theta}{ds} = 1 - \frac{dg}{dy} \bullet \frac{\partial y}{\partial w} \bullet \frac{\partial w}{\partial s}$

The subsequent discussion summarizes the results obtained by Uzawa (June 1963) and Inada (April 1964). For detailed proofs refer to these articles. Inada shows without using the capital intensity condition that, $d\theta/ds > 0$. It is further assumed that

(10.4.8) $\quad 0 < \varepsilon_1 < g(y) < 1-\varepsilon_2$

for some positive numbers ε_1 and ε_2. This is needed to ensure a non-trivial solution to s.

Since $\partial g/\partial s < 1$ and from (10.4.8) it follows that the g(y) curve will look as in Figure 10.11.

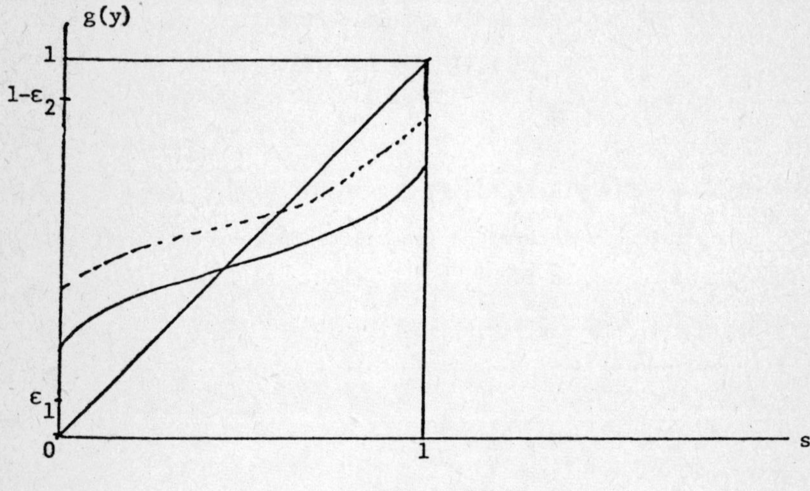

Figure 10.11

Thus there exists a unique s satisfying (10.1.9) for a given k. Next consider the process of capital accumulation.

$$\frac{\dot{k}}{k} = \frac{y_1}{k} - (\delta+n)$$

Let

$$\phi(w) = \frac{y_1}{k} = g(y)f_1'(k)\,\frac{k+w}{k}$$

from (10.2.4) and (10.2.5). Assume that the consumption good industry is more capital intensive than the investment good industry ($k_2 > k_1$). Then we saw earlier that for a given s, $\partial y/\partial w > 0$ and $\partial y/\partial k > 0$. Thus $\partial y/\partial k > 0$ and since g is non-decreasing in y, $g[y(k,s)]$ shifts upwards as s increases. Therefore $ds/dk \geq 0$ from which it can be shown that $dw/dk \geq 0$. Using all these Inada shows (April 1964, p. 135) that $\partial\theta/\partial w < 0$.

Thus there exists a unique s* (from which k*, y* etc. can be determined) satisfying the relation

$$\phi(w) = g[y(w)]f_1'[k_1(w)]\;\frac{k(w)+w}{k(w)} = \delta+n$$

Because $\partial\phi/\partial w < 0$ and $\partial k/\partial w > 0$, the system is globally stable.

REFERENCES

[1] Corden, "The Two-Sector Growth Model with Fixed Coefficients," Review of Economic Studies, July 1966.

[2] Drandakis, E., "Factor Substitution in the Two-Sector Model," Review of Economic Studies, October 1963.

[3] Hahn, "On Two-Sector Growth Models," Review of Economic Studies, October 1965.

[4] Inada, "On a Two-Sector Model of Economic Growth: Comments and Generalization," Review of Economic Studies, June 1963.

[5] Inada, "On the Stability of Growth Equilibria in Two-Sector Models," Review of Economic Studies, April 1964.

[6] Inada, "On Neo-Classical Models of Economic Growth," Review of Economic Studies, April 1965.

[7] Inada, "Investment in Fixed Capital and the Stability of Growth Equilibrium, Review of Economic Studies, January 1966.

[8] Kemp, Murray, International Trade and Investment, Prentice-Hall, 1969.

[9] Rybczynski, T.N., "Factor Endowments and Relative Commodity Prices," Economica, November 1941, pp. 58-73.

[10] Sato, R., "Stability Conditions in Two-Sector Models of Economic Growth," Journal of Economic Theory, June 1969.

[11] Solow, "Note on Uzawa's Two-Sector Model of Economic Growth," Review of Economic Studies, October 1961.

[12] Stolper, W.F. and Samuelson, P.A., Protection and Real Wages," Review of Economic Studies, November 1941, pp. 58-73.

[13] Uzawa, "On a Two-Sector Model of Economic Growth: I and II," Review of Economic Studies, 1961-62 and June 1963.

[14] Takayama, "On a Two-Sector Model of Economic Growth--A Comparative Statics Analysis," Review of Economic Studies, June 1963.

EXERCISES

10.1 Verify equations (10.1.17), (10.1.18), (10.1.19) and (10.2.5).

10.2 In the static model presented in Section 10.1, derive the sensitivities to changes in k, s_r and s_w (or s).

10.3 In the dynamic model presented in Section 10.2, derive the long run sensitivities to changes in s_r, s_w and n.

CHAPTER 11

INTERNATIONAL TRADE AND ECONOMIC GROWTH

The final chapter of the book is devoted to an extension of the two-sector model of economic growth to an open economy. We thus consider two countries, denoted as the "home" country (HC) and the "foreign" country (FC, or the rest of the world). The two goods will be, as before, consumption and investment.

Dynamic theories of international trade have, until very recently, concentrated on a barter situation where either goods are exchanged for goods (Oniki and Uzawa, 1965), or goods are exchanged for securities, (Fischer and Frenkel, 1972). In the last few years, several papers have introduced a monetary model to the dynamic trade literature. For instance, Allen (1972) considered a one-sector (complete specialization) two-country model with a monetary asset. A monetary model with trade in capital and securities has been considered for a small country by Sakakibara (1974). Onitsuka (1974) has analyzed a one-sector model with trade in securities but it has no monetary sector. Hori and Stein (1977) have extended this to a two-sector complete specialization situation. Ramanathan (1975) has examined the impact of monetary expansion with a two-sector trade model but he assumes a small country with no trade in securities. Roberts (1978) considers a two-sector monetary growth model for two intermediate size countries, but he does not allow for trade in securities.

In Section 11.1, the Uzawa-Oniki model is presented in the static form. This is then extended to the dynamic case in Section 11.2. Section 11.3 deals with the role of monetary expansion in a two-country, two-sector model of accumulation.

11.1 A Static Two Sector Trade Model

In the last chapter, we showed that given the price ratio p and overall capital intensity k, the supplies of consumption and investment goods, real wages and rents can be determined in terms of those variables. Let C be the supply of consumption goods and I be the supply of investment goods. We thus have, using the linear homogeneity property,

(11.1.1) $C = C(k,p)L$

(11.1.2) $I = I(k,p)L$

(11.1.3) $Y = C + I\,p$

(11.1.4) $y = Y/L = y(k,p) = C(k,p) + I(k,p)p$

where Y is aggregate output (a GNP measure) and y is per capita GNP. In international trade theory, p is often referred to as the "terms of trade". Equations (11.1.1) and (11.1.2) are the parametric representation of the production possibility frontier (for given L). At a point on the frontier, per capita output y (= C +Ip) is maximized with respect to p. Therefore, $C_p + pI_p = 0$, because of the tangency of the frontier with the price line C.

$$y_p = C_p + pI_p + I = I > 0$$

By the neo-classical conditions on the production functions, it is easily seen that $y = kr + w$, where w = real wages and r = real rents. Hence $y_k = MPK = r$ and $w = y - ky_k > 0$. To summarize, we have the following inequalities:

(11.1.5) $y_p = I > 0;\quad y_k > 0 \quad \text{and} \quad y_k - ky_k > 0.$

Let s be the overall saving rate. Therefore investment demand I_d is given by

(11.1.6) $pI_d = s\,Y$

The budget constraint is

(11.1.7) $C + Ip = C_d + I_d\,p$

where C_d is the demand for consumption goods.

For the foreign country, there will be equations similar to the ones presented above. Equilibrium in the world market is determined by the following market clearing condition.

(11.1.8) $\quad I_d + I_d^f = I + I^f$

where the superscript f stands for the foreign country. Equations (11.1.1) through (11.1.8), excluding (11.1.5), determine the equilibrium values for the endogenous variables, C, I, Y, I_d, C_d, y and p.

A natural question that arises is: "will the consumption goods industry be in equilibrium?". From (11.1.7) we see that $C + C^f + p(I+I^f) = C_d + C_d^f + p(I_d+I_d^f)$. Now use (11.1.8) we have $C_d + C_d^f = C + C^f$, which means that the consumption goods industry is also in equilibrium. Before analyzing the world trade equilibrium, it will be convenient to express it in terms of excess demand functions. Define z(k,p) to be the excess demand for capital goods, expressed in per capita terms.

(11.1.9) $\quad z(k,p) = (I_d - I)/L$

$$= s\ \frac{y(k,p)}{p} - I\ (k,p) = s\ \frac{C(k,p)}{p} - (1-s)\ I(k,p)$$

Given k and k^f the world terms of trade is determined by

(11.1.10) $\quad z(k,p) + \lambda\, z^f(k^f, p) = 0$

where $\lambda \equiv L^f/L$ is the relative size of the labor force in the two countries.

If $p \leq p_\ell\,(k)$, then the home country specializes in consumption goods production. In this case I=0 and hence $z = s\ C(k,p_\ell)/p$, which is a rectangular hyperbola. When $p \geq p_u(k)$, the home country specializes in the production of capital goods with C=0. Hence, $z = -\ (1-s)\ I(k,P_u) < 0$ and constant. For $p_\ell < p < p_u$ both goods are produced. In this case,

$$\frac{\partial z}{\partial p} = \frac{sC_p}{p} - \frac{sC}{p^2} - (1-s)\, I_p < 0$$

because $C_p < 0$ and $I_p > 0$.

For the foreign country the excess demand function will be the negative of this. International equilibrium with both countries non-specialized will be as in Figure 11.1. Trade pattern is dictated by where the intersection lies. In the diagram, $z(k,p_e) > 0$. Therefore the home country has an excess demand for investment goods. Thus, it will import investment goods and export consumption goods.

<u>Effect of a change in k</u>

To examine the effect of a change in the home country's overall capital-labor ratio, differentiate (11.1.10) partially with respect to k.

$$z_k + z_p\, p_k + \lambda\, z^f\, p_k = 0$$

Therefore

$$\frac{\partial p_e}{\partial k} = \frac{-z_k}{z_p + \lambda\, z_p^f}$$

Because the denominator is negative, the sign of p_k depends on that of z_k.

$$z_k = s\, C_k/P - (1-s)\, I_k$$

$k_C > k_I \Rightarrow C_k > 0,\ I_k < 0$ by Rybczynski's Theorem $\Rightarrow z_k > 0,\ p_k > 0$

$k_C < k_I \Rightarrow C_k < 0,\ I_k > 0 \Rightarrow z_k < 0,\ p_k < 0$

Henceforth we assume that $k_C > k_I$ in both countries, that is, that consumption goods are more capital intensive.

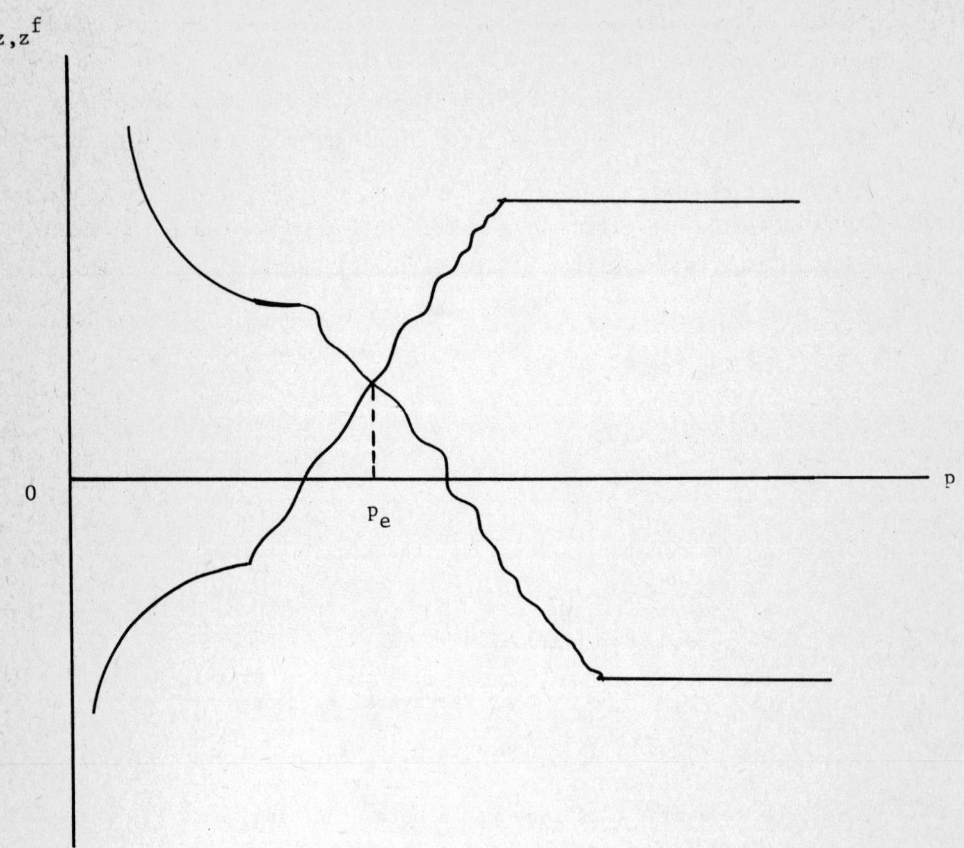

Figure 11.1

Effect of a change in s

The world trade equilibrium condition is

$$0 = s\ \frac{C(k,p)}{p} - (1-s)\ I(k,P) + \lambda s^f\ \frac{c^f(k^f,p)}{p} - \lambda(1-s)\ I^f(k^f,p).$$

Therefore,

$$\frac{\partial p}{\partial s} = \frac{C/p + I}{s\frac{C}{p^2} - \frac{sC_p}{p} + (1-s)\ I_p - \lambda s^f\ C_p^f + \lambda(1-s^f)\ I_p^f}$$

Because $C_p, C_p^f < 0$ and $I_p, I_p^f < 0$, we have $\frac{\partial p}{\partial s} > 0$. If the saving rate goes up, I_d goes up and hence world demand for capital goods will go up, thus driving the equilibrium TOT up. It is easily verified that the direction of the volume of trade (i.e., $\partial z/\partial s$) is also upwards.

11.2 A Dynamic Two-Sector Trade Model[1]

The equations of motion for the dynamic trade model are (ignoring depreciation):

(11.2.1) $\dot{K} = I_d$

(11.2.2) $\dot{K}^f = I_d^f$

(11.2.3) $\dot{L}/L = \dot{L}^f/L^f = n$.

This leads to the following equations:

(11.2.4) $\dot{k} = s\ \frac{y(k,p)}{p} - nk \equiv \phi\ (k,k^f)$

(11.2.5) $\dot{k}^f = s^f\ \frac{y^f(k^f,p)}{p} - nk^f \equiv \psi(k,k^f)$

where

(11.2.6) $p = P\ (k,k^f \mid s,s^f)$.

The long-run equilibrium is given by:

(11.2.7) $s\ \frac{y(k^*,p^*)}{p^*} = nk^*$

---

[1]This is a modified version of parts of the paper by Uzawa and Oniki [(1965)]

(11.2.8) $s^f y^f (k^{f*}, p^*)/p^* = nk^{f*}$

(11.2.9) $p^* = P(k^*, k^{f*} \mid s, s^f)$

Several cases are possible and these are examined one by one.

Case 1: Each country always produces both commodities

In this case of incomplete specialization, the above differential equations stand as they are. The standard neo-classical conditions on the production functions will guarantee the existence of a solution. $\phi(k,k^f) = 0$ gives the values of k and k^f for which $\dot{k} = 0$.

$$\left(\frac{dk^f}{dk}\right)_{\dot{k}=0} = \frac{-\phi_k}{\phi_{k^f}}$$

$$\phi_k = s\frac{(y_k + y_p P_k)}{p} - \frac{sy}{p^2} P_k - n$$

$$= s\frac{(y_k + y_p P_k)}{p} - \frac{sy}{p^2} P_k - \frac{sy}{pk}$$

$$= \frac{s}{pk}(ky_k - y) + \frac{sP_k}{p^2}(py_p - y)$$

In Section 11.1 we showed that $y - ky_k > 0$ and that $y_p = I$. Hence,

$$py_p - y = pI - y = -c(k,p) < 0.$$

Therefore, $\phi_k < 0$, provided $k_C > k_I$. Also,

$$\phi_{k^f} = \frac{sy_p P_{k^f}}{p} - \frac{sy}{p^2} P_{k^f} = \frac{sP_{k^f}}{p^2}(py_p - y) ,$$

which is also negative, provided $k_C^f > K_I^f$. Therefore, the $\dot{k}=0$

curve is downward sloping. By symmetry, so is the $\dot{k}^f=0$ curve. Sufficient conditions for these are (i) no factor intensity reversal and (ii) consumption goods industry is more capital intensive than the investment goods industry.[1]

The absolute value of the slope of the $\dot{k}=0$ curve is given by:

$$-\left(\frac{dk^f}{dk}\right)_{\dot{k}=0} = \frac{p}{kP_{k^f}}\left(\frac{y-ky_k}{y-py_p}\right) + \frac{P_k}{P_{k^f}}$$

$$= \frac{Pk}{P_{k^f}}\left[1 + \frac{p}{kP_k}\left(\frac{y-ky_k}{y-py_p}\right)\right] > \frac{P_k}{P_{k^f}}$$

under the capital intensity condition. By a similar procedure we can show that

$$-\left(\frac{dk^f}{dk}\right)_{\dot{k}^f=0} = \frac{\psi_k}{\psi_{k^f}} = \frac{P_k}{P_{k^f}} \cdot \frac{1}{1 + \frac{p}{k^f P_{k^f}}\left(\frac{y^f - k^f y^f_{k^f}}{y^f - p y_p^f}\right)} < \frac{P_k}{P_{k^f}}$$

Therefore $\dot{k}=0$ curve is steeper than $\dot{k}^f=0$ curve. The phase diagram is as in Figure 11.2 and conclusively demonstrates global stability when (i) both goods are produced in both countries, (ii) $k_C > k_I$ and (iii) $k_C^f > k_I^f$ for all w and p.

Case 2: HC always specializes in I

The differential equation in k is now

$$\dot{k} = s\, I\,[k, p_u(k)] - nk$$

which is independent of k^f. Therefore, the $\dot{k}=0$ curve is vertical at k^*. Two sub-cases arise depending on whether or not FC is completed specialized in C . In the case of incomplete specialization, $\dot{k}^f=0$ curve is downward sloping. It is easily seen that this is also a globally stable equilibrium. The case of complete specialization is left to the reader as an exercise.

---

[1] See Kemp (1974, p. 81 on factor intensity reversal).

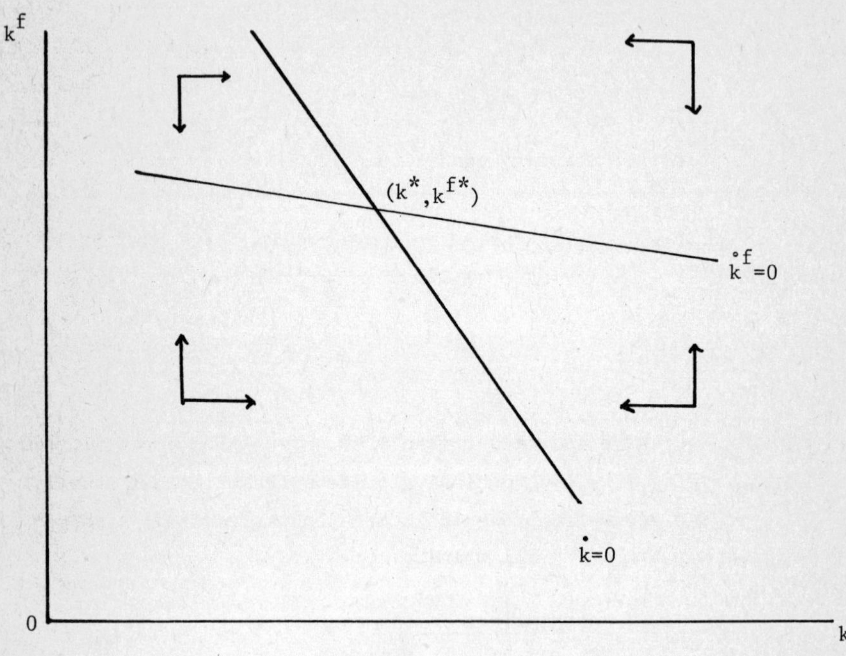

Figure 11.2

Case 3: HC specializes in C always

The differential equation in k is

$$\dot{k} = \frac{sC\ [k,p_e]}{p} - nk$$

$$\frac{\partial \dot{k}}{\partial_k f} = -\frac{sC}{p^2} p_{k^f} < 0 \text{ if } k_C^f > k_I^f$$

$$\left(\frac{\partial \dot{k}}{\partial k}\right)_{\dot{k}=0} = \frac{sC_k}{p} - \frac{sC}{p^2} - \frac{sC}{p^2} p_k - n \lessgtr 0$$

Thus the $\dot{k}=0$ curve could be upward sloping as in Figure 11.3. Suppose FC is completely specialized in I. Then

$$\dot{k}^f = s^f\ I\ [k^f,\ p_u^f\ (k^f)] - nk^f$$

The $\dot{k}^f=0$ curve is therefore independent of k and is horizontal as in Figure 11.3. The diagram indicates that the steady state is now a saddle point.

Changing patterns of specialization

Over time the pattern of specialization in a country may change depending on the time patterns of k and k^f. Given $k_C > k_I$, we saw that as k increases, for a fixed p, that C increases and I decreases (Rybczynski's theorem). It is clear from Figure 11.4 that $p_u(k)$ and $p_\ell(k)$, the critical price ratios that determine specialization in I and C respectively, are upward sloping.

Given a world TOT (p_e) if HC's capital intensity is between $\underline{k}^e$ and $\bar{k}^e$, then HC will be incompletely specialized. As k^f increases so does p_e, for a given k. Thus, there exist two curves $\underline{k}$ and $\bar{k}$, as in Figure 11.4 which give patterns of specialization. By looking at cases 1, 2 and 3 discussed earlier, we see that several long run possibilities of specialization exist. Two of these are drawn in Figure 11.5. Other cases may be worked out as exercises.

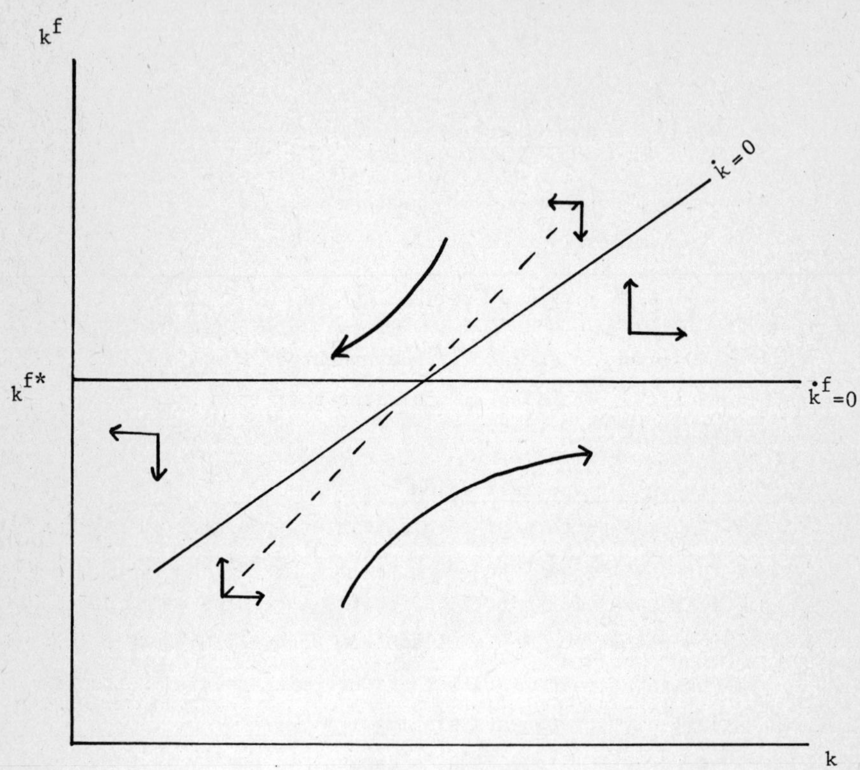

Figure 11.3

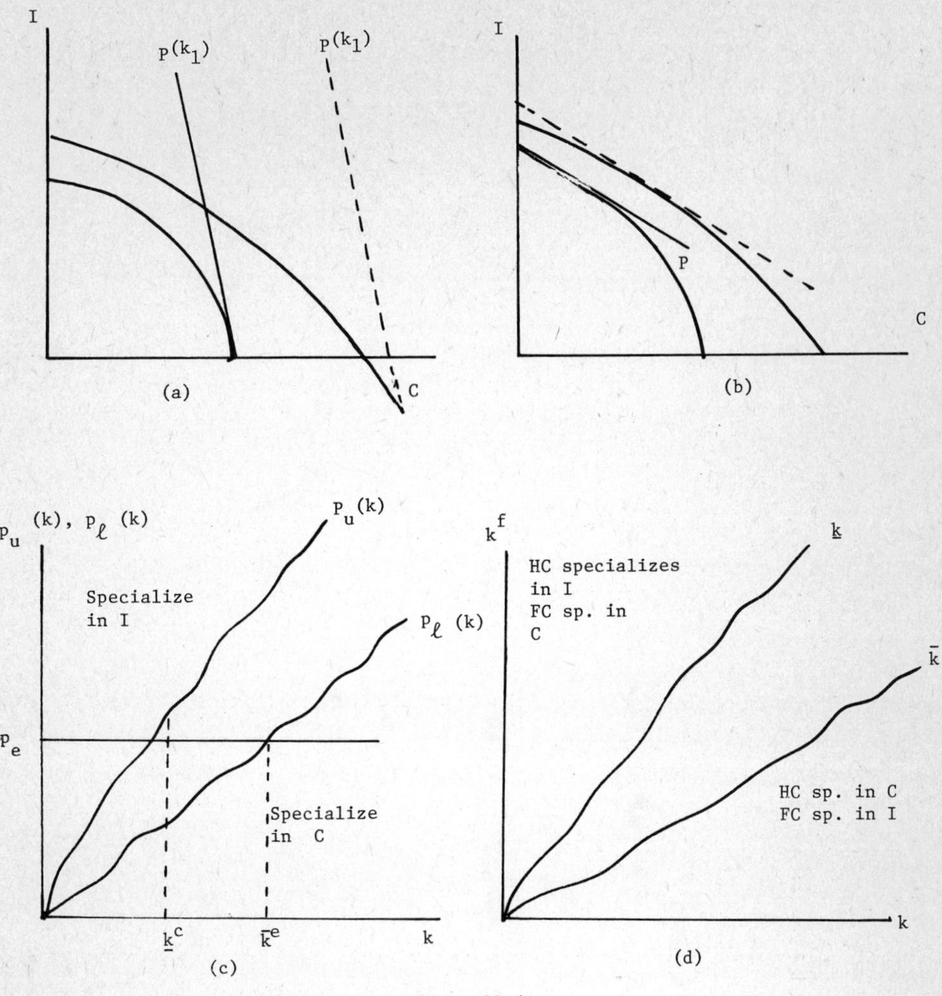
I
p(k1)
p(k1)
C
(a)
I
P
C
(b)
pu (k), pℓ (k)
Pu(k)
Specialize
in I
Pℓ (k)
pe
Specialize
in C
k^c
k^e
k
(c)
k^f
k
HC specializes
in I
FC sp. in
C
k
HC sp. in C
FC sp. in I
k
(d)

Figure 11.4

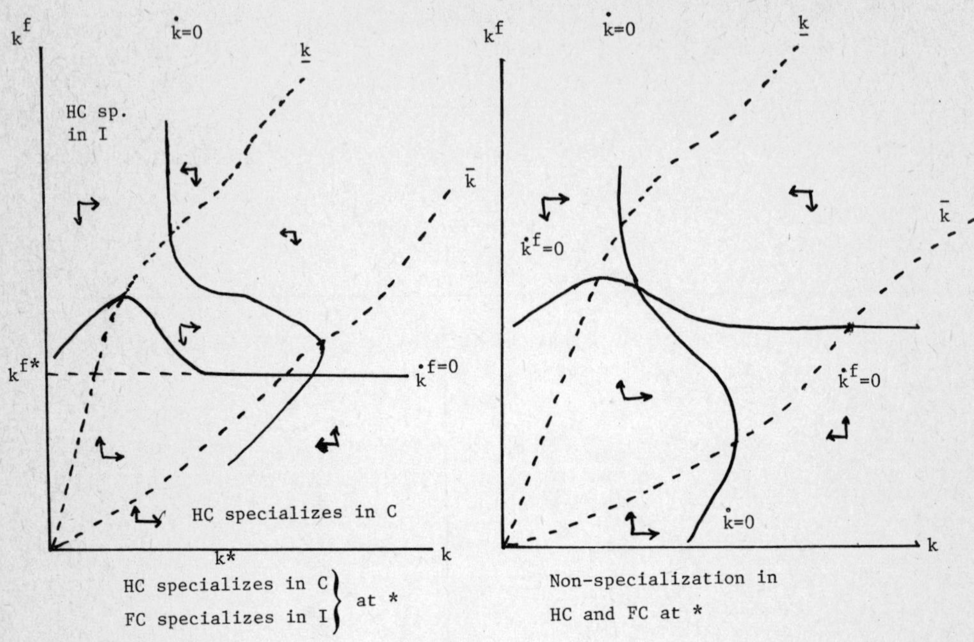
k^f
$\dot{k}=0$
$\underline{k}$
HC sp.
in I
$\bar{k}$
k^{f*}
$\dot{k}^f=0$
HC specializes in C
k^*
k
HC specializes in C
FC specializes in I
at *
k^f
$\dot{k}=0$
$\underline{k}$
$\bar{k}$
$\dot{k}^f=0$
$\dot{k}^f=0$
$\dot{k}=0$
k
Non-specialization in
HC and FC at *

Figure 11.5

Both steady states are stable and the pattern of specialization can change over time depending on s, s^f and n and the initial k_0, k_0^f.

Long run sensitivities for a non-specialization case

Let $A=((a_{ij}))$ be the partial of the ith steady state condition with respect to the jth variable $(j=k^*, k^{f*}, p^*)$. The steady state conditions are in (11.2.7) through (11.2.9). It is easy to see that $a_{12}=a_{21}=0$. Let $((a^{ij}))=A^{-1}$. We then have

$$\partial k^*/\partial s = - a^{11} y^*/p^* = (a_{22} + a_{23}\, P_{k^f})/\Delta$$

$$\partial k^{f*}/\partial s = - a^{21} y^*/p^* - a_{23}\, P_k/\Delta$$

$$\partial p^*/\partial s = - a^{31} y^*/p^* = a_{22}\, P_k/\Delta$$

where

$$a_{22} = \frac{s^f y^f_{k^f}}{p} - n = \frac{s^f y^f_{k^f}}{p} - \frac{s^f y^f}{pk^f} = \frac{s^f y^f}{pk^f} (\eta^f_{y^f k^f} - 1)$$

$$a_{23} = \frac{s^f y^f}{p^2} (py_p^f - y^f) < 0$$

$$a_{11} = \frac{sy}{pk} (\eta_{yk} - 1)$$

$$a_{13} = \frac{sy}{p^2} (py_p - y) < 0$$

$$\Delta = - a_{11} a_{22} - P_{k^f}\, a_{11}\, a_{23} + P_k\, a_{22}\, a_{13}$$

Stability of the model implies that $\Delta=\det(A)$ is negative. Because $a_{23} < 0$ and P_k, $P_{k^f} > 0$, we have, unambiguously,

$$\frac{\partial k^{f*}}{\partial s} < 0$$

Also,

$$\eta_{y^f k^f}^{f} \lessgtr 1 \quad \Rightarrow \quad \begin{array}{l} \partial p^*/\partial s > 0 \text{ and } \partial k^*/\partial s > 0 \\ \partial p^*/\partial s < 0,\ k_s^* \text{ ambiguous.} \end{array}$$

$$\eta_{yk} = \frac{ky_k}{y}$$

Similar sensitivities for n are possible.

11.3 A Monetary Growth Model of an Open Economy

In this section we introduce a monetary asset and examine the role of monetary expansion in the presence of both terms of trade effects and trade in securities. This model was analyzed by Ramanathan and Roberts (1981) and differs from other recent contributions in a number of ways. First, the model assumes non-specialization so that both goods are always produced. As such, the output of the investment good may be altered by not only shifting factors of production between sectors but also through changes in the domestic supply of factors of production. Although non-specialization is an assumption rather than a generalization, it is perhaps more realistic. In addition, the model permits trade in securities, a feature absent in Allen's model. Unlike the small country case examined by Fischer, Frenkel and Ramanathan, this model permits an analysis of the effects of monetary expansion and trade in securities on the terms of trade and the world interest rate. For a small country, both of these prices are exogenously determined whereas in this model they are endogenous. The effects of monetary expansion on trade in securities is also a feature absent from the Fischer-Frenkel model.

The working of the model is as follows. At any given instant, each country has given stocks of capital, labor, a stock of money (outside money) supplied by the government as a transfer payment, and a net holding of securities which transfers interest income between the two countries. Each country produces both a consumption good and an investment good. At the current levels of the terms of trade, world interest rate, domestic capital labor ratios, and expected rates of change in the domestic price level, there is a certain demand for the investment good. Also, there is a current supply of investment and consumption goods and a domestic demand for the consumption good. The world market for the two commodities is cleared through adjustments in these demands and supplies which occur through changes in the terms of trade and the world interest rate. If, at the resulting terms of trade and interest rate, a country is a net importer (exporter) of goods, the payment for the goods is handled through export (import) of securities which pay interest at the world rate. Monetary expansion enters the model by altering demand conditions which adjust prices, supply in both countries and the balanced growth paths. Capital accumulation is determined through investment demand and labor accumulates exogenously. In the next section, the model is specified in more detail.

11.3.1 The Model

It is assumed, as before, that there are two countries, the home country and the foreign country, each producing both consumption goods and capital (or investment) goods with labor and capital. For convenience of exposition, the algebraic equations describing specific relationships are grouped into four categories, (a) goods market, (b) asset markets, (c) factor accumulation, and (d) foreign sector. Each of these is described below.

(a) Goods Market

The following equations describe the goods market in the home country.

(11.3.1) $C = C(k,p_k)L$

(11.3.2) $I = I(k,p_k)L$

(11.3.3) $k - K/L$

(11.3.4) $Y = C + Ip_k$

(11.3.5) $D = (1-s)Y_d$

(11.3.6) $I_d = J(k,p_k,\pi,r)L$

(11.3.7) $Y_d = Y + Mp_m(\mu+\pi) + Zr$

The first two equations determine the supplies of consumption (C) and investment (I) goods for given levels of total labor (L), the price of the investment good (p_k) with the consumption good as the numeraire, and the capital-labor ratio (k) defined in equation (11.3.3). The production relations are assumed to be linearly homogeneous in capital and labor and to obey the standard neo-classical conditions. Equation (11.3.4) is aggregate real output (Y, a GNP measure). Equation (11.3.5) expresses the demand for the consumption good (D) as a fixed fraction(s) of disposable income (Y_d). Investment demand per unit of labor (I_d) is given in equation (11.3.6) as a function of capital intensity (k), the terms of trade (p_k) the expected rate of change in the price of money (π) and the world interest rate (r).[2] Disposable income (Y_d) is defined in equation (11.3.7) as the sum of the value (in units of consumption goods) of real output, the net earnings from foreign securities (Zr) and changes in real balances due to an exogenous change in the rate of monetary expansion and the expected rate of change of the price of money (π)[3]. To simplify the analysis, changes in the value of capital are not included in disposable income. This implicitly assumes that the marginal propensity to consume due to changes in the value of capital is zero.

(b) Asset Markets

The flow demand for capital goods has already been specified in equation (11.3.6). The assumptions regarding money and foreign securities are stated below.

---

[2]The signs of partial derivatives of J with respect to its arguments are discussed later on.

[3]Note that because consumption goods are treated as the numeraire, p_m is the reciprocal of the usual price level and hence $\pi > 0$ means expected deflation.

(11.3.8) $\dot{M}/M = \mu$

(11.3.9) $\pi = n - \mu$

(11.3.10) $Mp_m/(Kp_k) = m(k,p_k,\pi,r)$

(11.3.11) $\dot{Z} = Y + Zr - D - I_d p_k$

(11.3.12) $z = Z/L$

The rate of growth of the nominal stock of money is given exogenously as μ. Equation (11.3.9) states that the expected rate of change of the price of money (in terms of consumption goods) is equal to the rate of growth of the labor force (n) less the rate of monetary expansion. This equation is well known in monetary growth models as the condition for long run equilibrium. We are assuming that expectations are rational in the sense that individuals consider only long run trends in the inflation rate rather than its day-to-day changes. In equation (11.3.10) the demand for money (equal to its supply in instantaneous equilibrium) per unit of capital is assumed to be dependent on k, p_k, π, and r. The dependence on k and p_k comes through both the transactions and speculative demands for money (by affecting income, wealth and the yield on capital). Changes in π and r affect the opportunity cost of holding money and hence would alter the demand for real balances. All assets are assumed to be gross substitutes. Specific assumptions on the partial derivatives of m are made later.

Equation (11.3.11) is the basic budget constraint and determines the time path of the stock of foreign securities (Z).[4] The first three terms on the right-hand side of equation (11.3.11) are the income of the domestic economy and the last two terms are expenditures on consumption and investment goods. To the extent that domestic production plus interest earnings (or minus payments) is not equal to domestic demand, foreign securities will be issued or retired by an

---

[4]By Walras law, if capital and money markets are in equilibrium then so is the foreign security market and hence we do not explicitly model the latter.

amount equal to the difference. Per capital holdings of securities are defined in equation (11.3.12) as z.

(c) Factor Accumulation

Labor force is assumed to grow exogenously at the rate n, so that

(11.3.13) $L/L = n$

Because firms can issue or borrow foreign securities, investment desires will be attained. Capital accumulation is therefore given by desired investment (ignoring depreciation). Thus

(11.3.14) $\dot{K} = I_d$

(d) Foreign Sector

The following equations refer to the trade sector and provide the links between the two countries. A variable with a superscript f refers to the foreign country.

(11.3.15) $B_T = C + Ip_k - (D+I_d p_k)$

(11.3.16) $I + I^f = I_d + I^f_d$

(11.3.17) $Z = - Z^f$

(11.3.18) $\lambda = L^f/L$

Equation (11.3.15) defines the balance of trade (B_T). Equation (11.3.16) is the market clearing condition stating that the world supply of investment goods must, in instantaneous equilibrium, equal the world demand for the same goods. Because the net credit (debt) of one country is the net debt (credit) of another country, $Z = -Z^f$. Equation (11.3.18) defines the relative size of the two countries' labor forces (λ).

A natural question that arises is "Will the consumption goods market also be in equilibrium?" The answer is yes, as is easily shown below. From (11.3.11) and (11.3.4)

(11.3.19) $$C - D = \dot{Z} - Zr - (I-I_d)p_k$$
$$= -\dot{Z}^f + Z^f r + (I^f-I_d^f)p_k$$

using (11.3.16) and (11.3.17). From Equation (11.3.11) for the foreign country, the right-hand side is $-(C^f-D^f)$. Therefore, $C + C^f = D + D^f$ which implies that the consumption goods market is also cleared. It is also easy to show that $B_T^f = - B_T$.

Equations (11.3.1) through (11.3.15) hold for each country and hence there are 30 equations. Equations (11.3.16) through (11.3.18) stand by themselves thus making a total of 33 independent equations. Each country has 15 endogenous variables; C, I, k, Y, D, I_d, Y_d, M, π, p_m, Z, z, K, L, and B_T. Both countries have three common variables, p_k, r and λ. There are thus 33 endogenous variables and the system is complete.

We should point out at this point that the model abstracts away from exchange rate considerations. It would be both interesting and more realistic to incorporate the exchange rate determination and its consequences explicitly into the model. But in view of the complexity that already exists we have abstained from that. Because the focus is on foreign security holdings, the model also ignores the holdings of domestic securities.

Assumptions on Partial Derivatives

Before carrying out any further analysis, we shall make certain basic assumptions on the various partial derivatives relevant to the model. Additional assumptions will be made later on.

An increase in the price of the investment good (p_k) will increase its supply and decrease that of the consumption good. Therefore $C_p \equiv \partial C/\partial p_k < 0$ and $I_p \equiv \partial I/\partial p_k > 0$.[5] By Rybczynski's Theorem, an increase in the capital-labor ratio will increase the supply of the capital intensive commodity and reduce the output of the other industry.

---

[5] Where there is no ambiguity, partial derivatives will be denoted by subscripts.

Thus if the consumption goods industry is more capital intensive [Uzawa's (1963) capital intensity condition], then $C_k > 0$ and $I_k < 0$. These inequalities are reversed if the capital intensity condition is reversed.

Ceteris Paribus, an increase in the expected rate of change in the price of money (implying deflation) makes the monetary asset more attractive (because of the gross substitutability assumption) and will hence reduce demand for capital goods. Similarly, as the interest rate on foreign securities increases, investment demand will decrease. Therefore, $J_\pi < 0$ and $J_r < 0$. Besides these two variables, investment demand is also affected by the stock of capital (k) and the price of capital (p_k). A rise in the stock of capital alone will increase overall income and wealth and hence induce additional demand for capital goods.[6] This implies that $J_k > 0$. Other things remaining equal, if p_k increases then investment demand will decrease and therefore $J_p \equiv \partial J/\partial p_k < 0$.

Let $y = Y/L$ be per capital aggregate output. Then from equations (11.3.1) through (11.3.4), we have $y = C(k,p_k) + I(k,p_k)p_k = y(k,p_k)$. By the "envelope theorem" and the tangency of the production possibility frontier with the price line discussed in Section 11.1, we have

$$y_p \equiv \partial y/\partial p_k = I/L > 0,\ y_k > 0 \text{ and } y - ky_k > 0$$

To explore the partial derivatives of m, write the demand for real balances per unit of capital as $MP_m/KP_k = m^d[y(k,p_k),i(p_k),r,\pi]$. The first term is per capita income y. The second term is the real rental on capital. The third and fourth terms are self-explanatory. Basic portfolio choice theory states that $m_y^d > 0$, $m_i^d < 0$, and $m_\pi^d > 0$ (see Foley and Sidrauski [1971]). Therefore, $m_k = m_y^d \cdot y_k > 0$ because $y_k > 0$. Also $m_\pi > 0$. A rise in r will decrease the demand for both money and capital and hence $m_r^d = m_r$ is ambiguous in sign.

---

[6] See Foley and Sidrauski (1971), pp. 44-45 for a more complete analysis of this. The reader should be aware, however, that the signs of some of the partial derivatives are not etched in concrete.

$$m_p \equiv \frac{\partial m^d}{\partial p_k} = m_y^d \cdot y_p + m_i^d \cdot i_p$$

We have, $m_y^d > 0$, $y_p > 0$, $m_i^d < 0$. But by the Stolper-Samuelson Theorem, $i_p > 0$ ($i_p < 0$) according as the consumption goods industry is less (more) capital intensive than the investment goods industry. Therefore, $m_p > 0$ unambiguously if the capital intensity condition holds. Otherwise, m_p could be positive or negative.

To summarize, all the assumptions that follow from basic theory are stated below.

(11.3.20) $C_p < 0$, $I_p > 0$, $J_k > 0$, $J_p < 0$,
$J_\pi < 0$, $J_r < 0$, $y_p > 0$, $y_k > 0$,
$y - ky_k > 0$, $m_k > 0$, $m_\pi > 0$.

In addition, if the capital intensity condition holds, we also have

$C_k > 0$, $I_k < 0$, $m_p > 0$

11.3.2 Partial Reduced Form

The analysis of the model will be vastly simplified if the system is condensed to a few partial reduced form equations. Initially assume that k, k^f and z are fixed. With appropriate substitutions, the market clearing conditions for the two commodities may be written as follows.

(11.3.15a) $$I(k,p_k) - J(k,p_k,n-\mu,r) = \lambda J^f(k^f,p_k,n-\mu^f,r) - \lambda I^f(k^f,p_k)$$

(11.3.16a) $$C(k,p_k) + \lambda C^f(k^f,p_k) = (1-s)\ [y(k,p_k) + zr + nkp_k m(\cdot)] + (1-s^f)\lambda[y^f(k^f,p_k) - zr + nk^f p_k m^f(\cdot)]$$

where $y(k,p_k) = Y/L$.

We assume that these two equations may be solved for the world terms of trade (p_k) and the interest rate (r) in terms of k, k^f, z and the parameters of the system, so that

(11.3.21) $p_k = P(k,k^f,z|n, \mu,\mu^f,s,s^f,\lambda)$

(11.3.22) $r = R(k,k^f,z|n, \mu,\mu^f,s,s^f,\lambda)$

It will be noted that λ is now treated as a known parameter that is constant for all t. This is equivalent to saying that the relative size of the two countries is always the same. This is essential as otherwise one of the countries will eventually be small and hence cannot affect world prices.

If the saving rates in the two countries are equal and $\lambda = 1$, then equation (11.3.16a) becomes independent of z. Thus the terms of trade and the world interest rate will be independent of the stock of securities if the saving rates and the labor forces are equal. The intuition behind this result is quite straightforward. The level of the stock of securities enters the demand functions only through Y_d. If $s = s^f$ and $\lambda = 1$, the extra consumption stimulated from one country's interest receipts is exactly offset by the reduction in demand in the other country due to a lowering of its Y_d. This is familiar from the transfer problem.

11.3.3 Equations of Motion of the System

The full dynamic analysis of the system can be carried out by specifying the differential equations of the system that determine the time paths of k, k^f and z which were held constant earlier. They are obtained from equations (11.2.13), (11.2.11) and (11.2.14) with appropriate substitutions from the other equations.

(11.3.23) $\dot{k} = J[k,P(\cdot),n-\mu,R(\cdot)] - nk$

(11.3.24) $\dot{k}^f = J^f[k^f,P(\cdot),n-\mu^f,R(\cdot)] - nk^f$

(11.3.25) $\dot{z} = s\cdot y[k,P(\cdot)] - (1-s)\ nkP(\cdot)m(\cdot)$

$$- J(\cdot)P(\cdot) + z[sR(\cdot)-n]$$

The above differential equations fully determine the time paths of k, k^f and z. In turn they determine the dynamic paths of the terms of trade and the interest rate. The remaining endogenous variables may be obtained from the appropriate structural equations.

11.3.4 Steady State

Along the balanced growth path, $\dot{k} = \dot{k}^f = \dot{z} = 0$, giving the following steady state conditions in k^*, k^{f*} and z^*.

$$(11.3.26) \quad J(k^*, p_k^*, n-\mu, r) = nk^*$$

$$(11.3.27) \quad J^f(k^f, p_k^*, n-\mu^f, r) = nk^{f*}$$

$$(11.3.28) \quad z^* = \frac{sy^* - nk^* p_k^*[1+(1-s)m]}{(n-sr)}$$

$$(11.3.29) \quad p_k^* = P(k^*, k^{f*}, z^* | n, \mu, s, s^f, \lambda)$$

$$(11.3.30) \quad r^* = R^*(k^*, k^{f*}, z^* | n, \mu, \mu^f, s, s^f, \lambda)$$

Our assumption that the economies in question are of intermediate size brings about a sharp contrast in terms of results as compared to models which allow the flow of securities but assume that the countries are small. For a small country, p_k and r are exogenously determined and hence the saving rate (s or s^f) is neutral in affecting the long-run capital intensities. Given p_k and r, firms will acquire or retire as many foreign securities as needed in order to carry out their desired investment. Thus, for a small country, the only role of fiscal policy (through changing s) is to affect the per capita level of security holding. This can be seen more formally by noting that when p_k and r are constant, k^* can be solved for from equation (11.3.26) alone.

In the case of intermediate size economies, even if the saving rates are always equal (which is unlikely in reality), changes in the common saving ratio will affect k^* and k^{f*}. This is because p_k^* and r^* will both be altered and hence consumption and investment demands will be different resulting in altered balanced growth paths. The direction of movement cannot be examined without imposing additional specific restrictions on partial derivatives. This is done in Section 11.3.6.

Another interesting result that can be derived is the relationship between disposable income and total assets (A) per capita in the steady state. They are as follows.

(11.3.31) $\quad y_d^* = y^* + k^* p_k^* m^* n + z^* r^*$

(11.3.32) $\quad A^* = k^* p_k^* (1+m^*) + z^*$

we therefore have

$$sy_d^* - A^* n = sy^* - nk^* p_k^* [1+(1-s)m^*] + z^*(sr^* - n)$$

We note from equation (11.3.28) that the right-hand size is zero. Thus,

(11.3.33) $\quad y_d^* / A^* = n/s$

In other words, the equilibrium ratio of disposable income to total assets is equal to the ratio of the natural rate to the domestic saving rate. It is interesting to note that this ratio is independent of the rates of monetary expansion in the two countries, the foreign saving rate as well as the relative size of the labor forces.

In order to have an economically meaningful long run solution, total wealth and disposable income must be positive. Fischer and Frenkel showed that the necessary and sufficient condition for this is $n > sr^*$. We shall presently show that this result no longer holds. From equation (11.3.28)

$$(n - sr^*) z^* = sy^* - nk^* p_k^* [1+(1-s)m^*]$$

Per capita output is distributed between wages and rents (because of linear homogeneity). If, as Fischer and Frenkel do, we assume that the rental on capital is equal to the world interest rate (which is the efficiency condition when asset markets are perfect), then $y = kp_k r + w$, where w is the wage rate. Substituting this in the above equation and rearranging terms we get

$$(11.3.34) \qquad (n-sr^*)\, A^* = s[w^* - k^* p_k{}^* m^* (r^* - n)]$$

In the Fischer-Frenkel model, $m \equiv 0$ and hence the right-hand side of equation (11.3.34) is positive implying that $n > sr^*$ is the required condition. But in our model the necessary and sufficient condition is stated below.

$$(11.3.35) \qquad y_d^*, A^* > 0 \text{ iff } (n-sr^*)[w^* - k^* p_k^* m^* (r^* - n)] > 0$$

An alternative form of this has better intuitive appeal. Using (11.3.33), $n - sr^* = s(y_d^* - A^* r^*)|A^*$.

Therefore, an alternative form of (11.3.35) is

$$(11.3.35a) \qquad y_d^*, A^* > 0 \text{ iff } (n-sr^*)\,(y_d^* - A^* r^*) > 0$$

$A^* r^*$ is the return on all assets computed at the rate of the world interest rate. If disposable income is larger than this return then $n > sr^*$. n can be smaller than sr^* but then y_d^* must be smaller than $A^* r^*$(which is possible if the world interest rate is large) for a steady state to exist. Thus we require a much stronger condition for a meaningful long run solution.

11.3.5 Security Holdings and the Balance of Trade

The long run level of per capital security holdings is given in equation (11.2.28) which is reproduced here:

$$(11.3.28) \qquad z^* = \frac{sy^* - nk^* p_k^* [1+(1-s)m^*]}{n - sr^*}$$

The condition for determining whether the home country will be a net creditor or debtor is given below.

(11.3.36) $\quad z^* \gtrless 0$ according as

$$(n-sr^*)[s(y^*+nk^*p_k{}^*m^*) - k^*p_k{}^*n(1+m^*)] \gtrless 0$$

The first term in square brackets is saving out of real output plus the change in real balances, evaluated at the equilibrium. The second term is the long run change in the capital and monetary components of wealth per capita (that is, exclusive of security holdings). If the above saving component exceeds the wealth component and $n > sr^*$, or if both inequalities are reversed, then the home country will be a net holder (i.e. creditor) of foreign securities in the long run. It is readily seen from (11.3.28) that z^* has a higher value when $m = 0$. Thus a model with a negligible monetary sector will imply a higher level of foreign security holdings. This is obviously because the availability of a monetary asset offers asset holders a substitute asset which will act to reduce the holdings of foreign securities.

The home country's balance of trade is

$$B_r = C - D + (I-I_d)p_k$$
$$= \dot{Z} - Zr \quad \text{using equation (11.3.19)}$$

Because $\dot{Z}/L = \dot{z} + nz$, per capita trade balance in the steady state

(11.3.37) $\quad b_T^* = z^*(n-r^*)$

Efficiency of the consumption path requires that $r^* > n$ (see Burmeister and Dobell [1970], Chapter 11). The trade balance is therefore opposite in sign to the level of security holdings. Thus a creditor nation (with $z^* > 0$) will have a deficit in the trade balance whereas a debtor nation will have a surplus trade balance.

Although we have not carried out the complete stability analysis of our model, it is possible to show that a cyclical approach to the steady state is feasible. Thus the debt/credit position of a country can switch back and forth because the saving and wealth components in inequality (11.3.36) can switch around to reverse the indebtedness. In the long run however, a permanent position of creditor or debtor is established. Because monetary policy (through changes in μ) and fiscal policy (indirectly through changes in s) can affect this indebtedness, it should generally be possible to arrive at an attainable combination of μ and s for which $z^* = b_r^* = 0$.

11.3.6 Sensitivity Analysis

We now examine the implications of changes in the parameters of the system on the long run equilibrium values of selected endogenous variables. Before doing that, however, we shall explore the short run impact (with $\pi = 0$, $\dot{k} = 0$, $\dot{z} = 0$ for all t).

Short Run Sensitivities

Differentiating equations (11.3.16a) and (11.3.15a) with respect to k and solving for $\partial p_k/\partial k$ and $\partial r/\partial k$ we get

(11.3.38) $$P_k \equiv \partial p_k/\partial k = (b_1a_{22}-b_2a_{12})/\Delta$$

(11.3.39) $$R_k \equiv \partial r/\partial k = (b_2a_{11}-b_1a_{21})/\Delta$$

(11.3.40) $$\Delta = a_{11}a_{22} - a_{21}a_{12}$$

where b_1, b_2 etc. are defined in the Appendix (Section 11.A.1). From the signs obtained in the inequalities in (11.3.20), assuming the capital intensity condition, it is clear that $a_{11} < 0$, $a_{21} < 0$, $a_{22} < 0$ and $b_2 < 0$ but the signs of a_{12} and b_1 are ambiguous. Also, assuming the stability of the static model (by involking the Correspondence Principle), we have $\Delta > 0$. All the above assumptions do not make the signs determinate. Several alternatives are discussed below.

b_1 is the response of excess demand in consumer goods as a result of a rise in the overall capital intensity in the home country. An increase in k raises supply but it also increases demand through income and wealth effects. Thus a positive b_1 means that, near the equilibrium, the demand effect dominates. a_{12} is the response of excess demand in consumer goods for an infinitesimal increase in r from the equilibrium position. Because m_r could be positive or negative, depending on whether asset demand shifts away from money or capital relatively more, a_{12} could be of either sign. Various alternatives for which the signs are determinate, are listed in the table below. It will be noted that in most cases R_k is positive.

	Sign of $\partial p_k/\partial k$ when			Sign of $\partial r/\partial k$ when		
	$b_1>0$	$b_1=0$	$b_1<0$	$b_1>0$	$b_1=0$	$b_1<0$
$a_{12}>0$	?	+	+	+	+	?
$a_{12}=0$	-	0	+	+	+	?
$a_{12}<0$	-	-	?	+	+	?

To obtain the short run sensitivities with respect to changes in z, the per capita stock of foreign securities, differentiate equations (11.3.16a) and (11.3.15a) with respect to z and solve the resulting relations. We then have

(11.3.41) $P_z \equiv \partial p_k/\partial z = c_1 a_{22}/\Delta$

(11.3.42) $R_z \equiv \partial r/\partial z = -c_1 a_{21}/\Delta$

where

(11.3.43) $c_1 = (1-s)r - (1-s^f)\lambda r$

Because a_{22} and a_{21} are negative and $\Delta > 0$, the signs of the above partial derivatives depend only on that of c_1. c_1 represents the excess demand in consumption goods due to a unit increase in the stock of foreign securities. This depends only on the saving rates of the two countries and the relative size of their labor forces. If the home country's elasticity of demand for consumer goods with respect to disposable income is high enough, then $c_1 > 0$. Because $\Delta > 0$, $a_{22} < 0$ and $a_{21} < 0$, it follows that $P_z < 0$ and $R_z > 0$. If the income elasticity is small, these signs are reversed. At any rate, P_z and R_z always have the opposite signs.

Long Run Effects

Appendix Section 11.A.2 has the detailed derivatives of the long run sensitivities of the capital intensities (k^* and k_f^*) and the per capita security holding (z^*) with respect to changes in the rate of monetary expansion (μ) and the saving rate (s). The expressions have not been fully worked out because the derivations are very tedious. Most neo-classical monetary growth models imply that $\partial k^*/\partial\mu > 0$ and $\partial k^*/\partial s > 0$. The small country assumption implies that $\partial k^*/\partial s = 0$. We readily see that these conclusions are no longer possible if the model is expanded to include a foreign sector with trade not only in commodities but also foreign securities, with full feedback through the offer curve. We need specific strong assumptions about the elasticities of investment and consumption demands (in both countries) with respect to changes in income, the terms of trade and world interest rate, as well as assumptions on the elasticities of demand for real balances with respect to the arguments in the money demand functions of the two countries. Although not explicitly shown here, it can be demonstrated after a considerable amount of algebra that the assumption that the model is dynamically stable is not adequate enough to weaken the specific assumptions on the various elasticities. A simulation exercise with Cobb-Douglas function forms and specific choices of parameters would throw more light on this issue but we have not made any attempt in that direction. At any rate, it is clear that the results from simpler models simply do not generalize without adding heroic assumptions.

11.3.7 Concluding Remarks

By relaxing the commonly made small-country assumption and introducing an offer curve effect and also allowing for trading of foreign securities, we have shown that many of the results consistently found in simpler models no longer hold. More specifically, the neutrality of the saving rate implied for a small country does not exist any more. Furthermore, unlike most monetary growth models, an increase in the rate of monetary expansion or the overall saving rate, can reduce the long run capital intensity. It is now possible to chosse combinations of μ and s for which the trade balance and foreign security holdings are at "desirable" levels. The conditions stated for the determination of whether a country will be a creditor or debtor in the long run is now stronger. The approach to this long run position can be cyclical so that a country may alternate from a debtor to a creditor position over the years.

We have not attempted to incorporate exchange rate considerations into our analysis, nor have we modelled fiscal policy in a more realistic way through government expenditure and taxation. These are clearly weaknesses in our model, but considering the inherent complexity of a model which incorporates the above features and the resulting intractability, we believe we have made a modest step in the right direction.

APPENDIX

11.A.1 Short Run Sensitivities

Differentiation of equations (11.2.16a) and (11.2.15a) with respect to k gives

$$a_{11}\partial p_k/\partial k + a_{12}\partial r/\partial k = b_1$$

$$a_{21}\partial p_k/\partial k + a_{22}\partial r/\partial k = b_2$$

where

$$a_{11} = C_p + \lambda C_p^f - (1-s)y_p - (1-s)nkm - (1-s)nkp_k m_p$$
$$-(1-s)\lambda y_p^f - (1-s^f)\lambda nk^f m^f - (1-s^f)\lambda nk^f p_k m_p^f$$

$$a_{12} = -(1-s)z - (1-s)nkp_k m_r + (1-s^f)\lambda z - \lambda(1-s^f)nk^f p_k m_r^f$$

$$a_{21} = J_p - I_p + \lambda J_p^f - \lambda I_p^f$$

$$a_{22} = J_r + \lambda J_r^f$$

$$b_1 = -C_k + (1-s)y_k + (1-s)nmp_k + (1-s)nkp_k m_k$$

$$b_2 = I_k - J_k$$

Solving this for $\partial p_k/\partial k$ and $\partial r/\partial k$, we get

(11.3.38) $\quad \partial p_k/\partial k = (b_1 a_{22} - b_2 a_{12})/\Delta$

(11.3.39) $\quad \partial r/\partial k = (b_2 a_{11} - b_1 a_{21})/\Delta$

where

(11.3.40) $\quad \Delta = a_{11}a_{22} - a_{21}a_{12}$

Similar sensitivites to changes in z are given by

$$a_{11}\partial p_k/\partial z + a_{12}\partial r/\partial z = c_1$$

$$a_{21}\partial p_k/\partial z + a_{22}\partial r/\partial z = 0$$

where

$$c_1 = (1-s)r - (1-s^f)\lambda r$$

Therefore

(11.3.41) $\quad \partial p_k/\partial z = c_1 a_{22}/\Delta$

(11.3.42) $\quad \partial r/\partial z = - c_1 a_{21}/\Delta$

11.A.2 Long Run Effects

To obtain the long run impacts of changes in the parameters, differentiate equations (11.3.26) through (11.3.28) with respect to the parameter in question, we get

$$\alpha_{11} k_\mu^* + \alpha_{12} k_\mu^{f*} + \alpha_{13} z_\mu^* = J_\pi^*$$

$$\alpha_{21} k_\mu^* + \alpha_{22} k_\mu^{f*} + \alpha_{23} z_\mu^* = 0$$

$$\alpha_{31} k_\mu^* + \alpha_{32} k_\mu^{f*} + \alpha_{33} z_\mu^* = (1-s)nk^* p_k^* m_\pi^*$$

where

$$\alpha_{11} = J_k + J_p P_k + J_r R_k - n$$

$$\alpha_{12} = J_p P_{k^f} + J_r R_{k^f}$$

$$\alpha_{13} = J_p P_z + J_r R_z$$

$$\alpha_{21} = J_p^f P_k + J_r^f R_k$$

$$\alpha_{22} = J_{k^f}^f + J_p^f P_{k^f} + J_r^f R_{k^f} - n$$

$$\alpha_{23} = J_p^f P + J_r^f R$$

$$\alpha_{31} = s(y_k + y_p P_k) - (1-s)\, np_k^* m^* - (1-s)nk^* P_k^* m^*$$

$$-(1-s)nk^* p_k^* m_k - np_k^* - nk^* P_k + z^* sR_k$$

$$\alpha_{32} = sy_p P_{k^f} - (1-s)nk^* p_k^* m_{k^f} - (1-s)nk^* m^* P_{k^f}$$
$$- nk^* P_{k^f} + sz^* R_{k^f}$$

$$\alpha_{33} = sy_p P_z - (1-s)nk^* p_k^* m_z - (1-s)nk^* m^* P_z$$
$$- nk^* P_z + sr^* - n + z^* sR_z$$

Let α^{ij} be the $(ij)^{th}$ element of the inverse of the matrix of α_{ij}'s. Then

$$\frac{\partial k^*}{\partial \mu} = \alpha^{11} J_\pi + \alpha^{13}(1-s)nk^* p_k^* m_\pi^*$$
$$\frac{\partial k^{f*}}{\partial \mu} = \alpha^{21} J_\pi + \alpha^{23}(1-s)nk^* p_k^* m_\pi^*$$
$$\frac{\partial z^*}{\partial \mu} = \alpha^{31} J_\pi + \alpha^{33}(1-s)nk^* p_k^* m_\pi^*$$

The sensitivities with respect to changes in the saving rate are obtained by differentiating equations (11.3.26) through (11.3.28) with respect to s. We get

$$\alpha_{11} k_s^* + \alpha_{12} k_s^{f*} + \alpha_{13} z_s^* = 0$$

$$\alpha_{21} k_s^* + \alpha_{22} k_s^{f*} + \alpha_{23} z_s^* = 0$$

$$\alpha_{31} k_s^* + \alpha_{32} k_s^{f*} + \alpha_{33} z_s^* = - y_d^*$$

From this we get the following partial derivatives.

$$\frac{\partial k^*}{\partial s} = - \alpha^{13} y_d^*$$
$$\frac{\partial k^{f*}}{\partial s} = - \alpha^{23} y_d^*$$

$$\frac{\partial z^*}{\partial s} = - \alpha^{33} y_d^*$$

REFERENCES

[1] Allen, P.R. (1972), "Money and Growth in Open Economies," Review of Economic Studies, 39, 213.19.

[2] Burmeister, E. and A.R. Dobell (1970), Mathematical Theories of Economic Growth, Macmillan Co.

[3] Fischer, S., and J.A. Frenkel (1972), "Investment, the Two-Sector Model and Trade in Debt and Capital Goods," Journal of International Economics, 2, 211-34.

[4] Foley, D., and M. Sidrauski (1971), Monetary and Fiscal Policy in a Growing Economy, MacMillan.

[5] Frenkel, J.A. (1971), "A Theory of Money, Trade and Balance of Payments in a Model of Accumulation," Journal of International Economics, 1, 159-87.

[6] Hori, H., and J.L. Stein (1977), "International Growth with Free Trade in Equities and Goods," International Economic Review, 18, 83-100.

[7] Kemp, M.C. (1974), The Pure Theory of International Trade and Investment, Prentice-Hall, Englewood Cliffs, N.J.

[8] Onitsuka, Y. (1974), "International Capital Movements and the Patterns of Growth," American Economic Review, 64, 24-36.

[9] Oniki, H., and H. Uzawa (1965), "Patterns of Trade and Investment in A Dynamic Model of International Trade," Review of Economic Studies, 32, 15-38.

[10] Ramanathan, R. (1975), "Monetary Expansion, Balance of Trade and Economic Growth," Economic Record, 51, 31-39.

[11] Roberts, W.W. (1978), "Monetary Expansion in an Open Economy of Intermediate Size," Economic Record, 54, 380-386.

[12] Roberts, William W. and R. Ramanathan, "Economic Growth and Trade in Commodities and Securities in an Intermediate Sized Economy," UCSD Discussion Paper 76-15.

[13] Sakakibara, E., (1975), "A Dynamic Approach to Balance of Payments Theory," Journal of International Economics, 5, 31-54.

[14] Tobin, J. (1965), "Money and Economic Growth," Econometrica, 33, 671-84.

[15] Uzawa, H. (1963), "On a Two-Sector Model of Economith Growth: II," Review of Economic Studies, 30, 105.18.

EXERCISES

11.1 In the static barter model, assume that tastes and production technologies in the two countries are identical and that the only difference is in factor endowment (i.e., $k > k^f$ or vice versa). Then prove Heckscher-Ohlin Theorem which states that a capital abundant country will export the capital intensive good and vice versa.

11.2 In the static barter model, examine the volume of trade when saving rate increases. Now do the same in the long-run model with non-specialization.

11.3 In the dynamic model of Section 11.2, choose one of the other possibilities of long-run equilibrium and examine stability and sensitivities.

11.4 Consider two countries, home (HC) and foreign (FC), and two commodities C and I. FC always specializes in $\bar{C}$ and exports a fixed quantity C to HC in exchange for I at p, the world TOT (C is numeraire). HC produces both goods. C is more capital intensive in both countries. Preferences and technology in the HC are homothetic. FC's behavior is reflected only through C. HC's capital accumulates by the amount of I it demands at any instant (ignore depreciation). In answering the following questions, clearly state any additional assumptions you make.

Static behavior

a. Write down the structural equations of the complete model for HC and the trade linkage. For each equation, state whether it is behavioral, an identity, technological, a definition or an accounting relation.

b. Derive the static equilibrium condition that determines p, the world TOT.

c. Separately examine the effects on the volume of trade $(I_s - I_d)$ of increases in (a) HC's capital intensity k, (b) HC's saving rate s, and (c) FC's exports, $\bar{C}$. Rationalize each of these sensitivities in intuitive economic terms.

Dynamic behavior

d. Derive the differential equation in k for HC and obtain the steady state condition (s).

e. Suppose $\bar{C}$ goes up. How does it affect HC's k*? Rationalize this in intuitive economic terms.

REVIEW QUESTIONS[1]

1. One of the principal conclusions derived from the Solow-Swan growth model is that the equilibrium growth rate is independent of the saving rate. Write out the model in equation form, make clear which are the critical assumptions, and derive this result. In what sense, if any, does this imply that the saving rate is unimportant

2. Imagine an economy with production function $Y = f(K)$; where Y is output, capital K is the only input, and f is a function shaped as shown. Further assume there are two classes of capital owners, holding capital K_1 and K_2 respectively ($K = K_1+K_2$). They receive incomes Y_1 and Y_2 ($Y = Y_1+Y_2$) in proportion to their capital ownership. The two ownership classes plow back constant fractions s_1 and s_2 of their incomes into new capital, which depreciates at constant rate δ; so $\dot{K}_1 = s_1Y_1 - \delta K_1$ and similarly for K_2. Assume $s_1 > s_2$.

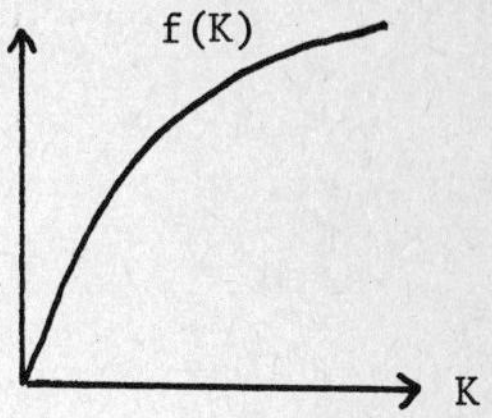

   a. State the entire model and list the variables it determines.

   b. Reduce the model to two differential equations in K_1 and K_2. Draw the corresponding phase diagram, and use it to describe what happens to the capital holdings of the two classes.

   c. Explain your results in terms of economic intuition.

3. Consider a neoclassical growth model of a socialist economy with the following characteristics.

   (i) Output Y is determined by a constant returns production function $Y = F(K,L)$ of capital K and labor L, with $F_1 > 0$ and $F_2 > 0$.

   (ii) Labor L grows at a constant given rate n.

[1] These questions are not arranged by Chapters.

(iii) All output is distributed to labor. The government (which owns the capital) charges a head tax of β output units per worker. The government plows back all the head tax revenue into new capital. Labor consumes all of its after tax earnings.

(iv) Capital depreciates at constant exponential rate δ.

In the following questions, denote the capital labor ratio by $k = K/L$.

a. State the equations of the model and derive from them a differential equation with k the only variable.

b. What additional conditions on F are needed to assure that your equation for k has a unique stable equilibrium.

c. Write down and fill in a sensitivity table of the following form. (Each entry should be +, -, or 0.) Explain your entries briefly.

Equilibrium Value of	β	δ	n
k			
K/Y			
Growth Rate of Y/L			

d. To make economic sense of the analysis, we must assume that the total head tax is less than output. Show that the needed assumptions are $\beta < F(k_0,1)$ and $\beta < F[\beta/(\delta+n),1]$, where k_0 is the initial value of k.

e. What does your lower left entry in the sensitivity table above imply about the usefulness of β as a policy instrument in pursuing growth goals?

f. Suppose the government wishes to set β at that (constant) level which maximizes equilibrium consumption per head. Derive that level for β.

4. Consider a country whose long-run growth behavior obeys the basic Solow-Swan model:

(1) $Y = F(K,N) = f(K/N)N$ (production function).

(2) $\dot{K} = sY - \delta K$ (capital growth equation).

(3) $\dot{N}/N = n$ (exogenous labor growth rate).

Here the production function displays constant returns; and the intensive form $f(k)$, where $k = K/N$, has the standard properties $f(0) = 0$, $f'(0) = \infty$, $f'(k) > 0$, $f''(k) < 0$, and $f'(\infty) = 0$. The savings, depreciation, and population growth rates are constants with $0 < s < 1$, $\delta > 0$, and $n > 0$. Now suppose this country, in return for agreeing not to criticize the United States, is awarded a capital subsidy from the U.S., in perpetuity, at a constant rate of σ units per head per unit time ($\sigma > 0$). Equation (2) changes to

(2') $\dot{K} = sY + \sigma N - \delta K$,

and (1) and (2) remain unchanged. Your problem is to analyze the model of (1), (2'), and (3).

a. Reduce the model to a single differential equation in $k = K/N$.

b. By drawing an appropriate graph (or by another technique if you insist), show that the model has a unique stable equilibrium k^* for k.

c. Construct a sensitivity table of the following form and enter a +, -, or 0 in each cell to show the direction of sensitivity of each of the indicated equilibrium magnitudes to an all-else-equal increase in σ. Explain each entry in terms of <u>economic intuition</u>. (You are not asked for mathematical derivation.)

Magnitude	k^*	$(K/Y)^*$	$(Y/N)^*$	$(\dot{Y}/Y)^*$
Sensitivity to σ				

d. Find the value of the savings rate which maximizes the equilibrium value of consumption per head c. More precisely, find the equation or equations whose solution yields this "golden rule" value for s; an explicit solution will not be available. What is the sensitivity of the golden rule s-value, call it s_g, to the parameter σ. Explain analytically and intuitively.

5. Consider a neoclassical growth model built around the production function $Y = F(K,L)$; where Y is output, K is capital, and L is labor. Assume:

(i) $F(K,L)$ displays constant returns, is smooth and differentiable, and obeys the usual Inada conditions [$F_1(k,1) > 0$, $F_{11}(k,1) < 0$, $F(0,1) = 0$, $F_1(0,1) = \infty$, and $F_1(\infty,1) = 0$].

(ii) The rate of return to capital is mandated by law to equal r, where $r > 0$ is an exogenously determined parameter. So marginal productivity factor pricing does <u>not</u> hold (except by coincidence). Income not accruing to capital accrues to labor.

(iii) Capitalists save a fraction s_1 of their income; and workers save a fraction s_2 of their income. Assume $0 < s_1, s_2 < 1$. Gross capital information equals total savings; and net capital formation equals gross capital formation less depreciation. Depreciation occurs at constant exponential rate $\mu > 0$.

(iv) Labor grows at constant exponential rate $n > 0$.

(v) $\mu + n + r(s_2 - s_1) > 0$.

Given these assumptions, answer all of the following five questions.

a. State the model as a system of equations. Then reduce the model to a single differential equation in the transform variable $k = K/L$.

b. Sketch a proof of the existence, uniqueness, and stability of a balanced growth path for the model. [Here the word "sketch" means that you may leave out mathematical details. However, your sketch must be persuasive evidence that you know how to prove the result. Be sure to show the role of assumption (v).]

c. Explain in intuitive economic terms why the balanced growth path comes about.

d. Construct a sensitivity table displaying the sensitivities of the equilibrium values of k, K/Y, and $\dot{Y}/Y$ to the parameters r, s_1, s_2, n, and μ. (Here $\dot{Y} = dY/dt$.)

e. Consider the "marginal productivity share" $(\partial Y/\partial K)K/Y$ of capital and the actual share rK/Y. They need not be equal in this model. Consider the sensitivities of these two shares to the parameter r. Either sensitivity could be positive or negative. For each sensitivity, state a simple condition on parameters of the function F determining whether the sensitivity is positive or negative.

6. Consider the following conventional Solow-Swan growth model.

$$Y = F(K,L)$$
$$\dot{K} = sY - \delta K \qquad (0 < s \leq 1,\ \delta > 0)$$
$$\dot{L}/L = n \qquad (n > 0)$$

Assume the constant returns production function Y = F(K,L), in the intensive form F(K,L) = f(K/L)L, obeys the Inada conditions: $f' > 0$, $f'' < 0$, $f(0) = 0$, $f'(0) = \infty$, $f'(\infty) = 0$. Each of the following questions can be answered with minimal algebraic effort. Fairly short answers are expected.

a. Let (K/Y)* be the equilibrium capital-output ratio. What is the elasticity of (K/Y)* with respect to s? Explain.

b. Would the long run qualitative behavior of the model change if the assumption n, $\delta > 0$ were replaced by the assumption $n = \delta = 0$? Explain. (For the remaining questions, assume n, $\delta > 0$.)

c. Explain in terms of <u>economic intuition</u> (not mathematics) why the sensitivity of $\dot{Y}/Y$ to s is what it is, both in and out of equilibrium.

d. Suppose the production function were changed to $Y = AK^{\beta}L^{\mu}E^{1-\beta-\mu}$. Here (A,β,μ) are positive parameters with $\beta + \mu < 1$; and the third factor input E represents environmental carrying capacity. If E is fixed, how does the qualitative long run behavior of the model change relative to that of the original model? Is the Cobb-Douglas nature of the new production function crucial to your answer?

7. The following model incorporates a "learning by doing" type of technical change.

(1) $Y = F(K,Z^{\sigma}N)$ $\quad (0 < \sigma < 1)$

(2) $\dot{Z} = Y$

(3) $\dot{K} = sY - \delta K$ $\quad (0 < s \leq 1,\ \delta > 0)$

(4) $\dot{N}/N = n$ $\quad (n > 0)$

In the production function (1), Y is output, K is capital, N is labor, and Z^{σ} is a labor-augmenting technology multiplier which needs explaining. The variable Z represents the serial number on the latest unit of output, where units of output are assumed to have been serially numbered since the beginning of time. This is all (2) says; the increment $\dot{Z}$ to the serial number Z equals the number of units Y currently produced. As the serial number, Z is a measure of the cumulative productive experience of the economy. Experience (or learning by doing) is assumed to lead to technical change through the technology multiplier Z^{σ}. The presence of the σ exponent (less than one) on Z implies that there are diminishing technological returns to the cumulation of experience. Equations (3) and (4) are standard. Parameter constraints are in parentheses. The production function is assumed to display constant returns; hence it may be written $F(K,Z^{\sigma}N) = (Z^{\sigma}N)f(k)$ where $k = K/(Z^{\sigma}N)$.

a. Reduce the model to two differential equations in $k = K/(Z^{\sigma}N)$ and $z = Z^{1-\sigma}/N$. You may assume that a unique equilibrium, which is globally stable, exists for k and z.

b. Derive the equilibrium growth rates of Y, K, and Z. Explain in intuitive economic terms why they are what they are. (Hint: You can answer this question and much of the following two questions even if you miss part a.)

c. Derive equilibrium expressions for K/Y and Z/Y. Then present a sensitivity table showing the sensitivities of the equilibrium values of $\dot{Y}/Y$, K/Y, and Z/Y to changes in s, δ, n, and σ. Briefly justify in intuitive economic terms the K/Y and Z/Y sensitivities.

d. Compare and contrast this model to the Solow-Swan model, explaining things in intuitive economic terms.

8. The economic growth literature has raised a number of issues about the nature of technical progress. These involved whether technical change is

   (i) neutral or factor biased.
   (ii) endogenous or exogenous.
   (iii) embodied or disembodied.

a. Carefully define the concepts involved in <u>each</u> issue.

b. Describe <u>at least two</u> major approaches which relate to <u>each</u> issue.

c. State the importance of <u>each</u> issue for the implications of growth.

In your answer avoid excessive algebraic detail.

9. Consider a neoclassical growth model with endogenously determined population growth.

(1) $Y = F(K,N)$

(2) $\dot{K} = sY - \delta K \qquad (0 < s < 1,\ \delta \geq 0)$

(3) $\dot{N}/N = \alpha(Y/N - \beta) \qquad (\alpha,\ \beta > 0)$

Equation (1) is a production function giving output Y as a function of capital K and the population of workers N; it is assumed to display constant returns to scale and other nice neoclassical properties. Equation (2) is the usual capital accumulation equation, where S and δ are constant saving and depreciation parameters. Equation (3) states that the population growth rate is proportional to the excess of per capita income over a given subsistence level; where α is the constant of proportionality and β is the subsistence level.

a. Reduce the system to a single differential equation in $k = K/N$.

b. State a set of conditions sufficient for stability.

c. Prepare a sensitivity table showing the sensitivities of important equilibrium magnitudes to changes in parameters.

d. Compare and contrast the sensitivities of this model to the more conventional model in which equation (3) is replaced by $\dot{N}/N = n =$ constant. Explain intuitively.

10. Monetary growth models may broadly be classified into two groups, (1) neoclassical and (2) Keynes-Wicksell. Neoclassical models can be further categorized according to whether money is (1a) purely a medium of exchange and store of wealth, (1b) a consumption good, i.e. enters into consumers' utility function and (1c) a producer good, i.e. enters into the production function. Carefully discuss each of the four types of models (1a, 1b, 1c and 2) in terms of both approach and results. More specifically,

    a. Contrast the assumptions embodied in each approach. If necessary, write down alternative structural equations which illustrate the differences.

    b. Identify the people who have made significant contributions in each.

    c. Contrast the results of each type of model (there is no need for any derivations).

d. Discuss the role played by price expectations and changes in them in altering, if at all, the results on neutrality of money and the stability of these models.

e. To what extent do each of these models adequately treat the long run impact of monetary and fiscal policy? How might one or more of them be improved in this respect? Carefully explain your answers.

11. Some of the research work in growth theory follows the Neo-Keynesian (also known as the Cambridge growth theory or Kaldorian) approach.

a. Clearly state the basic differences in assumptions between the above approach and the neo-classical approach.

b. Construct a simple neo-classical model and a simple neo-Keynesian one which reflect the differences stated in (1).

c. Carry out an analysis of each of the two models and identify the differences in conclusions which result from the differing assumptions.

d. Critically examine the two approaches and state which one seems superior. Carefully justify your choice. If a mix of the two is preferable, present such a model and explain why it is superior to either approach.

12. Consider the following growth model:

(1) $Y = F(K,L)$

(2) $\dot{K} = sY - \delta K$ $\quad (0 < s < 1,\ \delta > 0)$

(3) $\dot{L}/L = \alpha(Y/L - \beta)$ $\quad (\alpha,\ \beta > 0)$

a. Describe in intuitive terms (with an appropriate diagram, if necessary) the meaning of the third equation and the parameters α and β.

b. Derive the "warranted" and "natural" rates of growth in terms of the capital intensity k and graph them in the same diagram.

c. Derive the basic differential equation of the model and briefly discuss the existence and uniqueness of a steady state. State any conditions you impose.

d. Assuming the appropriate conditions, describe intuitively the economic mechanism that will take the economy to the steady state in the long run.

e. Suppose the saving rate increases. Examine what happens to the long run rate of growth of output. Describe in intuitive terms the economic mechanism behind your result.

f. Derive the Golden Rule saving rate in terms of the parameters and the steady state k*. Compare that with the relative share of capital.

13. Consider the following "learning by doing" model:

$$Y = K^{\beta}N^{1-\beta} \qquad N = TL \qquad T = e^{\lambda t}K^{\alpha}$$

$$\dot{K} = sY - \delta K \qquad \dot{L}/L = n \qquad k = K/N$$

a. Derive the Golden Rule saving rate (s*) that maximizes (C/N)*, i.e., per capita consumption per unit of efficient labor in the steady state. Assume that $0 < \alpha, \beta, s < 1; \delta, n > 0$.

b. Suppose that the actual saving rate (s) is less than s*. Then show how the government can tax, at the proportional rate t, and invest so as to achieve Golden Rule. Compute the tax rate needed in terms of the parameters of the model. Will t lie between 0 and 1?

c. Assume that labor is paid its marginal product ($\partial Y/\partial L$) and the balance is paid to capital. Furthermore, workers consume all their disposable income but capital-owners save all their disposable income. As before, the government invests all tax proceeds. Compute the above tax rate needed to achieve Golden Rule in this case.

14. In a Solow-Swan (SS) model, the demand for capital is determined by the equality of real rents to the marginal product of capital. Suppose that rents are regulated to be fixed at $\bar{r}$ which is high enough so that the SS long run equilibrium cannot be attained.

a. Without going through much of derivations, describe how and why the usual economic arguments for reaching the steady state break down here. Where will such an economy end up (in terms of capital intensity) in the long run? Will there be unemployment and/or excess capacity in the long run?

b. Carefully outline step by step how fiscal policy (i.e. taxing, etc.) can be an effective tool in bringing such an economy to a full employment (of K and L) equilibrium even with a rigid rental rate.

15. With reference to a Putty-Clay model carefully describe each of the following.

a. The differences in the optimization procedure between a firm with a perfect foresight and one with zero foresight (not the full model, just the differences). How do the necessary conditions for maximization differ?

b. The economic rationale behind the statement "under perfect foresight, the operating life of a machine is longer and the level of output higher than under zero foresight."

16. In a given economy, aggregate output (Y) is given by the linearly homogeneous neo-classical production function $F(K,N)$ where K is aggregate capital and N is employed labor. Firms' demand for labor (N) is determined by the equality of real wages (w) to the marginal product of employed labor. Real returns to capital (r) equal its marginal product. The supply of labor (L) responds to the wage rate according to the relation $\dot{L}/L = g(w)$ thus giving the labor supply equation. Because supply and demand for labor may not equal at a given point in time, the wage rate responds to the disequilibrium according to the relation $\dot{w}/w = \lambda(N-L)/L$, where λ is a scalor. The fraction of income saved is given by $s(r)$, that is, the saving rate is not constant but depends on the rate of return to capital. All saving is invested into additional capital. For simplicity there is no depreciation. Let $k \equiv K/N$ and $x \equiv K/L$.

a. Write down the structural equations of the above model for the endogenous variables Y, K, N, L, w, r, k and x.

b. What assumptions would you make about the signs of λ, $g'(w)$ and $s'(r)$? Provide an economic rationale for each of the assumptions.

c. Reduce the system to differential equations in k and x.

d. Assume that $\dot{k} = 0 = \dot{x}$ in the steady state and derive the long run equilibrium conditions. Briefly discuss the existence of a solution.

e. For a given K, assume that the labor supply grows faster than its demand. Describe the economic mechanism (consistent with the model and the assumptions you made in 2) that eventually makes the two grow at the same rate (no mathematics).

f. Suppose capital grows faster than labor supply. Describe the economic mechanism that makes the two grow at the same rate in the long run.

g. Check the model for local stability. Draw a phase diagram and examine global stability.

h. Suppose the economy is initially in steady state. Suddenly there is an influx of new women workers who at each wage rate make the labor supply grow faster. Trace the economic mechanism (no mathematics) that brings about a new long run equilibrium at which K, L and N grow at the same rate.

i. In which direction do the new k^*, w^* and $(\dot{Y}/Y)^*$ change? Describe the economic rationale behind such a change.

17. Describe in intuitive/economic terms (no mathematics) the rationale behind each of the following statements.

   a. If technical progress is both Hicks-neutral and Harrod-neutral then the production function must be of the Cobb-Douglas type.

   b. In a perfect foresight vintage model, an increase in the saving rate will lower the rate of time discount and increase the operating life of equipment.

   c. In an induced bias model with the Kennedy technical change frontier, if the elasticity of substitution $\sigma < 1$ then an increase in capital intensity (k) will result in an increase in labor-augmenting technical progress.

18. a. Describe the <u>essential</u> features of the structure (not results) of a monetary growth model that synthesizes the neo-classical and Keynes-Wicksell approaches. What weaknesses of the two approaches does the synthesis eliminate and in what manner? In what way are the results of the synthetic model different from those of each of the separate approaches?

   b. Critically evaluate the synthetic model from the point of view of the adequacy of its treatment of the long run impact of monetary and fiscal policy. Suggest possible modifications to the model that will eliminate any weaknesses you stated.

19. Consider an economy with a neo-classical production function $Y = F(K,L)$. Labor force grows at the rate n. Capital accumulation $\dot{K} = I$. For simplicity there is no depreciation. Also $Y = C + I$ where C is consumption expenditures. Consumption C = a fraction $c(k,p)$ of wealth W where $k = K/L$, $p = \dot{P}/P$ and $W = K + (M/P)$, M being the money supply, P the price level and $\dot{P}/P = p$ the rate of change of price level. Demand for real balances (i.e. money) is given by $m(k,p)$ and equals the supply of money in real terms. Money supply grows at the exogenous rate μ, i.e. $\dot{M}/M = \mu$.

   a. Write down the structural equations of the above model for the endogenous variables Y, K, L, C, k, M, p, P, W.

   b. What assumptions would you make about the signs of the derivatives of $c(k,p)$ and $m(k,p)$ with respect to k and p? Provide an economic rationale for each of the assumptions.

   c. Reduce the system to differential equations in k and p.

   d. Assume that $\dot{k} = \dot{p} = 0$ in steady state and derive the long run equilibrium conditions. Briefly discuss the existence of a steady state.

   e. Check the model for local stability. Draw a phase diagram and examine global stability.

   f. Examine the impact of an increase in μ on the equilibrium rate of inflation and that of capital intensity.

20. a. Describe the essential features of the structure (not results) of a Induced Bias Model using the Kennedy Frontier. In what features is the structure of this model different from that of a Solow-Swan model with Harrod-neutral technical progress?

b. In what ways are the results of the two models different? Carefully contrast the results.

c. Suppose the frontier itself is endogenous. State the formulations in growth theory literature that incorporate this endogeneity into the model. State the results of this model and contrast it to the case when the frontier is exogenous.

21. A given economy has the neo-classical production function $Y = F(K,LT)$ where the symbols have the standard interpretation. Technical progress is endogenous and changes according to the rule $\dot{T}/T = \lambda + \alpha Y/(LT)$. Demand for real balances per unit of capital is given by $m(k,p)$ where $k = K/(LT)$ and $p = \dot{P}/P$. Also $\eta = 1 + (km_k/m)$, m_k being the partial derivative of m with respect to k. The rest of the relations are as in the Tobin model.

a. Write down the complete set of structural equations of this model (ignore depreciation).

b. For each equation, state whether it is a behavioral equation, equilibrium condition, accounting relation, definition or of any other kind. Justify your answers.

c. Assume for the rest of the questions that the government maintains the inflation rate at p_o. Derive an expression for the rate of monetary expansion that is needed to achieve the target inflation rate in terms of $\dot{k}$, k and the fixed parameters.

d. Reduce the system to a single differential equation in k (be careful not to make algebraic errors here).

e. Write down the steady state condition for obtaining k^*.

f. Derive the long-run rate of growth of per capita income (call it g^*).

g. Suppose the saving rate goes up. Describe the economic mechanism (no mathematics) that takes the economy to a new steady state. Is the new steady state k^* higher or lower? Is the new growth rate of per capita output higher or lower? Carefully provide enough justification.

h. What is the economic meaning of an increase in α? Without using any mathematics, argue the direction of movement of k^* and g^*. Using the arguments just given, compare the values of g^* between two economies, one given by the above model and another in which technical progress grows at the exogenous rate λ.

i. Now suppose that the rate of monetary expansion is exogenous. State (no detailed mathematics needed) whether you expect this model also to exhibit a saddle point instability. To answer this, it is enough to state why the Tobin model has the saddle point instability and whether or not the present model exhibits this and if so, how?

22. The following reasoning has received a great deal of attention in recent years.

(1) To households, social security represents a form of wealth which, al else equal, reduces savings.

(2) Reduced saving leads to reduced investment which in time leads to a lower capital stock.

The usual exposition elaborates (1) and takes (2) for granted. You are to reverse the emphasis. That is, you are to take (1) for granted and develop a model which embodies the logic of (2) - that a downward shift in the savings function (upward shift in the consumption function) leads to a lower capital stock. Since change in the capital stock is the issue, your model should emphasize long-run forces. Your model should have the following characteristics: there should be an aggregate neoclassical production function $Y = F(K)$, where Y is output and K is the capital stock (treat labor as fixed). There should be a capital accumulation equation $\dot{K} = I - \delta K$; where $\dot{K} = dK/dt$, I is gross investment, and δ is a constant depreciation rate. There should be separate behavioral equations for savers (consumers) and investors; and there should be adequate mechanisms to show how the decisions of these two groups are brought into conformity. Social security should be handled in the following very simple way. Put a real-wealth argument in the savings (or consumption) function; and include a term X, representing social security wealth, in this wealth argument. Treat X as exogenous and suppress whatever tax-transfer mechanisms you might otherwise associate with social security. In this context, let K^* represent the long-run equilibrium value of K. The conclusion of logic (2) that $\partial K^*/\partial X < 0$ is to be expected.

a. Specify your model - list structural equations, state restrictions on functions, name variables, distinguish endogenous from exogenous variables, and so on. Simplicity is welcome so long as it does not undercut the purpose of the model.

b. Either derive an expression for the long-run multiplier $\partial K^*/\partial X$ or, if your model is too complicated to make the derivation feasible in limited time, do the following: make any simple substitutions or eliminations to compact the model; then describe in clear and specific terms how one would derive $\partial K^*/\partial X$ from the compacted model.

c. Discuss the economic substance of your model as it bears on the sign and magnitude of $\partial K^*/\partial X$. What forces in the model tend to make $\partial K^*/\partial X$ negative? What is the economic intuition of their operation? What forces work the other way, and what is the economic intuition?

d. In discussing K^*, you have been discussing the long-run equilibrium of the model. Explain how you would demonstrate that K^* is a stable equilibrium. Consider the dynamics of adjustment. Suppose that the model is initially in long-run equilibrium with $X = 0$. Suppose then that X increases once and for all to $X > 0$. Can you tell whether K will move monotonically from the old to the new equilibrium, or whether something else happens? Explain your answer (explain how to get an answer if your model is too complicated to yield it in reasonable time).

23. Suppose the saving-income ratio is s(r) where r is the rate of return to capital. Also let $\dot{T}/T = g(y)$ where y is per capita income (Y/L) and T is a labor-augmenting technical progress factor.

1. What signs will you expect for s'(r) and g'(y) and why?

2. Derive a differential equation in k, the capital effective ratio. Supply additional equations as needed.

3. Suppose the rate of growth of the labor force goes up by one percent. Describe the economic mechanism (no math) that will take the economy to a new steady state. Is the new steady state per capita income higher than the one before? Explain in intuitive terms.

4. Will the long run growth rate in output change by less than one percent or more than one percent? Justify your answer.

Vol. 101: W. M. Wonham, Linear Multivariable Control. A Geometric Approach. X, 344 pages. 1974.

Vol. 102: Analyse Convexe et Ses Applications. Comptes Rendus, Janvier 1974. Edited by J.-P. Aubin. IV, 244 pages. 1974.

Vol. 103: D. E. Boyce, A. Farhi, R. Weischedel, Optimal Subset Selection. Multiple Regression, Interdependence and Optimal Network Algorithms. XIII, 187 pages. 1974.

Vol. 104: S. Fujino, A Neo-Keynesian Theory of Inflation and Economic Growth. V, 96 pages. 1974.

Vol. 105: Optimal Control Theory and its Applications. Part I. Proceedings 1973. Edited by B. J. Kirby. VI, 425 pages. 1974.

Vol. 106: Optimal Control Theory and its Applications. Part II. Proceedings 1973. Edited by B. J. Kirby. VI, 403 pages. 1974.

Vol. 107: Control Theory, Numerical Methods and Computer Systems Modeling. International Symposium, Rocquencourt, June 17–21, 1974. Edited by A. Bensoussan and J. L. Lions. VIII, 757 pages. 1975.

Vol. 108: F. Bauer et al., Supercritical Wing Sections II. A Handbook. V, 296 pages. 1975.

Vol. 109: R. von Randow, Introduction to the Theory of Matroids. IX, 102 pages. 1975.

Vol. 110: C. Striebel, Optimal Control of Discrete Time Stochastic Systems. III. 208 pages. 1975.

Vol. 111: Variable Structure Systems with Application to Economics and Biology. Proceedings 1974. Edited by A. Ruberti and R. R. Mohler. VI, 321 pages. 1975.

Vol. 112: J. Wilhelm, Objectives and Multi-Objective Decision Making Under Uncertainty. IV, 111 pages. 1975.

Vol. 113: G. A. Aschinger, Stabilitätsaussagen über Klassen von Matrizen mit verschwindenden Zeilensummen. V, 102 Seiten. 1975.

Vol. 114: G. Uebe, Produktionstheorie. XVII, 301 Seiten. 1976.

Vol. 115: Anderson et al., Foundations of System Theory: Finitary and Infinitary Conditions. VII, 93 pages. 1976

Vol. 116: K. Miyazawa, Input-Output Analysis and the Structure of Income Distribution. IX, 135 pages. 1976.

Vol. 117: Optimization and Operations Research. Proceedings 1975. Edited by W. Oettli and K. Ritter. IV, 316 pages. 1976.

Vol. 118: Traffic Equilibrium Methods, Proceedings 1974. Edited by M. A. Florian. XXIII, 432 pages. 1976.

Vol. 119: Inflation in Small Countries. Proceedings 1974. Edited by H. Frisch. VI, 356 pages. 1976.

Vol. 120: G. Hasenkamp, Specification and Estimation of Multiple-Output Production Functions. VII, 151 pages. 1976.

Vol. 121: J. W. Cohen, On Regenerative Processes in Queueing Theory. IX, 93 pages. 1976.

Vol. 122: M. S. Bazaraa, and C. M. Shetty,Foundations of Optimization VI. 193 pages. 1976

Vol. 123: Multiple Criteria Decision Making. Kyoto 1975. Edited by M. Zeleny. XXVII, 345 pages. 1976.

Vol. 124: M. J. Todd. The Computation of Fixed Points and Applications. VII, 129 pages. 1976.

Vol. 125: Karl C. Mosler. Optimale Transportnetze. Zur Bestimmung ihres kostengünstigsten Standorts bei gegebener Nachfrage. VI, 142 Seiten. 1976.

Vol. 126: Energy, Regional Science and Public Policy. Energy and Environment I. Proceedings 1975. Edited by M. Chatterji and P. Van Rompuy. VIII, 316 pages. 1976.

Vol. 127: Environment, Regional Science and Interregional Modeling. Energy and Environment II. Proceedings 1975. Edited by M. Chatterji and P. Van Rompuy. IX, 211 pages. 1976.

Vol. 128: Integer Programming and Related Areas. A Classified Bibliography. Edited by C. Kastning. XII, 495 pages. 1976.

Vol. 129: H.-J. Lüthi, Komplementaritäts- und Fixpunktalgorithmen in der mathematischen Programmierung. Spieltheorie und Ökonomie. VII, 145 Seiten. 1976.

Vol. 130: Multiple Criteria Decision Making, Jouy-en-Josas, France. Proceedings 1975. Edited by H. Thiriez and S. Zionts. VI, 409 pages. 1976.

Vol. 131: Mathematical Systems Theory. Proceedings 1975. Edited by G. Marchesini and S. K. Mitter. X, 408 pages. 1976.

Vol. 132: U. H. Funke, Mathematical Models in Marketing. A Collection of Abstracts. XX, 514 pages. 1976.

Vol. 133: Warsaw Fall Seminars in Mathematical Economics 1975. Edited by M. W. Loś, J. Loś, and A. Wieczorek. V. 159 pages. 1976.

Vol. 134: Computing Methods in Applied Sciences and Engineering. Proceedings 1975. VIII, 390 pages. 1976.

Vol. 135: H. Haga, A Disequilibrium – Equilibrium Model with Money and Bonds. A Keynesian – Walrasian Synthesis. VI, 119 pages. 1976.

Vol. 136: E. Kofler und G. Menges, Entscheidungen bei unvollständiger Information. XII, 357 Seiten. 1976.

Vol. 137: R. Wets, Grundlagen Konvexer Optimierung. VI, 146 Seiten. 1976.

Vol. 138: K. Okuguchi, Expectations and Stability in Oligopoly Models. VI, 103 pages. 1976.

Vol. 139: Production Theory and Its Applications. Proceedings. Edited by H. Albach and G. Bergendahl. VIII, 193 pages. 1977.

Vol. 140: W. Eichhorn and J. Voeller, Theory of the Price Index. Fisher's Test Approach and Generalizations. VII, 95 pages. 1976.

Vol. 141: Mathematical Economics and Game Theory. Essays in Honor of Oskar Morgenstern. Edited by R. Henn and O. Moeschlin. XIV, 703 pages. 1977.

Vol. 142: J. S. Lane, On Optimal Population Paths. V, 123 pages. 1977.

Vol. 143: B. Näslund, An Analysis of Economic Size Distributions. XV, 100 pages. 1977.

Vol. 144: Convex Analysis and Its Applications. Proceedings 1976. Edited by A. Auslender. VI, 219 pages. 1977.

Vol. 145: J. Rosenmüller, Extreme Games and Their Solutions. IV, 126 pages. 1977.

Vol. 146: In Search of Economic Indicators. Edited by W. H. Strigel. XVI, 198 pages. 1977.

Vol. 147: Resource Allocation and Division of Space. Proceedings. Edited by T. Fujii and R. Sato. VIII, 184 pages. 1977.

Vol. 148: C. E. Mandl, Simulationstechnik und Simulationsmodelle in den Sozial- und Wirtschaftswissenschaften. IX, 173 Seiten. 1977.

Vol. 149: Stationäre und schrumpfende Bevölkerungen: Demographisches Null- und Negativwachstum in Österreich. Herausgegeben von G. Feichtinger. VI, 262 Seiten. 1977.

Vol. 150: Bauer et al., Supercritical Wing Sections III. VI, 179 pages. 1977.

Vol. 151: C. A. Schneeweiß, Inventory-Production Theory. VI, 116 pages. 1977.

Vol. 152: Kirsch et al., Notwendige Optimalitätsbedingungen und ihre Anwendung. VI, 157 Seiten. 1978.

Vol. 153: Kombinatorische Entscheidungsprobleme: Methoden und Anwendungen. Herausgegeben von T. M. Liebling und M. Rössler. VIII, 206 Seiten. 1978.

Vol. 154: Problems and Instruments of Business Cycle Analysis. Proceedings 1977. Edited by W. H. Strigel. VI, 442 pages. 1978.

Vol. 155: Multiple Criteria Problem Solving. Proceedings 1977. Edited by S. Zionts. VIII, 567 pages. 1978.

Vol. 156: B. Näslund and B. Sellstedt, Neo-Ricardian Theory. With Applications to Some Current Economic Problems. VI, 165 pages. 1978.

Vol. 157: Optimization and Operations Research. Proceedings 1977. Edited by R. Henn, B. Korte, and W. Oettli. VI, 270 pages. 1978.

Vol. 158: L. J. Cherene, Set Valued Dynamical Systems and Economic Flow. VIII, 83 pages. 1978.

Vol. 159: Some Aspects of the Foundations of General Equilibrium Theory: The Posthumous Papers of Peter J. Kalman. Edited by J. Green. VI, 167 pages. 1978.

[illegible]er Programming and Related Areas. A Classified [illegible]ed by D. Hausmann. XIV, 314 pages. 1978.

[illegible]n Rank in Organizations. VIII, 164 pages. 1978.

Vol. [illegible] Systems, Economic [illegible] R. Mohler and A. Rube[illegible]

Vol. 163: [illegible] ganisationen. VI, 143 Seiten. [illegible]

Vol. 164: C. L. Hwang and A. S. M. Masud, Multiple Objective Decision Making – Methods and Applications. A State-of-the-Art Survey. XII, 351 pages. 1979.

Vol. 165: A. Maravall, Identification in Dynamic Shock-Error Models. VIII, 158 pages. 1979.

Vol. 166: R. Cuninghame-Green, Minimax Algebra. XI, 258 pages. 1979.

Vol. 167: M. Faber, Introduction to Modern Austrian Capital Theory. X, 196 pages. 1979.

Vol. 168: Convex Analysis and Mathematical Economics. Proceedings 1978. Edited by J. Kriens. V, 136 pages. 1979.

Vol. 169: A. Rapoport et al., Coalition Formation by Sophisticated Players. VII, 170 pages. 1979.

Vol. 170: A. E. Roth, Axiomatic Models of Bargaining. V, 121 pages. 1979.

Vol. 171: G. F. Newell, Approximate Behavior of Tandem Queues. XI, 410 pages. 1979.

Vol. 172: K. Neumann and U. Steinhardt, GERT Networks and the Time-Oriented Evaluation of Projects. 268 pages. 1979.

Vol. 173: S. Erlander, Optimal Spatial Interaction and the Gravity Model. VII, 107 pages. 1980.

Vol. 174: Extremal Methods and Systems Analysis. Edited by A. V. Fiacco and K. O. Kortanek. XI, 545 pages. 1980.

Vol. 175: S. K. Srinivasan and R. Subramanian, Probabilistic Analysis of Redundant Systems. VII, 356 pages. 1980.

Vol. 176: R. Färe, Laws of Diminishing Returns. VIII, 97 pages. 1980.

Vol. 177: Multiple Criteria Decision Making-Theory and Application. Proceedings, 1979. Edited by G. Fandel and T. Gal. XVI, 570 pages. 1980.

Vol. 178: M. N. Bhattacharyya, Comparison of Box-Jenkins and Bonn Monetary Model Prediction Performance. VII, 146 pages. 1980.

Vol. 179: Recent Results in Stochastic Programming. Proceedings, 1979. Edited by P. Kall and A. Prékopa. IX, 237 pages. 1980.

Vol. 180: J. F. Brotchie, J. W. Dickey and R. Sharpe, TOPAZ – General Planning Technique and its Applications at the Regional, Urban, and Facility Planning Levels. VII, 356 pages. 1980.

Vol. 181: H. D. Sherali and C. M. Shetty, Optimization with Disjunctive Constraints. VIII, 156 pages. 1980.

Vol. 182: J. Wolters, Stochastic Dynamic Properties of Linear Econometric Models. VIII, 154 pages. 1980.

Vol. 183: K. Schittkowski, Nonlinear Programming Codes. VIII, 242 pages. 1980.

Vol. 184: R. E. Burkard and U. Derigs, Assignment and Matching Problems: Solution Methods with FORTRAN-Programs. VIII, 148 pages. 1980.

Vol. 185: C. C. von Weizsäcker, Barriers to Entry. VI, 220 pages. 1980.

Vol. 186: Ch.-L. Hwang and K. Yoon, Multiple Attribute Decision Making – Methods and Applications. A State-of-the-Art-Survey. XI, 259 pages. 1981.

Vol. 187: W. Hock, K. Schittkowski, Test Examples for Nonlinear Programming Codes. V. 178 pages. 1981.

Vol. 188: D. Bös, Economic Theory of Public Enterprise. VII, 142 pages. 1981.

Vol. 189: A. P. Lüthi, Messung wirtschaftlicher Ungleichheit. IX, 287 pages. 1981.

Vol. 190: J. N. Morse, Organizations: Multiple Agents with Multiple Criteria. Proceedings, 1980. VI, 509 pages. 1981.

Vol. 191: H. R. Sneessens, Theory and Estimation of Macroeconomic Rationing Models. VII, 138 pages. 1981.

Vol. 192: H. J. Bierens: Robust Methods and Asymptotic Theory in Nonlinear Econometrics. IX, 198 pages. 1981.

Vol. 193: J. K. Sengupta, Optimal Decisions under Uncertainty. VII, 156 pages. 1981.

Vol. 194: R. W. Shephard, Cost and Production Functions. XI, 104 pages. 1981.

Vol. 195: H. W. Ursprung, Die elementare Katastrophentheorie. Eine Darstellung aus der Sicht der Ökonomie. VII, 332 pages. 1982.

Vol. 196: M. Nermuth, Information Structures in Economics. VIII, 236 pages. 1982.

Vol. 197: Integer Programming and Related Areas. A Classified Bibliography. 1978 – 1981. Edited by R. von Randow. XIV, 338 pages. 1982.

Vol. 198: P. Zweifel, Ein ökonomisches Modell des Arztverhaltens. XIX, 392 Seiten. 1982.

Vol. 199: Evaluating Mathematical Programming Techniques. Proceedings, 1981. Edited by J.M. Mulvey. XI, 379 pages. 1982.

Vol. 201: P. M. C. de Boer, Price Effects in Input-Output-Relations: A Theoretical and Empirical Study for the Netherlands 1949–1967. X, 140 pages. 1982.

Vol. 202: U. Witt, J. Perske, SMS – A Program Package for Simulation and Gaming of Stochastic Market Processes and Learning Behavior. VII, 266 pages. 1982.

Vol. 203: Compilation of Input-Output Tables. Proceedings, 1981. Edited by J. V. Skolka. VII, 307 pages. 1982.

Vol. 204: K.C. Mosler, Entscheidungsregeln bei Risiko: Multivariate stochastische Dominanz. VII, 172 Seiten. 1982.

Vol. 205: R. Ramanathan, Indroduction to the Theory of Economic Growth. IX, 347 pages. 1982.